Choices We Make in the Global Village

From Fantasy Land
to
Tomorrow Land

by Stephen P. Cook

Parthenon Books

This book is dedicated to people eager to understand the human experience, and to work to make it a better one for all of us.

Looking back, it's dedicated to the memory of **Donella Meadows**.
Looking ahead, it's dedicated to
Greta Thunberg, Xiuhtezcati Martinez,
and young activists fighting for a sustainable, more just world.

Acknowledgements
The author wishes to thank the following people:

Bill Clinton for leadership as Arkansas Governor that supported my 1979-1985 environmental and energy education efforts, solar photovoltaic demonstration projects, and helped establish the Arkansas School for Mathematics and Sciences where I later taught from 1998-2003

Attila Grandpierre for facilitating my attending and presenting at the 2009 International Year of Astronomy conference in Budapest

Kate Raworth for use of the Doughnut Economics Diagram figure licensed under Attribution –Share Alike 4.0 International (CC-BY-SA-4.0). This appears at the lower right on the book's cover and later as Figure #22

Seth Wynes and **Kimberly Nicholas** for use of what appears as Figure #30, originally published on July 12 2017 in "The climate mitigation gap: education and government recommendations miss the most effective individual,actions" in *Environmental Research Letters* Volume 12 074024 and used under terms of Creative Commons Attribution 3.0 license

the creators of the public domain graphics
appearing in Figures #12, #19, #20, #21,and #25, courtesy of NASA, the USGS, the Institute for European Environmental Policy, the National Park Service, and the US Forest Service, respectively

Parthenon Books / a division of *Project Worldview*
Prescott, AZ 86301
parthenonbooks@projectworldview.org

Table of Contents

Preface: My dad went to work for Walt Disney in 1938, washing art off celluloid. He retired in 1980 as head of the animation camera dept. I first visited Fantasyland in 1955 as Disneyland opened. I recall hearing the song "There's a Great Big Beautiful Tomorrow" there in 1966 and thinking "We'll see." I won a scholarship from the Disney Foundation in 1969. As phi beta kappa 1973 graduate from UCLA, I entered a physics graduate program with a prestigious fellowship. The road to success beckoned—but I chose a different path. I think of my life as growing up in Fantasy Land, headed to Tomorrow Land, by way of Adventure Land.

Ten years removed from Fantasy Land —and thoroughly grounded in Reality—I began looking back at those trying to live the American Dream. By 1990 I'd finished a book in which The Reality Marketplace was born. By 2006 that moved online to a website I created. Cynics may say I'm still living in Fantasy Land, that I'm very naïve for imagining a rational, caring world in which people make better choices. I dispute that suggestion. This book, a sequel, is for those searching for meaning in life— and privileged to have choices, hope, and much to look forward to. (My heart goes out to those who do not.) It's a global education effort that promotes "we're all in this together." It hopes to shape healthy worldviews that nurture "people, planet, and prosperity." It's grounded in stories drawn from my experience. It charts paths to "the promised land."

I'm a humble, imperfect creature. But here I am again with a book saying "I define who I am, I magnify my identity." That's how Dana Meadows described the "True Believer" in us. As before, "I have written this book as if I were a great prophet." I'm not—and have no wish to be lifted out of obscurity. But I believe in where my "search for truth and ethical way to live" has led. I call it Tomorrow Land—where critical thinking, fair play, "Enoughness," and "Respect for Nature" are valued. A good global education and good leaders can get humanity there. But I don't have all the answers. I'm a seeker. My thought-provoking speculations scattered throughout the text — some quite "out of the box" — attest to that.

With its *Choices We Make* framework for global education in Appendix A, and resources on the *Project Worldview* website, this book is part of a learning package. Alas, I apologize for including choice #s. They aid learning, but add clutter. Life is full of tradeoffs. Choice #3 has one: "Humbly Unsure" and "I Know What's Best for You" worldview themes. Taking a middle path, come with me as your "selfless leader willing to helpfully step up and point the way forward." Let's humbly proceed together. Thank you for joining me in this wide-ranging journey.

Chapter 1: Global Education, Character Education

A. An Overview of this Book

This book's *Choices We Make in the Global Village* title pulls together two reasons for its existence. First, it's built around "Choices We Make" found in a similarly named deck of playing cards—created from 104 worldview themes paired on the flip sides of each of its fifty-two cards. This card deck is presented in its booklet form in Appendix A. Second, the book represents the sequel to the *Coming of Age in the Global Village* book published in 1990. This initial chapter will help you understand that earlier book's content, appreciate the form the fifty-two choices take, and make connections that enrich your experience.

This book's *From Fantasy Land to Tomorrow Land* subtitle can be understood in two ways. First, based on a two-word characterization of fantasy as "not real," this book promotes the ability to separate fantasy from reality—a big part of critical thinking. Second, it does this in a way that involves the "imagining" aspect of fantasy in a "fight for the future." It asks us to imagine a future Tomorrow Land—a world built by critical thinkers who accept Earth's biosphere imposed limits, and value sharing and fair play. Not a business as usual, throw-away society Fantasy Land of rich consumers raised on fairy tales like what Figure #1 offers.

The heart of Figure #1 is an ad from 1984. It's from the *Coming of Age...* book —whose back cover described American consumers as "the spoiled children of the western world." Thirty-five years later a sixteen year old girl got the world's attention with her words at a UN Climate Summit: "We are at the beginning of a mass extinction and all you can talk about is money and fairy tales of eternal economic growth." Greta Thunberg, named *Time* magazine's 2019 Person of the Year, serves notice that her generation's critical thinkers will fight for the future by telling global "powers that be" they need to get out of Fantasy Land.

Twenty months later, American embrace of fantasy and unwillingness to accept reality has taken an ominous turn. As headlined in a *CNN* May 25, 2021 story—reporting on a survey of Americans with respect to the 2020 presidential election outcome—"A majority of Republicans are living in a fantasy world built around the Big Lie." Ominous because not being grounded in reality can be dangerous—thousands of young adults who shunned science / Covid-19 vaccine would agree if they were still alive. No doubt reality can be depressing and many prefer Fantasy Land.

Rather than pushing a pretend world and some unsustainable thing or selfish activity, this book embraces escaping a consumerist lifestyle in "alternative hedonism" fashion. In promoting "the freedom to choose personal responsibility," it embraces a "we're all in this together" mentality. It portrays a lifestyle full of meaning, and urges readers to join in helping to create a hoped for future world we'll call Tomorrow Land.

Figure #1— From Fantasy Land to Tomorrow Land
Fantasy Land: there are no limits—you can wish for anything…
excerpt from *Coming of Age in the Global Village*, set at Christmas-time 1984 This was inspired by an ad urging you to choose "A Gift That Matters" that the author saw shortly after reading about famine and death in Ethiopia.

Back in affluent Southern California, many are browsing the Robinson's Christmas "Believe in Magic" catalogue, and contemplating gifts they could give. Inside are complete descriptions, prices, and ordering instructions for 412 consecutively numbered, high-priced gifts.
    "I invite you to join these joyful celebrations of tradition and to share in the fantasies and spirit of our childhood," says a message from Robinson's chief executive officer. You turn the page to a magical picture of Gift #1…
    It was Christmas morning. You became the baron. Home was now a castle in Scotland with a 700 year old legacy of glamour, chivalry and magic…the ghosts of Christmases past welcome you to Castle Lee…
A modernized medieval mansion with a tennis court, wine cellar, stable, kennel, helipad, etc. is described. The price is $5,750,000—availability subject to prior sale. (To aid imagining, see French castle photo in lower left corner on cover.)

Tomorrow Land: the diagram in the lower right corner on the cover defines what we wish for: A Safe, Just Space for Everyone—see Figure #22

Simple living based on ecosharing and alternative hedonism, and "Build Bridges, Not Walls" provide this book with two other important themes. I'll save discussion of the former for chapter 6. As for the latter, at rallies in recent years I've carried these words on a sign—along with an image of two hands reaching out. Those hands might signify two legislators on opposite sides of the political aisle trying to bridge the ideological divide separating them. The contrasting beliefs, values, etc of the *Choices We Make* cards, can spur finding common ground, and resolving conflicts.

Stories in this book include tales of my experiences and others'. The former offer something of a life story. They do a better job in this regard than the previous book, given that I'm roughly twice as old now as I was then. A few are built around poor choices, not ones I advocate: they're "live and learn" offerings. Some are not "politically correct," a few are blatantly irreverent. Some have names changed to protect privacy.

As for the book's more formal essays, I offer three comments. First, be prepared for global education experiences. These typically start with painting "the big picture" or presenting "first principles," before focusing on particular educational objectives. Thus, after a long informal story, the next ("History and Freedom...") chapter literally starts with "the Big Bang." And chapter 6 ("Economics, Ecology, Ecosharing,") after looking at word origins, stakes out "People, Planet, Prosperity" territory.

Second, some readers, with bad experiences related to organized religion, may cringe upon encountering (mainly in chapter 4) words like "God," "Jesus," etc. While I sympathize with you, we know many people take traditional religion very seriously, and they matter. While this book may appeal more to those who are "spiritual, but not religious," it nonetheless reaches out to traditionalists in bridge-building fashion. So, I hope you cringing folks can do an (choice #49) attitude fix and "Get over it!" Third, some readers might find some material in this book—especially in chapter 5 "Science: Sky, Earth, Life"— too "textbook-like."

I'd like to address these concerns with a couple of stories. The first, rather spread out, story, involves my setting foot in "New Age" territory. It starts long ago with frustration, and ends very recently with great inspiration. Before getting into it, I need to provide some background. In the last five decades I've attended many programs and events—even being a facilitator or featured speaker at a few—typically billed as about sky events, pagan / indigenous peoples / earth-centered spirituality, connecting to Earth's rhythms, equinox or solstice celebrations, New Age, etc. The latter refers to an affluent Western society movement that grew out of mind-expanding experiences of the 1960s, and really blossomed in the 1970s. It blends older religious and spiritual traditions from both East and West with more modern ideas about human consciousness, human potential, psychology, physics, and ecology.

While New Age enthusiasts possess diverse (and sometimes conflicting) beliefs, one notion embraced by many of them is the idea that all living things—and, for many, all matter in general—are fundamentally interconnected (either spiritually, by some life force, energy, consciousness, light, God, etc). The movement provides a large umbrella under which one finds mystics, psychics, astrologers, alternative health practitioners, those who value meditation / ancient wisdom, believers in reincarnation, angels, the magic powers of crystals, Atlantis, UFOs and space aliens, etc. Given my interest in things like the human potential movement and astronomy / earth science education, while I've found some to be worthwhile experiences, I've suffered through others.

My story begins at a gathering of environmental activists / bioregional thinkers[1] in northwest Arkansas in the fall of 1985. I was giving a talk about (soon to appear) Halley's comet. At its conclusion, no one asked about seeing this object, but many wondered about its metaphysical / astrological significance. This was a disturbing encounter, similar to what I later experienced in group-settings after I moved (first to New Mexico and then to Arizona) many years later. I came to associate it with a (choice #1) positive expectations / wishful longing for metaphysical connection with earth and sky— and relative lack of interest in Reality as revealed by observations your own eyes could make, or by evidence gathered by instruments that enhance human senses.

In recent years, I've many times participated in (what some consider sacred) ceremonies where we, in turn, face each of the four directions and listen to / repeat / chant words including, among others, the four ancient elements of earth, water, air, and fire. During one event, I'd imagined interrupting to quiz the assembled group with reality check questions like, "Hey, can someone point out how far behind the times we are here? Or with a simple request like, "Those of you who can, will you please point to where you'd expect the Sun to be at noon on the day of the winter solstice…What about on the day of the summer solstice?" I suspect many of the people in these gatherings lack the basic science literacy to recognize the "celebrating ancient misconceptions" nature of the event, and to correctly point out or point as requested.

A beautiful mountainside near Sedona, Arizona[2] was the scene of another disturbing experience I had about five years ago. Coaxed by a friend, I'd joined a large group hiking to a place of supposed metaphysical significance. The last part of this hour-long excursion required traversing a narrow ledge—and avoiding falling hundreds of feet. Quite frankly it scared me. I'm an accomplished mountain climber and don't scare easily, but I was surprised at how nonchalantly people trusted leaders and charged across this passage. Once safely across and comfortably seated, I mostly tuned out the guy lecturing on the spot's spiritual significance, and simply soaked up the natural beauty. But my reverie abruptly ended with a noisy drone that the event organizers unleashed to film the event for PR purposes. Again I was surprised I was the only one who was upset enough to refuse to be part of a group photo these folks commissioned.

Readers might conclude I'm setting up a science vs. spirituality conflict, in which I'll be on the (choice #20) "Rational / Dispassionate" side of science and against feelings-infused quests, metaphysical exploration, spirituality, etc—right? Wrong! I hope that by the time you reach what I consider the book's climax (chapter 8 "Four Dispatches from the Front Lines in My Battle to Find Meaning in Life" / Dispatch #3,) also set in Sedona, you'll feel differently. I hope you'll feel I've succeeded in my attempt to paint an open-minded picture of Reality that helps caring, intelligent people "make sense out of the confusion of existence." (See question #20 in Appendix C to better understand my motivation.)

With a second story I provide another example of a science education failure—perhaps in elementary school. This resulted in an incorrect childish belief being carried throughout one's life— until it was embarrassingly exposed. A man in his seventies who has risen to a prominent place in society—American President Donald Trump— is asked why he gave up sports after college despite some success. He did so, he answers, because he "believed the human body was like a battery, with a finite amount of energy, which exercise only depleted."[3] This man's appalling failure to understand the basics of how living things use energy was later parodied. "This is exactly right. The body is a battery. The key to longevity and power is to sit perfectly still and keep the body constantly full of food. It will last indefinitely."[4]

One goal of this book is increase scientific literacy. According to the National Academy of Sciences, this is "the knowledge and understanding of scientific concepts and processes required for personal decision-making, participation in civic and cultural affairs, and economic productivity. It also includes specific types of abilities." This can be had with a good science education—which should also increase critical thinking ability. The above shooting down of Trump's "human body is like a battery" idea illustrates critical thinking at work.

Critical thinking skills are an important part of (choice #29) "Education for Democracy"—especially the part about promoting "the ability to ultimately select good leaders." If education fails to provide this, authoritarian demagogues and self-centered corrupt politicians are better able to get the ignorant to follow where they lead. I suspect many people who believe the (choice #38) conspiracy theories they hear on right-wing news channels or encounter on social media lack those skills. Sadly, they may not be able to recognize a real conspiracy if they watched or listened to it unfold in front of them. Thus, after a sustained blitz of misformation he propagated regarding supposed (and imaginary) fraud in the 2020 USA presidential election, millions of Americans failed to see the conspiracy their president Donald Trump put squarely in front of them when he attempted, in a lengthy phone call, to recruit the Georgia Secretary of State to join him in some real election fraud.

My interest in promoting scientific literacy has another surprising dimension—one linked to another of this book's goals: to connect science with spirituality. This is best explained by citing something Carl Sagan said[5]. "A religion that stressed the magnificence of the universe as revealed by modern science might be able to draw forth reserves of reverence and awe hardly tapped by traditional faiths." This book, while respecting cultural heritages and diversity, can promote the growth of such a futuristic religion out of today's earth centered spirituality by helping its enthusiasts—or disgruntled refugees from mainstream religions— gain new understanding and make new connections.

I suspect many of those disgruntled refugees are turned off by the moralistic / judgmental God aspects of organized religion. This book, like its predecessor, aims to expose this for what it is—a historic relic of a long-ago time when a powerful few sought to maintain control over the masses. It seeks to move beyond this in a "pie in the sky" sense by broadening the concept of spirituality. And in a more practical, down to earth sense, by promoting ethical behavior and encouraging young (or forever young) people to become responsible stewards. Good global citizens are stewards of both democracy and planetary well-being.

Accordingly, another goal—one especially driving this book's creation —is to promote meaningful change. It shares the hope expressed as a caption underneath the global education logo on the box housing the deck of *Choices We Make* cards: "It's just a humble card deck, but it can burst bubbles, change minds, and just perhaps... CAN CHANGE THE WORLD." I know the likelihood of this happening is very low, but I'm enough of a hopeful idealist (choice #1) wishful thinker to at least put the possibility out there. Besides urging folks to make their own card decks!

Choices We Make in the Global Village   page 11

You've noticed the choice #s I'm using, right? If you haven't already, you may want to spend some time looking over those *Choices We Make* cards presented in booklet form in Appendix A, before returning to finish reading the rest of this first chapter. Of course the other alternative—to simply turn there to find needed information when the book prompts you with a "choice #"—may be an equally good plan. So—do you turn to the Appendix or keep reading? You have a decision to make—but wait, please read the last three paragraphs of this section before you decide.

How do you make decisions? Later in this chapter I shall describe what is called the computational model of the human brain. Its development was spurred by findings such as those communicated in the summary of an April 15 2008 report on research done at the Max Planck Institute for Human Cognitive and Brain Sciences. That began: "Contrary to what most of us would like to believe, decision-making may be a process handled to a large extent by unconscious mental activity."

No doubt the uncertain extent to which important human decisions depend on unconscious feelings—unexplained whims—precludes our having a great deal of confidence in predictions made based on methods for characterizing worldviews such as *Project Worldview*—or any other available methodology—provides. Prospects for doing a good job at predicting future human societal decisions are especially poor if leaders in key positions are neurotics—given their "poor ability to adapt to one's environment." But having said that, I'm nonetheless confident that using a worldview theme-based approach to characterizing worldviews—both of individuals and society— is a valuable tool for understanding human behavior. (Likewise for *Project Worldview*'s worldview analysis tools.)

So, having thrown around the term "worldview" and teased with suggestions related to using it to make predictions, or as to how it might be related to personality factors like neuroticism, let's move on. Let's consider worldviews and related topics—including *Project Worldview* — in more formal presentation fashion as this first chapter continues. (Bye to those of you who have whimsically decided to look over the *Choices We Make* cards presented in booklet form in Appendix A—see you later at the beginning of the next section.)

B. About Worldviews

Roughly speaking, your worldview is about your beliefs, your values, your answers to life's big questions— including where you come from and how you fit into the bigger scheme of things— and where you look to find meaning in life. More precisely your worldview can be thought of as a conceptual framework and a set of beliefs used to make sense out of a complex, seemingly chaotic reality based on your perceptions, experience and learning. Besides incorporating a purpose or "raison d'etre," it provides an outlook or expectation for the world as it exists, or is perceived to exist. It's something that you base predictions about the future on. It continually evolves—indeed, you spend the rest of your life testing and refining it, based on feedback you get. As it develops, it increasingly becomes the source of your goals and desires, and as such it shapes your behavior and values.

How do worldviews develop? After stories—one about the worldview of a seven-year old kid, and some from my experience—we'll work backwards in describing how worldviews, and the brains that contain them, develop from infancy. We start with the following discussion.[6]

Eric: Dad, what happens to us after we die? Is there a heaven?
Dad: Well, some people believe that after we die we go to Heaven where we live forever, and other people believe that when we die, our life is over and we live on through the memories of people who have known us and loved us.
Eric: What do you believe?
Dad: Well, some people believe that after we die we go to Heaven, and other people believe...
Eric: But what do *you* believe?
Dad: OK. I believe that when we die we live on through other people but not in Heaven.
Eric (after a long pause): I'll believe what you believe for now, and when I grow up I'll make up my own mind.

Before considering when kids like seven-year old Eric—and symbolically all intelligent young people—are ready to make up their own minds, background is needed to understand the "worldview as a conceptual framework" point of view. This begins with a definition of concepts: the abstract generalized ideas and understanding that replace a set of sensory experiences and memories. The two concepts involved in this discussion—death and Heaven—are not easy ones to think about. Death, while fairly straight-forward for a child to understand—think of green leaves turning brown and falling off a tree, or that bug you squash with your foot— is unpleasant to consider. Heaven on the other hand is an impossibly fuzzy concept. Is it a real place, if so where? What is it like, and how do know? Given these difficulties, let's replace them in our discussion with two other concepts. Having grown up in southern California, I offer instead: oranges and the Sun.

We imagine a young mind connecting oranges with other concepts it's grasped as part of a process of growing, experiencing the world, seeing relationships, categorizing, discriminating and generalizing about what the senses reveal. At a very young age I put oranges into a food category, at some point qualifying this with "food that grows on trees," and further categorizing them as a fruit. Of the physical object, I learned the orange's skin was not food, but that its overall shape fit into another category. After handling many similar but different objects—marbles, rectangular blocks, a beach ball, a tennis ball, toy cars, a globe, etc— perhaps I'd formed a concept of "roundness." I soon included oranges in this group. And maybe I realized that, like leaves, oranges die and fall from trees.

Death can simply be thought of as the end of something being alive— like the green leaf or the crawling bug. But describing it starting from the concept of life presents an extraordinary challenge. What does it mean to say that something is alive? How do we define life? I recently read that scientists had come up with something like 123 different definitions of life[7]—definitions which typically depend on other concepts—like matter, cells, reproduction, food, energy, metabolism, homeostasis, etc. Linking death to its opposite, birth, suggests a bigger scheme with a dynamic aspect. One's concept of death may eventually lead to thoughts of one's own death—and the question Eric asked his father.

As the above suggests, the conceptualization process—often driven by questions—extends to fitting many concepts together into schemes, and structuring conceptual schemes into a framework. Can we fit the orange and the Sun together in such a scheme? Yes. Eventually many children learn that the Sun powers a process called photosynthesis going on in the leaves of an orange tree. Solar energy input, along with water and carbon dioxide gas pulled from the air, drives the formation of the tree's fruit. The orange, photosynthesis, and the Sun all are part of a complete description of a bigger something we conceive of: the Earth's life or biosphere. The Sun fits into a still bigger scheme—as one of hundreds of billions of other stars that make up our Milky Way Galaxy.

My own concept of the Sun—which by age twelve extended to include the above fact —began outdoors with feeling its warmth on my skin as a toddler. And realizing it was so bright I couldn't look directly at it for long. I came to love it and depend on its warmth. Though seemingly gone on cloudy days, I knew the Sun was still there behind the clouds. Likewise, I came to understand the Earth blocks our view of the Sun at night. Will it always be around in its current form? During junior high years, I learned the Sun shines by turning matter into energy. And it is so massive it can do this for billions more years. I appreciated that, like many conceive of God as responsible for the creation of the Earth, the Sun and Earth were born together as part of something that took place 4.5 billion years ago. And that Earth exists only because of the Sun.

Is the Sun alive? No, says the scientific consensus view I'd long accepted as an adult. Yet in 2009—after I gave the opening talk at a conference in Budapest celebrating the International Year of Astronomy—I chatted with a Hungarian physicist and out-of-the box thinker who insisted the sun is alive. I remained skeptical. Seems our worldviews are continually challenged. Seems we grow by considering others' questions, and ones we raise ourselves. The above suggests that, though the rate of acquiring new concepts generally slows as you age, your conceptual framework can change as new experiences provide new insights. In this way, your comprehensive conception of the world as a whole, that is, your worldview, develops. But how, and where, does this process begin?

Starting as an infant with crying to get your mother's attention, what you do to better fit into the surrounding environment becomes increasingly sophisticated. Worldviews develop not only with your increasing language capability and concept acquisition, and as you emotionally mature, but also with learning about the surrounding environment. Such learning proceeds via a feedback process that begins with sensing you're uncomfortable and taking steps to rectify the situation. Perhaps a diaper needs changing, and you holler to let your parents know. Aided by both parents and formal schooling, the tabula rasa or blank slate of your mind steadily fills as you experience and learn. Your worldview and behavior change accordingly—as does information content stored in your brain.

As scientists conceive of it, the basic unit of information is called a bit, a contraction of "binary digit" with but two values: 0 or 1. Accordingly, information is linked to questions framed to be answered yes or no: a yes puts a 1 in some register, a no means a 0 goes there. Human brains are capable of rapidly processing incredible amounts of information they receive as sensory input. For example, our eyes can send ten million bits of information per second to our brains. Whole images—where 1 means bright, and 0 dark—can form from individual pixels containing 1s or 0s. Brain processing power depends on neurons— cells transmitting electrical impulses. In simple terms, a neuron that turns on to transmit or "fire" can be linked to a 1, one that stays off is linked to a 0.

Your brain contains roughly one hundred billion neurons—each of which may be connected to up to a thousand other neurons in links called synapses. To some extent, infant brains come hard-wired—with connections between neurons already in place or pre-programmed— along with other instinctual behaviors you need to survive. Many of the neurons are specialized. Consider mirror neurons. They turn on (or fire) both when you initiate a particular action and when you observe another individual performing the same action. Thus their sympathetic firing "mirrors" the action of another. Some neuroscientists trace the roots of empathy to neural networks in the brain with such mirror properties.

In addition to hard-wired neural connections, as you experience the world and learn, your brain creates soft-wired connections. Thus your unique experience, shaped by both the physical and cultural learning environment you grow up in, leads to the storing of critical information you need to survive and thrive in your brain. This is part of a feedback process where information gleaned from the environment modifies the soft wiring and potentially changes your future behavior. Ideally this happens so that you fit into the environment better, with behavior that improves the fit reinforced, and behavior that does not discouraged. Such learning, associated acquisition of knowledge, and changing neural connections at the most basic level, ultimately is reflected at a much higher level with changes in that product of your mind: your worldview.

A computational theory of the mind explains how the mind arises from the activity of the brain. Responding to sensory input (from eyes, ears, nerve endings, etc,) information is processed, put into memory, etc. This involves signals initiating action, neurons encoding information, networks forming data patterns, and rules / logic employed in comparing patterns / doing computation. Using this model, neuroscientists describe brain function in terms of predictive processing—a name that gets us thinking of worldviews in terms of something you base predictions on.

Your brain, they say, continually updates a mental model of the external environment you live in—a model ultimately internalized inside your head in endless numbers of neural connections. This model generates predictions of what should be perceived by human (or higher animal) senses, which are compared to sensory input received. Differences uncovered in this comparison provide feedback used to update / improve the model, and guide subsequent behavior like activation of the motor system, etc. This can function at a low level without involving conscious thinking. Something similar, but more abstract, happens at a higher level within your conscious thinking mind. We call this comprehensive higher-level mental model of the world you inhabit your worldview.

Consciousness of some type emerges once a worldview's complexity reaches a certain point. This can be linked to a (choice #13) metasystem transition, defined as the formation of a new, more complex system from simpler systems, where the new system includes a mechanism that controls the production and behavior of the subsystems. Conceivably, from a choice #9 scientific materialist perspective, such a "reorganizing event" may mark the moment when a person (or other complex living thing?) becomes conscious? It may mark the moment—if there is one—when, using terms from linguist Ray Jackendoff and philosopher Ned Block, one acquires two things. One is self knowledge (including the ability to recognize one's self in a mirror); the other is sentience (knowing "what is it like" to be someone because you are that someone.)

Pondering the problem of consciousness triggers thoughts about long-standing related problems. Questions about how the mental world of intangibles (your perceptions, beliefs, desires, thinking, feeling, intentions, etc.) connects with tangible matter inside your brain, puts us in the mind–body problem territory. Thoughts about Darwinian evolution —with survival of the fittest / natural selection, and passage of time— may help answer another question: "Why is the human mind what it is, and how did it get that way?"

In real person terms, suppose you're seven-year old Eric and realize your beliefs will be refined as you get older. Ideally your growing up will bring increasingly sophisticated understanding of how the world works, and better tools for analyzing all of the diverse beliefs you see people around you buying into. Hopefully, by the time you reach adulthood, the mental model you long ago began building—your worldview— can be characterized as intelligent and healthy.

Alas, for many this process is corrupted. Many parents rightly help their kids learn basic values (honesty, sharing, etc), but wrongly force their beliefs on them with respect to life's big questions. Young children aren't ready to ponder: "Why am I here?" " What is the meaning of life?" "How does nature work?" "How can I please God?" They should be allowed to grow up free of prejudices, and mature until they're capable of freely selecting beliefs and values from a range of possible choices.

Instead, some devout Christian parents teach their toddlers to pray; start their church and Sunday school attendance before kindergarten; choose for them the theocracy of religious home school rather than the democracy of public schools. Christian parents may send their younger kids to summer vacation Bible schools, their older ones to belief indoctrination events like "Worldview Weekends,"[8] and encourage college applications to schools such as Jerry Falwell's Liberty University. Islamic parents may enroll their children at madrassas.

In contrast, some atheistic parents deny their child's request to visit a friend's church. They may force young minds to cope with beliefs they aren't ready for: there is no God; the universe has no Creator; existence can be explained as a byproduct of billions of years of impersonal forces and random processes acting on matter; life has no intrinsic purpose or meaning; only knowledge based on observation and science is valid.

Rather than allowing (choice #12) free inquiry / liberty of thought, these approaches tyrannically wrap young people in intellectual strait jackets. Many equate such indoctrination with child abuse. The discussion between Eric and his Dad illustrates how parents and teachers of youngsters can proceed in a way that encourages curiosity by honestly responding to young questions in non-dogmatic fashion. But sadly, many parents are increasingly ill equipped to answer questions and gently shape their children's worldviews into healthy, reality-based ones given the proliferation of social media conspiracy theories and extremist news networks providing "alternate facts."

Facts are occurrences in the real world, independent of belief, which can be verified and demonstrated to be consistent with experience of reality. Worldviews develop as facts are fit together into beliefs about how the world works. But if the "facts" are heavily distorted by preconceived notions, political agendas, or misinformation designed to produce "clicks" and bolster someone's profits, the process is again corrupted.

I grew up without social media or extremist cable news channel misinformation. By the time I reached high school, I'd matured to where I was ready to make up my own mind on many belief-related issues. But—as I'll share in chapter 4—I had my own troubled history of religious indoctrination at the hands of others, which led to disturbing nightmares. Out of this, I later sought to help others get non-dogmatic, reality-based answers to questions, and develop healthy worldviews

Guided by this, and a desire to help others resolve conflicts, in 1984 I began work developing a structure for analyzing worldviews. I soon recognized that worldviews "should build on fragments of worldviews as a starting point"—an approach that the Apostel group at VUB in Belgium would later advocate.[9] I called my fragments of worldviews "worldview themes," and composed formal descriptions of them for use in characterizing worldviews. As I worked, I gradually appreciated the complexity of this task, and began longing for a place where people could "shop" for answers to life's big questions.

C. About *Project Worldview*

The beginnings of *Project Worldview* can be traced to the fall of 1984, when I began writing what was published in 1990 as *Coming of Age in the Global Village*. Along the way I acquired a collaborator in the person of Donella Meadows (1942-2001), systems thinker, teacher, gardener, global citizen, MacArthur Prize winner, and co-author of the 1972 widely read and influential MIT study and book *Limits to Growth*. The *Coming of Age...* book described something called "The Reality Marketplace." This, I imagined, is where important ideas, beliefs, values, etc. are bought / sold, and where someone might go to find answers to life's important questions.

I got the idea for The Reality Marketplace from the 1985 book *Perfect Symmetry*, by physicist Heinz Pagels. His wife was Elaine Pagels, professor of religion and author. After Heinz died in a 1988 skiing accident, I discovered Elaine's books—beginning with the 1979 *The Gnostic Gospels* effort about the early history of Christianity. While the interests of this academic heavyweight couple spanned science and religion, about the time I read Elaine's 2005 book *Beyond Belief* book, I realized "my worldview project" was even broader.

So when *Project Worldview* was launched in 2006, the reality marketplace it provided extended far beyond physics. Both a "shopping to piece together a worldview" imagined activity, and another phrase, gave it something of an economics flavor. That other phrase — "free to choose" —came from the title of famed economist's Milton Friedman's 1979 book (co-authored with wife Rose.) I liked how it fit nicely with *Project Worldview* promoting itself as a place for "free inquiry."

Whereas the *Coming of Age...* book's initial (version 1) structure for characterizing worldviews used twenty-six so-called worldview themes, what went online (version 2) in 2006 as part of *Project Worldview* used eighty of them. Given a formal name and description, a worldview theme refers to the beliefs, thoughts, feelings, and behavior that come together in a way that is articulated in similar fashion by lots of people.

That book's first worldview theme was "The Humble Skeptic Worldview." Its description began with a sentence written by Donella Meadows, "Skeptics never forget the complexity of the world or the smallness and ignorance of any one person." I identified with worldview theme #1—but also liked, though to a lesser extent, that book's worldview theme #2: "The True Believer." The first two sentences of its paragraph description—also written by Meadows—were, "I understand what it is to be a Believer. I like to think of myself as devoted to noble causes." From that start over thirty years ago, the structure evolved to include 104 worldview themes paired to define fifty-two choices.

To illustrate the use of such themes, let's analyze the worldviews of the people who wrote the lyrics to two national anthems: American and British. With its fixation on the American flag, bombs falling, and bravery, certainly the "Proud Identification / Tribalism" theme of choice #36, and the "Military Backers" theme of choice #50, are valued. Critics `of America's "Star Spangled Banner" have suggested using the "America" song instead. This song starts with "My country 'tis of thee...," and is sung to the same tune as the British "God Save the Queen" anthem. Lyrics in this latter song celebrate (choice #5) the "Belief in a Personal God" theme, an acceptance of royalty / (choice #30) "Elitism," and (choice #31) "Valuing Traditions / Status Quo."

In my later years, I developed an interest in writing new lyrics for old songs. As I'll explain in chapter 3, in 2013 I began composing songs for worldview themes. These can be found in various places: online on the *Project Worldview* website, in *The Worldview Theme Songbook*, and in Appendix B. There, as Song #11 in an imagined church service program, you'll find one newly penned song, "My Planet 'Tis of Thee." This is something a (choice #36) "Global Citizen" might sing to the tune of "America" and "God Save the Queen."

Worldview themes were formulated with the idea that many of them could be used to characterize a person's worldview. The initial version 1 effort had too few themes to adequately distinguish one person's worldview from another's. This limited resolution problem led to the second version provision of eighty themes. With it "The Humble Skeptic" theme was split into two separate themes—one designated #1A about humility, the other labeled #1B about skepticism. What had been theme #5, "The Mechanistic Worldview," was reworked and became #5A "Scientific Materialism," while what had been theme #8 "The Vitalist Doctrine" was reworked and renumbered as #5B "Vitalism." This change was an early pairing of themes with diametrically opposite viewpoints together to frame a choice (now choice #9.)

Version 2 incorporated several new themes. One, inspired by Meadows[10] was #13 "Dancing With Systems." A nice complement to themes emphasizing belief in the value of procedures—like #6 "The Scientific Method"—the first sentence of #13's description read, "I value solving problems with computer-aided modeling and systems thinking." Reworking and refining of the worldview theme structure continued, with the 2009 publication of *The Worldview Literacy Book,* and the 2015 *The Worldview Theme Song Book* offering. This ushered in Version 3, with eighty-one themes. Additional expanding and revising of the structure—combined with renumbering and pairing of themes to define choices —has culminated with the latest (version 5) worldview theme structure, with 104 themes paired to make fifty-two choices.

One can thus imagine curious people going into a *Reality Marketplace,* with fifty-two stalls and vendors opposite each other selling quite different potential additions to worldviews. Or—to use another metaphor —those people picking up a deck of fifty-two *Choices We Make* playing cards. Or pursuing a global education course built on the framework of fifty-two choices the *Choices We Make* booklet provides. In some (including online manifestations) fashion, all of these have come to pass.

These educational settings are part of a bigger global education effort. In whatever form I've presented lessons in over the last four decades, I've sought to ambitiously tackle something big and important in appropriate fashion. Big as in "helping you see the big picture." Important as in how your life—and all lives it inspires—turns out. Important as in the title of the independent study course I've put together: *Nurturing Global Citizens*. Ambitious in that help in "making sense out of the confusion of existence" is offered. Ambitious as expressed in that "change the world." caption beneath the logo on the box holding the *Choices We Make* playing cards. Appropriate as in employing a free inquiry approach, exercising "the freedom to choose responsibility," promoting the ability to make responsible choices and helping people find meaning in life.

Undoubtedly parts of this *Choices We Make in the Global Village* book read like a textbook—although certainly no one would characterize other, more personal parts of it as such. Yet what it presents is but the tip of the iceberg.[11] The bigger hidden portion lives on the *Project Worldview* website. There, along with much else, you'll find:
1) background needed for assessing each of the fifty-two choices, with relevant definitions/ descriptions of words / terms from excerpted from *The Project Worldview Cultural Literacy Encyclopedia*, 2) self tests for each of those choices to check your understanding of that background material—totaling over 1100 questions altogether, 3) thousands of "more to explore" links to click on—making your web surfing into a curiosity-driven learning experience, 4) *Global Education, Worldview Literacy, and Nurturing Global Citizens* courses can more formally structure that experience, and 5) computer programs for analyzing your worldview.

Along with studying physics and astronomy at UCLA, I took courses in educational theory. There I learned that educational activities and associated objectives have been categorized using three domains:
1) cognitive—relating to comprehending and intellectual processing of information and knowledge in forming concepts, having ideas, and holding beliefs, 2) affective—relating to the emotions associated with learning experiences, and 3) psychomotor—relating to the physical activity and motor skills component of learning.[12] More recently some have added 4) social—relating to communication, teamwork, management, leadership, etc.

These four learning domains inspired *Project Worldview*'s worldview theme categorization scheme, along with four fundamental things the human experience involves: thinking, feeling, joining, and doing. A playing card analogy—as in likening one's worldview to cards held in a card game— extends this by putting playing card suits to work. Thus 104 themes are split into four groups (of twenty-six each,) with categories as follows: 1) thinking <==> cognitive <==> diamonds, 2) feeling <==> affective <==> hearts, 3) joining <==> social <==> clubs, and 4) doing <==> psychomotor / behavioral <==> spades.

I'll elaborate on this scheme with three comments. First, given the human experience typically can't be neatly split into four components, and often it's impossible to separate, for example, where the "feeling" associated with something stops and the "thinking" begins, this categorization has its limitations. Second, the last (spades) category typically focuses on behavior where something is done that impacts nature. Third, of the twenty-six themes in each group, the most basic four are called "meta themes." These are featured on the "aces" and "kings" cards, and outline two basic choices. Multiplied by four groups, these define eight basic choices that a person makes, ones representing an important step in characterizing a worldview.

We pause to note that, while *Project Worldview* began with my imagining a place which acquired a cyber-reality with the website launch years later— The Reality Marketplace place is still there. Along with it is a "Neutrality Pledge," which includes the words, "Your worldview should be uniquely yours...We won't force our beliefs on you!" This pledge has one important qualifier: "we will not knowingly spread misinformation, nor engage in tactical deception."

Let's use this to provide an illustrative example. One of the fifty-two choices you'll encounter in the booklet is choice #43. This is presented on the jack of spades card, with the "Valuing Honesty, Learning" theme on one side, and the "Spreading Disinformation / Tactical Deception" theme on the other. Consistent with our important qualifier—but generally unlike how other choices will be handled—we'll unabashedly promote the former theme. Back to the "Neutrality Pledge," you might ask, "Isn't this pledge too constraining? Won't it prevent you from taking sides in political debates or squarely coming down in favor of one theme or the other when considering one of those fifty-two choices?" The short answer is no. How so? Two reasons.

First, citing the above qualifier, I go after what's not true, what's deceitful, or what's illogical. If it seems that, despite my steady movement in recent decades toward the American political center, I prefer the Democrats to the Republicans, it could be this reflects what

Nobel Prize winning economist Paul Krugman said in a late January 2021 *New York Times* op-ed[13], "One of America's two major political parties has parted ways with facts, logic, and democracy and is not coming back." (Let's hope they do.) Second, many of those fifty-two choices have themes where reasonable people might find good reasons to like—or dislike—both themes and have no clear preference.

Seems I can find some value in nearly all of the 104 worldview themes if I try hard enough. For example, I'm very uncomfortable around people who are (choice #8) religious fundamentalists, and (choice #16) worry lots about salvation—based on the judgment of a moralistic God. When I must interact with them, I typically try to ignore where my worldview conflicts with theirs. If this proves impossible, rather than immediately put down statements I find offensive, I instead try to build on any common ground we share. Thus I might deflect a *Bible*-toting-quoting person who lets drop "For all have sinned and fall sort of the glory of God" (Romans 3, verse 23) by first agreeing, "Yes, certainly we're all imperfect creatures."

And follow that with a story that begins, "Long ago I didn't value the concept of people's actions being judged according to some idealized behavior." I go on to recall my college days and reading the 1970 book *The Greening of America* by Yale professor Charles Reich. I describe being initially taken with what Reich described as Consciousness III— and what is now seen as a sketch of the personal freedom / egalitarianism heavy worldview of the 1960s hippie counterculture. One of three "commandments" Reich identifies is, "No one judges anyone else." "Eventually," my story continues, "I came to see this as—despite constraints placed on it by the other two commandments—unacceptably moving human behavior too much in the direction of 'anything goes'."

If pressed I'll say, "The *Bible* is great literature, has amazing stories, and much to teach us—but I much prefer the (choice #19) *New Testament*'s loving, forgiving God, to the *Old Testament*'s harshly judging, vengeful one." And perhaps gently drop in that I think the *Bible* often speaks to us in metaphorical language, not literally. And, if necessary, even praise the person for his or her belief in something—noting too many people these days are (choice #32) drowning in cynicism.

You might be reading this and thinking, "Why doesn't he just totally avoid such people?" Why doesn't he build a wall and, as gatekeeper, only let certain people, who he knows more or less share his worldview, in?" I think this strategy—amplified by website / social media filters that allow in only news or information consistent with what we believe—is largely responsible for the polarized society we live in. If people with different beliefs interacted more frequently in low-key, friendly, small talk ways, perhaps we'd have fewer blowups in culture war type confrontations? Is it easier to live in a bubble, with the reality you're comfortable with, among like-minded friends? In the short run, probably yes. But I think this is part of the problem, not part of the solution. "Build bridges, not walls," describes the interaction and interpersonal communication solution we need more people practicing.

In considering each of this book's fifty-two choices, I will sometimes argue for a preferred theme. But in putting down the other theme I may nonetheless point out some value it might have and avoid too strongly forcing my beliefs on you. Rather I'll encourage your own thinking and exploration, and metaphorically urge, "As you shop in 'The Reality Marketplace' avoid spending your 'reality cash' too early, before you have seen everything." Where I have no preference I will typically explain why both themes are valuable—or should not be encouraged—or try to find common ground perhaps associated with some bigger goal.

The *Project Worldview* home page offers "Our Logo and Our Hope." This wishes everyone "a healthy worldview…that brings happiness and promotes planetary well-being." My comments: I know there are many paths one can take to arrive at this outcome, many choices one can make, many slates of worldview themes that will get us there. Rather than lobbying for a particular slate, I urge people to do what they have done for millions of years, since our species' earliest days on the African savannah: "Use your brain, think and be mindful!" Seems that the alternative—mindlessness —now as then, is the route to extinction. (Final comment: see Appendix C for more on the framing of choices.)

D. Worldviews and Global Education

Consider four facts: 1) "world" is part of the term "worldview," 2) both for mapping and symbolical representation purposes, a globe can take the place of the world, 3) "view" refers to seeing, a process necessarily involving light, and 4) the phrase "an enlightening experience" has been used (by the *Oxford Languages Dictionary*) to define education. These four facts bolster the argument that the topics of worldviews and global education naturally belong in the same discussion.

I link global education with (choice #2) global vision. Thus (choice #36) global citizens' perspective is such that they "try to be knowledgeable of people, customs and culture in regions of the world beyond where they live." Beyond that I often interject vision when introducing global education with talk of "seeing the big picture." I hesitate throwing in "making sense of reality" as it may make some people uncomfortable. Given (capital R) Reality presents the ultimate in complexity, us simple-minded humans need help in making sense of it, and in seeing how its parts fit together in big picture wholeness.

While following a vision perhaps implies using it as a map, mature worldviews provide better help. But we aren't born fully equipped with these outstandingly useful mental models—they take time to develop as previously described. But having a vision and having a worldview are different things. While both involve a sense of how the world works, having a vision is much simpler than developing a worldview. While we might think of having a vision as coming to us all at once, it's often something we "feel" as much as we "see." Stanford University African-American economist Thomas Sowell, in his book *A Conflict of Visions*, describes a vision as "a sense of causation...[and] more like a hunch or 'gut feeling' than it is like an exercise in logic or factual verification." And, following Joseph Schumpeter (1883-1950), he refers to a vision as a "pre-analytic cognitive act...[that] we sense or feel *before* we have constructed any systematic reasoning that could be called a theory."

Worldview development involves many visions being tested. Just as (choice #10) dreams and "Non-Rational Knowing" experiences can be subjected to analysis / "Scientific Method" before acting on content they communicate, our brains consciously and unconsciously shape visions before they become part of our worldviews. But where Sowell speaks of "conflicting visions," I prefer to approach conflict resolution in terms of conflicting values and worldviews.

Sowell distinguishes between constrained and unconstrained visions. He writes, "The constrained vision sees the evils of the world as deriving from the limited and unhappy choices available, given the inherent moral and intellectual limitations of human beings." He associates thinkers like, Thomas Hobbes, Edmund Burke, Adam Smith, Alexander Hamilton, and later Milton Friedman, with such constrained vision. Their ideas contrast sharply with those of people like William Godwin, Jean-Jacques

Rousseau, Thomas Paine, and later John Kenneth Galbraith—who he links with the unconstrained vision. This tradition he describes as "the conviction that foolish or immoral choices explain the evils of the world—and that wiser or more moral social policies are the solution."

The constraint, as Sowell describes it, arises from different views of human nature. One is the Hobbesian view of human nature. According to 17th century English philosopher Thomas Hobbes, human beings should be viewed (choice #32) rather cynically as selfish, aggressive, fiercely competitive, highly acquisitive creatures, incapable of self-restraint. With this dim view of human nature, he saw the (choice #29) authoritarian state as the only way to keep human beings from killing each other in constant warfare, and destroying civilization. The other, noble savage view of human nature, is build on belief that people, if they lived in a natural state away from the corrupting influence of social institutions, are fundamentally peaceful, co-operative, and altruistically concerned with each other's well being. Popularized by 18th century French philosopher Rousseau, it argues humans are not aggressively greedy, acquisitive, competitive, and merely out to advance their own self-interest—a view those seeing with constrained vision don't share.

In contrast to traditional education, which looks to human nature to identify fundamental constraints, global education emphasizes the limits provided by the finite nature of Earth's life support system. These are different things. Thus economists linked with Sowell's constrained vision, like Milton Friedman, don't want to (choice #40) limit freedom to choose, nor restrict economic activity based on certain environmentally imposed limits. Just as a global citizen / progressive like Donella Meadows would be more comfortable linked to Sowell's unconstrained vision, in economic policy she is associated with *The Limits to Growth*.

The terms (choice #36) global citizens and global education mean different things to different people. By the former, we aren't referring to some narrow-minded jet-setter business elites, who fly all over the world in pursuit of profit. We conceive of global citizens— dating back to the *Coming of Age…*book and Meadows' long running *Global Citizen* column—differently. We like Oxfam's description: "A global citizen is someone who is aware of and understands the wider world—and their place in it. They take an active role in the community and work with others to make our planet more peaceful, sustainable, and fairer."

Ideally global citizens have been shaped by a global education. This seeks to expand individual worldviews by providing a "big picture" look at whole systems and encourages people to use that understanding to aid global human development. It emphasizes the interconnections and interdependencies that traditional, reductionist education often overlooks. It extends boundaries of concern, and strives to involve the whole person—seen as a thinking, feeling, joining, and doing creature.

As accessed in August 2021, *Wikipedia's* global education article includes a lengthy definition of global education. This begins by describing it as "a human mental development program that seeks to improve global human development." Fearing this implies an "everyone ends up sharing a common mental outlook" outcome, I've been tempted to put on my *Wikipedia* editor cap. I'd rewrite the article to 1) emphasize goals of expanding individual worldviews, and (choice #24) celebrating cultural identities and diversity within the global village by cultivating a "we're all in this together" mentality; 2) weave in the main points of a Global Teacher Project "What is Global Education?' article[14] — portraying it as "an extra filter to help children make sense of all the information and opinion the world is throwing at them;" 3) recognize worldviews and human behavior are profoundly affected by emotions.

Given all the interconnections between how we learn, acquire concepts, relate to language, interact with other people, come to value certain abstract ideals, etc. and our feelings, it seems pointless to try and distinguish where thinking—or any of these other activities—ends, and feelings begin. Certainly as we grow, our worldviews change as we 1) learn to protect our feelings (with emotional armor,) and 2) both acquire and discard so-called emotional baggage, or shed armor. Mature, healthy worldviews are linked to emotional intelligence. And, in employing coping mechanisms to (choice #14) shield ourselves from pain and feeling hopeless, we may find laughter has a place in attempts to made sense of a world that sometimes seems nonsensical.

Many who survive the emotional wringer known as junior high, find the high school environment kinder and emotionally gentler. After a K-12 experience and a year or two of college, many people seek to become specialists. Ideally that transition should occur only when one is equipped with a good general educational foundation. Accordingly, many people first establish basic working knowledge and cultural literacy in various fields. These might variously be labeled health and safety, liberal arts, financial literacy, scientific literacy, technological literacy, etc. They then move on to specialized study set in a particular field of knowledge. While this specialization can provide worldviews with important input, its (choice #2) typically narrow focus is a concern. Seems many move on and never re-examine childish beliefs, perhaps relics of parental biases, from a more mature perspective.

Global education seeks to broaden that perspective. I appreciate that when I take off my STEM teacher hat and put on my global educator one. STEM programs refer to efforts to encourage student pursuit of careers in Science, Technology, Engineering, and Mathematics fields, improve the education they receive, and in general build science literacy. From 2010 to 2012 I worked (part-time and mostly remotely) to develop such a program in astronomy education with a NASA funded team at New Mexico State University[15]. Years earlier I'd designed a physical science lab course at Arkansas Tech around a related STS approach.

Peter Mahaffy has been involved in a chemistry-related STEM effort at Kings University in Canada. Upon encountering his comments[16] I felt he could be speaking for me. "...We've become so good at specialization in STEM education, that we divide knowledge into smaller and smaller pieces, and we understand those little pieces exceptionally well...But it's not enough. We need to equip citizens and scientists to think bigger, to think outside and across the boundaries of their disciplines."

Peter's comments were part of a recent *Time* magazine with a "Climate is Everything" special section. In justifying this focus, *Time* editors write, "As the world emerges from the Covid-19 pandemic, it's becoming clear: in every aspect of what comes next—how we plan, build, sell, educate, legislate, move, create—the shared ingredient is addressing climate change." Certainly building climate literacy—see chapter 7—is part of global education. Indeed, I see an important goal in producing global citizens who think, behave, and vote based on protecting our planetary home and the well-being of all its inhabitants. This "People, Planet, Prosperity" goal goes beyond, and is distinct from, related educational efforts to promote what might be called worldview literacy.

Worldview literacy refers to mastery of the concepts, terminology, and background related to a wide range of beliefs and worldview component themes, and at least basic understanding of these beliefs and themes. Such mastery and understanding are indicative of someone with a well-developed worldview—one that's benefited from consideration of many diverse beliefs and worldview themes, and selectively incorporated a few of them into his or her worldview after examining their compatibility with the rest of the framework. Well-developed worldviews can be shaped by global educational experiences that broaden (choice #8) narrow, childish religious orientations, and reflect how one connects to spirituality. We'll turn to this topic in chapter 4 "On Religion" — redefining it to build around concerns deemed fundamentally important.

University philosophy classes might consider worldviews in terms of epistemology, ontology, axiology, teleology, theology, metaphysics, anthropology, and cosmology. We believe our global education approach, starting with seeing ourselves as thinking, feeling, joining, and doing creatures and using thus sorted worldview themes to characterize worldviews, is a more accessible one. One that makes sense, given your worldview is behind what you perceive, think, feel, do, how you treat other people, work with them, and join with them in bigger pursuits

Hopefully the eight words from that philosophy class context didn't intimidate you. Regarding getting help with unfamiliar vocabulary, each *Project Worldview* theme has its own web page, with a links to the other theme it's paired with, and to a related words / background information page where you'll find definitions / mini encyclopedia descriptions. There you'd find the first one, epistemology, defined as "the branch of philosophy concerned with knowledge, its nature, where it comes from, the methods used to obtain it, and limits faced by humans as they attempt to broaden knowledge." Ontology is a word philosophers like that I relate to the building conceptual frameworks part of worldview development.

So far we've emphasized individual worldviews— but we can also consider collective, consensus efforts. From that perspective a "best fit" worldview that humanity collectively assembles can be seen as its current best effort in the ongoing attempt to describe or map Reality. The central tenet in the search for objective reality, claims E.O. Wilson in his 1998 book *Consilience: The Unity of Knowledge*, is the unification of knowledge. He writes, "When we have unified enough knowledge, we will understand who we are and why we are here." If one omits the word "objective," capitalizes "Reality," broadens knowledge to include tacit knowledge[17] and thinks of unifying in terms of connecting as "making whole that which belongs together," I believe he is right.

E. Character Education and Personality Development

Besides promoting worldview literacy and global education, *Project Worldview* values character education, which also means different things to different people. It certainly involves teaching manners and promoting socially acceptable behavior. It can involve teaching values clarification, morals, civics, ethical reasoning, critical thinking, and conflict resolution skills. In the past, that list has extended—sometimes unsuccessfully—to include social and emotional learning, violence prevention life skills education, and health education. Regarding this last topic, stay tuned for chapter 3 visits with a wildly popular (but imaginary) high school health and safety teacher. Here we turn to a real middle school English teacher Jessica Lahey —a lady once skeptical about character education only to gradually become a firm convert. Consider what she had to say in a 2013 article in *The Atlantic*.[18] (And note its relevance to choice #18, choice #24, choice #29, choice #36, and choice #43.)

"As Gallup polls show that over ninety percent of American adults support the teaching of honesty, democracy, acceptance of people of different races and ethnic backgrounds, patriotism, caring for friends and family members, moral courage and The Golden Rule in public schools, it seems odd that this facet of American education has disappeared from public debate over curriculum and academic content. The core values—prudence, temperance, fortitude, and justice—make it into every lesson we teach at our school and every facet of our daily lives on campus. The curriculum we use…is a non-sectarian education in intellectual, moral, and civic virtues through literature, and can be used in conjunction with any academic curriculum." A character education curriculum I value weaves it into global education and includes promoting "healthy bodies." In considering it, a good starting point is "healthy mind" related history.

Famed psychologist Abraham Maslow (1908-1970) was known for promoting understanding of what he described as the ultimate personal development state: self actualization. Happy, self-actualized people, Maslow said[19], have achieved, "the full use and exploitation of talent, capacities, potentialities, etc." They're confident and find their way through life better partly due to a better understanding of themselves. Getting to this state begins with a healthy self-concept. This part of one's worldview includes an organized mental framework of concepts and conceptual schemes a person needs for self-understanding. It provides a structure of knowledge upon which explanations of one's behavior can be based, along with future behavioral plans and expectations.

A (choice #26) healthy self-concept is an important part of a healthy worldview—but sadly many people struggle along the road to emotional maturity. This is not surprising. As Maslow wrote[20], "The struggle between fear and courage, between defense and growth, between pathology and health is an eternal, intrapsychic struggle." The early teenage years represent a particularly difficult time in this struggle—partly due to puberty-related physiological / hormonal changes, and partly due to the fact that children in this age group are often lacking in fellow feeling or empathy. Some are simply hurtfully mean. While one's self-concept can suffer from painful lessons in this "School of Hard Knocks," learning to meaningfully relate to others begins during these years.

Empathy begins with overcoming shyness / fear and talking to other people. The struggle between (choices #14, #18) fearing and finding courage to be yourself often plays out in learning to value authenticity. This refers to the extent an individual's actions (both intended and actual) are consistent with his or her beliefs, values, and deepest desires — despite peer, family, economic, legal, and other pressures. It's said that an authentic person takes this wisdom to heart: "Don't just know thyself—be thyself!" This can involve courageously choosing "the road less traveled," instead of "the path of least resistance."

Individuals lacking courage or conviction often succumb to pressure to (choice #12) conform based on their fear of, or unwillingness to displease given possible consequences, some authority figure. While parents fill that role during early growing up years, increasingly those at the top of some (choice #27) social hierarchy ("the in crowd") occupy it for teenagers. As traumatic as displeasing parents or fending off peer pressure episodes can be, they're often insignificant compared with the authenticity struggles of those where (choice #37) sexual identity is involved. Given that finding courage is typically viewed favorably by society, a "Sharing What Many Consider Very Private" decision to "come out of closet" as gay or trans should be viewed accordingly.

Growing up can bring increasing realization that joining with others can be a powerful way to accomplish things—like (choice #31) changing the world—that would be much more difficult to do by yourself. And you may discover the occasional need to (choice #49) change your attitude / modify your behavior to better fit in. Doing this, you may find, can also increase your comfort in relating to others. Ideally behavior is both driven by, and consistent with, sense of right and wrong (ethics), beliefs and values. Such coherence in an individual's worldview can be an important source of strength. Something one uses to bolster (choice #26) self-esteem, increase effectiveness in interacting with others, and in becoming a healthy, more authentic, more self- actualized person.

Beyond understanding one's own worldview, most find relating well to other people depends on understanding where those other people are coming from: their feelings, beliefs, values, etc. Encounters with people whose behavior, lifestyle, and values are quite different from our own is important in both understanding ourselves and the society we're part of. Many find that making sense of others' behavior requires understanding their worldview—something that may present challenges to one's own beliefs and values. Likewise, if others understand your worldview, they can better understand your behavior and values.

When one makes a value judgment, one makes a statement about the way the world "ought to" be. Clarifying your values and both 1) affirming them in terms meaningful to others, and 2) exploring the implications of practicing and applying them— and being able to do both of these in relation to different cultural traditions or within the framework of various diverse belief systems / worldviews— is known as (choice #49) values articulation. Certainly living your values / "practicing what your preach" is an important part of helping other people come to understand you. And engaging with them in conflict resolution (should disputes between you arise) is easier if you have this mutual understanding, and if you respect each other despite disagreement.

Differences in underlying worldviews and conflicting values are behind disputes all over the world that arise over ethical concerns, societal stresses, technology assessment, environmental quality of life issues, etc. Finding common ground, identifying bridge values, etc. is an essential part of working to resolve intractable conflicts. These typically involve complex issues, communication difficulties, and deep-seated, often unacknowledged differences in worldviews. The people on opposing sides often feel threatened by the other side— indeed they may feel that their sense of identity, cherished beliefs or way of life is being attacked.

Such conflicts often also involve material goods, resources, or real or potential impacts on people and their environment— impacts that are threatening. Sadly, many conflicts—especially in (choice #43 and choice #38) disinformation / conspiracy theory plagued parts of the world—

increasingly involve "alternative facts." In 21st century USA, a culture war polarizes society and, many feel, threatens (choice #29) democracy. Some feel a related conflict poses an even more serious long-term threat: between (choice #1) wishful thinking climate change deniers, and those concerned about growing evidence of global climate change impacts.

The above discussion has taken us beyond character education territory — we've landed back in global education territory. We can ease back into character education by noting that China—under Xi Jinping—is promoting it in connection with Confucius' teachings—as we'll describe in chapter 6.   Before moving on to relate character to personality and psychology, we note US character education has a long history of people 1) not agreeing on what it seeks to achieve—as in what constitutes a "good" person for example, and 2) having difficulty measuring educational outcomes—partly due to vagueness of objectives. Some even advocate dispensing with using the word character altogether, claiming it's a vague concept that "blends personality and behavior components."

Personality has been defined[21] as "the dynamic organization within the person of the psychological and physical systems that underlie that person's patterns of actions, thoughts, and feelings." In the last decade, academics have begun using a five-factor model to facilitate discussion of individual personality differences. These factors are: 1) openness to experience, 2) conscientiousness, 3) neuroticism, 4) agreeableness, and 5) extraversion.   Four of these terms need no comment—neuroticism being the exception.

Neurosis, as Boeree[22] thinks of it, involves a "poor ability to adapt to one's environment, an inability to change one's life patterns, and the inability to develop a richer, more complex, more satisfying personality." Severe cases are linked to emotional disturbance characterized by high levels of stress, anxiety, depression, low self-confidence, and/or emotional instability. All humans at some time may exhibit symptoms of neurosis, and it can take different forms. Those chronically plagued with such symptoms, whose suffering interferes with their normal functioning, are said to have a neurotic disorder and are labeled neurotic.   Many neurotics are emotionally needy. German / American psychologist Karen Horney (1885-1952), who developed a still highly regarded theory of neurosis, felt it originates with parental indifference.

Neurotic disorders differ from character disorders. Unlike people suffering from character disorders, who accept little or no responsibility for problems (preferring to blame them on external factors beyond their control), neurotics tend to accept too much responsibility (or blame themselves). When problems arise, neurotics often assume they're at fault—due to a (choice #26) poor self image and feelings of inferiority and guilt over past (believed to be) wrong choices.

The unhealthy personality and behavioral problems that preoccupied Horney, were not Maslow's focus. The titles of these two psychologists most important books—Horney's *The Neurotic Personality of Our Time*, and Maslow's *Motivation and Personality*—suggest the difference. Maslow was especially interested in the characteristics of, and what motivates, self-actualized people. "Probably the most universal and common aspect of these superior people," Maslow believed (according to biographer Frank Goble,) "is their ability to see life clearly, to see it as it is, not as they wish it to be."[23] In other words, they avoided (choice #1) wishful thinking. In particular, Maslow studied Lincoln, Jefferson, Einstein, Eleanor Roosevelt, Jane Addams, William James, Spinoza, Albert Schweitzer, and Aldous Huxley. Understanding such people, Maslow felt, could be a first step in humanity eventually attaining the (perhaps) utopian dream of universal self-actualization.

Were Karen Horney and her equally prominent psychologist colleague (and sometime lover) Eric Fromm (1900-1980) alive today, they might find themselves especially interested in Donald J. Trump. Neurosis, character disorder, and especially narcissism—they'd look for it all in this man. In his book *The Heart of Man*, Fromm describes narcissists in terms of vanity, self-admiration, self-satisfaction, and (choice #28) self-glorification. He sees the associated antisocial behavior as the anti-thesis of brotherhood/sisterhood/comradery and greatly hindering co-operation.

Donald Trump plays an important role in this book. With the exception its author, Trump is the person whose character as defined by choices he's made, his words, his actions is most closely examined (chiefly in chapters 2 and 3). Why? Given his (choice #43) lack of respect for the truth, as you might expect I'm not one of his admirers. Rather, seeing him through character education and psychology lenses, I believe he provides a useful example of behavior—both as private individual and elected public official—not to emulate, of choices not to make.

Indeed, in contrast to Maslow's humanistic, human potential driven focus on studying the best examples of self- actualized people, students may someday study Trump for opposite reasons. Surprisingly his own niece—Mary Trump, a woman with a Ph.D. in clinical psychology who characterizes her uncle as "a narcissist" and "the son of a sociopath" — may spur this study with her July 2020 book, *Too Much and Never Enough: How My Family Created the World's Most Dangerous Man.*

F. Critical Thinking and Worldview Analysis

In his *The Power of Critical Thinking* text—now in its sixth edition— Lewis Vaughn identifies "egocentric thinking" and "psychological factors such as our fears, attitudes, motivations, and desires" as fitting into the first of two categories of what hinders critical thinking. He links this category to <u>how</u> we think, and notes it also includes (choice #12) "conformist pressures" and (choice #36) "ethnocentric urges to think our group is superior to others."

Vaughn's second category, of what interferes with critical thinking helping our constructing a worldview with a solid belief foundation, is linked to <u>what</u> we think. Within this category he most notably identifies three traps to avoid: 1) a (choice #1) wishful thinking / believing that something is true makes it true, 2) a (what we'll call in chapter 5) cultural relativism that proclaims truth depends on society's beliefs, and 3) only believing in something if we can do so with absolute certainty— otherwise being hostilely (choice #4) skeptical toward it. As chapter 5 will fully discuss, scientific knowledge based on observation and measurement is always associated with some amount of uncertainty. And as Vaughn notes, to become knowledge, "claims need not be beyond all possible doubt, but beyond all <u>reasonable</u> doubt."

In a May 2021 *Skeptical Inquirer* article "How to Repair the American Mind," Guy P. Harrison argues that the need for critical thinking "is too vital now to be left to university philosophy classes" or put down as (choice #30) elitism / "intellectual snobbery." He describes it as "a collection of skills" that help one "figure out important things based on reason more than emotion, and on analysis more than trust and tradition." And as "the conscious attempt to dodge lies and false beliefs while moving in the general direction of truth and reality." Like Vaughn who writes, "A consequence of not thinking critically is loss of personal freedom," Harrison sees critical thinking as a "safeguard against becoming someone's fool or the sad pawn of an empty fantasy."

While often applied at the level of finding the faulty premises that arguments are based on, critical thinking can involve overall assessment of your worldview. This can reveal the basis for your beliefs (such as reason, faith, etc,) which of your beliefs or values are justified based on evidence, which beliefs are important to your emotional / mental health, etc. And it can help you find its internal inconsistencies / contradictions.

For example, a person strongly valuing both (choice #3) "Humbly Unsure" and choice #4's "The True Believer" themes would trigger a *Project Worldview* computer program raising a red flag. Note a contradiction: the latter theme proclaims "My faith in what I believe is free from doubt"—whereas a "Humbly Unsure" someone is full of doubt.

Detailed assessment of your worldview using the one-person analysis tool on the *Project Worldview* website (in file cwm1.htm) includes comparing it with twelve "generic" worldviews. Each of these is based on the twenty choices (of the fifty-two defined) that one feels most strongly about, and which therefore form the core of this worldview. The names of these generic worldviews are shown in Figure #2. In chapter 4 we'll consider how the two Christian generic worldviews in the Figure #2 list have been formulated. And at that chapter's conclusion, I shall bring together results of exploration (mostly conducted in the last sections of chapters 2 and 3) of choices global citizens make.

Figure #2: Twelve Generic Worldviews Defined by *Project Worldview*

HUMANIST PROGRESSIVE
USA CONSERVATIVE
PRO SCIENCE
PRO ENVIRONMENT
PRO BUSINESS
WORLD'S POOREST / STRUGGLING
EARTH-CENTERED SPIRITUALITY / PAGAN ANARCHISM
EXTREME ALT RIGHT
USA AUTHORITARIAN / PATRIARCHAL
CHRISTIAN LOVE / STEWARDSHIP
CHRISTIAN SALVATION / HAVING DOMINION OVER
NEW AGE SPIRITUALITY / MYSTICISM

Hillary Clinton's 1996 book *It Takes A Village* has inspired this attempt at describing the global citizen inhabitants of the global village. She writes, "Technology connects us to the impersonal global village it has created. To many this brave new world seems dehumanizing and inhospitable...But by turning away, we blind ourselves to the continuing, evolving presence of the village in our lives, and its critical importance for how we live together. The village can no longer be defined as a place on a map, or a list of people or organizations, but its essence remains the same: it is the network of values and relationships that support and affect our lives." Later in this book, I'll attempt to identify the choices global citizens make that define these values and relationships.

Two lists—each of twenty worldview themes—will identify global citizens' most strongly preferred choices (Figure #10) and additional preferences (Figure #11.) Likewise I'll identify specific choices and values global citizens will typically detest, and most definitely not want to promote. Two things for you to realize: 1) admittedly, this will be strongly shaped by my own perspective, and 2) others might characterize global citizens somewhat differently.

Beyond quickly comparing your own worldview with the twelve generic ones of Figure #2 using the one-person analysis tool, you can use the two-person analysis tool on the *Project Worldview* website (file cwm2.htm) for more detailed assessment. You can do that in conjunction with a real person with whom you're trying to assess your compatibility. If you're thinking of this person as a potential life partner, the results of your analysis could inform one of life's most important choices. Or that second person could be our hypothetical global citizen— with chapter 4 Figure #10 and Figure #11 lists serving as input data. Based on choices you've made and input data submitted, both one-person and two-person analysis tools will provide Pearson correlation coefficient based output to gauge how compatible your worldview is with either the generic, hypothetical or real person's worldview.[24] (This can be used to address concerns others have expressed about difficulties measuring success of global citizenship courses and character education programs.)

Enough of setting the stage for your exploration of knowledge, beliefs, spirituality, values, etc., and subsequent characterization and assessment of your worldview— it's time to "turn you loose" and encourage your active participation in this drama. I hope the global / character education program, etc. that this book, and support the website offers, 1) provides

help as you examine your attitudes, beliefs, values, etc, and attempt to
sort out "the confusion of existence;" 2) like a good life coach, helps you
with much that's important, including figuring out what you believe in,
value, and why; 3) helps shape your worldview into a happy and healthy
one; 4) helps you make good choices. Regarding this, and the "stupid
choices" you'll encounter in the next chapter, see choice #20. No doubt
use of the rational choice theory approach of the Rational, Dispassionate
alternative found there would preclude one making many poor choices.

Notes

1 Bioregionalism uses naturally defined areas as an organizing principle in
   seeking sustainable and socially just solutions
2 Sedona has been called "The New Age Capitol of North America"
3. detailed in 2016 book *Trump Revealed* by M. Kranish and M. Fisher
4. in a May 15 2017 article in *The Atlantic* by James Hamblin
5. *Pale Blue Dot: A Vision of the Human Future in Space* by Carl Sagan 1994
6. Doherty, William "Home Grown Unitarian Universalism" *UU World*, 2008
7. "Vocabulary of definitions of life suggests a definition" by E. Trifonov
   PubMed 2011
8 it appears that worldviewweekend.com has grown from promoting the
   Christian worldview to young people into a broadcast network that peddles
   conspiracy theories / misinformation.
9 Apostel, Leo etal "Worldviews: from Fragmentation to Integration" 1994   at
                  http://pcp.vub.ac.be/CLEA/reports/WorldviewsBook.html
10 She tragically died of meningitis in 2001.
11 plans for making *Choices We Make* cards on *Project Worldview* website
12 This domain is increasingly thought of in more terms of observable
   behavioral than using psychomotor language.
13 "This Putsch was Decades in the Making" *The NY Times* January 11 2021
14. "The Global Teacher Project" globalteacher.org. uk retrieved August 2021
15 The team was led by Dr. Nicole Vogt. see astronomy.nmsu.edu/geas
16 See *Time* April 26 / May 3 2021 double issue
17 Tacit knowledge is knowledge that is ineffable: it can't be put into words.
   Explicit knowledge can be expressed in words, symbols and be abstracted.
18 Lahey, J. "The Benefits of Character Education" in *The Atlantic* May 6, 2013
19 Maslow, A. *Toward a Psychology of Being*, Van Nostrand, New York 1962
20 Maslow, A. Motivation and Personality, Harper and Row, New York 1954
21 Carver, C. and Connor-Smith, J. "Personality and Coping" in *Annual Review
   of Psychology* Vol. 61:679-707 Jan 2010
22 Boeree, C. George "A Bio-Social Theory of Neurosis" 2002
23 Goble, Frank *The Third Force: The Psychology of Abraham Maslow* Pocket
   Books, New York 1970
24 complete compatibility gives +100% score, incompatibility a minus 100%.
   Given (choice #37) privacy concerns, the results vanish when program ends

Chapter 2: History and Freedom to Choose
A. An Autobiographical Sketch of My Own History
I was born in southern California in 1951. After a conventional middle class, suburban, conservative upbringing—and six years of university, increasingly specialized education—I made a drastic break with my past. I chose to live close to the land in semi-wilderness, and metaphorically attend "The School of Hard Knocks." By the time I was thirty-three, I began writing a book—one that would be described as "providing an inspiring story of the author's own search for truth and an ethical way of life... [and] providing lessons in global citizenship."

As I write, over three dozen years have passed since late 1984 when I began writing *Coming of Age in the Global Village*, which would be published six years later. Along the way I gained a collaborator in the person of Donella Meadows. Unbeknownst to her, "Dana" had long ago played a key role in shaping my worldview, and in my subsequent change of career path and lifestyle. She did this by co-authoring (as part of an MIT team) the best-selling, earth-shaking book *The Limits to Growth*. I first encountered this in 1972 in an undergraduate UCLA geography class I was taking as an elective. After getting my degree, the book influenced a decision I later made. In fall, 1973 I dropped out of a Ph.D. program in astrophysics at UC Santa Cruz / Lick Observatory that I'd worked my tail off to get into. In justifying that decision, I still find myself occasionally using my hands to describe the choice I made.

I start by holding them— as if to clap—a foot apart at chest level. I then move them forward and together. This represents, I tell listeners, my past intellectual path of narrow specialization. Then, after returning them to their starting position, I move my hands forward, but this time apart, as if to embrace something much bigger. I tell people I chose breadth, not depth; a big picture perspective rather than narrow focus; the down to earth "School of Hard Knocks" over the rarefied air of ivory towers. In abandoning astrophysics and embracing global education, I turned away from learning all I could about a single highly technical, esoteric topic that few people cared about. I turned toward experiencing and learning about what matters in being human—and pursuing an ethical lifestyle. In making this transition, I came to think of myself as a global citizen.

I returned to UCLA, but left grad school for good in 1976. After getting an M.S. in physics and a teaching credential, I moved to the Ozarks, and pursued self-sufficient living. This involved house building, installing a wind and solar electricity system, gardening, tending goats /chickens, working as a solar educator / engineering consultant, and starting a family. I lived on twenty-two acres of beautiful, snake and tick infested, mountain bench land. I recalled those years—and described what I called "The Ecosharing Experiment" in the *Coming of Age...* book.

After that experiment ended in mid-1985, I began working at Arkansas Tech University (ATU). There I helped the chemistry program get ACS accredited, developed and taught an innovative general education science lab course, and taught a graduate "Science, Technology, and Human Values" class using the *Coming of Age...* book. And I helped establish a campus observatory—serving as its first director. Leaving ATU after fourteen years, I worked with gifted high school students for five years at what I've described as Bill and Hillary's Clinton's dream school: The Arkansas School for Mathematics and Sciences (ASMS.)

In late 1999, I bought 10.3 acres of Ponderosa pine scattered, devoid of snakes and ticks, land at 7000 ft. elevation in the Sacramento Mountains of southern New Mexico. I spent the next four summer vacations living in a small shed, and building an 1100 square foot passive solar house. I did all the work myself—including digging trenches for foundation footings by hand. By the time the last building inspectors left in late 2003 and I again moved "back to the land," I'd spent around $20 per square foot. This can be compared to the $100 per square foot that people paid building contractors around there to build houses. While the house was not as "pretty" or nicely finished as most professionally built homes, structurally and functionally it was wonderful.

Having helped pay for my two children's college education, I retired from full-time teaching in mid-2003 at age fifty-two. When asked how I was able to retire so young, I credited a lifetime of (choice #45) "Enoughness" / frugal living, a (choice #48) "Work, Play, Pay As You Go" approach, a willingness to invest "sweat equity" in meeting housing needs, and a disdain for notions like "you need a new car every three years." Despite a resolve to stay retired from full-time work and pursue variable star photometry from the dark sky observatory I soon built next to the house, I was continually challenged by a desire to "give something back." Thus I (choice #32) worked as volunteer firefighter, helped local community groups and friends in various ways, taught physics for a year at a Fort Worth prep school, and part-time for New Mexico State

University. Occasional giving back pursuits further characterized my life after moving to an Arizona mountain town in 2014.

As I write, 2020 is about to become 2021. I'll use the story of my Christmas Day 2020 to help you better understand who I am. Normally I would have traveled to spend the holidays with my adult children Dayton and Ruth. They live twenty-five miles apart in the San Francisco Bay area. But the Covid-19 pandemic relegated my 2020 visiting them and their families to iPhone facilitated talk and video.

My in person holiday celebration began around 2:30 PM when I loaded my vegetable casserole contribution to a Christmas dinner, and a few presents, into my Toyota Prius. I drove the 2.5 miles over to my partner Lena's (the name I gave her in *The Worldview Theme Song Book*) house. Since the 1990 breakup of my first marriage, I have found myself fitting into various "families." The local representation of my current one is provided by Lena, her adult son, and her cat. Watching others open Christmas presents I've gifted them renews my feeling of being a bit different. Since I don't do (choice #46) "The Consumerist" thing very well, most presents I give are items (choice # 45) I'm recycling or have made or refurbished. I especially like giving gently used books.

Christmas dinner followed. The evening ended with piano-accompanied singing carols and discussion about this and past Christmases. In other years I might have stayed later, but I headed home to celebrate something I've been doing for over fifty years and hold dear. As part of "citizen science" related observational astronomy work, I had a date with a star—actually a binary star known as AP Andromeda, and an eclipsing one at that. I'll continue this story at the beginning of chapter 5— preceded by a story that speculates as to what helped wire my brain as a kid.

In a way, my Christmas night 2020 experience had its beginnings on Christmas morning 1963, when my parents gave me *The Picture History of Astronomy* by Patrick Moore. The book expanded the worldview of my twelve-year old mind, forcing me to revise my separate concepts of space and time, given the finite speed of light. And in acquiring a new (space-time) concept, my concept of the Sun expanded. I realized, since it takes light eight minutes to travel (at 186,000 miles per second) the 93 million mile distance between Sun and Earth, when we see the Sun we're seeing it as it existed eight minutes ago—not right at the instant we look.

Finishing Moore's book—he was later knighted and became Sir Patrick—spurred my desire to get a telescope. I share this story in chapter 8. Looking out in space to the next nearest star besides the Sun— and vastly farther away— we similarly see alpha Centauri[1], not as it exists at that moment, but as it was roughly four years ago. Looking out in space unavoidably means looking back in time. As I write, the most distant object I've knowingly caught a glimpse of —using the same telescope I bought as a kid and still have—is the bright center, known as 3C 273, of a giant elliptical galaxy[2]. Based on its estimated distance, in seeing it I was looking 2.5 billion years into the past. Pondering that leads to questions about the long-ago history of the universe.

B. History—The Big Picture, and Narrowly Focusing It

When did history begin? Evidence supporting the Big Bang theory suggests our observable universe began 13.8 billion years ago. Earth history began with our planet's formation 4.55 billion years ago. The history of life on Earth began roughly 3.6 billion years ago. Initially essentially confined to the oceans, life didn't significantly move to dry land until roughly a half billion years ago. Until now, life history has been marked by five major extinction crises—the last dating to 66 million years ago with asteroid impact / vulcanism ending the reign of dinosaurs. One can chart human history beginning with Homo Sapiens —our species evolved roughly 300,000 years ago in Africa. But we have increasingly more primitive ancestors dating back to the last common one we shared with chimpanzees roughly eight million years ago.

Human (choice #49) technological history goes back (three million plus years ago) to production of stone cutting tools via flint knapping. Certainly harnessing fire (half a million plus years ago) was a key milestone in the technological progress that separated us from animals. Key advances have not happened at the same time all over the world— there have been geographical differences. Use of the wheel occurred thousands of years earlier in the Old World than it did in the New World. Regional development differences are not surprising given migration out of Africa took a long time—with North and South America starting to fill in significant numbers only 15,000 to 20,000 years ago. .

Regarding human knowledge and worldview development, Jo Marchant writes[3], "The big innovations of the Neolithic are often said to be stone monuments and farming. Yet both of these can be traced back to a deeper shift, as humans began appreciating individual boundaries, and mentally separated themselves from nature." With this (choice #41), human manipulation of nature led to our increasingly dominating it— culminating with the beginning of agriculture (~ten thousand years ago.)

Some historians use this to mark the beginning of civilization—but several advances that together define "civilized behavior" greatly predated it. We traded participation in the "tooth and claw" animal world for coming into our own as "thinking, feeling, joining, and doing" creatures— able to conceive of, and appreciate, planning for a future time, empathy, co-operation, and restraint. Eventually most of us learned "might does not mean right" and became "gentle men." Long before that we became teachers, with recognizing survival depended on transmitting skills and information to children. This first happened automatically given human capacity for imitating others, then progressed into conscious instruction—spurred by the great co-operative, joining to agree on meaning venture known as language development

Philosophers have debated whether language grew out of thinking / need to logically explain (Kant's position,) or need to express feelings (Rosseau's position.) Certainly human activity in the psychomotor domain led to later capability for (choice #47) creative expression / art over 25,000 years ago, and writing, around five thousand plus years ago.

A much less appreciated milestone came with the discovery of counting—which archaeological evidence (of notches cut in bone) suggests happened roughly 50,000 years ago.[4] Without fingers to facilitate counting, modern human minds would never have evolved. Indeed, both mathematics and human consciousness can be thought of as emergent products of (choice #13) brains / complex systems composed of neurons. It seems, both metaphorically and literally, genetically programmed minds are grounded, but culturally programmed ones can soar. Human cultural evolution, guided by memes, took off and left behind biological evolution, guided by genes.

Memes are abstract theoretical units of cultural information—such as a particular behavior, a procedure or recipe for doing something, an idea, a story, etc. —that propagate from mind to mind. Whereas genes are transmitted in reproduction, memes spread by imitation—a process that spoken language, written words, and later electronic sounds and images shape. Just as genes compete in a Darwinian survival of the fittest / natural selection battle, memes similarly compete. Battles are ongoing.

A tame example of this competition involves today's consumers preferring a product—perhaps a book or a song—and buying it. So, as a "winner," more of it is made and it has a longer lifetime than all of the similar, but not preferred, books or songs that are "losers." A dark example of such competition occurred in the 1930s, when memes promoted by Adolf Hitler—such as the belief that Jews were less than human and were to blame for Germany's World War I defeat—resulted in intolerance, hate, fear, and death on an unprecedented scale. Out of Hitler's (choice # 24) scapegoating—and Allies' blaming Germany for starting World War I and forcing the harsh Treaty of Versailles on it— came World War II, and the deaths of over 50 million people.

Surely memes like Hitler and Nazis promoted—and others such as the white supremacist beliefs behind the USA Civil War— have clearly lost, are dead, and will never live again, right? Not so—sadly, related hateful memes are spreading rapidly. Likewise, (choice #24) discrimination against minorities and (choice #17) violence directed at them is growing. Many memes based on lies are pushed by those (choice #43) spreading disinformation and (choice #12) unthinking conformity /censorship—not Valuing Honesty, Learning, openness humanity needs to prosper. Still, numbers of people who value books exceeds those wanting to burn them.

It's been said we must study history so we don't repeat past mistakes. What type of person gets involved in this study? Imagine two idealized people who have different choice #2 preferences: person A, with worldview and associated behavior dominated by the "Mind Narrowly Focused" theme, and Person B, who similarly values the "Mind Open, Vision Global" theme. Key differences between these two person's worldviews can be described using a space vs. time plot.

This is a graph in which distance from the current location is plotted vertically, and time elapsed since the present moment is plotted horizontally (with points to the right in the future, points to the left in the past.) Suppose we locate the thoughts and concerns in each individual's mind in this plot—plotting one point for each of them. Looking at our finished products (Figures #3a, b), note person A's points cluster around the center or origin of the graph. In contrast, person B's points typically extend out from the origin, much farther in all directions. Why? Person A spends more time mentally living in the present and operating nearby, whereas person B's thoughts more frequently take him or her back into the past or forward into the future. Likewise Person B thoughts more frequently involve distant places

Figure #3: Concerns Plotted in Space-Time Diagrams

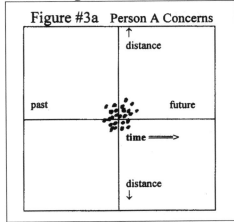

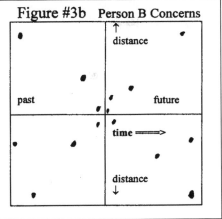

We conclude that Person A's worldview is 1) more here and now centered, and 2) takes in a smaller space-time field of view than Person B's. And that Person B—who knows "the past provides insights into dealing with today's problems" —is more likely to become a historian. And he or she is more likely to visit museums, archaeological sites, cemeteries, old houses where famous people lived, etc. than Person A. Person B, with mind open, vision global and whose "mind ranges freely over the intellectual terrain," is more likely to travel widely —both physically and mentally—than Person A, who "often refuse[s] to deal with issues requiring my mind range widely in space and time." We might also conclude that Person B handles abstract things better than person A—who more concretely often needs to put his or her hands on something, or see it with his or her own eyes.

Making additional distinctions between people who have diametrically opposed choice #2 preferences is less certain —but we might imagine other theme preferences to follow in a predictable pattern. For example, given Person A has not traveled widely, we might expect prejudice against people who look or behave differently than those he or she is used to seeing. That is, Person A types fit into a "small-minded prejudice" stereotypical group, reject (choice #24) a Culture of Tolerance and lean toward Blaming / Scapegoating. Such a person might also prefer narrowly focused themes such as Religious Fundamentalism, Fatalism,

Group Think Imperative, Bitterness and Vengeance, Authoritarian Followers, Valuing Traditions / Status Quo, and Proud Identification / Tribalism. In terms of loyalty to people or particular beliefs, person B, who is capable of "simultaneously holding conflicting beliefs" and more curious to learn about others different from himself or herself, might show less such loyalty. In contrast, person A might, to "keep it simple, stupid," lock unto certain beliefs or people he or she is comfortable with.

Are we making too much out of this open-minded / vision global vs. mind narrowly focused thing? I think not. Indeed, in chapter 4 we'll meet a person who holds out hope for fundamental change in the world's most troubled region—the Middle East—only to the extent to which "Opening the Muslim Mind" occurs. For now I wish to stay closer to home and use person A and person B in reflecting on American history.

C. American History Coming Back to Bite Us?

It's naïve to think the same ideological camps that opposed each other in the Civil War are today squaring off in today's American culture war. Yet the sight of a large Confederate flag carried through the US Capitol Building after insurrectionists breached it on January 6, 2021 perhaps had some wondering? Likewise identifying the opposing worldviews with Person A's and Person B's as sketched in the last section is far too simplistic. And it's naïve to assume people trying to resolve ideological conflicts by talking and finding common ground in "Build bridges, not walls" fashion can always avoid conflict. Sometimes this simply won't work: it's both impractical and the ideological gulf is too wide to bridge.

Might the Civil War with its 620,000 deaths been avoided? Might the huge US Covid-19 pandemic death toll (which exceeds the Civil War death count) have been much lower if Americans had initially been urged to take it seriously? And if their leader had promoted health-conscious behavior as patriotic? Something you do when asked by your president, because you (choice #36) love your country and fellow citizens? Certainly putting the complex societal and economic changes that needed to be made in pre Civil War 1860 America— with its legalized (choice #23) slavery and putting a $ price tag on the lives of black human beings—on an equal footing with simply asking Americans to wear masks, socially distance, get vaccinated etc. today is questionable.

But just as 2020 America has leaders ignoring the law in pursuit of self interest and culture war victories, so too did 1860 America. Some ignored a law passed in 1808 that prohibited the importing of slaves. All told some 12 million Africans were kidnapped and forced to endure the horrors of crossing the Atlantic to America in slave ships in the years between 1619 and 1860. Those numbers should have fallen to zero after 1808— but they didn't. Given a recent discovery, no one can dispute the importing of 110 to 160 slaves into the Mobile, Alabama area aboard the *Clotilda* in 1860—a ship its owner soon burned to cover up the crime.

Chapter 9 in Howard Zinn's *People's History of the United States* begins: "The United States government support of slavery was based on overpowering practicality. In 1790, a thousand tons of cotton were being produced every year in the South. By 1860, it was a million tons. In the same period, 500,000 slaves grew to 4 million." Might that growth of slavery never have occurred if founding father Thomas Jefferson had courageously stepped forward? What if, in late 1791as the Bill of Rights was being ratified, he'd promoted something like the 13th Amendment (finally ratified in early 1865 as the Civil War was winding down)?

On August 19, 1791, son of a freed slave, and talented black man Ben Banneker, wrote to Jefferson. He had taught himself enough math and astronomy to predict a solar eclipse, and publish a scientific almanac. He would later serve as part of a surveying / planning team laying out the US Capitol in Washington. Banneker's letter—which came with a gift copy of that almanac—was long, articulate, and poignant.

He quoted Jefferson's *Declaration of Independence* words: "We hold these words to be self-evident, that all men are created equal, and that they are endowed by their creator with certain unalienable rights, that among these are life, liberty, and the pursuit of happiness." And pointed out Jefferson's slave-owning hypocrisy. He wrote, "How pitiable it is to reflect, that although you were so fully convinced of the benevolence of the Father of mankind, and of his equal and impartial distribution of those rights and privileges which he had conferred on them, that you should at the same time counteract his mercies, in detaining by fraud and violence so numerous a part of my brethren under groaning captivity and cruel oppression, that you should be at the same time guilty of that most criminal act, which you professedly detested in others."

On August 30, 1791, Jefferson wrote back, saying "Nobody more ardently wishes to see a good system commenced for raising the condition of [blacks] to what it ought to be." He could have followed that up by freeing his slaves—something wealthy Virginian Robert Carter III did one week later on September 5, 1791 in freeing 500 slaves. He could have called for a constitutional amendment that embodied the spirit of those noble words he wrote in America's most treasured, founding document...But he didn't. Perhaps it's too much for us to imagine that this one gifted American founding father could have possessed the (choice #2) "long-term foresight" to see seventy-five years into the future when 620,000 Americans had died, and half the country lay in ruins? Might his strong and forceful action have prevented this?

Seventy years after that moment in 1791 when Jefferson failed to act— failed to elevate himself to the next level of greatness—in 1861 President Abraham Lincoln began work to clean up the mess Jefferson and others had left to fester. It was long, bloody work defeating the slaveholders-Jefferson Davis-Robert E. Lee led Confederacy. Let's fast forward over 140 years to a hopeful moment on election night in 2008. 200,000 people have gathered in Chicago's Grant Park—including my daughter Ruth. They're celebrating a black man's election as US President.

As Barack Obama recounts in his book *A Promised Land*—which both my son and daughter gifted me with many years later—"The rest of the night is mostly a blur to me now. I remember [his Republican opponent, Arizona Senator] John McCain's phone call, which was as gracious as his concession speech. He emphasized how proud America should be of the history that had been made and pledged to help me succeed." He ends by recalling what happened at the Lincoln Memorial in Washington, DC later that night. He describes "a small gathering of people on the stairs, their faces obscured by darkness, and behind them the giant figure shining brightly, his marble face craggy, his eyes slightly downcast. They're listening to the radio, I am told, quietly contemplating who we are as a people—and the arc of this thing we call democracy."

That was a night to celebrate America's preference for both (choice #29) democracy and working to build a (choice #24) "Culture of Tolerance." But alas, seemingly (choice #2) small-minded Americans did not see it that way. Rather than bringing the country together in building bridges, not walls fashion, those folks fanned the flames of a long-smoldering culture war. Sadly, a decade later, US President Donald Trump, with repeated references to "the China virus," "the Kung Flu," and "the Wuhan virus," was one of them. Many connected those labels with a surge in hates crimes against Asian Americans in the following months.[5]

Choices We Make in the Global Village   page 49

As US President Joe Biden previously imagined it, July 4, 2021 was supposed to be a day proclaiming success in battling the Covid-19 virus, with long-separated family reuniting in celebrating America's Independence Day. But alas, with many—chiefly young people and Republicans—resisting vaccination, the hoped for goal of 70% of USA adults vaccinated had not been reached. Rather than on the pandemic, many thoughts that day are of July 4, 1776. The Minute Men with muskets and American Revolutionary War sadly take millions of Americans to a fantasy land in which their guns play an important role. But they aren't imagining themselves as long-ago patriots fighting King George's repressive laws, they're seeing themselves finally acting on the hate they feel today for the federal government—one that others (mistakenly) tell them wants to take away their guns.

As Florida Congressmen Matt Gaetz put it, "The Second Amendment is about maintaining, within the citizenry, the ability to maintain an armed rebellion against the government if that becomes necessary." Fueled by such views—and (choice #18) fear— American civilians own 393 million firearms, according to the Small Arms Survey. According to a 2015 *Mother Jones* report[6] this legacy and all those guns come back to bite Americans in the form of staggering costs. Beyond the suffering and death, gun violence annually costs $229 billion—$700 per person every year— to pay the costs for medical treatment, first responders, long-term care, lost wages, legal costs, incarceration of criminals, impact on victims' quality of life, etc ($169 billion of it falls into this last category.)

During Biden's first months in office the US epidemic of innocent people dying, as someone who (choice #17 and choice #24) hates uses an assault rifle to kill, continues. As do Republican efforts—backed by the National Rifle Association (NRA) lobbying and campaign dollars— fighting gun control. Their 2005 success in passing the Protection of Lawful Commerce in Arms Act makes it nearly impossible for victims and families to sue gun makers. By the end of 2021 laws allowing carrying guns without obtaining permits or required training will take effect in nineteen states. Mass murderers are virtually all men, as is membership in hate groups. While these men are extremists, it seems how typical men see themselves has changed in the last 200 years.

Twenty years ago, Fritjof Capra in his book *Hidden Connections*, described a shift from real men once being (choice #46) "those who produce more than they consume," to now manhood "measured in terms of ownership of valuable goods—land, cattle, or cash—and in terms of power over others, especially women and children," with "this image being reinforced by the universal association of virility with 'bigness'…" Possession of a gun vastly increases its owner's power, even if the weapon is not discharged but simply used to magnify one's forceful presence in a dispute. Even if never displayed, just having it can give an insecure male's sense of masculinity a boost.

Over the last half century those (choice #45) seeking bigness, power, stronger, faster, richer, etc have discovered semi-automatic assault rifles. Numbers of AK47, AR15, etc assault rifles in private hands have increased from a few thousand to around 20 million. And their pursuit of bigness / power helps answers the question Angie Schmitt asks in her March 11 2021 *Bloomberg* story "What Happened to Pickup Trucks?"

Schmitt reports American made pickup trucks have added 1300 pounds in weight since 1990. So at 7000 lbs they now weigh three times as much as small cars (like Honda Civics.) And they've become more expensive: the average U.S. pickup truck sells for nearly $50,000, up 41% in the last ten years. The first half of her lengthy article tells the story behind these trends, and what she calls "the truckification of the family car." In sections entitled " make way for petro-masculinity" (a term coined by Virginia Tech professor of political science Cara Daggett,) "built for battle," and "only in America," she makes some surprising connections. She says petro-masculinity glorifies burning of fossil fuels; built for battle implies more than just a place to store guns on racks: these vehicles increasingly resemble tanks, some are even bulletproof; only in America suggests these trucks might play a violent role if American culture wars blow up into civil war.

Some monster truck drivers are already fomenting conflict. They have driven into pedestrians at protest marches. Schmitt describes an illegal, polluting practice known as "rolling coal." With this "drivers of modified diesel trucks blow black smoke at targets of their disapproval (often Prius drivers or bicyclists.)" This behavior would not be worth dwelling on if only Prius drivers and bicyclists[7] had to worry, but fans of (choice #29) democracy should also be concerned. This, and related behavior, is all part of, as Daggett puts it, "a reassertion of white masculine power on an unruly planet that is perceived to be in need of violent, authoritarian order." Schmitt also quotes author Dan Albert who says[8], "…the

American Way is to affirm climate denial, petrol-adventurism, and American exceptionalism."

My last story involves a group supposedly promoting the American Way. It has a large chapter in Yavapai County, Arizona, where I live: the extremist, right-wing militia Oath Keepers. My first confrontation with one of its members came in very public fashion years ago at a city council meeting, when I presented a petition signed by over 800 people. It asked our city and its mayor to sign onto the US Conference of Mayors Resolution on Climate Change, something over one thousand communities had already done. My plea, supported by power-point slides presented in a packed auditorium, was met with climate denial. The petition never even got a proper hearing from the full Council.

Years later a Yavapai chapter Oath Keepers meeting on November 22, 2020 made headlines[9] after one of its members posted a video on *You Tube*. It showed US Congressman Paul Gosar replying to the question, "Do you think we're heading into a civil war?" Gosar replied, "We're in it. We just haven't started shooting at each other yet."

That shooting could start in 2024 in the aftermath of another presidential run by the man who incited the January 6 2021 insurrection. Long before that, the Biden administration needs to act to defuse this real threat to American democracy. Here the remedy is rule of law simple: use section 3 of the 14th amendment to the Constitution to disqualify this man in a simple majority vote of Congress. There is no such simple solution to averting a second "history coming back to bite us" tomorrow if we fail to act today with respect to an even bigger threat: climate change. Giving increasingly obvious signs of looming climate catastrophe, can the Biden administration act to help make the world in the distant year of 2100 a better place? Greta Thunberg and other young people hope so. As she points outs in her frequent talks, she would be 100 years old in 2103

D. Recent American History— narrow-minded view

The 1930s Great Depression brought massive USA government intervention into the country's economy to help the jobless and poor. After victory in World War II fighting Nazi hate and Japanese militarism, and success rebuilding Europe with the Marshall Plan in the war's aftermath, America stood undisputed as the global economic powerhouse and free world leader. But alas, tired of its liberal, big government policies, many wanted America to metaphorically leave the world stage. That did not happen. But, by the late 1950s and early 1960s, the voices of two critics—later to become beloved figures on the American political right—began to be heard above the Cold War white noise chatter that otherwise might have drowned them out.

The first voice was Ayn Rand's—expressed most eloquently in the epic 1957 novel *Atlas Shrugged.* The modern libertarian movement (see choice #39) grew out of Rand's philosophy. Her book celebrates "the virtue of selfishness." Its title refers to the industrial giants who rebel in disgust with a society that fails to respect the (choice #40) "Freedom From Limits" they stand for. Its climax involves "John Galt" speaking as follows, "We will rebuild America's system on the moral premise which had been its foundation...the premise that man is an end in himself, not the means to the ends of others, that man's life, his freedom, his happiness are his by inalienable right."

The second was Milton Friedman's, who like Ayn Rand was a big fan of (choice #34) free market capitalism. In his 1962 book, *Capitalism and Freedom*, Friedman essentially argued that there's no freedom without capitalism, and no capitalism without freedom. By 1979 his fear that "ever bigger government would destroy the prosperity that we owe to the free market and the human freedom proclaimed so eloquently in the Declaration of Independence," led to publication of *Free to Choose*. It proclaimed, "We are still free as a people to choose whether we shall continue speeding down the 'road to serfdom' as [Austrian economist] Friedrich Hayek entitled his profound and influential book, or whether we set tighter limits on government and rely more heavily on voluntary co-operation among free individuals to achieve our several objectives."

While the 1980 American presidential election brought a repudiation of big government, cheered up libertarians, and ushered in the Reagan era, the last four decades have not brought the change some hoped for. The dream of a revitalized, small farm and business-based, (choice #34) competition-based free market economy has not come to pass. Instead, (choice #35) multinational corporation led globalization resulted in factories shut down, and millions of jobs transplanted overseas. Given the extent to which its leaders are in bed with big government, someone might say, "I'm no fan of "Corporate Capitalism." Only to qualify it by saying "But I nonetheless prefer it to 'Social Welfare Statism' —the part of American society that caters to those who want hand-outs."

Such a person might argue that what made America great—an abundance of individual freedom, and self-reliant rugged individuals working hard in pursuit of wealth, dreams, etc. —is increasingly becoming a thing of the past. And add that Americans are increasingly forced to be (choice #28) team players, (choice #24) to be tolerant, to co-operate, be politically correct, and (choice #27) increasingly considerate of the common good. All of this has resulted in limited choices. Given the environmentalists' agenda, the argument continues, those who like the incandescent light bulbs they grew up with are out of luck. And those who want to work developing the land / mining resources, are increasingly told, "No way—we have to protect endangered species!" They counter with, "We'll pick the economy, jobs, and side with the developers (choice #41) over environmental protection / the damned spotted owl or whatever, every time!" And add, "Used to be you could buy a piece of land, build whatever you wanted, and no one cared as long as you weren't hurting them. But today—as a builder, producer, and shaper of the landscape— there are so many damned regulations I have to comply with."

Many see the regulatory morass as worse for (choice #46) consumers because it affects even more people. They suggest a look back to 1979 when the Friedmans asked[10], "Who protects the consumer?" They answered with a summary of what they saw as the failure of various American government regulatory agencies to do the job without negatively affecting economic growth. They concluded, "Insofar as the government has information not generally available about the merits or demerits of the items we ingest or activities we engage in, let it give us information. But let it leave us free to choose what chances we want to take with our lives."

Critics, of the decades-long effort the government has made to protect us from everything, might use automobiles in continuing to rant. "Look at where the trend Ralph Nader started with his 1960s *Unsafe At Any Speed* book [about what they claim turned out to be a perfectly good car] has gone. We got mandated unleaded gasoline, seat belts, air bags, catalytic converters, crash resistant bumpers, anti-lock brakes, and all kinds of things. Consumer protection comes at a price—seems cars that could cost $10,000, now cost $25,000. Operating costs—including insurance—continue to rise. California has led the way in imposing state-sanctioned wisdom on consumers. The result? Air pollution controls, higher gas prices due to excessive taxation to pay for assorted regulations, and—I'm told—it may soon be impossible to even buy a car with a gasoline powered engine there."[11]

"The common good sucks," they might say, agreeing with Reagan's friend British leader Margaret Thatcher. She said[12], "There is no such thing as society —only individuals." Adding, "Their regulations limit our (choice #40) freedom to choose and say, "You aren't capable of making your own decisions." One of the more out-spoken might say, "The government's paternalistic (choice #3) "I Know What's Best for You" orientation is condescending. As a freedom-loving, fiercely independent person, I don't want those corrupt government folks telling me, with their 'one size fits all' approach, how I'm to live my life. This must end."

Many Trump voters sought such an end. They hoped his 2016 election would "Make America Great Again" and "Drain the Swamp." While conceding "the man is not perfect," many of them nonetheless became convinced Trump wanted what they did. They liked his business know-how and background. And hoped he could cut regulations, cut taxes, bring back the manufacturing jobs that left, lead a national economic boom, and reign in the supposed socialist tendencies of his political opponents. And they counted on him to appoint conservative judges to the Supreme Court who would end (choice #42) abortion.

After Trump became president in 2017, he supposedly began keeping promises. He pushed through a big tax cut which put additional money in an ordinary person's take-home pay check. Many applauded as the stock market surged and the value of retirement accounts increased. With respect to America's relations with other countries, narrow-minded (choice #36) American patriot types liked his "America First" orientation. They liked how he stood up to China on trade policy, got out of the nuclear treaty with Iran. And left the World Health Organization. They liked his prioritizing the economy over acting to meet far in the future possible environmental threats. They liked his getting rid of automotive fuel economy standards, power plant emission standards, and pulling America out of the Paris Climate Agreement.

They'll tell you, "Trump was unfairly attacked from all sides. Take his tax returns— he's admitted doing what everybody else tries to do: pay as little tax as possible. He has every right to want to keep them private, just as he does information about how he made his money, his sexual indiscretions, etc." They supported Trump's attacks on the mainstream "lamestream" media, believed his claim that he won the 2020 election, and, long into 2021, continued to see him as the leader of their conservative (choice #36) Republican party tribe.

E. Recent American History— big, open-minded view

Let's recall something Galileo wrote almost four hundred years ago. In his book *Dialogue Concerning the Two Chief World Systems*, he invented a character named Simplicio into whose mouth he put narrow, uninformed, simple-minded arguments—which he later demolished. Alas, my task in demolishing the arguments advanced in the previous section won't be so straightforward. Some of the frustrations expressed have validity. Many are suffering. Certainly life is full of tradeoffs and tough choices—indeed this premise underscores the need for this book and the structure behind it. And while—to pull some words from the (choice #3) "Humbly Unsure" theme—"I can't forget the complexity of the world or the smallness / ignorance of any one person," — I nonetheless will proceed to challenge much of what you've just read.

As I write, 2020 draws to a close. Weeks earlier, in territory occupied by the planet's (choice #29) oldest democracy, millions of Americans made a single choice. Previously, they and their ancestors had individually and collectively made trillions of mostly small choices. Those choices had shaped their lives and society. Many of them were made involuntarily without thinking. Many were made separately, anonymously, informally and without fanfare. But the big choice we refer to here was different—it was part of a formal election process in which people on both sides made their preference known. Indeed many worked tirelessly to promote their voting preference. Many donated money to bolster their side's chances.

Many of those who voted for Joe Biden did so in support of (choice #27) his "Egalitarian Progressive" positions on many issues, or based on their (choice #44 and choice #52) environmental protection concerns. But many of Biden's votes were anti-Trump votes (choice #18) cast out of fear— fear that the continued existence of their democracy was at stake should Trump win. And the firm conviction that Donald Trump had demonstrated he was unfit to lead. That his character was badly flawed.

Let's begin Trump's story[13] with his parents, and a parenting style choice (choice #25) they made: preferring "Tough Love" to "Love as Family Glue." As for many of the fifty-two *Project Worldview* defined choices, there is no clearly preferred choice here. My own parenting style—an estimate, based on my initial two decades as a father—was about 25 % tough love and 75% unconditional love. Of the latter, young Donald got virtually zero. Since his mother has been described as "perfunctorily attentive, but not loving," and "at best a marginal figure in the Trump family," his father Fred Trump, Sr.'s parenting style was critical. Of him, one of young Donald's early mentors and a leader at the military school he attended, Theodore Dobias, said, he "was really tough on the kid."

Mary Trump—along with referring to Fred Trump Sr. as "a high-functioning sociopath"—describes him as "controlling, unrelenting, inflexible, with a heartless view of human worth." While on one hand he repeatedly stressed "the power of positive thinking," his abuse "warped the family," she claims. Fred Sr. verbally terrorized his oldest son, leading to alcoholism and death at age forty-two, Mary Trump charges in describing what happened to her father. Witnessing what his father did to his older brother, Mary says Donald had no "option but to be positive, to project strength, no matter how illusory, because doing anything else carries a death sentence; my father's short life is evidence of that." In summarizing the family life Donald's parents provided him, she writes, "In the end, there would be no love for Donald at all."

Born in 1946, Donald Trump grew up in New York City, continued the family tradition of working in real estate development, and promoted himself as a celebrity By the time he was a reality TV star and neared seventy years old, he first sought elective office: his country's highest. In a winning campaign, he portrayed himself as a successful businessman, and defined himself in largely black and white terms. He was outspokenly against many things, outspokenly for others. But as weeks turned into months, then years, it was what he did, as much as what he said, that really defined him.

Shaped by his father's stern hand and his desire to please him, our future alpha male learned to value strength. Perhaps at the military school he learned to size up situations for what they were, to "see the handwriting on the wall" and make decisions based on evidence. But later in his life his behavior revealed the (choice #1) Positive Expectations side of him. This "wishing makes it so" magical thinking is characteristic of many childish minds. Thus, in early March 2020 as his country's leader, this man, after being thoroughly briefed on the seriousness and catastrophic global potential for the Covid-19 made an unfortunate statement. In an extraordinary exhibition of wishful thinking, he totally downplayed the threat posed by this virus —which had then knowingly infected only fifteen of his countrymen—and suggested it might just disappear. Following this, as the months went on and the virus spread relentlessly, he refused to appear in public wearing a protective mask, and even mocked those who did.

From the start of as his term, Trump had his (choice #2) Mind Narrowly Focused on his own re-election. Everything else, including his country's global reputation based on values it stood for, and its national security, did not matter. Thus he notably threatened the leader of a small nation (Ukraine)— by withholding support as it fought a war against a large neighbor (Russia)—unless that leader said bad things about Donald's political opponent. This blackmail attempt resulted in Trump's (first) impeachment. Later, to boost his re-election chances, he approved of tear-gassing folks peacefully protesting on June 1, 2020 in Lafayette Square near the White House. Within minutes of clearing protestors, he marched to a nearby church for a photo op of him holding a *Bible*.

Years earlier, possibly recognizing his own incredible arrogance, Donald Trump chose the code name "Humble" for use by security forces protecting him.[14] During an early October 2020 hospital stay, while recovering from Covid-19 infection his wishful thinking suggested would never happen, he disregarded the health of those security forces. He insisted they drive him around the hospital in another re-election publicity stunt. Donald's (choice #3) "I Know What's Best for You" campaigning—which ignored mask-wearing, social distancing guidelines—led to untold numbers of virus infections. Several of his own staff were infected, as were 130 of his security forces. By the time 2020 election votes were counted, those fifteen infections had grown to ten million—with roughly one in forty, or a quarter million of his countrymen, dead as a result. Near its peak, 200,000 new USA cases were being added daily and American deaths reached over 3,000 per day—more than perished in the terrorist attacks of 9/11/2001.

Although Christian evangelicals overwhelmingly supported Trump, if their adopted torch-bearer were to stand with them as a (choice #4) "True Believer," it would not be because he, like they, claimed to be (like Jesus) other-oriented. His faith — "faith…free from doubt" —was in himself. Sharing their preference for faith and wishful thinking over reason, their leader is no fan of the "Scientific Method" (choice #10). His scientific illiteracy extended to promoting injection of disinfectant to kill

Covid-19. His pandemic "leadership" routinely ignored advice of medical science professionals, just as he ignored science as a climate denier. In late summer 2020, while talking with leaders in California as it suffered from record extreme climate driven forest fires, he countered their science-based concern for future climate change impacts by saying, "Science doesn't know."

Donald Trump has cultivated a loyal base of supporters. These folks demonstrate a (choice #12) "Group Think Imperative"—where he is the "authority [they put their] faith and trust in feeling obligated and beholden to..." In trashing the "...Intellectual Freedom" other side of this choice, he has consistently identified the professional journalists of the reputable news media—whom he calls "fake news" — as the enemy. Like other strongmen in foreign (choice #29) authoritarian regimes, he has mocked and even threatened them.

This American strong man has his own (choice #17) "Taking Charge➔Violence" style. His "intimidating and instilling fear, by verbally... threatening," often employs the "more modern approach... to file / threaten a lawsuit." He's been involved in a staggering 6,000 lawsuits—many of which he initiated. These— and aspects of cultivating his base and election campaigning —are part of a (choice #18) "Culture of Fear" strategy. Trump undoubtedly won many votes by distorting Joe Biden's centrist leaning and promoting fear that an extreme (choice #38) socialist, freedom-trashing regime would follow a Trump defeat.

In demanding loyalty, Trump turned on many fellow Republicans, including in his own administration. He attacked those who were unable to ignore reality, those who questioned his way of doing things—ousting several with a surprising display of (choice #19) "Bitterness, Vengeance." He has notably taken down inspector generals tasked with making sure government leaders follow legal procedures, and military leaders, he initially appointed, when they displeased him. Such attacks are part of his blaming others style— behavior testifying to a clear preference for (choice #24) Blaming / Scapegoating. Rather than take responsibility for his own failures, Trump looks for someone to blame. Thus, of the reported twenty-six or so women who have accused him of sexual misconduct including rape—they are all lying, he says.

Political opponents and supposedly biased news media are frequent assigning blame targets. They were behind the massive voter fraud that, he charged, explained his loss of the popular vote in the 2016 election. Though a commission he created to investigate the matter found no evidence of this and quietly disbanded after months of investigation, he leveled the same charge as the 2020 election played out.

Children and immature adults often seek someone to blame for their failures—and no one has praised Donald for being "one of the adults in the room." During his 2016 election campaign he used scapegoating to appeal to potential small-minded supporters—often choosing "people who don't look like us" as targets. The highlight of many of his rallies came when attention turned to the wall he sought to build along the Mexican border. It would, he said, keep out the (supposed) bad guys— "many of them rapists." "Who will pay for the wall?" he'd ask. Perhaps those shouting "Mexico!" were really naming people they wanted to blame for their own misfortune or fears? Given his father's history of discriminating against black people (in renting out properties,) Donald's behavior disdains the (choice #24) Culture of Tolerance theme.

Trump's race-based discrimination and efforts to divide people along racial, ethnic, and ideological lines reflects his support for (choice #27) "Hierarchical Rigidity." In finding places for others in this social ladder way of viewing society, his judgment is typically based on wealth. With his 2016 election victory, his taking the top spot in a political power-based national hierarchy was undoubtedly a crowning achievement in his life-long quest for "Individual Glory" (choice #28). Taught by his father to egotistically see the world in zero sum game "I win, you lose" terms, winning became all that mattered. He came to loathe losers.

Trump's opponents cast the 2020 election as a choice between "Democracy or Dictator?" Donald realized that much of his appeal was to those who sought a strong leader to obey, and were (choice #29) "Authoritarian Followers." His disdain for education for democracy was flaunted during the 2016 campaign when he celebrated victory by saying[15] "I love the poorly educated." Upon becoming president, he appointed Betsy DeVos, a wealthy donor and backer of private—often religious, not public— schools, to be Secretary of Education. Despite Trump's supposed embrace of populism and being on the side of ordinary people, this woman—like the vast majority of his appointees— reflected his obvious long-time membership in the exclusive, wealthy world of (choice #30) "Elitism."

Was Trump's appointment of "foxes to guard the chickens" —including foes of public schools, public lands, environmental regulations, etc to lead key federal departments like education, interior, environmental protection, etc — how he sought to keep his promise to "drain the swamp?" Hardly. Rather, with his characterization of long-time public servants as crooks—including promoting "Lock Her Up" chants directed at 2016 election rival Hillary Clinton—Trump showed his disdain for the (choice #32) "Service to Others" theme. His "tear it down," sometimes even (metaphorical) "bomb-throwing," style was pure cynicism.

The 45th USA president's opponents found few if any instances of Trump acting as unselfish public servant. They instead viewed his behavior as consistent with his (choice #33) "Seeking Wealth and Power." He'd learned from his father: you do whatever it takes to succeed, and you celebrate success as evidence of your superiority. His coming of age start along this path was greased by Daddy's loans and pulling strings. From his father, Donald eventually got gifts worth $413 million as reported by *The New York Times* in an October 2, 2018 story.

Trump's progressive critics viewed him as one of those people who was (to borrow Ann Richards' words) "born on third base and made the mistake of thinking he got there by hitting a triple." With respect to his business-related decisions, Trump refused to consider questions—like those from the "Ethical Orientation" (flip side of choice #33) theme— such as "What would happen if everyone did this?" That certainly could be asked of his failure to pay meaningful taxes for many years despite $ millions of income. Answer: they'd be no money for even universally deemed essential public sector services.

Trump's ethics problems go far beyond these questions: they include numerous criminal and conflict of interest charges. Not only has he failed to follow laws, he has great difficulty being honest and telling the truth. At rallies and on Twitter he seemingly would lend support to some of the unbelievable things his base believed in—like in QAnon and other (choice #38) "Conspiracies." Those folks loved his embrace of anti-big government, cutting taxes, (choice #39) Libertarian policies, his opposition to even common sense regulations with a (choice #40) "Freedom From Limits" stance, and his (choice #41) "Human Centered" pro development, "nature should serve people," positions.

Many outrageous conspiracy theories Trump either embraced, or failed to distant himself from, were part of what some called "truth decay." To America's rather humble, often low key 44th president Barack Obama, this lamentably meant "not only do you not have to tell the truth, but the truth doesn't even matter." The often arrogant 45th USA president established quite a record of failing to tell the truth. According to *The Washington Post*, he told 30,573 lies during his presidency, with nearly half coming in the final year. This behavior shows his clear preference for (choice #43) "Spreading Disinformation / Tactical Deception."

Trump's initial political appeal to many hinged on his business background— in creating jobs and cheerleading for (choice #44) "Economic Growth." In seeing him as a successful businessman, they overlooked his numerous setbacks—including those involving treating workers and contractors unfairly, and with paying debts. In his pursuit of wealth, power and more of everything, Donald embodies the (choice #45) "More is Better Mentality..." Yet, despite his father staking him with lots of money as a young adult, he has not embraced "Pay As You Go," but rather has been become a poster child for the (choice #48) "Borrowing Mentality." He's achieved this by suffering six actual bankruptcies, and one instance of a (Chicago-based) bank forgiving a nearly $300 million loan. Those bankers made that decision out of respect for Donald's notoriety for bullying, long-drawn–out lawsuits, and "muddying the waters" delaying tactics. In short, he has walked away and stiffed others out of colossal sums of money. Again, one might ask from an (choice #33) ethical point of view, "What would happen if everyone did this?"

Trump's role in national policy advocacy can be similarly characterized in two ways. First: he's been a cheerleader for reckless borrowing and incurring ecological debt: compromising clean air and water, destroying natural beauty, failing to reduce greenhouse gas emissions, etc. His big tax cut—which exacerbated inequality by giving lots of money to wealthy folks who didn't need it—ballooned the USA national debt by roughly $2 trillion. Second, he childishly tried to undo much of what his predecessor did, without having anything to replace it with. He did this most notably with (unsuccessfully) trying to kill the USA Affordable Care Act, pulling the US out of the Joint Nuclear Treaty With Iran signed by seven nations and the European Union, and out of the 2015 Paris Climate Agreement—undermining that global accord signed by 190 countries to limit climate-disrupting greenhouse gas emissions. This latter action indicated his unwavering support for (choice #52) "Big Business Pushes Global Limits."

In (choice #49) technological or attitudinal fix terms regarding big important problems, Donald Trump didn't try to fix anything. Both his "oppositional defiant" attitude and eagerness to either walk away from, or not acknowledge the reality of existing messes, underscore his childish mentality. And in general, it seems Donald failed to learn lessons that most of us learn in kindergarten: to tell the truth, share, and "clean up your mess". He failed to learn you can't have all the toys—or the prettiest girls— to play with. And—despite his cynical use of a song whose creators[16] blasted him for illegally using—failed to learn "you can't always get what you want."

Donald Trump did not get the victory he wanted in the 2020 election, and his childish wishful thinking / lifelong preoccupation with winning / loathing losers prevented him from accepting the result. 81 million voters repudiated him. But he still had the support of many of the 74 million people who voted for him even after he committed two more outrages: 1) he attempted to get the Georgia Secretary of State to "find votes" to overthrow that state's election results, and 2) he incited the January 6 2021 siege of the U.S. Capitol that killed five people and sent lawmakers, including the Vice President, running for their lives.

While masquerading as a populist who preferred the wisdom of ordinary people to experts, the 2020 election aftermath clearly revealed Mary Trump's uncle—not as a (choice #29) democracy-loving man of the people, but as an authoritarian (choice #30) elitist. But unlike some well-educated deep thinkers, his problem with democracy was simple: it was with those who voted against him—and he heavy-handedly attempted to overturn those verdicts. Alas, Trump's appalling behavior had many supporters. Even on January 7, 2021, 145 Republican U.S Congress representatives and senators voted against following the law, as laid out in the U.S. Constitution. They refused to accept the results of all the states certifying Joe Biden's victory in the 2020 election. This group's members, who failed to uphold oaths they swore on taking office, included two people from Arizona we'll discuss in the next section.

Votes for Trump signal colossal educational failure. Using words in the (choice #29) "Education for Democracy" theme, they suggest America's "ability to ultimately select good leaders" is highly questionable. And that idealistic (choice #30) populist hopes to "promote their continuing education" are naïve in this modern day—given how people can be (choice #43) manipulated in our social media / profit-making corporation dominated information (and misinformation) world. Certainly the growing power of money from corporations and wealthy individuals to influence election outcomes and policy is a big threat to American democracy. According to OpenSecrets, such money (in constant dollars) grew from $4.6 billion in 2000 to $14.4 billion in 2020. Another threat: Republican efforts to make voting more difficult and give state legislatures they control power to overturn voting results they don't like.

F. The Freedom to Make Stupid Choices

"The USA is a special nation," argue those spouting (choice #36) American Exceptionalism, "superior to others because of its <u>unique heritage of freedom</u>: throwing off tyranny, liberty, equality before the law, democracy, individualism, etc." Many Americans have historically added a religious dimension to this: "It is our manifest destiny;" "God is on our side;" "We are God's shining city on a hill," etc. And a duty: "America must provide a beacon for other nations to follow." Given the recent behavior of its 45th president and his supporters—including "banana republic" type 2020 election antics—making the above argument for American Exceptionalism is downright laughable. Rather than being a shining beacon for freedom, a big part of American political leadership seems to be pushing its constituents in a direction that devalues truth, law and order, promotes corruption, intolerance and hate, and celebrates "the freedom to make stupid choices."

Two Republican Arizona congressmen have been leaders in this regard. Paul Gosar was formally objecting in U.S. House chambers to accepting Arizona's presidential election results as rioters raged outside on January 6 2021. His political career started with denying the legitimacy of the first African-American president, and promoting the "birther" conspiracy fiction that Obama is not a US citizen. Years later he distinguished himself as being the only one of 538 US legislators to boycott the appearance of Pope Francis before a joint session of session of Congress. He cited the Pope's position expressing concern about climate change, and calling him "a leftish politician." In January 2021 shortly after Paul's role as the siege of the Capitol unfolded, *CNN* interviewed two of his six siblings. (All six have publicly opposed their brother's past candidacy.)

His brother Tim said, "Paul has lost sight of what character and integrity mean, what we were taught as kids growing up...He lies consistently to the American people and his constituents." Later his brother Dave told *The New York Times*, "He's been involved with anti-Moslem groups, and hate groups. He's made anti-Semitic diatribes. He's twisted up so tight with the Oath Keepers it's not even funny."

After rioters broke in and lawmakers fled, Andy Biggs, House Freedom Caucus Chair, was one of four Republicans who refused to wear a mask to protect against Covid-19 transmission in the crowded room. There, roughly 100 people "were hiding from the Trump mob that stormed the Capitol." A January 12, 2021 story by Laurie Roberts in *The Arizona Republic* blasted his refusal on put on a mask, when asked to do so and offered one by a colleague. Roberts' scorn for his "to heck with common decency" action earned him her label of "a class A jerk." As a result, a known four people in that room tested positive for Covid-19 soon after.

In justifying this behavior, anti-mask folks typically cite (choice #40) impingement of personal freedom. Protecting individual freedoms including (choice #23) freedom of speech is a big part of Republican fundraising efforts. Trump forces used this—and their leader's endlessly repeated "Big Lie" that he actually won the 2020 presidential election—to raise over $200 million after his loss. Some Trump voters got as many as thirty emails a day begging for money. With this, they seemingly validated the old adage: "a fool and his money are soon parted." Of course behind national collective stupidity are uncounted multitudes of poor choices that ordinary individuals make. The following stories provide details of a few of these—two of which tragically end in death. We begin with a story about the tradeoffs involved in riding a motorcycle.

Certainly Karl Pohl hasn't forgotten what happened in Michigan in April 2012, when lawmakers lifted the requirement of mandatory helmets for motorcycle riders.[17] Shortly after, his son Scott, an experienced rider, bought a Honda Shadow VLX motorcycle. Karl begged Scott to wear a helmet, texting him with a plea on May 23. Scott, after respectfully citing his love for his Dad, replied, "I'm always going to be more of a risk taker than you ever were. That's where I get a thrill out of life. You may call it stupid, but I call it living." Exactly one month later, he was dead, after a Ford Explorer turned left into his oncoming motorcycle without seeing it. Both his parents believe he might have lived had he been wearing a helmet.

Eighteen months after Scott's death, *The Economist*, in its November 16 2013 issue, reported that American state legislatures were increasingly thinking about the true costs involved, before caving in to pressure to repeal motorcycle helmet laws. With respect to head injuries suffered by helmet-less riders involved in accidents, the article noted, "Such patients typically run up $1.3 million in direct medical costs. Fewer than a third work again." In summing up the opposing sides in this debate, they write, (choice #39) "Libertarians often demand: 'Let those who ride decide,' says Jacqueline Gillan, who heads Advocates for Highway and Auto Safety, an insurer-funded lobby group. Her retort is: 'Let those who pay have a say.'"

I view this issue in terms of freedom vs. restraint. Many years ago Lynton T. Caldwell, in characterizing American beliefs, wrote[18], "The most pervasive and invalid belief of all is that 'freedom' is free—that is it exacts no price, that freedom exists when each individual does whatever he pleases..." Here the issue involves the freedom of motorcycle enthusiasts to enjoy the feel of the wind in their hair—and avoid the hassle of putting on a helmet— vs. the legal restraint that government can place on their activity, given the costs to taxpayers of accidents associated with the exercising of this particular freedom. Those arguing motorcyclists should be free to decide for themselves whether or not to wear a helmet, say people should be free to choose how to live their lives. It's basically Milton Friedman's same message.

Such issues can be resolved by individuals exercising "the freedom to choose responsibility" —meaning they make choices that go beyond their own self interest and factor in society / the common good. But if individuals repeatedly make unwise choices, many would say restraint should be legislated. Though you might expect laissez faire free market capitalists to object to more government intervention in looking out for the welfare of everyone, *The Economist* article's tone suggests otherwise. As does the caption beneath an accompanying photo of a helmet-less motorcyclist: "Born to be wildly irresponsible."

There's more to the text twenty-five year old Scott Pohl sent his Dad before his death. He'd added, "I say a prayer every time I get on my bike too. I ask to be protected. It makes me feel safer so I hope you can relax

Choices We Make in the Global Village
a little more." Many would label this (choice #1) wishful thinking—
something young people, besides their feeling of invincibility— are
notorious for. How often have we heard a young person say (choice #22)
"I don't inhale cigarette smoke, so I won't get addicted?" Despite
decades of public health campaigns —such as the one launched on
February 8 2008 by the World Health Organization (WHO), which
argued that unless governments and societies act quickly to reverse
trends, tobacco use could kill more than one billion people around the
world by the end of the century—over five trillion cigarettes are still
consumed globally every year.

In America, which spends a growing fortune on health care, the Center
for Disease Control (CDC) figures put the annual cost of medical care to
treat adult smoking-related disease at $170 billion per year. Despite this
agency's and others' efforts to point out that "tobacco use is the leading
cause of preventable disease, disability, and death in the United States,"
nearly 40 million US adults still smoke cigarettes. And about 4.7 million
middle and high school students use at least one tobacco product,
including e-cigarettes. Exercising the freedom to make stupid choices,
some would say.

Even a helmeted Scott Pohl could have been killed by someone else
making a poor choice: choosing to drive while drunk. The year after
launching its campaign against tobacco, the WHO launched one against
(choice #22) alcohol abuse. At the time it estimated there were two
billion consumers of alcohol worldwide, with Europeans consuming the
most. It linked alcohol to one-third of all auto accidents, 3.2 % of all
deaths, and 20% to 30% of all cancer. By May 2010, delegations from all
193 member states of the WHO reached consensus at the World Health
Assembly on "a global strategy to confront the harmful use of alcohol."

The WHO, a UN agency founded in 1948, seeks "the attainment by all
peoples of the highest possible level of health." Besides promoting
(choice # 21) human health and well-being, it works for universal health
care, monitors public health risks, and co-ordinates responses to public
health emergencies—including pandemics. It was dealt a financial blow
in 2020 when its long-time largest financial contributor, the United
States, withdrew. This was done as Covid-19 infections and deaths were
mounting, and the American president childishly sought someone else to
blame for his administration's failure to better control the virus' spread.

As September 2021 ended, the USA had recorded 700,000 people dead from Covid-19, and nearly 44 million infections. By then it was clear the extent to which the pandemic would be contained depended on people choosing to wear masks and get vaccinated. Consider two examples of people dying from failing to make those choices and, given their history of urging people to make similar poor choices, and no doubt contributing to other deaths. Before he died in Texas at age thirty, Caleb Wallace helped organize anti-mask protests in the name of freedom. And dead in Florida: radio host Marc Bernier who called himself "Mr. Anti-Vax."

The worldviews of who oppose the vaccinations are shaped by diverse factors, including dislike (choice #39) of government telling people what to do (libertarians and anarchists), and (choice #38) conspiracy theory motivated books or (choice #43) internet websites spreading misinformation in claiming a (non-existent) link between autism and vaccines. Thus some parents choose to shield their children from what they perceive to be dangerous vaccinations—fearing the risk outweighs the benefit. Such parents face (choice #33) an ethical consideration: "What would happen if everyone acts in this manner?" Answer: bad diseases that vaccines have conquered will return. As one reporter[19] wrote in 2012, "...today's parents are the first in history with no memory of the maiming and killing caused by polio, tetanus, diphtheria or measles. At some point an epidemic will remind them." Yes: Covid-19.

The consequences of poor choices—motorcycling without helmet, failing to fasten seatbelt, smoking cigarettes, drinking alcohol and driving, not getting vaccine, etc—can be death. No one suffering that fate celebrates they were "free to choose." Since Milton Friedman's book appeared, the American media information environment has changed dramatically. In 1987, the Federal Communications Commission (FCC) eliminated its 1949 Fairness Doctrine. This required broadcasters cover controversial issues of public importance in fair, honest, balanced fashion so that contrasting viewpoints were at least presented, if not allotted equal time. Its demise allowed those (choice #43) spewing nonsense / spreading disinformation to reach a wider audience. Thus Caleb Wallace sought livestock anti-wormer ivermectin to treat his Covid-19 symptoms.

Since the 1987 FCC decision, cable TV, internet and social media have totally reshaped the information landscape that consumers—and voters—depend on. Many people now get the bulk of their information—not from three major TV networks required to even-handedly share best practices suggested by government, corporate leaders or academia—but from places like Fox News and social media. Consider the story of then twenty-eight year old North Carolina resident Maddison Welch. Alarmed by social media reports of a Washington D.C. child sex ring linked to Hillary Clinton and Democrats, just after the 2016 election he set out driving there to take action. During the drive, according to a June 14 2017 *Washington Post* story, he texted his girlfriend, citing a Biblical verse behind his feeling he had been anointed by God. He asked her to pass a message to his two daughters as to the potential danger he faced, and expressing hope they'd one day understand what he'd done. Hours later he arrived at the pizza place where the pedophiles supposedly operated, armed with fully-loaded AR-15 military weapon and pistol. After terrifying employees and customers, using his weapon to blow open a back door, and finding no sex ring, Welch surrendered to police.

Welch "came to D.C. with the intent of helping people," but later realized "...just how foolish and reckless my decision was." It was based on websites pushing (choice #38) supposed evildoers conspiring and plotting. Sadly, many social media platforms are profit-minded corporations, who care more about getting clicks than their role in (choice #43) spreading misinformation, undermining democracy, etc. Facebook, with 2.8 billion users and valued at $1 trillion, is the biggest.

Consider what whistleblower Frances Haugen, who worked on civic integrity issues for the social media giant has concluded. After releasing thousands of pages of internal documents, an October 3, 2021 CNN Business report says she "says the documents show that Facebook knows its platforms are used to spread hate, violence, and misinformation." She says "there were conflicts of interest between what was good for the public and what was good for Facebook, and Facebook over and over again chose to optimize for its own interests like making money."

Making money from conspiracy theories can be traced to supermarket tabloid pages and talk radio in the 1960s-1970s —including the phony story that NASA faked the whole lunar landing. This undermined trust in government and science & technology. Since then, loud mouth entertainers and the psychologically unbalanced caring nothing about truth, have transformed the field. Aided by internet platforms / social media, pushing conspiracy theories has morphed into a multi-billion $ industry with huge political influence. Before the consequences of its extremism brought it down, infowars.com was a favorite site of right-wing conspiracy enthusiasts. Likewise, tens of millions of Americans are entertained by— and many believe—the bizarre fiction, and rants of extremists with a political axe to grind they encounter on talk radio and online. Believers share the same prejudices as the originators, but with additional gullibility, propensity for (choice #1) wishful thinking, and lack of critical thinking skills / common sense.

By 2020 the situation had gotten so serious that PBS's Frontline devoted a fifty-minute documentary *The United States of Conspiracy* to it. There, infowars.com founder Alex Jones' story becomes a chilling tale when it describes his hooking up with political dirty trickster, and long-time Donald Trump friend, Roger Stone. By 2017, the US President begins promoting conspiracy theory fiction, and "PizzaGate" morphs into the QAnon conspiracy theory. This involves good guy patriot Q battling evil collusion between deep state forces embedded in the US government, Satan worshippers, child molesting pedophiles, and cannibals. As it evolves, Q's battle is increasingly identified with Donald Trump's. It will supposedly culminate with the "A Great Wakening": when everyone realizes QAnon believers have been right about the threat all along. The final victory of the forces of good / God will follow.

Who are these QAnon believers? According to February 2021 American Enterprise Institute poll, they're typically white, and often Christian evangelical Protestant. 27% of those folks said they   "mostly" or "completely" believed, and overall 50% were extremely proud to be Americans. These data, QAnon content, and research into similar beliefs, suggest QAnon believers' worldviews are built around (choice #8) Religious Fundamentalism, (choice #12) Group Think Imperative, (choice #13) Apocalypticism, (choice #17) Evil is Out There, (choice #24) Blaming / Scapegoating, (choice #29) Authoritarian Followers, (choice #36) Proud Identification…, and (choice #38) Conspiracies.

As the Group Think Imperative theme suggests, QAnon believers typically give up making certain choices based on their own critical analysis and let others dictate what they believe. If it were otherwise, they might come to see the forces (choice #43) "Spreading Disinformation / Tactical Deception" as the real evil—not supposedly child molesting Democrats such as Hillary Clinton. To put Hillary into this category—author of *It Takes a Village: And Other Lessons Children Teach Us*, and big fan of *Children's Defense Fund* founder Marian Wright Edelman—is especially sick. Likewise that QAnon promoters often spread their hateful lies under a "Save the Children" banner—the name of an international charity / aid group founded in 1919 and instrumental in helping to establish the UN Declaration of the Rights of the Child—is similarly disgusting.

During the 2020 election campaign, many of the (choice #29) authoritarian followers of the incumbent president believe he is heroically working with Q. Fortunately the alternate reality inside the White House does not extend to the FBI, which labels QAnon believers a major domestic terrorist threat. It breaks up a plot to kidnap and execute Michigan governor Gretchen Whitmer, in which—according to one version— 200 men would storm, bomb, and set fire to the state capital. Even after losing this state by 150,000 votes, Trump lobbies to overturn the will of those voters. Elsewhere, Alex Jones headlines a "Stop the Steal" rally in Maricopa County, Arizona, whose election board there—composed of four Republicans and one Democrat—certifies Biden's victory. This comes after the Republican governor and Secretary of State Democrat Katie Hobbs attest to the lack of evidence of election fraud or wrong-doing. Hobbs receives death threats.

One of those at the Maricopa County rally, Jake Angeli, dressed in fur hat, horned, face-painted, fashion carrying a "Q is Watching" sign, later joined the lawless mob that stormed the U.S. Capitol on Wednesday January 6, 2021. Also with them was thirty-five year old freedom-loving Air Force veteran, and avid Fox News viewer, Ashli Babbitt. Given her rebellious, unwilling to conform tendencies, her military career ended in 2016. Soon after she started what became a debt-ridden pool supply business, she found new causes—one being QAnon, another was opposing efforts to fight the Covid-19. She called it the "controla virus" and "a F___ING JOKE" In July 2020 she wrote, "We are being hoodwinked...The sheep need to wake up."

According to a January 10 *The Washington Post* story, "She avidly followed the QAnon conspiracy theory, convinced that Trump was destined to vanquish a cabal of child abusers and (choice #17) Satan-worshipping Democrats. She believed Wednesday would be 'the storm' when QAnon mythology holds that Trump would capture and execute his opponents." The video she streamed to *Facebook*, prior to attempting to jump through the broken glass of a door inside the Capitol, proclaimed, "It was amazing to get to see the President talk." Her beaming face went on to report "three million-plus" people were marching with her.

Ashli—later identified by her brother as "my beautiful sister" —was happy, and "believed she had found a cause that gave her life purpose." Like virtually all of crowd, numbering in the thousands, who protested that day, she wasn't wearing a mask—but it would not have protected her. This woman—once part of "an Air National Guard unit whose mission is to defend the Washington region and respond to civil unrest"—never completed that January 6 attempted leap. She was shot and killed by U.S. Capitol police.

Given the authoritarian president and his supporters spreading lies and successfully (choice #17) inciting violence, for the first time in American history since the Civil War, the transition of power was not peaceful. With millions believing the election had been stolen— in what Republican commentator Chris Christie called "a national embarrassment" that "something happened that didn't happen"[20] — many were asking, "What has happened to American democracy?" Do a significant number of Americans really prefer (choice #29) authoritarianism to democracy?

Given their inability to select good leaders, of equal concern is where those folks are getting their information. Conservative Republicans have largely depended on the sometimes "alternate reality" provided by the right-wing dominated Fox News network. But that network greatly disturbed the childish, wishful thinking President on election night when it called the outcome in Arizona for Biden. He soon began urging followers to instead watch even more extreme, more removed from reality networks such as One America, and Newsmax. The words of Trump and others (choice #43) spreading disinformation dispute American politician Daniel Patrick Moynihan's statement, "Everyone is entitled to his own opinion, but not to his own facts."

Many fear that, unless "the adults in the room" prevail, American democracy can't survive if a majority of citizens are poorly informed and repeatedly make childish, stupid choices. Should Americans' (choice #23) basic rights include the freedom to make stupid choices? An answer, it seems, should only be given after serious discussion about freedom of speech in this new era. Sadly, we live in a brave new world where "the free marketplace of ideas" has been increasingly hijacked by extremists spreading misinformation, lies, and hate—with voices dramatically amplified by social media.

For many, the October 2019 publication of the book *Antisocial: Online Extremists, Techno-Utopians and the Hijacking of the American Conversation* by Andrew Marantz began a reexamining of freedom of speech by its liberal, once unquestioning, supporters. They'd accepted (choice #40) limits such as not allowing yelling "Fire!" in a crowded theater, but had long fought reining in speech full of lies, misinformation, and hate unless it triggered imminent violence and harm. Most notably progressive groups such as the American Civil Liberties Union have a reputation for fighting censorship even to point of defending the rights of neo-Nazis, etc. to express themselves.

In March 1989, roughly thirty years before Marantz' book, Dana Meadows wrote a "Freedom of Speech—Up to a Point" essay.[21] There she asks, "Who should be the censor?" And eventually answers, "The only entity I'm willing to trust with the critical judgment of public words is the public as a whole, just as the First Amendment says." But could she have anticipated a situation where a very significant portion of the American adult electorate—roughly one-third—believed something blatantly and repeatedly shown to be false: that the 2020 election was fraudulent and Donald Trump really won?

One reviewer of Marantz' book chided him for "skepticism about freedom of speech" and the need to balance it "against other liberal principles." But one can argue that, if American democracy is to continue to function as the Constitution intended, those who value truth need to act. Speaking just hours after rioters had been cleared from Senate chambers, former Republican 2012 presidential nominee Mitt Romney warned those who claimed they were standing up for those who felt the election was stolen in opposing election certification efforts. He said, "The best way we can show respect for the voters who are upset is by telling them the truth." A few days later, commentator and advisor to four presidents David Gergen compared the Trump years to Hitler's years in Germany. He wrote[22], "Trump's greatest strength is his ability to convince large swaths of people that what is true is false and what is false is true. He has become a master of 'The Big Lie'—just as Adolph Hitler was." (Reports suggest Trump has some admiration of Hitler.[23])

Up until shortly after the January 6 2021 siege of the Capitol when his Twitter account was suspended, Trump could instantly reach a reported 88 million plus followers. That "bullhorn" helped not only amplify "The Big Lie," but also promote the notion that Donald Trump was a victim.

These beliefs fueled the (choice #19) "Bitterness, Vengeance" that much of the rampaging mob, chanting "Stop the Steal," felt as they stormed the Capitol in an effort to overturn the democratic process. After Trump's expressed anger against the Vice President's lawfully carrying out his duty in that process, many chanted "Hang Mike Pence."

Will (choice #29) American democracy end as Lenin supposedly (not actually) said, "The capitalists will sell us the rope with which we hang them"— but with a (choice #43) twist? (In this version, the capitalists are talk radio loudmouths spewing hate with self serving agendas, and social media / cable news operators concerned with profits not facts, "us" refers to authoritarian demagogues, and "rope" refers to disinformation posts, conspiracy theory promotions to click on, and talk radio / cable news channels to turn to.) Will authoritarian single party rule replace it? Will that be a party of kleptocrats as in Russia, or one that embraces the notion that "democracy means ruling in the public interest,"[24]something many Chinese say in asserting their Communist Party rule is democratic. Can American democracy survive if voters resemble those exercising the freedom to make stupid choices more than informed citizens capable of making responsible choices and selecting good leaders?

G. Choices: Children Make, Global Citizens Make

This section might otherwise be titled "Small Stupid Selfish Choices People Make—And Big Responsible Caring Ones." Besides making this distinction, it also begins an effort to formally define "Choices Global Citizens Make." This will continue in the last section of chapter 3, with discussion of how such citizens view world governance issues, and conclude at the end of chapter 4. There, after factoring in religious perspectives, a sort of generic worldview of global citizens will be presented with Figures #10 and #11. As we head in this direction, we start our list of choices global citizens make by fleshing out our conception of them in four ways.

First, ideally global citizen worldviews have been shaped by a global education as discussed in chapter 1. Second, given the nature of this education, global citizens possess a maturity seldom found in children. They have a much broader perspective than a child's, which is typically confined in (choice #2) "Mind Narrowly Focused" fashion to the here and now—like person A in Figure #3. A global citizen might thus say, in the words of one valuing the Mind Open, Vision Global theme, "I am capable of long-term foresight, am open-minded and curious...my worldview extends in space and time," adding, "I realize the world is complex." Such a person will typically not engage in simplistic thinking — (choice #1) "wishing makes it so" and (choice #7) magical thinking.

Third, realizing "the complexity of the world" and "the smallness / ignorance of any one person"—to use words from (choice #3) the "Humbly Unsure" theme—global citizens can be tentative. I mention this after recalling British philosopher Bertrand Russell saying, "The whole problem with the world is that fools and fanatics are always so certain of themselves, but wiser people are full of doubts." Fourth, as mature adults, global citizens nonetheless take to heart lessons they learned (and haven't forgotten) at a very young age. Some they learn at their parents' knee, like "Don't tell lies," ""Don't cheat," etc. Once in school, according to *All I Really Need to Know I Learned in Kindergarten*, Robert Fulghum says they may learn additional things like, "Don't take things that aren't yours;" "Don't hit people;" "Say you're sorry when you hurt somebody;" "Play fair;" "Share everything;" and "Clean up your own mess."

Based on this list of lessons global citizens have mastered, in recounting recent American history we note Donald Trump's smaller minded, more self-centered, sometimes temper tantrum behavior, falls short. That's to put it mildly. In just one failed lesson area— "Don't tell lies" — his (choice #43) fact-defying, spreading disinformation, has threatened the very "honesty and respect for laws" ethical foundation (choice #33) upon which modern society sits. Donald Trump has been the most simple-minded, narrowly-focused, "childish thinking" president in American history. Evidence in two more areas further illustrates this man's (choice #1) "wishful thinking / wishing makes it so" mentality.

First, in refusing to accept election defeat (by seven million votes,) he complained, about widespread voter fraud. He childishly fired the (widely praised by members of both parties) cyber security chief, who had stood by the integrity of the election. His complaints continued— even intensified—after his own Attorney General announced that Justice Department investigations had found no evidence to support his claims. Second, he claimed[25] in wishful thinking fashion, the Covid-19 virus was vanishing or would soon vanish, thirty-eight times between (the date of the first confirmed American death) February 6, 2020 and October 31, 2020. With a childish-thinking president downplaying the threat—and certainly not modeling responsible behavior—the number of Americans (over 400,000) who died from the virus during the last year of his presidency was far higher than it might have been.

Let's leave Trump behind, but continue contrasting childish and global citizen choices. While on matters of health, consider the choice presented between (choice #21) "Hedonistic Orientation" and "Healthy Orientation" themes. For me personally, a growing up transition came as childhood trips to a neighborhood market to buy candy began to decrease. No doubt much of what Americans buy is purchased with short-term, feel good instant gratification in mind—sometimes in a (choice #20) Passionately Impulsive manner or with (choice #22) lack of self-restraint. Where money is limited, credit cards facilitate the childish "have now, pay later" (choice #48) Borrowing Mentality behavior.

Much buying can be traced to child-like fascination with "experiences / things that are richer, bigger, louder, longer, faster, stronger" (choice #45) More is Better Mentality. One can argue that it was entirely appropriate for Americans to elect a poster child for this mentality— someone who constantly spoke using words like big, great, tremendous, huge, incredible, fantastic, wonderful, terrific, etc. Long before Donald arrived as a big player on the political scene, critics had described Americans as "the spoiled children of the western world." In bolstering this argument, I cite (choice #46) American consumerism. And offer lyrics from another Rolling Stones song ("Wild Horses"): "Childhood living, it's easy to do. The things you wanted, I bought them for you."

As a child of the 1950s, as American consumerism ramped up, by 1970 (when those lyrics were written) I'd learned to refrain from acting on childish impulses. But during those years, America's exuberance of growing up and facing the seemingly limitless frontier with increasingly in-your-face embrace of (choice #40) individual freedom soared. Thus Walter Szykitka, in the preface to the 1974 book *Public Works*, described an (choice #39) anarchist fantasy in which a newly elected US President burns the US Constitution "to symbolize our release from the institutions and procedures it mandates, and to symbolize our freedom from the need to draw up fixed rules and regulations to guide our conduct." Years earlier in 1961, after historians concluded the traditional frontier had closed, newly elected youthful president John F. Kennedy reinforced the "there are no limits" mentality by launching America into the new frontier of outer space, and aiming for the Moon.

For decades I was an unabashed fan of this man—and still think highly of his presidency—but I eventually changed my opinion of Kennedy's character. I realized he was not what he seemed. In many respects he had lots in common with Donald Trump—including his rise to power being greased by Daddy's money, his (choice #21) hedonistic womanizing behavior, and the extent to which he was a fraud. He wasn't healthy and vigorous, plagued only by occasional back problems from a war injury. He hid the chronic, debilitating Addison's disease he suffered from—something destined to leave him a cripple had he lived. His celebrated *Profiles in Courage* book was mostly written by Ted Sorensen.[26]

Nonetheless, unlike Trump, Kennedy had mature critical thinking skills, and was firmly grounded in reality. This is something the world was thankful for, as they facilitated his and his administration's handling the Cuban Missile Crisis with diplomacy. Given this conflict resolution effort—largely built on finding an (choice #49) "Attitudinal Fix" —the world (choice #50) avoided nuclear war. This was built on agreement between Kennedy and Soviet Premier Nikita Khrushchev, one largely based on promises and mutual trust. But even with good choices from clear-thinking leaders, we now know "only the purest luck saved the world from nuclear catastrophe."[27] Human history nearly ended in 1962.

The year before, in 1961, Frank Drake published what we now call "The Drake Equation." It calculates the number of intelligent civilizations in the Milky Way galaxy—those possessing the capability of establishing contact with each other. While it inputs and multiplies together estimates of seven factors, in actuality its output most heavily depends on just one value: L, the average lifetime of the civilization. Drake, in calculating twenty such civilizations existed, optimistically assumed L= 1000 years.

Had different people making stupid choices led the US and Soviet Union back then, humanity's intelligent civilization lifetime, dating from its unintentionally sending radio signals into space in the 1920s, might have spanned but forty years. We'll return to this topic near the book's end. First, we turn our attention, at the beginning of the next chapter, to a key factor behind intelligent humanity's future lifespan: leadership.

Notes

1 Technically the much fainter star Proxima Centauri is a bit nearer. Alpha Centauri is another far southern very bright star. I finally saw it in 2018, along with the Southern Cross, from a wind-blown penthouse room in Costa Rica.

2 3C273 is also a quasar, short for quasi-stellar object since it looks like a star

3 Marchant, J *The Human Cosmos: Civilization and the Stars* Dutton, NY 2020

4 Earliest best-documented evidence for counting comes from a set of notched bones found at Border Cave in South Africa. They are 46,000 years old.

5 An *NBC News* report from Kimmy Yam on March 9, 2021 says hate crimes against Asian-Americans rose 150% in 2020 compared to 2019 levels, while overall hate crimes decreased by 7%

6 Follman, Mark etal. "The True Cost of Gun Violence in America" *Mother Jones* April 15, 2015

7 Most of my transportation comes from driving a Prius or riding a bicycle

8 Albert, Dan *Are We There Yet?: The American Automobile Past, Present, and Driverless* W.W. Norton New York 2019

9 Kelety, Josh "Paul Gosar Allegedly Met with Oath Keepers and Said the U.S. is in a Civil War" *Phoenix New Times*, February 1, 2021

10 Friedman, Milton and Friedman, Rose, *Free to Choose: A Personal Statement* Harcourt Brace Jovanovich, New York, 1979

11 On September 23, 2020 California Governor Gavin Newsom signed an executive order that bans sales of new gasoline powered cars by 2035

12 said during interview given to *Woman's Own* in September 1987 found on margaretthatcher.org website

13 Much of what follows is either from Mary Trump's 2020 book *Too Much and Never Enough: How My Family Created the World's Most Dangerous Man*, or has been widely reported

14 Johnson, J. and Leonnig, C. "Donald Trump's Secret Service Code name is less humble, more mogul" in *The Washington Post*, November 10, 2015

15 said as widely reported on February 24 2016 in Nevada after primary election

16 *BBC News* in story headlined "Rolling Stones warn Trump not to use their songs or face legal action" June 28 2020

17 Counts, John "Son prayed for safety, but chose not to wear a helmut; now parents grief is doubled" story on mlive.com posted December 2, 2012, updated April 3, 2019

18 Caldwell, L.K. *Environment: A Challenge to Modern Society* Anchor / Doubleday, New York 1970

19 see *The Economist* May 5, 2012 or www.economist.com/node/21554252

20 said on *ABC News* November 22, 2020

21 find her writings in the Donella Meadows Archives at donellameadows.org

22 Gergen, D. "The Perfect Symbol of the Trump Years" *CNN* Jan 13 2021

23 according to a 2021book by Michael Bender of the *Wall Street Journal* , Trump told Chief of Staff Gen. John Kelly, "Hitler did a lot of good things."

24 according to Bruce Dickson in his 2021 book *The Party and the People*

25 Wolfe, D. and Dale, D. "It's Going to Disappear" *CNN* October 31, 2020

26 Parmet, H. *Jack: The Struggles of John F. Kennedy* Random House NY 1980

27 the quote is from a review of *Nuclear Folly* by Serhii Plokhy in *The Economist* April 17, 2021. The book draws on new information from Soviet files, such as only luck prevented a Soviet sub from firing a nuclear torpedo.

Chapter 3: Sociology: People, Trust, Institutions

A. Leadership

Early in 2021 I found myself studying a colorful ad (Figure #4A) in *The Economist* that promotes an MBA program at "the Business School of the Future." It features a strong looking, attractive young woman standing on Mars, and surveying—perhaps directing— the activity pictured around her. Starting at the bottom, as your gaze moves upward, the background transitions from dark reddish ground to gray mountains to brighter sky. The top third contains a sphere, slightly offset upwards from being centered on the woman's head. Blazoned across her chest is an invitation: "Learn to be CEO of Mars, Inc."

For me, the ad recalled a similar scene I'd created over thirty years earlier: the cover of the book I'd spent years writing (Figure #4B). There, as your gaze moves upward from the bottom, a dark mountain landscape background—with photovoltaic solar array in the foreground—gives way to white sky containing a sphere. The sphere, representing the global education symbol and covering the top of the open pages of a book, is centered on a much younger, smaller, fragile looking girl's head. She's standing on the open book's spine—although it also looks like she could be riding on top of a bird in flight. Just below her waist is centered the book's title: *Coming of Age in the Global Village.*

After the book appeared, many people asked me if the girl on the cover was my daughter. No, I'd tell them, it's a girl in Indonesia I never met, just supported through charitable contributions. But my daughter Ruth does have a role in this story: the subscription she gave me over ten years ago—and continues to renew—facilitates my regularly reading *The Economist.* Thus many of the thousands of "More to Explore" links on the *Project Worldview* web pages are to articles in this publication.

I'd been working on the *Coming of Age...* book for about a year when Ruthie wowed them at Head Start by counting to1400 by fives as a three year old! As I write, after graduating from Harvard she's about ten years removed from getting a Ph.D. in economics—a route she chose over an MBA program. I will be very upset if she ever becomes CEO of Mars, Inc. I don't like one message the ad seems to be sending: "there are no limits to what you can do." This is in direct conflict to the message at the very top of the *Coming of Age* book cover, where reference to *The Limits to Growth* book appears.

Figure #4: Contrasting Images

Figure #4A	Figure #4B
	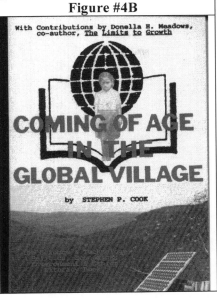

These conflicting messages play out in choice #40—between Freedom From Limits and Limits and Ethics themes. The contrasting words each of the theme descriptions end with are especially relevant to the messages associated with future CEO of Mars vs. humble global village girl images.

excerpt from the Freedom From Limits theme

"If we ever do run out of living space / resources on Earth, we'll simply go elsewhere in space for them."

excerpt from the Limits and Ethics theme

"Going elsewhere in space to live is a fantasy: If we ruin Earth, we have no viable Plan B."

To three keywords they contain, freedom, limits, and ethics, we add two others: individualism and capitalism. Behind the development of the system named by this last word is the thinking of John Locke (1632-1704). As described in the *Coming of Age...* book, Locke identified three ethically-based limitations to individual appropriation of common wealth. He then argued that when people consent to the use of money, these limitations no longer apply. He concluded that individual pursuit of self-interest was the only logical basis for society. He greatly influenced both Adam Smith—often considered the founder of (choice #34) capitalism (more on him in chapter 6)—and the American founding fathers.

Locke and Smith, with his 1776 book *The Wealth of Nations*, laid the (choice #33) ethical foundation for the pursuit of wealth. That same year, the American founding fathers' *Declaration of Independence* launched a movement that celebrated individual freedom. Shaped by the wildness of the American frontier, for many that became a rugged individualism. Two centuries later, critics of the excessive pursuit of wealth began referring to toxic individualism. Key words in the contrasting images in Figure #4— "CEO" and "village"—draw attention to (choice #28) two fundamentally different orientations: "Individual Glory" and "Celebrating Team Accomplishments." The CEO stands in for reaching the pinnacle of individual "Seeking Wealth and Power" success; the village represents a contrasting orientation based on sharing / team-player concern for the common good.

A CEO can also represent something beyond highly paid individual success: he or she can be seen as the influential leader moving a team in a new direction. The subtitle of the 1991 book *The Good Society* by UC Berkeley sociologist Robert Bellah and colleagues—"Shaping the Institutions That Shape Us"—names the broad (choice #31) "Working for Change" effort involved. In a *Commonwealth* magazine summary[1] of this book they wrote, "One of the greatest challenges, especially for individualistic Americans, is to understand what institutions are—how we form them and how they form us—and to imagine that we can actually alter them for the better." Thirty years later, this remains a great challenge—one this chapter is devoted to.

Institutions can be both formal and informal. They all have a social purpose—indeed sociology is sometimes defined in terms of them.[2] Both specific, generic, and loosely defined examples of them can be found associated with words like family, religious, traditional, political, economic, money, etc. For example, the Donnelly clan in Ireland heads a list (on *Wikipedia*) of oldest (at 1073 years) family institutions still in continuous operation. The Catholic Church (nearly 2000 years old) heads another list of oldest religious institutions. Besides tradition, interactions between people are guided by institutions, which typically have rules that structure social interactions. Political institutions promulgate rules known as laws; economic institutions are built on rules related to the concept of money, which itself is something of an institution based on agreement of what will be accepted as payment for goods and services.

Let's return to the word our list begins with—family. We note *The United Nations Economic and Social Development Web*, in a "General Introduction to Major Trends" report, writes, "The institution of family is a basic unit in society, and the multi-faceted functions performed by it makes it a much-needed institution in a society. Some of the important functions performed by the family include reproduction of new members and socializing them, and provision and care for older persons or young. Family... is an institution which resolves or eases a large number of social problems." If a particular family can be thought of as an institution, so can, I would argue, a particular individual. Growing up as a baseball fan in southern California, a story I'll continue in chapter 5, I loved listening to Los Angeles Dodgers' broadcaster Vin Scully. By the time he retired in 2016, after sixty-seven years in this role, many characterized Vin as an institution.

Shortly before I started listening to Vin Scully, the institution known as NASA was created in 1958. With the July, 1969 USA Apollo 11 landing on the Moon, this institution became a household name. Several individuals rose to prominence in association with NASA's moon landing and space program, including astronaut Neil Armstrong, CBS news anchor Walter Cronkite, and NASA administrator James Webb, who the successor to the Hubble Space Telescope is named after. These people all exhibited the capacity to lead, influence, and affect the behavior of others. Besides (choice #3) persuading people to follow, charismatic leaders motivate and inspire them to accomplish great (sometimes extraordinary) things, either (choice #28) individually, or as part of a team. Such leaders communicate their vision and attract followers by infusing them with energy and eagerness for undertaking a particular mission.

MBA programs—like the one future CEO of Mars, Inc. hopefuls might attend—bill themselves as teaching leadership skills. A recent CNBC story on MBAs and leadership, begins with the question, "Is the MBA the most valuable degree in the world?" "Perhaps," it answers, then notes "MBAs don't come cheap" —citing US tuition averaging "$100,000."[3] Prior to learning how to become CEO of some corporate or business institutional enterprise, from an "individuals can be thought of as institutions" perspective, learning to successfully manage yourself—as in

page 82   *Choices We Make in the Global Village*
"Learn to Be CEO of Yourself, Inc." seems a good first step. Later in this chapter we describe how that might work, using this book and *Project Worldview* website as resources. First, we'll identify and discuss the personal characteristics behind successful leaders. Then delve into real world interactions between people, and their pursuit of livelihoods, as related to trust— sharing many stories involving several institutions.

Another early NASA employee, George Mueller, is featured in "Leadership Through Stewardship: A Foundation for Organizational Success Across Cultures"[4] The essay—having choice #15 relevance—connects stewardship to leadership, to individuals leading institutions, and to global citizens. It says, "Stewards are institutional leaders. They act as responsible caretakers for organizations, large and small, which seek to improve and expand. For stewards the pressures of short-term performance, financial or otherwise, threaten to compromise long-term goals, and the challenge for institutional stewards is to navigate these external pressures…Despite the diversity of the types of organizations around the world, we believe there are certain qualities of stewardship, in particular, long-term foresight, effective listening, humility, and trust that are universally applicable…The steward creates a system of enduring values, and then empowers others to perpetuate them…Leadership through stewardship should be a foundational aspect of not just successful organizations, but of our shared culture as citizens of this 21st century global society."

As Paul Hawken notes in his book *The Ecology of Commerce*, originally published in 1994 and revised in 2011, collectively business represents the largest institution. He urges business leaders make decisions (choice #1) based on evidence, and, in (choice #2) global vision fashion, take a long term perspective that values (choice #15) stewardship, (choice #41) respect for nature and (choice #44) sustainability. More generally, long-term success of institutions depends on leaders practicing (choice #22) restraint and (choice #24) tolerance, embracing (choice #43) honesty and (choice #28) co-operation, and not succumbing to (choice #32) cynicism. Trust in something or someone is behind all of these attributes.

B. People and Trust
In his 2020 book *Trust*, Pete Buttigieg writes, "We need trust to negotiate daily life, to participate in an economy, to engage in relationships, and to maintain a democratic society." While trust can be considered from a neurobiological human brain perspective, in psychological and

sociological terms the degree of trust one places in another person, or in an agreement where people are involved, measures one's belief in their honesty, fairness, good intentions, and competence. If the trust turns out to be misplaced, the breach can more readily be forgiven if the other party's failure is due to incompetence, rather than dishonesty or bad intentions.

Measures of trust, based on whether they agree with the statement, "Most people can be trusted," vary widely both with country one lives in and over time. In the USA 46% answered "yes" to this question in 1975, but that fell to 32% by 2012 based on General Social Survey data. In 2014 in Sweden and China over 60% answered yes, in the UK only 30% did, whereas in Brazil and Columbia less than 10% did.

While not necessarily true for people in many countries, generally speaking how much people in the USA trust other people or institutions has declined over the last several decades. Trust in USA government has fallen from 73 % saying they trusted it "to do what is right always or most of the time" in 1958, to just 19% agreeing with this in 2019. Trust in USA mass media—as measured by Gallup surveys—has similarly fallen from 72% in 1976 to 41% in 2019, with only 15 % of Republicans registering such trust.

Such numbers—and events surrounding recent USA elections, the ongoing culture war, and a barrage of (choice #38 and choice #43) conspiracy theories / disinformation—concern Buttigieg. He writes, "The ability to trust in institutions and each other—the ability to trust that we are subject to the same facts, even *living in the same reality* —is now endangered." Globally, a late 2020 survey, conducted by the Edelman Trust Barometer of thousands of people in twenty-seven countries, found "57% of people believe government leaders, business chiefs and journalists are spreading falsehoods or exaggerations."

Once I thought people could be trusted..." begins the (choice #32) "Cynicism" theme. Most would say a decline in trust correlates with an increase in cynicism, and extend that to an increase in (choice #18) the culture of fear. Correspondingly—with an increasingly dim view of human nature —you'd expect 1) naysayers to be less likely to engage in kind, public-spirited service, and 2) expect those increasingly scared of strangers less likely to practice Golden Rule / offer Good Samaritan help. Sadly, in interpersonal relationships, often all it takes is one big hurtful, cheating-related breach of trust to permanently change a predominately (choice #14) "Relaxed, Generous, Loving" orientation into a more "Cautious Processing" one. Or end it completely.

Besides typically being "feelings" infused, marriage is one of the biggest "joining" commitments a person can make. This is especially true when caring for children is involved. As its *Wikipedia* article points out, "marriage is an institution in which interpersonal relationships, usually sexual, are acknowledged or sanctioned...It usually creates normative or legal obligations between the individuals involved... [it may be] performed by a religious institution " Were I to put on my *Wikipedia* editor's cap I'd replace the word "normative" in the sentence above with "ethical" — the study of right and wrong in matters of conduct.

Given its importance, and my experience as part of three marriages—the first producing two children, the second and third presenting step-parenting challenges—not surprisingly I have "wisdom" to impart. Given my associated experience with divorce, I use that word in a "live and learn" way. My first marriage to Annie—and our many years of working well together in making a livelihood, as environmental activists, building a homestead and raising a family—was described in the *Coming of Age...* book. It ended as that book was being published in 1990. The committed relationships behind my second and third marriages spanned the 1993—1999, and 2005—2013 periods, respectively.

In assessing the prospects of a marriage, one needs to consider differences in both worldview[5] and personality. An important part of my personality is conscientiousness. In choice #15 terms, I do "Conscientious, Efficient Stewardship" much better than "Easy-Going, Disorderly, Cavalier." While I took marital and parenting commitments as part of a (choice #25) family very seriously, I also realized that a certain easy-going, accommodating flexibility was needed for the marriage to work. I learned to balance (choice #28) my sense of individual accomplishment, with the need to be fully committed to the marriage team / family. Ideally both partners grow together as their relationship deepens—something neuroticism can preclude. In that regard, famed psychologist Abraham Maslow identified neurotic needs as those that don't promote health or growth if they are satisfied. Certainly both (choice #26) psychological and physical challenges complicate many marriages.

As with life in general, being happy in a marriage involves coming to terms with, and accepting, the tradeoffs involved—and finding a good balance between extremes. Consider in this regard the two themes that make up choice #25: Love as Family Glue and Tough Love.[6] Ideally unconditional love—most fundamentally between husband and wife, but also growing bond between parents and children—holds families together through good times and bad. That, and all members—especially husband and wife—behaving in ethical, considerate, fashion. Doing this requires valuing (in choice #18, choice #19, choice #22, choice #24 respectively) Golden Rule, gratitude / forgiveness, self-restraint, and tolerance, much more than themes they're paired with. When a "child's or spouse's behavior falls short...he / she should be confronted" to borrow words from the Tough Love theme description. How this is done depends on the magnitude of the transgression, the delicacy of the relationship between transgressor and the one confronting him or her, "hurt feelings" factors, etc.

Occasionally one marital partner's behavior is so unreasonable that, when subsequent events unequivocally establish this, no confronting this unreasonable person—not even an "I told you so" — is needed. Thus my second wife apologized to me in the middle of a trip between Arkansas and Virginia when an accusation she'd previously made turned out to be obviously false. The accusation involved our cat, which—confined in a cat carrier— had traveled with us. While initially not pleased, I'd grudgingly accepted her reasoning as to why the creature should come along. But I couldn't accept what she'd concluded as to why the cat was nowhere to be found as we sought to leave a motel room one morning: that I'd either intentionally or carelessly left the room's door open and the cat had escaped. After an hour of her increasingly distraught blaming me, a faint "meow" from the inside the bed's box springs put an end to her (choice #24) scapegoating me.

Looking back on all three of my marriages, I'd say failure of each of my wives to apply the Golden Rule as in (Donella Meadows' words on moral leadership) "You don't want your spouse to commit adultery, so don't do it yourself" was a factor. As was, in the case of the first marriage, my less than delicate, tough love way (roughly five years before she left with the kids) of confronting my wife. Seems I gave her no face-saving way out, other than to admit she was lying. How might I have handled that differently? I have no answer—but I might have done something differently six weeks after she left.

A July 1990 phone call—which both of us expected would be short and confined to details of my picking up / returning the kids as non-custodial parent—ran unexpectedly long. Surprisingly, Annie got emotionally distraught, expressed doubts as to her decision to break up the family, and invited me to accompany her and the kids the following weekend on a trip to St. Louis. I was shocked. I had literally been through an emotional hell during the previous six weeks, but was emerging and facing life with new resolve. Having to respond immediately, I told her I'd gladly make the trip if it could be seen as a first step in putting the family back together—but I did not want to recommit if she would not also. She said she'd think about this.

I have no idea why, but she had a change of heart. When I saw her again three days later she acted like she'd never extended the invitation. She even made a veiled threat of legal action unless I agreed to something she wanted in the divorce / child support agreement. What if I'd just immediately said yes to her previous invitation? Might I still be married to this woman? Had everyone involved suffered in the thirty years since the divorce, I might have regrets—but in actuality, despite a few ups and downs, we've mostly thrived.[7]

My marital history is such that—without becoming (choice #32) very cynical about prospects for two people to make marriage work—I'm now much less willing to unconditionally extend trust. I thus operate in (choice #14) "cautious processing" mode more than I once did. I'm certainly more aware of the potential for emotional factors to disrupt married life—and the "emotional volatility" marriage involves. Something that's volatile is likely to change in a sudden and extreme way. Many have applied the term to financial investments, where stocks are generally more volatile than bonds, which typically behave much less erratically. Something similar can be said about emotionally investing in another person in a committed relationship. While passion can drive such a relationship, in (choice #20) terms, marrying a relatively dispassionate person may make for metaphorically smoother sailing than hooking up with a passionately impulsive one, given emotional volatility considerations. (Might be duller and less fun too—tradeoffs again.)

Over seven decades of human interaction, I've been able to gradually defuse the passion bomb inside me, become less impulsive and more thoughtful. And to find a certain stoic wisdom / serenity and value tranquility—which long ago[8] Seneca in *Letters from a Stoic* described as: "a certain equality of mind which no condition of fortune can either exalt or depress." He added, "There must be sound mind to make a happy man; there must be constancy in all conditions... True joy is serene."

Sustained living in a state of tranquil serenity—without emotional crises that trigger excessive release of stress-related hormones like cortisol—is nice. A life of many high highs and no low lows may be better—but it's riskier in terms of emotional volatility. While eliminating passion in one's life may be too drastic to contemplate, making good choices often involves consciously avoiding passionate impulses and exercising (choice #22) restraint. My next story is from my early, pre-marital days of committed relationships. It involves a woman — I'll call her Sheryl —who failed in matters of restraint on two noteworthy occasions: one marking a key turning point in my life, the other ending with her tragic death.

Sheryl was my high school sweetheart. She was both a kind, caring, considerate person and an academic high achiever. Rather surprisingly, she wanted to have a child and seemingly didn't care if she got pregnant while still in high school. Although I thought she'd be a fine person to eventually raise a family with, I wasn't ready to start at such a young age. Thus, I made sure that the frequency of our liaisons, the precautions taken, etc. minimized the chances of pregnancy.

Suffice it to say Sheryl found something lacking, and as our sophomore year in college ended she had a brief affair with someone she knew was unsuitable for a long-term relationship. She much regretted her fling, and months later came apologetically begging back, but her dalliance ended something we thought would end in marriage. Looking back, although I suffered short-term pain, Sheryl's trust-breaking affair knocked me off the (choice #2) "Mind Narrowly Focused" path I was on. As I described in the *Coming of Age...* book, "The resulting emotional turmoil led me to re-examine my attitudes and values. I began a search for meaning in life. I started doing things I'd never done—reading Eastern philosophy, writing poetry..."

My writing poetry eventually evolved into writing song lyrics. During my months of inner turmoil, I discovered new musical terrain, appreciating, in particular, musicians who were also talented songwriters, such as Carole King, Joni Mitchell, David Bowie, and Neil Young. Later in this chapter I'll continue the story of my inner struggles and adventures along the road to emotional maturity with song lyrics highlights—and continue Sheryl's story.

But first, before leaving my recollections of that summer of 1971, I need to describe how I changed in outward appearance terms. Not only did my hair lengthen considerably, I underwent a political conversion / change in (choice #36) "tribal affiliation": from rather conventional, straight-laced, conservative Republican to hippie, leftist anti-establishment guy. While this didn't happen all at once, it began that summer when I started questioning the trust I'd placed in a certain idealized view of American history, and in its leaders.

C. Trust and Livelihood; Health

One question to consider before tying the marriage knot is, "What prospects do you and your potential partner have for working together as a team?" While teamwork is essential in making the exhausting job of parenting manageable, marriages can flounder long before children enter the mix if husband and wife aren't a good "making a livelihood" match. From a narrow perspective, livelihood refers to what individuals do to secure the basic necessities of life such as food, water, shelter, clothing, etc. My conception of it eventually broadened to include doing this in a healthy way that contributes to the common good—in other words also enhances the prospects for others making a living. Trusting in something to provide a livelihood is unwise if that something is basically (choice #21) unhealthy.

Trusting in the future means having confidence in how things will turn out: in the predictability of certain outcomes. Emotional volatility factors typically make outcomes less predictable. Predictability and trust increase when backed by experience—especially when trusting yourself to do a job similar to ones you've successfully done before. As Naomi Oreskes and Erik Conway write in their 2010 book *Merchants of Doubt*, "If we don't trust others or don't want to relinquish control, we often do things for ourselves. We can cook our own food, clean our own homes, do our own taxes, even school our own children. But we cannot do our own science." They're referring to decisions that depend on scientific assessment of competing claims—like whether smoking is dangerous to one's health.

Their book's title refers to a 1969 tobacco industry memo. This concisely summarized the campaign strategy to combat charges that cigarettes cause cancer and other health problems by saying, "Doubt is our product since it is the best means of competing with the 'body of fact' that exists in the mind of the general public." After discussing a number of issues beyond smoking and health where scientific assessment is critical—such as the effectiveness of a proposed "star wars" missile system, acid rain, the depletion of the ozone layer, dangers of second-hand smoke, danger of pesticides, and global climate change—Oreskes' and Conway's concluding remarks involve trust and cynicism.

They write, "...Our trust needs to be circumscribed, and focused. It needs to be very particular. Blind trust will get us into at least as much trouble as no trust at all. But without some trust in our designated experts—the men and women who have dedicated their lives to sorting out tough questions about the natural world we live in—we are paralyzed, in effect not knowing whether to make ready for the morning commute or not...C.P. Snow once argued that foolish faith in authority is the enemy of truth. But so is foolish cynicism." To which I add, "So is (choice #4) foolish skepticism—where choosing not to believe defies (choice #1) evidence-based reason."

Before turning to questions of trust between individuals, let's consider trust between people and (choice #35) large corporations. Despite the 2010 Supreme Court *Citizens United* decision, few would claim they act like individuals. The *Coming of Age...* book devoted several pages to corporate crime, including tobacco companies' promotion of their deadly products. Recently, Nobel Prize economist William Nordhaus has provided us with his own list of crimes worthy of membership in what he calls "The Ninth Circle of Corporate Irresponsibility"—the title of his April 26 2021 *Time* magazine article. One of the corporations he believes resides there "languishing in their ethical filth" is the maker of my first car: Volkswagen. With respect to its behavior in the last decade he writes, "[it] not only hid the emissions of its diesel automobiles and fabricated the results but designed the equipment to falsify the results. It did this to save money on the production of purportedly 'clean' diesel engines." In wondering about the health effects of the resulting air pollution, he asks, "How many people died as a result?"

Those who have succumbed to (choice #32) cynicism feel people can't be trusted, and are fundamentally self-serving and corrupt. Cynics question whether people are capable of being totally honest, and doubt their ability to overcome emotional bias and reason clearly. Some darkly view (choice #14) loving kind-heartedness and seemingly (choice #18) altruistic good intentions as instances where these basically selfish people are fooling themselves—"deluded, not seeing misguided self-interest for what it is."

Two truly cynical people perhaps should not marry, as shared belief in humans as untrustworthy is not something to build a marriage on. While trust destroying experiences with various women beginning with Sheryl—and other lessons in the School of Hard Knocks—added to my cynicism, the tally has never been such that cynicism consumed me. I still think of Sheryl as basically a loving, kind-hearted, good person. To continue that story, I forgave her transgression. We tried to "pick up the pieces"—but, after previous months of suffering and broadening my worldview, I'd become a different person. I realized we wanted different things, and too many choices we'd individually make would be different enough to prove problematic if we were married. Given my doubts about the prospects for us pulling together as a team and living the life I wanted, we eventually went our separate ways.

Sheryl's desire to have a child abated. After graduate school, she was hired by a major university hospital where she had increasing nursing-related responsibilities. She had married, and seemingly was living a busy, but fulfilling life when I last saw her in late 1984. The same could be said of me—and I was also the father of two beautiful children. Unbeknownst to me, family matters weighed on her mind that day, and she surprised me by sharing two things. First, even though she and her husband worked as professionals pulling down a combined salary that exceeded my family income by roughly fifteen times, given mortgage, and wining / dining, (choice #46) consumption-based lifestyle, they had trouble making ends meet. Second, her marriage was at the point where, she said, either they would decide to have kids, or they would split up.

I heard nothing about her for eighteen months. Then one day I got a call from my mother with sad news. Sheryl had died in childbirth. Many years later in 1997, long after hearing the grim details of Sheryl's pregnancy, and the toxemia that killed her from her mother, I watched the PBS documentary film "Affluenza." This film, and thoughts of my last conversation with her, led me to conclude that affluenza was what really killed Sheryl.

That film defined affluenza as "a painful, contagious, socially transmitted condition of overload, debt, anxiety, and waste resulting from the dogged pursuit of more." After noting a (choice #45) connection, I point out affluenza is a derogatory term most frequently employed by critics of (choice #46) consumerism. I make a choice #21 connection by adding, "Those afflicted often fail to pay attention to what should be fundamentally important to them: their health." My disdain for consumerism and a wasteful lifestyle—something that grew out of my months of "finding myself" after her long-ago affair— is ultimately what kept Sheryl and I from marriage. Although we resumed our friendship after her March 1972 apology—even being occasional lovers on and off for the next three years—I knew that she valued shopping, having nice things, fine dining, etc, and I didn't. And if forced to choose between hedonism and health, she'd pick the former and I the latter.

How does health fit into the "trust and livelihood" theme of this section? Very naturally in that trusting your body and mind is something to build a life on—one with good prospects for a physically and psychologically healthy future. In my naïve conception of how one's life ideally might unfold—and how health education might fit into global education— I imagine a wildly popular high school class called "Health and Safety," taught by the football coach. He is young, fun, trim, sexy, *Friday Night Lights*[9] famous, and a healthy living fanatic. Early in the semester, class one day consists of eating some of the most delicious pizza you've ever tasted, followed by discussion of "What's different about this pizza?"

Our heroic instructor— also big on the learning by discovery approach to teaching—tells students, "The answer is 'three things'—represented by what I'd got here in front of me." In one hand he's got what you later learn are soybeans, in the other are wheat berries, and he's standing in front of a hand crank mill. The question is eventually answered: the pizza is homemade, vegan, and has whole-wheat crust. We soon appreciate both the alternative (choice #21) hedonism and health, and the (choice #46) "Small Producer" implications of that unusual pizza.

Class moves to the home economics kitchen, where we learn how easy it is to make the crust by mixing flour with cold water and olive oil, and using a rolling pin. We see how the flour can be made by grinding wheat berries. And, from a *You Tube* video, how to make tofu from soybeans. We learn how to top the crust in tasty, nutritious fashion: chopping up onions and veggies, stir-frying in olive oil, adding dice-sized, herbal seasoned tofu pieces and finishing with tomatoes to turn it into a sauce.

One day class features our teacher / gifted story teller holding forth on "Dumb Ass Things You Can Do To Kill Yourself Quickly or Slowly." Other classes provide global education / big picture lessons designed to help you quantitatively argue the nutritional superiority of natural food over "junk" food, and also attest to its psychological superiority. The latter testimony starts with a rhetorical question: "Would you rather go to sleep at night recalling the junk or the healthy food you put into your body that day?" And attest to its (choice #44) environmental superiority, including why "Fight Climate Change With Diet Change" bumper stickers make more sense than "Beef—It's What America Eats" ones. Many years later you credit that class with getting you (choice #22) "unhooked" from coffee, fast food addiction, never starting smoking, and eventually adopting a healthy lifestyle. Enough imagining...

My own health education blossomed in the summer of 1975. Helped by *Diet for a Small Planet*[10], I discovered cooking with natural foods, quit eating red meat, and got nutritional common sense. In leaving California for good in 1976, in giving up on a career as an astrophysicist, I sought to become a teacher who made a difference in students' lives. By that fall I was teaching math and science at a tiny Missouri Ozarks high school. That year left me with many memories: of being over-worked and exhausted; of the day I played radio celebrity DJ "Danny Decimal Point" and taught math with help from "Wonder Dog Buster" whose number of barks provided answers to algebra problems; of awarding the kid who improved the most the honor of getting to trim my beard as the class watched.[11] And more seriously, of berating and rather violently pinning a kid against a wall after I saw him harass the school's lone black girl.

My July 1977 move to the Arkansas Ozarks facilitated integrating physical labor into my lifestyle. Whereas "affluenzacks" would pay big bucks for gym membership and invest untold hours in getting exercise with treadmill, lifting weights, etc, I learned to get mine as I also got some other task done. I soon came to see many "labor-saving" devices as health-compromising, and robbing people of needed exercise (See chapter 6 for more on using muscle power, the associated house building, gardening, etc.)

I also found that simultaneously accomplishing two or more things—or solving two or more problems—represented efficiency that I liked. In (choice #21) culinary / hedonism vs. health tradeoffs, finding foods I liked that were also healthy became a lifelong pursuit. One early success involved satisfying my sweet tooth in a way that provided fiber.[12]. This story begins in the summer of 1977, with bulk purchase of several hundred pounds of food—including, in particular, wheat berries, sunflower seed kernels, and raisins. I used my human muscle-powered flour mill to turn the wheat berries into fiber-rich, tasty bread, and learned to snack on a sunflower seed / raisin (or other fruit) combination. I became more enthused after reading of an eye doctor's report of the wonderfully healthy eyes he saw throughout a region of heavy sunflower seed growing operations in Romania. I decided a daily serving (one-fourth cup) of those seeds might be what my eyes—nearsighted, 20/100 since I was a pre-teen—needed. Dried fruit's sugar—unlike refined sugar in soft drinks or typical pastries—comes with nutritious fiber and other healthy compounds. I began regularly (three or four times a week) munching this snack.

Thirty-five years later in 2012, I put away the glasses I'd worn for decades after a driver's license renewal eye test said I didn't need them. A 2016 visit to an ophthalmologist put my vision at 20/20 in one eye and 20/30 in the other, and my overall eye health as something seldom seen in people my age. Granted, I don't know for sure if the sunflower seeds were behind my improving eye health. But my current overall health is outstanding, and I attribute it to a natural foods-based diet and lots of exercise. (Aside: for those needing another healthy snack recommendation, consider homemade popcorn with extra virgin olive oil, nutritional yeast, low sodium soy sauce to taste.)

Certainly (choice #22) self-restraint is an important aspect of health maintenance. I learned at a young age to view "Addiction" (initially to smoking cigarettes) as both an unhealthy choice and as a prison that determined self-restraint could conceivably prevent being trapped inside. No doubt certain people are genetically pre-disposed to addiction, and inappropriate treatment of pain is behind much opioid addiction. But I think (choice #12) peer pressure leads many to addiction to more socially accepted recreational drugs—chiefly tobacco and alcohol.

Consider an incredibly bad choice that a young friend of mine made after I'd lost contact with him. I first met JB, when I was in fifth grade. Over the next year I got to know him well enough to realize that—although he looked and acted fine—he was born with a serious birth defect. JB had only one lung. This surprised me as I'd never noticed him short of breath during strenuous basketball games we'd played. But, sure enough, when he removed his shirt an obvious sunken depression confirmed what he'd told me. I last saw JB as a high school senior, twice at an off campus gathering spot. Each time he was smoking a cigarette. I was shocked. From a common sense, self-interest based, personal health perspective, JB should absolutely not have become a smoker—but somehow this happened. Was it parental failure to educate their son as to health realities he faced? Or school failure? Or plain rebelliousness? Or simply JB's own need to fit in that explained his failure to muster restraint and not cave in to peer pressure?

Health was an important part of my decision to avoid a sedentary American lifestyle and make an attempt at self- sufficient living in the Arkansas Ozarks. Given its pioneering aspects— such as clearing land, pulling out tree stumps, putting in a garden, and building a house—many have concluded I'm something of a self-reliant "rugged individualist." That's partly true. But when I tell them of how well Annie and I worked together at establishing a homestead, and then at raising a family, they see me as more of a (choice #28) team player. This choice—and one of my best moments as a parent—was involved in an issue that many years later threatened the relationship between my son and daughter. It occurred during Dayton's freshmen year in college. He was still back in northwest Arkansas for Christmas break; Ruth had just resumed her junior year at Fayetteville High School (FHS).

One Friday morning, before physics class at ASMS began, I overheard conversation. Two of my students were talking about Ruth. Her picture accompanied a story in that morning's edition of Arkansas's leading newspaper. Ruth, the story reported, was one of only seventy students in the entire country who'd registered perfect scores on both SAT and ACT college board aptitude tests. One of the students talking had attended FHS the previous year and knew my daughter. I overheard him saying, "She's a f—-king genius!" Whereupon the other replied, "Doesn't surprise me—look at her dad."

I recalled this conversation during the four hour after school drive I made from the Hot Springs area, where I lived, to Fayetteville. It provided, I realized, a rare chance in my years as non-custodial parent to bask in the glory of my children's accomplishments. But after that, I wondered, "How Dayton is handling his sister's sudden fame?" I wondered if he'd outgrown feeling jealous of, and perhaps threatened by, Ruth's successes? Upon arriving, my concerns grew, and I knew I had to take Dayton aside and say something important. Say it as his dad—not in the "older brother role" I'd loved to play during our "checking in" talks, joking, banter during one on one basketball games, etc.

I began recalling his numerous accomplishments and how proud of him I was, but then confronted my concerns head on. "Yeah know Dayton, rather than feel threatened or slighted by all the attention your sister is getting, you ought to celebrate your own key role in her success. During those key formative years when she was making sense of the world, when the neurons in her brain were wiring to facilitate that, YOU, more than anyone else taught her and helped her understand reality. Given the isolated way you two grew up and demands on me and your mother, YOU—more than anyone else— helped her learn."

I pointed out that Ruth might not even be alive if her brother hadn't rescued her as a toddler from the rattlesnake on the porch (a story told in the *Coming of Age*...book.) I added a (choice #28) something about when one person succeeded all of those on the team that made it possible should share in the glory. And perhaps I said that the greater the success, the more glory there was to go around. While I don't recall exactly what else I told my son, I might have told him that I'd personally been trying to move away from being an arrogant, egotistical, glory seeker, and toward being a more humble, gracious, team player. And, that I was much more comfortable in that role.

Nearly four years later, I was again concerned about Dayton. Though he graduated with two degrees from UC Berkeley—including one in computer science—with the "dot com bubble" bursting, the job market was horrible. During a "waiting for a security clearance" period that one job offer depended on, he lived with his grandmother for several weeks. I remember, toward the end of this period, missing him when I phoned— but talking instead with his grandmother. She gave me a glowing report about what a helpful, caring, considerate, good guy Dayton was. Hanging up the phone, I realized that I too was glowing.

I'd just been provided with evidence that a "hoped for" outcome—here a parent wanting a child to grow up into a responsible adult—had become a reality. Dayton was born during my "back to the land" years of working hard building a rural homestead, and (choice #47) struggling to make a living. The night before he was born, I finished teaching a 7:00 to 10:00 PM community college class, and began the two-hour drive to the town where my wife was staying near the hospital. Had my car not broken down an hour later, Dayton might have been born that night Annie said the next morning. Roughly twenty-two years after the day I became a father—after many other dreams had faded, and many hoped for outcomes had not materialized despite my best efforts—I realized that venture into (choice #25) raising a family firmly belonged in the "experiencing life's biggest joys" category.

After I left graduate school at age twenty-five, in a sense I lived in two worlds. One was the practical material world of accepting reality as encountered and common sense explanations for the workings of the world.[13] I also lived in a "hoped for" world I mentioned in the last paragraph. That world also included trying to bring about change. As an adult, I spend lots of time (choice #31) Working for Change. This notably takes three different forms. First, where possible, I try to "live the change" I want to see others in society make. In a sense I'm advertising / modeling lifestyle choices I've made. Some of this has involved energy and resource use (described in chapter 7.) Second, some has involved working for a livelihood at doing something that I see as part of the solution, not the problem. Third, I've worked with several groups as an environmental activist.

One notable such effort involved a 1978 trip to Washington DC—paid for by the Sierra Club—to successfully lobby the EPA and USFS in a fight against use of herbicides in the national forest. This was described in the *Coming of Age...* book, as was my work as solar energy educator and engineering consultant between 1979-1985. After that, I taught for nineteen years: the first fourteen at Arkansas Tech University (ATU), and the last five at (previously mentioned) ASMS. In the latter half of my years at ATU—I designed and taught a general education physical science lab course. This introduced thousands of students to solar / renewable energy basics / environmental / global climate change concerns, and taught lab and critical thinking skills. It also promoted science literacy, and better understanding of technologically (and sometimes ethically) complex issues. This is important with respect to the (choice #29) "Education for Democracy" theme. I have no doubt that if we had more capable and dedicated teachers doing this, we'd have fewer "Authoritarian Followers" —the other choice #29 theme.

In returning to our "trust and livelihood / health" theme, let's revisit our imaginary "Health and Safety" course teacher. Were I to assume that role, I might build a safety lesson around "Trusting With Confidence in the Predictability of Future Outcomes." And begin with a School of Hard Knocks story that helped me learn that (choice #1) positive expectations / wishful thinking can be dangerous. Soon after I turned nine, we moved from a modest two-bedroom home in a relatively flat neighborhood, to an upscale four-bedroom one in the hill section of town. Unfortunately the coaster cart my dad built for me—with a big steering wheel but no brakes—also made the trip. Whereas coasting down small hills had previously provided lots of fun, my dad warned me not to try coasting down the much bigger hill offered by the school parking lot across the street from our new home.

Encouraged by a "friend," I ignored this warning. We wheeled the cart to the top of the hill and I got in. Pushing off with my feet—and confident that those same feet could stop me when the time came—I had fun for two seconds before a terrifying reality set in: my "foot brake" would not work. I had three choices. I could 1) crash into the wall two hundred feet away where the parking lot ended, 2) turn out into the street and—after going through several intersections— perhaps coast to a stop two miles away, or 3) turn sharply and stop by intentionally rolling the vehicle over. I chose the last option. During the painful, weeks-long, healing aftermath, my School of Hard Knocks lesson firmly settled into my brain: wishful thinking nearly killed me.[14]

Growing up, I often recalled this incident and factored a (choice #14 and choice #20) cautious, dispassionate "If it can happen, it will happen" into my assessment of situations requiring "look before you leap." Without that, as a fifty-year old roofing the house I was building in a remote New Mexico location, I might have fallen to death or serious injury. This story starts with me about to step onto a two-ladder configuration I'd put together for support. Rather than just trusting it, I asked myself, "What will happen if one of these ladders fails?" I reckoned there was just a tiny chance this could happen, but that risk, I decided, was unacceptable. So I took a few minutes, and installed a rope to grab if catastrophe occurred. As you've probably guessed, soon after venturing onto it, the support structure failed. I had perhaps one-quarter second, as my descent started, to grab the emergency rope.

After successfully doing this—and relocating to safer footing—I found myself shaking. Looking down twenty feet below to where I would have landed, I could see rocks and cactus. While emotionally shaken, I celebrated the fact that my cautious planning had prevented something really bad. Even if I survived the fall, with nearest neighbor over one quarter mile away, cries for help from my bloody, immobile, busted body might have gone unanswered. But prior to that near disaster, I was thinking clearly. I was focusing on the job I was doing—the structure I was building—and in control of my emotions.

D. Controlling Emotions, Becoming CEO of Yourself

In that long-ago summary of their *The Good Society* book, Robert Bellah and colleagues, after describing institutions as "essential bearers of ideals and meanings" put them in the context of real, imperfect individuals. After writing, (choice #33) "all institutions…are necessarily involved to some degree with both wealth and power," they lament these things can become ends in themselves, and lead to corruption. After noting, "Suddenly an institution we thought we understood well begins to look like the institutions we don't understand at all," they allude to someone too often absent from the real world of American society: the hero.

They write, "The heroic individual who cleans up the corrupt institution is a staple figure of our lore in movies and television." In recent years America has learned a hard lesson: with respect to heroic individuals fighting corruption, the gulf between the world portrayed on the screen and the real world can be very large. They elected as President a reality TV star, a man who promised to "drain the swamp." In reality they elected a highly flawed individual—a psychologically challenged person, who as an institution stood for nothing other than personal enrichment. We will confront the reality of this deranged person's assault on American institutions later in this chapter. For now, we put that (choice #32) Cynicism aside and think about what goes into making truly heroic individuals capable of great "Service to Others."

If individuals are thought of as institutions, like all institutions they're subject to rules that structure social interactions. And they need responsible care taking. Seeing a person's physical body as a key part of this corporation isn't a big leap, given the word derives from the Latin word *corpus* meaning body. The human body operating without thinking / "on automatic" has a great deal of built-in functioning know-how as modern neuroscience confirms—recall chapter 1. And with thinking conscious brain serving as its steward or CEO, it's capable of great things. It's capable of becoming a respected institution.

Accepting the challenge of being CEO of Yourself, Inc, and aspiring to greatness, means you are <u>not</u> (choice #26) "Struggling With a Basic Need: Self-Esteem." Nor are you heavily burdened with an attitude built around (choice #32) Cynicism. It suggests that you think of yourself (choice #15) as capable of being a good steward, since you typically don't apply for a job if you don't think you can do it well.

My transition, from being not very emotionally together into a confident manager of crises or of whatever life threw at me, is a story that spans many years. I recall a night in 1973 when my battle with self-esteem had escalated into introspective trauma. Previously engaging in introspection —the process of looking inside one's mind, recalling events, memories, sensory experiences, etc, and reflecting—had typically been a healthy activity. But that night, with harsh critical inner voices tearing at me, it was unhealthy war. I know some people of (choice #5) faith think of their "consciences" in terms of "God's voice" talking to them. And some psychologically distraught individuals can't escape a nagging parent's voice in their head. I didn't have those problems. I had difficulty—long before I fully realized "We are all imperfect creatures"— accepting anything less than perfection.

Writing a poem titled "Me and Myself" helped me get through that night. Forty years later— during a burst of song- writing to deal with pain I was suffering after the breakdown of my third marriage—I would set a reworked and expanded version of this poem to the music of the Moody Blues' song "Nights in White Satin." It begins, with first verse and the refrain as follows:

I'm scared and vulnerable—I need a friend
And this war inside me, I know it must end
What do I care, what others may think?
Make peace with myself, without it I'll sink
End the war [echo] the war
Me and myself [echo] myself
End the war [echo] the war

In those young, not very together days, I wasn't thinking of the need to assume a successful CEO of Myself, Inc. role. Rather, another of my poems suggests a "captain of my ship" metaphor. Forty years later, I likewise used this poem as the basis for a song I called "Sail With Serenity." It was to be sung to the tune of Neil Young's "After the Gold Rush." I replaced his words[15] with "If I'm trusting enough to close my eyes, there's no way I can see..." The song has a message which nicely complements the "Me and Myself" effort. (Both songs can be found in *The Worldview Theme Song Book*.)

Besides writing poetry, getting together to talk and hang out with a friend—I'll call him Craig—also helped. We got comfortable talking about wrestling with emotional issues—something many male conversations avoid. Many years later, on an Arkansas Ozarks morning in the fall of 1980, Craig also inadvertently helped me. His antics led to my conceiving of the CEO of Myself role and giving it some structure. Visiting from southern California, Craig was greatly impressed with two developments since his previous visit months earlier: 1) my infant son Dayton, and 2) the encounter (very pregnant) Annie and I had with a black bear.

Having shared that story in the *Coming of Age* ...book, I won't repeat it. But I will say when Craig showed up were we still spooked. We still imagined this bear lurking behind every tree at the edge of the forest where our house was set. Sensing this, the next morning Craig staged a prank—I still maintain he was actually growling— that had me convinced the bear was really back!

Months passed without any sight of the bear. I began to realize the creature had actually acted maturely and exercised a great deal of restraint when confronted with my laughable—and potentially very dangerous to me—attempts to run him off the previous summer. He first became something of a totem / my power animal.[16] Later I came to think of him as (choice #15, choice #22, and choice #25)) "The Growling Bear": the organized, rational, conscientious, restrained, tough love, no-nonsense chairman of "the board of directors in my head." I'll spare you details of other imagined members of this board, except to say they each embody aspects of my personality.

Sometimes, in conversations with close friends / family, I'll describe some decision I've made and refer, in a strange way, to my relationship with this executive in charge. I'll use an objective "me" personal pronoun, not the subjective "I" —as in "The Growling Bear told me to do this." Just as the personal growth tool known as "The Voice Dialogue Method" offers psychologists' support in one's use of sub-personalities, so does "distanced self talk." As Noam Shpancer describes in a December 2020 *Psychology Today* article, using something other than the first person "I" pronoun, "leverages the structure of language to promote emotion regulation by cueing people to reflect on self." He claims such talk has emotional intelligence benefits—something to point out to friends who think I'm crazy for talking this way!

Before heading back into advantages of being "The CEO of Yourself, Inc." I must share the sad ending of this story. My interaction with Craig helped me grow up and cope with my emotions, and I once similarly assumed it helped him. Alas, in early January 1991 his (choice #26) lack of self-esteem and feeling of hopelessness led to his suicide. Apparently he'd never banished all the negative messages planted in his brain by critical parents during a difficult childhood and adolescence. The shock and sadness of this smart, talented, beautiful, and caring person was compounded by his failure—or trying and failing—to contact me with cries of help.

Craig's tragic demise underscores the importance of emotional intelligence, a term first described by John Mayer and Peter Salovey in 1990, and later popularized by Daniel Goleman.[17] According to Mayer, *etal* in a 2008 *Annual Review of Psychology* article[18], emotional intelligence "concerns the ability to carry out accurate reasoning about emotions and the ability to use emotions and emotional knowledge to enhance thought." Goleman sees four abilities as contributing to it: the ability to 1) be aware of one's own emotions, 2) control those emotions, 3) sense, comprehend, and respond to other individual's emotions, and 4) help other people's emotions develop in the context of a relationship. Some feel that EQ (emotional intelligence quotient) is as important as IQ in predicting a student's future success. Many schools now mount efforts to help students build emotional intelligence.

In truth, rather than thinking of myself as a "corporation," I prefer substituting "institution" since it seemingly carries less emotional baggage. And I like its use in discussions of values, and especially in confronting the question "As an institution, what do you stand for?" Rationally composing an answer, then following the resulting mission statement is quite a task. Suppose you start such a statement—with choice #1— by writing, "I will make decisions based on evidence." Perhaps you can justify this as a thinking creature, but besides doing that and engaging in joining and doing behaviors, you have feelings. So, in what follows, I offer my humble opinion on choice #1 between Evidence-Based and Positive Expectations themes.

With "the adults in the room," I strongly prefer the Evidence-Based theme. This signals I've outgrown childish needs to be taken care of, engage in wishful thinking and accept simplistic explanations. Growing up brings new opportunities for learning by paying attention to outcomes, and from continuing feedback as one interacts with people, culture, and the environment. If self-reliance is the goal, the (choice #25) tough love / School of Hard Knocks is a better teacher than deceiving, sheltering parents playing Santa Claus and Tooth Fairy—or even worse—indoctrinating ones promoting saying prayers.

Eventually most of us learn that continuing to delude ourselves and believing hoped for outcomes can be had simply by wishing them to be, is not a good recipe for success. Certainly it's no substitute for critical thinking and hard work. And that constantly acting on (choice #10) intuitive "hunches" without thinking can be dangerous. Investigating what you can depend on—say the daily sunrise or your iPhone working —and the (choice #7) "why" behind it, builds confidence in the rational / science / technology side of the cultural divide preferred themes in both choice #1 and choice #7 represent. And diminishes the influence of those pushing magical thinking, and the faith-based side of "In God We Trust," "good boys and girls go to heaven," etc.

Despite my preference for the evidence-based theme, I see some emotional coping value in positive expectations. Sometimes knowledge is lacking and an evidence-based answer is not to be found. And that provides space for otherwise evidence-driven people to do a bit of wishful thinking. I'm referring to believing in something that, despite (choice #4) skepticism, is not demonstrably false. I call this believing in "useful fiction," and link it to adopting healthy beliefs. This is especially true when adopting certain beliefs with psychological benefits. Into this category I put widely held beliefs in a (choice #5) Personal God, and in a "life after death" afterlife. While I don't believe in either of these, I recognize they can offer great comfort and psychological benefits to those with unmet emotional needs. Similarly, the less widely held notion that human beings are all (choice #6) mystically connected to each other in an unseen has great psychological health benefit potential.

In addition, I like the way the (choice #1) Positive Expectations theme includes optimism and hope. Consider an alternative appraisal. Margaret Weis[19] has said, "Hope is the denial of reality." While evidence-based types may link hope with self-deception and wishful thinking, I disagree. For me, hope is dwelling on the possibility that your view of a certain aspect of reality—which you believe to be correct—is too grim of an assessment. While some have no place for faith, hope and wishful thinking, many very rational people are willing to admit they have found a place for them in their lives. Many do so to keep (choice #19, choice #20, and choice #23) strong feelings associated with sadness, grief, suffering, and pain from otherwise paralyzing them, or wreaking havoc.

In continuing this task of addressing "As an institution, what do I stand for?" let's return (recall chapter 1) to what Abraham Maslow decided makes one a self-actualized individual. To paraphrase him, he felt such people "see life more clearly than others due to a better understanding of themselves." And that self-actualized individuals have the "ability to see life clearly, to see it as it is, not as they wish it to be." From a feelings perspective, we imagine such people possess emotional intelligence, and can rationally characterize their worldviews.

I began this chapter with an ad from an MBA program trying to recruit students. After distancing my values from theirs, I nonetheless built on the idea that training to become CEO of Yourself—especially acquiring emotional intelligence—was valuable. I traded the corporation metaphor for the institution one—and even alluded to a ship captain metaphor. In the *Coming of Age...*book I used single word metaphor chapter titles. One of them, "Grabbers," conjured up images of (choice #33) greedy, aggressive, people taking more than their fair share to the detriment of others. The contrast between lives of greedy rich grabbers and struggling dirt-poor people, touched people and triggered lots of comments.

Given the thorough coverage of Grabber excesses this earlier book and its *Updates* provide, I'm limiting this book's detailed depictions of grabber behavior. Consider two stories set in the USA health care sector. The first involves a friend who gets fifteen minutes of instruction from a physical therapist in performing simple exercises requiring no equipment other than a bed upon which to lay. She gets a bill for $450—which the government Medicare program is expected to pay. Were all the money directed to the worker involved, the rate of pay would be $1800 / hour. Note at a nearby high school, many teachers work for under $20 / hour.

The second story involves rural Missouri physician assistant /health care provider Patricia Derges. (Recall I lived and taught school in a similar area.) There, in the heart of "the Bible Belt" — in "Christian" County where 50% of its people have identified as "Evangelical Protestant" in a survey—Patricia was recently elected to a seat in the state legislature. This was soon followed by her being indicted—twice. Patricia's indictments were related to charges she perpetuated Covid-19 fraud.

At the three health clinics she owned, and in TV ads, Patricia offered a "potential cure" for Covid-19. According to federal agents, it was actually a (choice #43) fake stem cell treatment. She "abused her privileged position to enrich herself through deception" the first indictment[20] charges. According to the second indictment[21], she helped herself to nearly $900,000 of CARES Act funding, but the Covid-19 testing and other services claimed on invoices submitted were never actually provided. This Covid-19 fraud scheme rip-off puts her in the company of roughly 500 other people the U.S. Justice Dept. has similarly indicted for ripping off collectively nearly $600 million of money provided to help fight the virus in a time of national crisis.[22] Her first indictment also included charges of (choice # 22) distributing highly addictive Oxycodone drugs over the internet without valid prescriptions.

Before leaving Patricia's story[23], I offer two comments. First, voters that elected her to a first term in November, 2020 also preferred Donald Trump. A whooping 75% preferred Trump over devout Christian Joe Biden. Patricia's election was surprising in that federal agents were questioning her as she was running for office. Seemingly, Christian County Missouri voters discount (choice #33) high ethical standards when choosing leaders. So do many other American voters. This does not bode well for (choice #29) democracy in America.

Second, she apparently screwed over two different groups: people who trusted her for their health needs, and voters. As such, what did the institution of Patricia Derges stand for? Not much—it looks like she let greed get the better of her. She seems like the embodiment of the (choice #33) theme description—which we summarize by saying, those who choose this path do not let ethical concerns get in the way of their pursuit of wealth and power. Such people turn their backs on what the world needs more of these days: a "We're all in this together" approach to living. Instead their behavior asserts, "I'm in it for myself."

Enough of this depressing story. To escape (choice #32) cynicism that accounts of human failing often provoke, we present another metaphor. And return to considering how one learns to become a confident executive fully capable of managing his or her life. Figure #5 employs playing cards in that regard.[24]

****

Figure #5: Self-Help
The Goal: Enjoying The Game of Life

In the game of life you constantly interact with people. The outcome of serious confrontations—constructive information exchange, compromise, dispute resolution, personal growth, or uncompromising standoffishness, fighting, relationship breakdown, fear—often critically depends on the participants' worldviews and how well they understand and accept them. As in playing cards, the better idea you have of the cards each person holds, the easier it will be to steer the game's outcome to your liking.

The starting point is understanding what cards you hold.

****

Shedding the playing cards metaphor, looking at this as a young person, and returning to the "you as an institution" metaphor, consider the following question. "As old person—as a venerable institution—what do I want to be remembered for?" Thoughts of "leaving a legacy" can provide a way of finding—or instilling— meaning in life (an important part of chapter 8.) And define a way to "live on, after death" — important to those who (choice #8) don't believe in an afterlife in Heaven. This reference can help set the stage for our next chapter look at religion. But before going there, we'll briefly return to that wonderful example of someone not to emulate: Donald Trump. This will be part of a bigger picture look at institutions—American and global, past and present.

E. National Institutions— past and present

Crises test both individuals and institutions. Certainly the Covid-19 pandemic has tested many national governments with respect to their ability to protect citizens. In the last century many of these have evolved, to some degree, into what can be called (choice #35) social welfare states, which provide social services. In a report entitled "The Future of the Welfare State," an early March 2021 issue of *The Economist* notes that such states provide "some form of social security and poverty relief." It credits Danish sociologist Gostra Esping-Andersen with identifying three models of such states: 1) market-oriented (especially in US) "where the state plays a 'residual' role," 2) family-oriented (mainland Europe) "where the state and employers play a supporting role," and 3) state-oriented (Scandinavia,) which provide "universal protections and services." The report notes, "The balance between state, market, and family shifts over the course of people's lives, but most take out about as much as they put in."

Since the 1990 date of Esping-Andersen's work[25], China has joined "the family of countries that have reasonably comprehensive systems of social protection in place," according to a September, 2013 UN Research Institute for Social Development working paper. In terms of deaths per capita, China seemingly has handled the pandemic better than all other large nations, surprising given the Covid-19 virus originated there. China also stands out in another way: its national government doesn't readily fit into the following way to categorize institutions.

In their book, *Why Nations Fail*, Daron Acemoglu and James A. Robinson distinguish between (choice #23, choice #27, choice #30, choice #33, choice #34, and choice #51) inclusive and extractive institutions. The former seek to include the widest possible strata of society in economic and political life, whereas the latter aim to exclude the majority of society from the process of political decision-making and income distribution. Western examples of extractive economic institutions include the medieval European feudal system, Russian serfdom, USA southern slavery, and capitalist economy monopolies.

In an eight page paper accompanying his April 16, 2013 presentation in Mexico City, "Why Regions Fail: The Mexican Case," Robinson notes, "Inclusive economic institutions create incentives and opportunities necessary to harness the energy, creativity, and entrepreneurship in society"—whereas extractive ones do not. He then discusses Mexico's *ejidos*. These are tracts of land held in common in villages, and farmed co-operatively or individually. He writes "the rules that governed access to land in *ejidos* were extractive because they meant that farmers did not have the security of property rights. This reduced their incentive to invest in the land and also to adopt better technology that could have boosted productivity."

The first chapter of the Acemoglu and Robinson book ends with a contrast between how two of the world's richest men—Bill Gates in the USA, and Carlos Slim in Mexico—(choice #33) made their money. Gates did it, besides being at the right place at the right time, with technological innovation; Slim got rich by acquiring a telecommunications industry monopoly during a wave of privatization advanced by the Salinas presidency (1988-1994.) Salinas also appointed a woman, known throughout the country as "La Maestra," to head the powerful teachers' union. In the words of Acemoglu and Robinson, "La Maestra used the union like a personal fiefdom for two decades, enriching herself and blatantly intervening in elections." That teachers count the votes in Mexico—which turns out to be particularly useful in close elections—facilitated this.

The role of unelected wealthy individuals can be especially critical, as Scott Robinson, in a review[26] of *Why Nations Fail* explains. "As wealth and power is concentrated, the ability of holders of power to propagate and enforce these institutions increases. Elites, not accountable to the population, create and protect monopolies, and resist any threats…to their supremacy." Beyond impeding the innovation that could spur economic development, it can extend to an attack on the political and economic rights of all those who do not belong to the elite.

Choices #27 and #30 are particularly relevant to this discussion. Those preferring Hierarchical Rigidity and Elitism themes align with the powerful. They argue for maintaining the extractive institutions they control, whereas those siding with common people prefer Egalitarian Progressive and Idealistic Populism themes. A person who prefers Hierarchical Rigidity might proclaim, "I accept the inequality inherent in such [hierarchy-based] society," whereas a social justice-minded Egalitarian Progressive will not stand for it.

In his Mexican Case paper, James A. Robinson refers to the Gini coefficient. This provides a measure of income inequality—with 0 meaning complete equality, and 1 meaning income totally concentrated in very few individuals. He uses it in asserting that higher levels of inequality correlate with "more extractive economic and political institutions." In particular he notes the prevalence of poverty in the southern Mexico region of Chiapas and Oaxca, where the Gini coefficient of over 0.8 greatly exceeds the nation's 0.55 average (compared to the USA average at the time he writes of 0.45.) He goes on to trace this to "historic exploitation of indigenous peoples through institutions such as the *encomienda* [royal land grants to conquistadors, soldiers, or officials] and *repartimiento* [division of land associated with grant of forced labor imposed on indigenous people]...[which] created a very hierarchical unequal society based on extractive economic institutions"—and to "the neglect of a weak state."

This Mexican history began with the early 16th century arrival of the Spanish conquistadors, followed by the Catholic Church—a pattern repeated elsewhere around the world in the following centuries with different national origins and religious motivations. From a global history perspective, the "Imperialism" theme of Choice #51 recalls the colonial era in which rich Western countries dominated poor Third World countries, often extracting their wealth and leaving the local inhabitants mired in poverty. The "Ethical Globalization" alternative promotes inclusive institutions / "nation transcending authority" that, among other things, "bust monopolies," and "promote wealth / technology transfer aiding the poor."

The role (choice #30) populism can play in this deserves comment. Idealistically it is related to appreciation of "the people," their heroic struggle, and their potential to unite and claim the political power that their numbers suggest they have to oust the self-serving elite who rule. But beyond "a social and political movement in which diverse groups bridge their differences and come together to work for meaningful change," the term can refer to something else: "use of appropriate, persuasive language in political appeals to common people." Practically speaking many so-called populist politicians are actually demagogues. These are corrupt leaders who play on popular prejudices, make false claims, and pretend to champion the causes of common people—all in an effort to get elected and gain power. Like Donald Trump, many have been associated with fooling voters with (choice #43) Spreading Disinformation / Tactical Deception, and (choice #38) conspiracy theory peddling.

To say the Trump presidency tested American institutions is an understatement. Trump's words and actions give the term institutional abuse a whole new meaning. His presidency was "Churchillian" in that, "Never in the course of human history has one person done so much damage to so many institutions." That damage begins with the institution of truth, and extends to include that of the rule of law, courts of law, the U.S. Justice Department, the FBI and US intelligence agencies, American democracy, the office of U.S. President, the US State Department, and the institution of journalism. His actions, and those of his appointees, damaged many other respected American institutions, including the Census Bureau, the Federal Reserve, the Post Office, the Department of Education, the National Endowment for the Humanities, the Voice of America, the Center for Disease Control, the Environmental Protection Agency, etc.

His support for extractive institutions and big money interests threatened national parks and monuments, wilderness, Native American cultural heritage, etc. Trump damaged professions, including science, public health—even professional basketball and football. With respect to the latter, he urged owners to "fire the sons of bitches"—referring to widespread player support for (choice #24) tolerance and Black Lives Matter. He did damage to the business leader / CEO brand. After a business career that included six bankruptcies, given another chance to use his supposed business acumen, and demonstrate leadership in running the country, he failed miserably. He damaged the institution of civilized behavior governing how males treat females with his "grab'em by the p_____" videotaped remark, numerous sexual misconduct and rape allegations.

Their leaders unwavering support of Donald Trump damaged the credibility and reputation of many institutions. This list begins with the Republican party and includes the US Vice President's Office, right-wing media (Fox News), and religious institutions like the National Prayer Breakfast. With respect to religious people, one wonders, "How could Donald Trump, someone whose own sister says has "no principles" and the Dalai Lama charges with "lack of moral principle," win the trust and support of so many Christian leaders and evangelicals?" And "Why did they overwhelmingly support him over Joe Biden, a lifelong devout Catholic?"

In a January 9, 2021 opinion piece posted on *Irish Central*, Niall O Dowd revealed what was headlined as "The truth about Trump the Antichrist …" He began "And so it came to pass in the final days of his presidency Donald Trump revealed himself as a fully flown fascist, ready to burn down the Capitol rather than accept defeat…" Before a last paragraph—that began, "And God saw that it was time and prepared the way for Joe Biden, a tribune of the people, whose very life was an example of a noble calling," and ended with "Let us pray" — O Dowd suggested some minds might change. He wrote, "Even princes of the church like Cardinal Dolan in New York, a true Trumpian believer, understood how much the time was out of joint and the murder and mayhem out of control." And suggested many "realized they had followed a false prophet." As we turn to religion in the next chapter, a question we'll consider is, "Can Christianity and it institutions become a force for good once more?"

F. International Institutions and Global Citizen Hopes

The United Nations (UN) was established in 1945, as its website describes, "following the devastation of the Second World War, with one central mission: the maintenance of international peace and security." Its establishment signaled a renewed determination of the widespread feeling that, after the First World War, the horrors the world had suffered must never be repeated. The (choice #50) militarists in Nazi Germany, Italy, and Japan made a joke of the first institution—The League of Nations. And the world learned that the pacifist appeasement policies were no way to respond to the aggression of military strongmen.

Seeking to learn from the earlier failure, the UN Charter recognizes a nation's right to self-defense in response to an illegal armed attack, but not to initiate a war. It grants powers the earlier League lacked—notably provisions to prevent outbreak of hostilities, to end hostilities already begun, and to order collective enforcement measures. These include economic sanctions and actions to prevent or halt military conflict with deployment of a UN peacekeeping force. These so-called "Blue Helmets" consist of over 70,000 people drawn from the armies of many nations. The UN's scope is much broader than the old League. Along with maintaining peace, according to the "What We Do" section of its website, it (choice #23) protects human rights, delivers humanitarian aid, promotes sustainable development, and upholds international law.

As the 75th anniversary of its founding approached, a mid 2019 Pew Research survey of nearly 35,000 people in 32 countries found 66% had a positive view of the UN, generally continuing a relatively stable history of positive public opinion. Younger people tend to like it more than their elders. Generally speaking, supporters of (choice #30) populist parties tend to view it less favorably. In America, 59% view it favorably—an opinion that has generally remained steady, but now reflects a more partisan divide, with 77% of Democrats approving, and but 41% of Republicans doing so.

For many Republicans, their feelings extend beyond "lack of trust in the UN" to outright hostility to anything resembling world government. This reflects a generally strong (choice #36) "Proud Identification..." flag waving American patriotism orientation, and lack of connection with the "Global Citizen" concept. No doubt many of these UN foes buy into (choice #38) conspiracy theories related to "the new world order." The common theme here is that, as *Wikipedia* puts it, "a secretive power elite with a globalist agenda is conspiring to eventually rule the world through an authoritarian world government—which will replace sovereign nation-states—and all encompassing propaganda."

Regional international institutions operate one level beneath the United Nations. Exempting the European Union, which often functions more like a single nation, examples include: 1) the North Atlantic Treaty Organization (NATO) spanning North America and Europe, 2) the Organization of American States (OAS) spanning North and South America, 3) the fifty-five countries of the African Union, and 4) various trade pacts, most notably the Regional Comprehensive Economic Partnership (RCEP) involving fifteen countries including China, Japan, and South Korea. The role of such organizations in promoting international co-operation and contributing to regional peace and stability can better appreciated in light of a recent statement suggesting problems in the Middle East could be partly attributed to it being relatively "de-institutionalized."

How individuals view institutions depends on their worldviews, which typically determine choices they make. Focusing on distinguishing between choices children make and those adults make, the previous chapter ended with an examination of choices global citizens make. We continue this effort, with focus here on how global citizens in America think about their country's relationship with the wider world. Picking up where that previous chapter ended with Donald Trump's presidency, unlike his predecessor, Joe Biden models adult, responsible behavior. He promises to trust (choice #1) evidence and science.

Thus, besides committing himself and his presidency to doing whatever it takes to defeat the Covid-19 virus, a second even bigger challenge on Biden's "to do" list is mobilizing America to take global climate change seriously. Despite just ended record setting western wildfire and Atlantic hurricane seasons providing more evidence justifying global climate change concerns, millions of Americans—including the outgoing president, refused to connect this evidence with human activity. Pledging that America would rejoin the World Health Organization (WHO) and the Paris Climate Agreement, Biden sought to set the nation on the path to responsible global citizenship.

After rectifying these mistakes, on February 19, 2021 the new American president told rich nation G7 leaders he was directing $4 billion of Covid-19 vaccine aid to poor countries. And he sought to find a balance that would provide enough regulation to insure that greenhouse gas emissions did not cause catastrophic climate impact, while at the same time preserving businesses' ability to make profits and enhancing people's efforts to make a good living. Global citizens with a "People, Planet, Prosperity" orientation applauded these moves.

One hopes responsible nation leaders will let other leaders know when their nation needs to rectify unacceptable behavior. Sadly, Donald Trump, with his admiration of Russian (choice #29) authoritarian Vladimir Putin, failed to do this with respect to a litany of outrages. Given his own relationship with (choice #33) unethical seeking of wealth, one hardly expected Trump to chastise Putin for his, and his oligarch cronies, looting kleptocracy / hoarding of the national wealth for themselves. But how could he keep silent after repeated poisoning of Putin's political opponents such as Alexi Nalvalny?

Mature superpower nations are expected to behave accordingly, but what about their individual citizens? Many, perhaps most, Americans would be comfortable saying, "I take pride in being a(n) _____ " —where they complete the sentence by inserting "American" (choice #36.) Those who are more *Bible*-toting than flag-waving might prefer to use "Christian" in completing this sentence. Male white supremacists might finish the sentence by inserting "white man" During the last two election campaigns, in which a majority of white Christian American men supported Trump, many chose to emphasize their identity as a "Republican" or "conservative" in completing the sentence. In contrast, those who prefer the other (choice #36) "Global Citizen" theme might say: "I do not primarily identify with any particular nationality, religious, or ethnic group. I think of myself first as a global citizen."

My global citizen connection began with my dad's (choice #24) endorsing the "Culture of Tolerance" theme by discounting racial or ethnic stereotypes, and saying, "People are people." By my mid-twenties, I'd come to feel strongly that (choice #23) human rights around the world should be protected. And increasingly "to think / behave / vote based on protecting our planetary home and the well being of all its inhabitants." As an old man, my charitable contributions are spread out to help many around the world.

With global citizens' concern for the well-being of all, they especially worry about (choice #47) those "Struggling With a Basic Need: Sustenance." Especially concerning are United Nation Refugee Agency (UNHCR) estimates that 79.5 million people have fled their homes, and 26 million people are refugees. Why have so many fled their homes and crossed national boundaries? It can be traced to poverty, violence, and political instability—especially in the Middle East.

Climate change may have also played a role—something that needs to be factored into future planning as Bill Gates explained. In a February 21, 2021 interview with *Fox News*, he noted "The migration that we saw out of Syria for their civil war…was somewhat weather dependent…" And went on to predict, "We're going to have ten times as much migration because the equatorial regions will become unlivable" unless we act. Either we act to achieve zero net greenhouse gas emissions by 2050, he said, or be prepared to face a grim future.

Humanitarian-minded global citizens' response has been to help refugees find places to live, and financially support global health-minded groups like Doctors Without Borders and the WHO. Sadly, led by its "America First" president, America severely restricted admitting displaced immigrants, built a costly, environmentally disastrous, wall on its southern border, and pulled out of the WHO. Whereas global citizens responded with love, the American government responded with indifference and scorn. Some charged that liberal globalists wanted to do away with national borders altogether. Practical minded global citizens responded by saying that wasn't so, given their (choice #51) valuing and wanting to preserve cultural heritages worldwide.

In recent years, the southern USA border has periodically been overwhelmed with refugees seeking asylum and poor people seeking jobs. The situation won't improve, humanitarians say, until the root causes of what's making desperate people flee their homes in Central America are addressed. Besides rampant poverty, problems include (choice #17) gang violence, governments controlled by drug cartels, and climate-related disasters. Cynics (choice #32) charge US government aid has largely gone into the pockets of corrupt officials. Global citizens support groups like Transparency International, which "seeks to end the injustice of corruption," and operates in over 100 countries. It works "to expose the systems and networks that enable corruption to thrive," and to "promote transparency, accountability, and integrity."[27]

Nearly twenty years earlier, America destabilized a whole region with its response to the 9/11/2001 terrorist attack. It started a war in Afghanistan, and then launched an illegal invasion of Iraq. These interventions were part of "the war on terror" that met the hate of *Qu'run*- toting extremists with bombs, guns, and death. The cumulative monetary cost of both wars has reportedly been over $4 trillion.[28] With a fraction of that, America could have reached out to (choice #29 and choice #18) educate the ignorant and help those in need. Education to combat extremist (choice #17) violent Islamic (choice #8) religious fundamentalist ideology could have positively transformed the region. But instead of a reaching out with a prevention-minded approach grounded in generous, loving hearts and helping hands (choices #14 and #18,) (choice #17 and choice #50) America violently unleashed bombs and launched wars. The August 2021 fall of Afghanistan to the Taliban extremists adds to this tragedy.

Rather than feeling "we're all in this together," engaging with the rest of the world and sharing their wealth with the world's poor, those who put "America First" and value "American Exceptionalism" feel differently. Many of them celebrate American freedom and embrace ethnocentrism, believing American society values and way of life are superior to those of other cultures. And, as the survey results cited earlier suggest, many of them do not support the mission of the United Nations, affiliated organizations, or other international organizations with similar missions.

(Choice #36) global citizens see things differently. While fully recognizing "we are tribal creatures," and some "Proud Identification and Tribalism" is to be expected, they bring a commitment to the well-being of all people that transcends national boundaries. Yet, despite their idealistic support for things like (choice #24) tolerance, (choice #29 and choice #43) education for democracy and fighting misinformation, and (choice #33) ethical behavior, they tend to be practical. They aren't pushing for a centralized (choice #38) socialist world government. Contrary to the fears of those concerned about a heavy-handed "new world order," global citizens generally accept the decentralized system of organization nation states provide. Many work to preserve unique cultural heritages. They support (choice #51) Ethical Globalization, and the international organizations listed and described in Figure #6.

Figure #6 International Organizations Global Citizens Support

1	the World Health Organization (WHO)—UN agency founded in 1948
2	the Intergovernmental Panel on Climate Change (IPCC)—the UN body for assessing the science related to climate change and making science-based policy recommendations
3	the International Criminal Court (ICC), an international "court of last resort," was set up in 2002 to prosecute people who have committed genocide, crimes against humanity, and war crimes
4	the International Monetary Fund (IMF), founded in 1944, works "to foster global monetary co-operation, secure financial stability, facilitate international trade, promote high employment and sustainable economic growth, and reduce poverty around the world"
5	UNICEF—the United Nations Children's Fund works "to save children's lives, to defend their rights, and to help them fulfill their potential."
6	UNESCO—the United Nations Economic and Security Council—with mission "to contribute to the building of a culture of peace, the eradication of poverty, sustainable development and intercultural dialogue through education, the sciences, culture, communication, and information."
7	World Trade Organization (WTO) —an international organization founded in 1995 to promote more international free trade, and regulate / resolve disputes involving international trade of goods and services. It replaced the General Agreement on Tariffs and Trade (GATT), an international body founded in 1947.
8	the Food and Agriculture Organization (FAO) —a United Nations agency that works with developing countries in an effort to raise levels of nutrition and standards of living, improve production and distribution of food and agricultural products, and promote rural development.
9	The United Nations High Commissioner for Refugees (UNHCR)— established in 1950 and also known as the UN Refugee Agency, it works to help and protect refugees, forcibly displaced communities, and people without a country. It does this by assisting their voluntary return to where they once lived, or local integration / resettlement in another country.

What choices related to freedom, growth, resource use, and global environmental concerns do global citizens typically make? With respect to choice #40 and choice #44, they chart a sustainable development course that recognizes limits. Seeing past a "wishful thinking" / childish rationalization of why we don't need to worry about American consumer excesses, global climate change, etc, they stand with the adults in the room in urging folks to take personal responsibility by embracing (choice #40) Limits and Ethics.

Global citizens argue that we live on a small planet already straining under the impact of the nearly eight billion humans it supports. With their long-term, big picture orientation, they prefer (choice #44) "Sustainability" to "Economic Growth." And accordingly say "I believe we need sustainable development: meeting present needs without compromising the future." With these preferences they are at odds with the majority of American adults—who like (choice #40) the "Freedom From Limits" theme, and might say "I value individual freedom and don't like regulations that restrict it." In response, global citizens reply, "I support common sense regulations that protect people and the environment." In addition, applying (choice #22) self-restraint to their resource and energy use, they prefer "Enoughness" to the "More is Better Mentality…" theme in making choice #45.

Global citizens recognize that national borders are porous, and that pollutants, viruses, people, hate, etc readily cross them. Perhaps the most positive thing one can say about the Covid-19 pandemic, which has killed millions of people, is that it's helped people realize this. As Dr. Tedros Adhanom Ghebreyesus, head of the WHO, put it in March, 2021, "We cannot end the pandemic anywhere, until we end it everywhere." Besides underscoring that the pandemic is a global problem that requires coordinated global response, such statements communicate global citizen feelings. Another metaphorically urges people everywhere to help each other by building bridges not walls. Another reflects the strong belief that, "We're all in this together. " Some folks acquire such beliefs through religious / spiritual experience—a topic we turn our attention to in the next chapter. There we'll also distinguish faith and trust.

Notes

1 Bellah, Robert etal. "The Good Society: Shaping the Institutions That Shape Us" July 12, 1991 issue of *Commonwealth* magazine
2 the Sociology Dept. at the University of North Carolina defines this discipline as "the study of human social relationships and institutions."
3 Wellins, R. and Sinar, E. "What an MBA program won't teach you about leadership" *CNBC* July 12, 2017
4 posted at nytimesineducation.com

5 Recall the help the two-person analysis tool on the *Project Worldview* website can provide was discussed in chapter 1 section F

6 My own parenting style—an estimate, based on my initial two decades as a father— was about 25 % tough love and 75% unconditional love

7 This is a much sanitized, version of the end of my marriage, giving ex-wife and her now husband "the benefit of the doubt" in (choice #14) fashion. I've avoided a less charitable, (choice #32) cynical rendering, with suggestions of (choice #17) violence, (choice #38) conspiracy—as it does no one any good.

8 Seneca the Younger (4 BCE – 65 CE) Roman stoic philosopher

9 first a book: Bissinger, H. *Friday Night Lights: A Town, a Team, and a Dream* Addison Wesley, Boston 1990, then a 2004 film, and then a TV series.

10 Moore-Lappe, Frances *Diet for a Small Planet* Ballantine Books, NY 1971

11 I got reports students cried when they heard I wouldn't be back the next year

12 Given soaring obesity and type II diabetes rates, I have no doubt that many millions of Americans have failed to meet this challenge.

13 On rare occasions I'd be jolted out of this mindset and forced to consider the opposite: a world not of cause and effect, but of mysterious coincidence. Both Chapter 5 and 8 provide evidence my worldview broadened to look beyond a trusting predictability, scientific, evidence-based perspective.

14 Wishful thinking, that a prayer would protect him so he didn't need a helmet, contributed to Scott Kohl's motorcycle death described in chapter 2.

15 "I was lying in a burned out basement, with the full moon in my eye…"

16 to anthropologists out there: I'm just throwing some words around here, and have probably read—and misinterpreted— too many Carlos Castenada books

17 Goleman, Daniel *Emotional Intelligence: Why It Can Matter More Than IQ,* Bantam Books / Random House, New York 1995

18 Mayer, J, Roberts, R., Barsade, S. "Human Abilities: Emotional Intelligence" *Annual Review of Psychology* 59: 507-536 2008

19 with T. Hickman, Margaret Weis wrote novel *Dragons of Autumn Twilight*

20 February 1, 2021 press release from US Dept. of Justice, US Attorney's Office, Western District of Missouri

21 March 26, 2021 press release from US Dept. of Justice as in the above note

22 Holzberg, Melissa "Nearly 500 People Charged with Covid Fraud Schemes DOJ Says" posted on *Forbes* website March 26, 2021

23 As I write, Patricia is only under indictment, she has not been found guilty.

24 Cook, S. *The Worldview Literacy Book*, Parthenon Books, Weed, NM 2009

25 Esping-Andersen, Gostra, *The Three Worlds of Welfare Capitalism* Princeton University Press   Princeton, NJ 1990

26 Robinson, Scott "Books for self-isolation: Revisiting Why Nations Fail" post on *The Interpreter* lowryinstitute.org March 18 2020

27 from transparency.org website

28 A Feb 2020 report from the Brown Univ. Costs of War Project estimated US taxpayers paid an average of $8,000 each and over $2 trillion for the Iraq war alone. As the US military exited Afghanistan in mid 2021, the PBS News Hour reported the twenty-year long war there had cost $2.26 trillion.

Choices We Make in the Global Village

Chapter 4: Religion /Imagining Change

A. Toward a Reality Check

Roughly 4.3 billion people—nearly 60 % of the world's population—subscribe to its two largest religions: Christianity and Islam. Most retain (choice #31) traditional religious—some would say ancient and backward—beliefs. In approaching the task of meaningfully describing the current state of traditional religion in terms of the individual choices involved, I'll use three words from the (choice #3) Humbly Unsure theme description: "I feel inadequate."

And I'm uncomfortable abandoning humility and, in "I Know What's Best For You" fashion, advocating changes in religious practice and culture as these relate to global citizenship. After all, "Who am I to challenge long-lived religious institutions and traditions?" Lacking humility, I might arrogantly blast religion from an overly (choice #32) cynical viewpoint. While I could (and will to some extent) use evidence to do that, my goal is to probe how religion might constructively change. I hope to (choice #3) come across as both humble and "selfless leader willing to helpfully step up and point the way forward."

Let's begin with a reality check. Just as fact checks can help dissuade belief in conspiracy theories, reality checks can bring those in fantasy land back to the real world. Oxford's English Dictionary defines a reality check "as an occasion on which one is reminded of the state of things in the real world." In this chapter—with a followup in chapter 8— religion gets a reality check. Despite the efforts of many to do this— notably Richard Dawkins in his 2006 book *The God Delusion*—religion persists.

Later I'll present ten different definitions of religion, of which the last two link it to childhood. A similarly linked reality check was provided by American lawyer and defender of evolution Clarence Darrow who said, "I don't believe in God as I don't believe in Mother Goose." Despite including such (choice #8) secular humanist putdowns, the reality check I provide also humbly assumes religion must offer something of value to have persisted for so long—and attempts to discern what that is.

Before heading there, we need to confront an "elephant in the room": (choice #32) cynicism. Conservative Christian and Southern Baptist Russell Moore, sees this, not secularism, as "the biggest threat facing the American church right now." Moore's own disillusionment, over his church's sexual abuse scandals, many white supremacists, and failure to seek racial reconciliation, was expressed in a February 24, 2021 letter. The letter, according to Peter Wehner in a June 7, 2021 *Atlantic* article, "The Scandal Rocking the Evangelical World," "has shaken the Christian world." At the time he wrote it, Moore was president of the Ethics and Religious Liberty Commission of the Southern Baptist Convention.

(Choice #32) cynics doubt the intentions of others, question their integrity, and are typically unable to extend the trust that co-operation requires. To borrow words from that theme description, it's easy to see religious "do gooders" as "hypocrites too stupid to see themselves as such." In a 2017 article in *The New Yorker*, Timothy Keller, an influential Christian evangelical, wrote, "Evangelical used to denote people who claimed the high moral ground, now in popular usage, the word is nearly synonymous with 'hypocrite'."

For decades the Catholic Church has endured the cynical wrath of those outraged by widespread sexual abuse of minors by priests. Reports document the problem as long ago as the 11th century and come from all countries where the Church has operated. Studies suggest 2% to 4% of all priests have been involved. By mid-2018, the Church had paid nearly $4 billion to settle sexual abuse claims dating back to the mid-1980s according to the group Bishop Accountability. The year before, Pope Francis reported the Vatican had a backlog of 2,000 sexual abuse cases that still needed investigating.

Islam has likewise not escaped cynical putdown. In the aftermath of the 9/11/2011 terrorist attacks, many linked it to violence. Where was God on September 11, 2001?" many Americans cynical of (choice #5) Personal God belief wondered. In the aftermath of Islamic extremists dreaming of heaven and striking a blow for Allah, some voiced concern about all religion. One of those was Sam Harris, who used how disturbed he was by the attack to motivate writing *The End of Faith.* There he points the finger at (choice #8) sacred books of great religions: "each making an exclusive claim as to its infallibility." He laments that "intolerance is... intrinsic to every creed" and that "certainty about the next life is simply incompatible with tolerance in this one."

With these cynics' broad strokes, it's clear that the big picture of religion we'll paint portrays it as more about imperfect human beings than God. Indeed, critics charge, the later concept is simply a product of deluded minds. Putting aside that charge, let's use stories from human experience to fill in details of that picture. Before sharing long-ago stories centered on my religious education growing up in America, I'll share two such tales from my more recent adventures as a world traveler.

B. Stories from My Own Experience

In 2009 I journeyed to Budapest at the kind invitation of an amazing man who had previously stumbled onto the *Project Worldview* website. I arrived thinking of my benefactor, Attila, as an astrophysicist. By the time I left Budapest four days later, I realized he'd become famous as something of a (choice #47) creative folk rock star musician. If the stories were to be believed, as the Soviets left Eastern Europe as the 1990s began, his band was drawing 80,000 + people to its concerts.

Attila Grandpierre seemingly refused fitting comfortably into roles of Hungarian astrophysicist or musical celebrity. He perhaps preferred the "forbidden" he territory staked out as a physicist dabbling (with lots of American friends) in what can be called New Age spirituality. This topic—which has religious overtones—will be thoroughly discussed in chapter 8. I mention Attila to help set the stage for that, and to express my (choice #19) gratitude for his role in introducing me to Europe and—what I came to love—experiencing its history.

That love began the day after I left Budapest, and encountered my first castles and cathedrals in Visegrad and Esztergom. Now, after roughly a dozen overseas excursions, I've come to see this pair of "c" words as spanning both sides of the themes paired in choice # 14 and choice #18: cathedrals as shrines celebrating Christian love and loving kindness deeds; castles as secure fortresses embodying the caution and culture of fear that surviving tumultuous times required.

Given my name, it's fitting that my first encounter with this pair came at Castle Hill and the ancient basilica in Esztergom. There, Hungary's first Christian king—known today as Saint Stephen—was both baptized and crowned. Years earlier, Stephen's pagan father promoted (choice #50) what might be called "an international peace conference" — two years before his son's birth in 975. According to legend, his coronation took place on the first day—January 1, 1001—of the new millennium, just as Europeans were learning to build those truly amazing cathedrals.

After visiting several cathedrals in many countries, I appreciated the extent to which Christianity was at the heart of European life for hundreds of years. Given how dear faith was to them, people in cities throughout Europe dedicated a significant part of their wealth—and labor they were capable of mustering— to glorifying Christianity. And it's not just visits to cathedrals where travelers can find abundant evidence to attest to the enduring importance of Christianity in Europe, it can be found in museums. There I've spent untold hours appreciating the (choice #47) creative expression, passion, story telling, and spiritual feeling communicated by religious-themed art filling room after room.

In contrast, my experience with Islamic shrines and art is limited to just a few locations— in Turkey, in Andalusia (Spain,) Morocco, and Jerusalem. My closest encounter with a Moslem cleric lasted but a couple of minutes. Having been warned that Konya, Turkey was a very conservative place, I didn't know what to expect as I removed my shoes and entered an ancient mosque there late one evening with my wife. After looking over this seemingly empty building, we were surprised when the imam entered. The language barrier hindered communication, but upon hearing we were from America, he surprised us with hugs.

My most meaningful reading about the Islamic world occurred rather recently when I finally read what is now something of as a controversial book. *Three Cups of Tea*[1] is mostly set in Pakistan and Afghanistan. I'll share comments on it later in this chapter. Suffice it to say here that, after completing this volume and delving into the controversy[2] that later surrounded it, I found myself in something of an unusual position in the (choice #4) Skeptic vs. True Believer battle. I "wanted to believe in" and was very sympathetic to what happened to the book's humanitarian hero, Greg Mortenson, after his scandalous fall from Nobel Peace Prize nominee stature. This was surprising since it seems I've tended to side with the skeptics—especially in religious or moral behavior matters— for as long as I can remember.

One of my earliest memories is of an adult Sunday school teacher. In between talk of Jesus, "he died for your sins, ""good boys and girls go to Heaven," etc, she insisted my name was "Stephan" (pronounced with a short e), not "Stephen" (pronounced with a long e.) I still recall the frustration of correcting her, only to be told, "No, you're wrong!" Years later in trying to sort out prejudices I've developed, I wonder if perhaps my recognition of her ignorance with respect to my name led to general skepticism as to the truth of religious lessons she and others provided?

A more painful early memory is set in southern California in January 1955. I was three and a half years old and my grandmother had just died. I barely knew this woman and her death doesn't upset me—but my parents' funeral plans did. They planned on being gone for three weeks. After putting Wanda, a teenage neighbor girl who helped out at her church teaching Sunday school, in charge, they boarded a train for Iowa. Wanda's baby-sitting difficulties grew until—perhaps in desperation— she began (choice #16) moralistically asserting that if I didn't behave, I'd burn in Hell when I died. Her sober, but earnest, description—deep underground burial chamber, flames hotter than those in the backyard's trash burning incinerator I kept my distance from, the lurking presence of the horned, tormenting Devil who maintains the hell-fires, etc.— terrified me. And I didn't like the guilt she instilled. She scared me into behaving.

This experience psychologically scarred me. When my parents returned, they were shocked to find their once articulate kid was a (choice #26) lacking self-esteem, stuttering emotional basket case. The psychological damage was long lasting. For many years thereafter I'd periodically have "burning in Hell" dreams—ones I would sometimes awake from in a cold sweat, screaming. I eventually decided that believing in the existence of the Devil—and by extension the (choice #17) idea that "Evil is Out There"—was psychologically toxic. Not interested in seeking out evidence in pondering whether to believe that (and make choice #16,) I employed some (choice #1) wishful thinking. I decided to emotionally distant myself from such (choice #21) unhealthy notions. Many decades of life experience has since confirmed the wisdom of that decision.

My subsequent involvement with the (choice #17) concept of evil has, fortunately, been mostly an academic one. I became acquainted with the problem of evil, which has plagued philosophers since ancient Greek times. It can be simply stated with a question, "Why does an all powerful, all knowing God allow evil to exist in the world?" At some point I recognized that, related to this problem of evil, (choice #8) religious fundamentalists face another question, "What do you say when your sacred book depicts God as behaving evilly?" For example, in the *Old Testament* book of *Deuteronomy,* God commands (Moses' assistant and eventual successor) Joshua to go into Canaan and—speaking about "the seven nations greater and mightier than you"—"conquer them and utterly destroy them." The latter description in *Joshua* of the resulting (choice #24) genocidal massacre is tough to read.

I have two stories related to my non-academic experience with themes related to evil and fearing people (as found in choice #17 and choice #18, paired respectively with themes about violence and helping people.) Both involve individuals whose behavior is better explained as (choice #24) Blaming / Scapegoating me and (choice #17) Taking Charge ➜ Violence —rather than involving the Devil. Alas, on two occasions—in two different states thirty years apart—someone threatened to kill me.

The first threat came from my Arkansas Ozarks red neck neighbor—I'll refer to him as Lee's son. (Lee was like a father figure to me as I describe in the *Coming of Age...*book, but he died a year after I met him.) I'd been guardedly friends with him for the previous six years and we'd worked well together on a couple of projects before—including one where he (choice #18) unselfishly helped me move a small building. Note I said "guardedly": I'd seen Lee's son become meaner and meaner as he got increasingly drunk. Given bruises his wife occasionally displayed, I suspected him of (choice #17) domestic violence.

My chance encounter with his wife, and perhaps his consumption of alcohol, was involved in his delivering a death threat. He did this by cutting into an evening phone conservation I was having on our shared phone line.[3] Earlier in the day I'd showed up at a gas station in town needing to fill five gallon buckets with water from a faucet there. The station's owner—who was also a politician and needed votes—had no problem with people using the faucet for hauling water.[4] Lee's son's wife coincidentally happened to also be there at the station for some unrelated reason. Unbelievably, this man accused me of stalking his wife.

Two things are (choice #49) funny about this incident. First, Lee's son and his wife later divorced. She married the backhoe operator who I had much earlier learned not to believe, when he promised his machine would show up at some time he named to do whatever digging job I needed done. My jobs were typically small, and the reality was this guy prioritized bigger jobs where the money was. Frustration with waiting led to a (choice#21) healthy choice. I decided to do my own digging, and eventually earned the nickname "The Human Backhoe." Second, many years later after I'd moved to New Mexico, a friend told me Lee's son had supposedly found Jesus, and thought of me as his long-lost buddy.

My second death threat came on December 10, 2012 as I was sitting in the driver's seat of my wife's Prius. We were stopped alongside a remote stretch of New Mexico highway. I remember the date because we were celebrating the seventh anniversary of our first meeting at fancy restaurant and mountain lodge. We were returning from that same place after a wonderful time. Heading home on the mountain road, I felt relaxed and like all was right with the world.

Roughly halfway home, after driving about fifteen minutes, we encountered a slow moving pickup truck. Its driver seemed to be behaving erratically, slowing down, speeding up and making it difficult for us to pass. I was caught up in conversation and didn't think a lot about it, but finally got a chance to accelerate and speed past the truck. Figuring to soon leave this vehicle behind, I was surprised to see that it too had sped up—so I watched it in the mirror. It stayed close behind for a couple of miles as we headed up a long hill, then, after we reached the top, I was surprised to see it suddenly pull over to the side of the road.

At that point, I made a poor choice—although at the time it seemed like it was the right one. I too pulled over. Had I known who I was dealing with, there's no way I would have also pulled over—but I didn't know. Given that it was a cold night, given my concern that someone had broken down on this middle of nowhere mountain road, I stopped to potentially offer help. In doing this I gave whoever it was the benefit of the doubt that their seemingly erratic previous driving was unintentional and harmless. I chose not to be fearful of this unknown driver now walking toward me, but to behave in (choice #18) "Golden Rule, Village Ethic of Mutual Help" fashion and stop. I'd stopped to help a stranger as I sometimes would—and as people would sometimes do for me, when it seemed help might be needed.

I hadn't entirely thrown (choice #14) caution to the wind. I'd stayed in the Prius ready to make a hasty retreat if necessary, but—with driver's side window rolled down—also ready to offer assistance if requested. Once I got a better look at who was approaching, I immediately sensed I'd be doing the former instead of the latter. Coming toward me, thirty or so years younger than I was and outweighing me by roughly a hundred pounds, was someone I recognized and knew was potentially dangerous. I 'd played basketball with him on a couple of occasions at a community gathering in an old gym. I knew he was a (choice #17) bully.

I doubt he recognized me as he started to make noise. He wasn't requesting help: he was yelling. He didn't like that I'd passed him earlier on the road. As he began swearing, I realized my mistake, and began moving the car forward to insure this guy got no closer. I realized I'd been wrong about his erratic driving, and now decided he'd been intentionally trying to provoke some highway incident. But I was right in recognizing a bully. After he threatened to kill me, I calmly said, "Kiss off pal!" and drove away.[5]

I now give this incident greater meaning than I did at the time —and use three of the fifty-two *Choices We Make* pairs in doing so. I view it in terms of someone (me) feeling Relaxed, Generous, Loving —one of the choice #14 themes. After initially acting in Golden Rule, Village Ethic of Mutual Help (one of the choice #18 themes) fashion, he realizes his mistake. In stopping to offer help, he is soon facing an intimidating large person he associates with (choice #17) Taking Charge➔Violence, upon which the mindset of our "would be Good Samaritan" totally changes. He goes into (choice #14) Cautious Processing mode and, instead of acting out of love, acts in fear as in (choice #18) Culture of Fear.

I like being in a Relaxed, Generous, Loving state, but recognize it's a potentially dangerous place to be. Undoubtedly dangers would be less if all people practiced the Christian "Love your neighbor" ideal—but clearly many don't. These days I encounter more news of people offering reasons to fear, even hate, others, rather than love and help them. I might practice loving kindness more often if I believed (choice #14) "God is love"—but from a (choice #41) Respect for Nature perspective this seems naïve. Where is this loving God in the predator killing prey painful death process behind the "tooth and claw" way the world works?

Given unusual, difficult to explain experiences I'll share in both chapter 5 and chapter8, I don't think of myself as an (choice #8) atheist, although I otherwise identify with Secular Humanism.   While I'd agreed to baptism in the Presbyterian church at age twelve to please my mother, I don't recall ever completely accepting what I later came to call (choice #5) Belief in a Personal God. Or thinking that praying did any good. As the story of my January 1955 experience shared above makes clear, certain aspects of the religion others were pushing scared me.

Consider the prayer my mother often insisted I say at bedtime: "Now I lay me down to sleep. I pray the Lord my soul to keep. If I should die before I wake, I pray the Lord my soul to take" Those words offer two disturbing thoughts: one, that you might die before morning, and two, that if you've been bad, God won't accept you to hang out in Heaven. Neither of these is a comforting, (choice #14) loving thought. Rather than help me drift off into peaceful sleep, they would more likely provoke guilt-ridden memories of (choice #16 and choice #25) tough love (well-deserved?) spankings I'd received.

C. Religion—Using Words Carefully

Defining religion is a challenge, as it means different things to different people. In his classic *The World's Religions*, Huston Smith defines it very broadly as "a way of life woven around people's ultimate concerns," and seeking "to align humanity with the transcendental ground of its existence." Synthesizing, and building on these, religion can be defined as involving beliefs, behaviors, feelings and devotion or obligation to faith in the divine, or what is held to be of ultimate importance. Two much narrower definitions are: 1) the worship of, and service to, God or the supernatural, and 2) a belief system associated with traditionally defined or formally institutionalized ceremonies or rituals.

Many find none of these descriptions adequate. So here, ranging from positive / upbeat to negative / downcast / cynical, are seven more definitions of religion, and (in parentheses) their links with particular people. Religion 1) is "man's response to ultimate concerns in terms of the ultimate" (Tillich); 2) "adds strength to frailty, fulfillment to frustration, wholeness to incompleteness" (Bewkes); 3) is "a feeling of creaturely dependence on God" (Schleirmacher); 4) is about healing the "brokenness" that happens when ego triumphs over spirit producing a condition of being "terribly and tragically alone" (Collier); 5) is "a technique for success...a desperate measure that people resort to when the stakes are high and they have exhausted the usual techniques for the causation of success" (Benedict & Pinker); 6) is "the childlike condition of humanity...knowledge of God is self-knowledge" (Feuerbach); 7) is "a childhood neurosis—God is a father projection" (Freud.)

Religion is sometimes linked to faith—but what is that? Faith and trust are terms often used in reference to believing in something or someone. They're similar except that faith is typically used in a spiritual context, whereas trust is employed in relationships—especially interpersonal ones. As commonly used, faith seems to have two different meanings—which can blend together in what many wordsmiths craft, like using two threads in making a fabric. This can lead to confusion, as many encountering the word as they read think its author is referring to one meaning, when actually the other is intended. Examples: the phrases "faith in the benevolence of God" and "a whole host of faith affirmations" illustrate the difference.

In the first example faith is used in a "firm belief" sense. In a (choice #1 positive expectations) sense, this can mean, "complete confidence and trust in something for which there is no proof." Note, in defining faith, this phrase alone isn't enough, it should be qualified by adding "often associated with religion and typically linked more to the one's feelings / emotions than one's rational / analytical side." The second example illustrates using faith as a synonym for "religion," or where the term "religious" might instead be used. Many descriptions of faith weave both meanings and much else together in a difficult to untangle way.

The "much else" for Christian philosopher Paul Tillich has him connecting faith with "ultimate concern" —as in to what one's life should be devoted. In his book *Stages of Faith*[6], James Fowler views finding faith as ultimately finding "an overarching, integrating and grounding trust in a center of value and power sufficiently worthy to give our lives unity and meaning." Elsewhere he writes, "One's faith qualifies and gives tone to one's entire way of interpreting, reacting to, and taking initiatives in the world. It is the awareness, the intuition, the conviction of relatedness to something or someone more than the mundane."

Finding clarity in the meaning of passages employing this term can be challenging. Sometimes it seems the deeper meaning additions to descriptions of faith make its meaning increasingly vague. Some writers, even in the same composition, use it to mean different things—such as William F. Schultz. He is the author[7] of "faith in the benevolence of God" and "a whole host of faith affirmations" which came from the same essay separated by just five paragraphs.

Even in liberal religious settings, one needs to choose words carefully. Both James Fowler and William F. Schultz have operated in such a setting: Unitarian Universalist (UU) congregations. Indeed many new UUers have referred to "our UU Church" only to be corrected by UU old timers who'll say, "You mean our UU congregation." Use of "religion" and "faith" have proved problematic as well. Years ago, many objected to referring to certain formal UU educational activities as "religious education." This happened despite educators like John A. Buehrens, writing, in a 1999 edition of *The UU Pocket Guide*[8], "To be human is to be religious. To be religious is to make connections. The word *religio* in Latin means to reconnect. To lead a meaningful life...each of us needs support in making meaningful re-connections to the best in our global heritage, the best in others, and the best in ourselves."

These are admirable words. Recalling historian of science James Burke's book *Connections*, I like them. But many UUers were unable to let go of all the negative connotations and emotional baggage they were carrying based on previous encounters with "religion." They raised such a fuss that the term "Faith Development" soon replaced "Religious Education" in many UU names. From a faith as synonym for "religious" perspective this doesn't cause problems, but from a faith meaning "firm belief" perspective it does. And adding the word "development" makes it toxic for many (me included.) Indeed, many hearing the term "faith development" instantly think "indoctrination" —something that Unitarian Universalism, which celebrates (choice #12) "a free and responsible search for truth and meaning," is <u>not</u> supposed to involve.

Having discussed meanings of religion and faith, let's consider a third word—reason—by distinguishing it from religion and faith. Certainly one's earliest rational awakenings involve important self-knowledge: of where you end and the surrounding environment begins. Down this religion and reason path, Valerie Tarico describes[9] a (choice #1 wishful thinking and choice #12 group think) problem, one she connects with many forms of organized religion. She writes, "Religion trains believers to practice self deception, shut out contradictory evidence, and trust authorities rather than their own capacity to think."

The reason vs. faith distinction is essentially between (choice #1) evidence-based belief, based on facts and concepts (ultimately linked to observation and experience) which fit together in a coherent way as part of a useful, logical framework, and belief which has no such basis. Often, the latter has only a (choice #10) feeling of "Non-Rational Knowing" — and an unshaken feeling of confidence, trust, and willingness to believe — behind it. Of course, when one's knowledge and experience is limited, as in children, belief can be extended based on trusting the authority of someone else—especially a parent—rather than doing one's own investigation into the rational basis for belief. (Recall the story of Eric and his dad in chapter 1.)

Sometimes, there is no way to rationally or scientifically decide, and anyone holding such belief holds it through faith. The term faith-based group suggests both its cohesion and a social interaction dimension. In this way, faith can be connected with belonging. Some such groups are associated with rituals designed to switch off one's rational mind in a (choice #12) Group Think Imperative way. Some see the (choice #10) Non-Rational Knowing aspect of faith as a valid basis for knowledge, others say it provides no such basis.

Harvard psychology professor Steven Pinker is one of the latter. In the 2006-2007 academic year, Harvard revamped its general education requirements. During this process Pinker strongly objected to a task force recommendation[10] that students take courses in an area they initially called "Reason and Faith." In criticizing this he wrote, "There is an enormous constituency of people who would hold that faith and reason are two routes to knowledge. It's a mistake to affirm that." He went on to add, "It's like having a requirement in 'Astronomy and Astrology.' They're not comparable topics." Others felt similarly. While the task force renamed this area "What It Means to Be a Human Being," co-chair English professor Louis Menand defended a widespread concern. "It's non-controversial that there is this thing called religion out there, and that it has an enormous impact on the world we live in. Scholars should be able to study and teach it without getting cooties…"

When I'm asked, "What do you have faith or trust in?" I start by referring to people around us. Then express hope that we—starting with myself—are worthy of trust, despite our individual failings and imperfections. After expressing my belief in the humanity's innate ability to (choice #34) co-operate, (choice #43) be honest and learn from feedback, I mention the power of (choice #14) love. This could provide some (choice #25) intangible "glue" to hold "the human family" together. A key part of that glue could consist of trusting loyalty / having faith in each other. This can help forge a (choice #36) global citizen pre-requisite feeling that "we're all in this together."

While I prefer believing based on (choice #1) evidence, I realize this concept can be tough to explain to young children. For them, "faith" is more naturally linked to "love" than "evidence," and that sometimes one just feels that trusting others is right. After hearing of my dislike of the term faith development, I've been asked, "Do you have faith in or trust in science?" After citing the "firm belief and having complete confidence in" meaning of faith, I reply, "Yes, I trust in science as long as (choice #10) accepted methods are followed, high ethical standards are maintained, and the limits / challenges it faces are appreciated."

Science is challenged by certain seemingly real phenomena, which don't fit into its conceptual framework. Scientists explain supposed benefits of certain alternative medicines, and "laying the hands on" type healing, in terms of the placebo effect. Placebos are defined as preparations with no medical or pharmacological value, and any positive effect they seemingly produce is believed connected to patient expectations. Recognizing that many people are predisposed to (choice #1) positive expectations, I accept such explanations of certain difficult-to-explain things. But I can't completely discount the value of (choice #10) intuition, synchronicity-based or paranormal type experience, and (rarer still) transcendent cosmic consciousness. While some may accuse me of (choice #7) being sympathetic to Magic, this is only true to the extent I hope that certain phenomena identified as mysterious will someday yield their secrets to our evidence-based understanding.

Some—like Martin Luther in the early 16th century— see reason as threatening faith. For others—like Valerie Tarico, a frequent contribution to *Free Inquiry* magazine—as one increasingly relies on reason and sets out down an evidence-based path, one's reliance on faith steadily diminishes. While many futurists read *Free Inquiry*, you don't have to think of yourself as a futurist to hope for a better tomorrow—and pin those hopes on education. Thomas Jefferson felt that well-educated citizens are "the ultimate guardians of their own liberty." The siege of the US Capitol on January 6, 2021—an attempted coup in which Christians were well represented among the insurrectionists as we'll describe later in the chapter— raises questions about the commitment of many Americans to (choice #29) Education for Democracy.

Even before this troubling event, one could say that challenges for American democracy extend beyond educating citizens to select good government leaders. Three additional challenges are, first, promoting critical thinking skills, and second, promoting understanding of scientific, (choice #49) technological, and (choice #33) ethical complexities that living in an increasingly integrated, interdependent world requires. The third is the most intractable: countering threats posed by the forces of mass indoctrination—both domestic and foreign. While other nations' weapons of mass destruction instill fear, so should those of mass indoctrination. These include Islamic religious fundamentalists' schools known as madrassas (choice #8) to be discussed later in the chapter. Before heading there, let's begin the process of considering how large numbers of Christians might become global citizens.

D. Imagining a Discovery and Q GAIA Conspiracy

What follows takes us to an imaginary world (ten years from now) in 2031. Presented below is the text of something I've written. We'll imagine it's a review article just published in a liberal, (choice #27) progressive Christian magazine. We suppose this publication is noted for its 1) appreciation of (choice #6) mysticism, (choice #18) the Golden Rule, and (choice #36) global citizens, and 2) disgust with (choice #8) religious fundamentalism, and (choice #16) salvation and moralistic God orthodoxy. Accompanying the article is a (choice #38) Conspiracies relevant disclaimer that reads in part: "What follows has been carefully fact-checked and is accurate to the best of our knowledge."
****

As Good Friday dawned in the Holy Land in year of our Lord 2030, rumors began leaking out of an amazing archaeological discovery. Before the year was out, this recovery of ancient scrolls focused attention on the meaning of an event that happened 2000 years earlier: Jesus' death. The discovery had long been hoped for by Biblical scholars such as Bart Ehrman, chair of the Department of Religious Studies at the University of North Carolina.

As Ehrman described in his 2003 book *Lost Christianities*, the authors of *New Testament* books *Matthew* and *Luke* (written 80 to 90 CE) clearly used the older book of *Mark* as the source of stories found in both books. But they also contained common passages not found in (earlier, 68 to 70 CE) *Mark*—suggesting they'd come from another source. According to Ehrman, "The German scholars who devised this theory decided to call this other source *Quelle*, the German word, conveniently enough, for 'source.' It is frequently called Q for short."

Spring 2030 rumors that Q had been found—along with a trove of other documents—were soon confirmed. Remarkably, there was an even more stunning find than the recovery of Q's book and other ancient books dating from the time the familiar Biblical gospels were composed. A book authored roughly 250 years later, detailing some sinister plotting, was found. Given all the social media posts, before the year was out a new conspiracy theory was spreading like wildfire. It came to be called

Q GAIA. Although New Age enthusiasts adamantly insisted the latter part of this name had all along referred to the ancient Earth goddess and its modern environmental movement connection, in truth it hadn't. Rather it was an acronym coined by religious scholars standing for a phrase found in one of the ancient texts: "God Always Inside us All."

The discovery of the ancient scrolls recalled that of texts buried outside Nag Hammadi, found eighty-five years ago. Decades-long study of their contents, which included, most notably, a complete copy of the gospel of *Thomas*, lead to significant revision of early Christian history. Preliminary study of the new batch, found in Iznik, Turkey, suggested its most significant ancient volume was one authored in the 325 to 330 CE era. It was the work of Alexis Josephus—although given his strong advocacy for the views expressed in the traditional gospel of *John* many of his contemporaries apparently referred to him as Alexis Johnes.

Alexis Josephus' work begins with recounting his illustrious ancestry, which he traced back to the Jewish historian and Romanphile Flavius Josephus. This earlier Josephus was born in 37 CE in Judea. By age sixteen, after studying Jewish sect writings, he became enamored with those of the Essenes, and went to live in the wilderness as a disciple of Bannus. After three years, he renounced commitments to their austerity and mysticism, and joined the Pharisees in Jerusalem.

By 64 CE Flavius Josephus made it to Rome, where he was greatly impressed with the city's magnificence. Returning to Judea, he reluctantly joined the Jewish revolt against Rome and became commander of forces, which came under siege at Jotapata. Rather than surrender, all of those Jews chose death by suicide—except Josephus and one other man. Impressed by his apparent gift of prophecy, Roman commander—and later Emperor—Vespasian spared Josephus. He began working for the Romans. Similarly, some 250 years later, Alexis Josephus began working for Roman Emperor Constantine. He was apparently hired to help stamp out Christian sects viewed as heretical.

After recounting his ancestry, Alexis Josephus' book describes his pilgrimage to Judea, and climbing to watch sunrise from Masada.[11] There he paid respects to his famous ancestor, who'd chronicled the siege of that stronghold in *The Jewish War*. Alexis Josephus' book, again following a path charted by his ancestor, took a shot at mysticism—this time at that of Christian sects. Like earlier Essene mysticism—which

Heinrich Gratz (1817-1891) would characterize as involving magic and miracles—early Christian mystics believed that "the image of God" is hidden within everyone. As his book makes clear, Alexis Josephus feels this belief, especially as bolstered by *Thomas*, is dangerous.

Thomas, according to Princeton University religious studies professor Elaine Pagels in her book *Beyond Belief: The Secret gospel of Thomas*, portrays Jesus as teaching his disciples to discover the light within them. This totally contradicts the gospel of *John*, which has Jesus proclaiming, "I am the light of the world." And, if people are to avoid walking in darkness, they can find God only through Jesus. As Pagels puts it, "John never tires of repeating that one must believe in Jesus, follow Jesus, obey Jesus and confess him alone as God's *only* son…Thus John's Jesus declares that 'you will die in your sins, unless you believe that I am he.'"

John's view of salvation is radically different from that presented in *Thomas*. According to Pagels' account of this gospel, "Jesus said: If you bring forth what is within you, what you bring forth will save you. If you do not bring forth what is within you, what you do not bring forth will destroy you." Ehrman claims Thomas' writing presupposes a view of salvation from writings of other Gnostic Christians. He writes, "Salvation…comes from saving knowledge. The Greek term for knowledge is gnosis. And so these people are called Gnostics, 'the ones who know'." He goes on to suggest that Jesus helped them in seeking that knowledge: by finding "the spark of the divine spirit within."

As Pagels describes it, John's book was written (90 to 100 CE) to promote his view of Jesus as God in human form—not just God's servant as the other three canonical gospels suggest. And written, she argues, to counter views of Jesus like Thomas presents, and what those other gospels hint at. The most explicit support there of Thomas's characterization is in *Luke*, where Jesus says, "The kingdom of God is within you." According to Ehrman, over half of the 114 sayings (seventy-nine by one count) that compose the gospel of *Thomas* are similar to sayings found in the four gospels (mostly in those other than *John*.) But only in John is Thomas portrayed as "Doubting Thomas" and—as Pagels puts it—'faithless' because he seeks to verify the truth from his own experience."

Alexis Josephus likes the gospel of *John*. Having the ear of the power brokers at the Bishop's Ecumenical Council in Nicaea in 325 CE, he argues against including the gospel of *Thomas* in what becomes the Christian *New Testament*. His is a practical argument: Thomas's book doesn't urge the reader to believe in Jesus—only to encourage each person's search for God. Unlike John's book, it does not promote a collective group think mentality that enshrines Jesus' authority. Nor can it be used to foster the power brokers' goal of unifying the Christian church. So, unlike John's book, it's not included in the *New Testament*.

Alexis Josephus's describes a coverup—a story that "powers that be" in the young Catholic Church do not want told. It recounts how Thomas's book, and many other Gnostic and early Christian sect's writing, is suppressed. Scrolls found with it provide additional documentation of how many Romans viewed Christians in the two centuries before Constantine made Christianity the Empire's official religion in 310 CE. Despite having outlawed their religion, these Romans were generally greatly impressed by Christians and their emphasis on helping each other, on love, loving your neighbor, and even, in accordance with the Golden Rule, loving your enemy. Though impressed, Roman leaders also realized that, for an empire held together with instilling fear, backed by violence not love, this "loving kindness" message was a threat.

So, as Alexis Josephus documents, power brokers decided this loving aspect of Christianity can only be used to attract new followers. Mention of such behavior is kept out of belief statements such as the Nicene Creed. There, Christians are required to affirm belief that Jesus is "the only begotten son of God," who "...for our salvation came down from heaven," "for our sake...was crucified...suffered death," then "ascended into heaven...[and] will come again in glory to judge the living and the dead." They must "confess one Baptism for the forgiveness of sins," and "look forward to the resurrection of the dead..." Missing is any mention of the widely praised Christian generosity or practice of loving kindness —not even a three word simple declaration such as, "God is love."

Into the large, earthenware jar he buried so long ago, Alexis Josephus not only put his written account of the coverup at Nicaea, but several other scrolls that he was told to burn. But he couldn't bring himself to do that. Thus, when recovered roughly 1700 years later, scholars found a treasure of works—some known, some they only possessed in fragmentary form, some totally unknown. In the latter category were additional writings of Flavius Josephus, ancient Hebrew scriptures, some written in Aramaic, and many early Christian tracts typically written in Greek. Most of these supported the characterization of Jesus offered by Thomas, not John, promoted the loving, generous "way of life" Jesus advocated, and downplayed—or even ignored—his death. One of them corroborates an account of Jesus and disciples dancing and chanting the words of a mystical hymn later known as "Round Dance of the Cross."[12]

As 2030 ended, two things had become apparent regarding the Q GAIA conspiracy theory that grew up out of the great archaeological find. First, other than the initial common letter designation and the ending in which people experience "A Great Wakening," it's totally unlike the crazy QAnon conspiracy popular ten years earlier. That story culminated with people in general finally realizing that QAnon believers have been right about the threat posed by the evil pedophiles, and with the final victory of the forces of good / God over the evil deep state / Satan forces.

But whereas QAnon is completely made up conspiracy, the conspiracy described in Q GAIA is real. Even before Alexis Josephus' account of the coverup, available evidence suggested plotting by evildoers with a hidden agenda. Even prior to the Nicaea meeting in 325 CE, they worked to infiltrate both the Roman court and what became the Catholic Church's Council of Bishops. And, as Alexis Josephus described in chilling fashion detailing brutal suppression, they manipulated events and successfully shaped outcomes to their liking.

Second, the Q GAIA conspiracy theory appears to be propagating in two versions. The "right-wing" version, popular among conservative Christians, expresses outrage that Christians were long ago deceitfully steered into being authoritarian followers. They were taught to not ask, like Thomas did, for evidence before they invested their faith. And taught—above all else—to fear a burning in Hell fate if they displeased God. This version predicts A Great Wakening in which Christians abandon the Christian Salvation / Having Dominion Over worldview in favor of the Christian Love / Stewardship one. It predicts their turning away from authoritarian theocracy, a renewed commitment to education and democracy, and enthusiastic rediscovery of The Golden Rule. The latter was apparently prompted by some blogger who mixed Q GAIA with the great Russian writer Leo Tolstoy's Christian beliefs.

In the 1890s, Tolstoy argued for a Christian reboot. In his book *The Kingdom of God is Within You*, he presented his vision of ethical living, based on what he'd decided Jesus was really about. In describing it, his biographer Henri Troyat wrote[13], "He held that the teachings of the Church had deformed the simplicity of *The Sermon on the Mount.* As the ally of the State, it had become the chief obstacle to human happiness on Earth. Therefore any fundamentally Christian mind should refuse all laws, both religious and secular, and adhere to the following precept: "Do not do unto others what you would not have them do unto you."

The "left-wing" version of Q GAIA builds on, but goes beyond, the right-wing version. Tolstoy would have liked it, as do liberal Christians, many New Agers, and Earth-Centered Spirituality enthusiasts. It emphasizes how the religious revolution, initially begun by kind-hearted, ethical, honest, and altruistic Christians and Romans 1700 years ago, successfully traded "In gods we trust" for "In God We Trust"—and that this is a victory to celebrate even today.

Likewise the importance of mysticism in early Christian belief (bolstered by documents recovered from what Alexis Josephus buried) should be similarly celebrated. This version of Q GAIA argues these are both routes for humans to feel connected to each other —either through "the God within each of us," or in a way that can be experienced. The archaeological discovery, it claims, and appropriate Christian reboot, can add a spiritual dimension to global citizenship— making it feel that hurting an innocent someone else is like hurting yourself

Q GAIA enthusiasts generally expressed outrage over the documented hijacking 1700 years ago of the religious revolution. That revolution should have unified humanity with the strong belief that "we're all in this together" —founded on the strong, psychologically healthy feeling that we're all fundamentally connected to each other in some way. It should have fully embraced the loving kindness Jesus practiced and preached. But instead, something else happened. A few evildoers stepped in and failed to point the revolution in the originally intended direction.

They succeeded in giving the Catholic Church unchallenged power for the next millennium and beyond. But it came at a heavy price. Instead of nurturing loving, generous, Golden Rule oriented, thoughtful adults, it produced obedient children. Until forced to make reforms by the Reformation, the Church kept the masses from even reading the *Bible.* And even then, Martin Luther in essentially arguing to keep the masses stupid, said, "Reason is the greatest enemy of faith." Sadly, Christianity, instead of encouraging people to join together to fight hate and injustice with loving kindness, kept them subservient, and fearful. Typical Christians became concerned less with helping others, and more concerned with their own personal salvation—and avoiding hell fire.

E. Christian Salvation /Having Dominion Over View

Preferences that emerge from the 104 worldview themes paired to make fifty-two choices depend on one's worldview. Recall (Figure #2) we previously named twelve generic worldviews for which twenty favorite themes—those most strongly preferred among those in all fifty-two choices—have been identified. Here we describe how these themes were selected for one of those twelve generic worldviews: The Christian Salvation / Having Dominion Over Worldview. The next section similarly does this for The Christian Love / Stewardship Worldview.

First used on US coins in 1864, the phrase "In God We Trust" became the official motto of the United States in 1956. Consider how earlier generations of Americans—who valued this motto and believed in the ultimate authority of the Bible— might have simplified their religious thinking.   They would have no trouble following the lead of Dutch Christian minister Abraham Kuyper (1837-1920). They thus would place themselves in the first of the two camps that Kuyper divided all humanity into: either faithful to God or unfaithful. His belief or unbelief way of simplistically seeing the world was based on whether one accepted the supreme authority of God as sovereign ruler.

Kuyper was a conservative (choice #31) traditionalist who counted monarchs and Catholics among his allies. Generally he saw modernism, especially its (choice #8) secular state manifestation, as the enemy, and, in particular, liberals and socialists as his organized opponents. Citing the *Bible*'s story of God's destruction of the Tower of Babel as a justifiable put down of humans attempting to unify and claim ultimate authority, he had no use for those we will increasingly refer to as global citizens.

Christians following in Kuyper's footsteps today, and considering our fifty-two choices, will find constraints that narrow their choices. For those tens of millions of Americans who 1) accept the literal view of God's instructions to man in the *Bible*'s book of *Genesis*, "Be fruitful, and multiply, and replenish the earth, and subdue it: and have dominion over...every living thing," and 2) see God in judgmental terms as a (choice #16) moralist, and especially value their own personal salvation, we think many of their choices are rather predictable.

Their top twenty expected preferences are shown in Figure #7. Those with strong evangelical tendencies to spread the "Good News" of the gospels and recruit new followers, will not be surprised to see their choice #3 preference for the I Know What's Best for You theme in this list. We note that Kuyper himself—and other Protestant Christians with Calvinist beliefs such as in a predestination type of determinism—might have wanted to add a preference for the Fatalism theme in choice #11. Given a "can do" —not resigned— American attitude, we have declined making that selection.

Figure #7: Christian Salvation / Having Dominion Over Worldview

Choice #	Preferred theme	Choice #	Preferred theme
1	Positive Expectations	14	Cautious Processing
2	Mind Narrowly Focused	16	Salvation & Moralistic God
3	I Know What's Best For You	17	Evil is Out There
4	The True Believer	27	Hierarchical Rigidity
5	Belief in a Personal God	29	Authoritarian Follower
7	Magic	31	Valuing Traditions and Status Quo
8	Religious Fundamentalism	34	Competitive Capitalism
9	Vitalism	36	Proud Identification and Tribalism
12	The Group Think Imperative	41	Human-Centered
13	Simply in God's Hands: Apocalypticism	42	Sanctity & Dignity of Life

But we have included (choice #34) Competitive Capitalism, given the lingering influence—beginning with John Calvin (1509-1564) —of the Protestant work ethic. Some link the beginning of capitalism to workers being encouraged to labor beyond what was required to meet their families' needs and producing a surplus. Whereas idleness and waste of time were viewed as sinful, self-reliant extra labor was celebrated as contributing to "the glory of God." This God was seen in personal and moralistic terms (preferences in choices #5 and #16.) And as a God who gave humans a dominion mandate as the (also preferred) Human Centered theme of choice #41 describes.

One suspects other preferences in Figure #7 are not much different from those feudal era (around 1000 CE) Catholic Church authorities would wish people to have. Given that organization embodying hierarchical rigidity, finding that theme in our list is not surprising. Recent events, which have allayed the fears of conservative priests, also justify that choice #27 preference over the social justice-oriented egalitarian progressive alternative. Those priests had worried that supposedly liberal Pope Francis would move the Vatican position on the hot button issue of same sex marriage in a progressive direction. These fears proved unfounded. On March 15, 2021, to the disappointment of the (choice #37) LGBTQ and (choice #23) human rights communities, the Church reasserted its (choice #16) moralistic stance that same sex unions are sinful. It also depicted a same sex preference as a choice. Researchers, who've built a strong body of (choice #1) evidence suggesting otherwise, wish the Church—like they finally did with Galileo—would accept the scientific evidence bearing on this question.[14]

Finally the choice #36 selection of Proud Identification would be made by inserting "Christian" in the first sentence in that theme's description. But, given competing forms of Christianity, that alone might not be enough. Many would feel the need to further identity their religious tribe by stipulating "Catholic," "Methodist," "Presbyterian," "Baptist,"—or even "Mormon" or "Jehovah's Witness."

Many Protestant and newer faiths aggressively push their members to recruit new followers. This evangelism is hardly new. Accompanying discovery, exploration, and eventual colonization of the New World, were Christian missionary efforts to convert indigenous people. The late 18th and early 19th century missions established by Spanish Padres (like Junipero Serra) throughout California attest to this. To some extent these evangelists, as they interact with the targets of their missions, are convinced (choice #3) "I Know What's Best for You!" As they see it, the message of Jesus Christ they bring to those ignorant of it can be the (choice #16) salvation of those who embrace it. Sadly, such contact brought a staggering death toll to New World tribes who lacked immunity to Old World germs.

The problem is still with us. In 2015, Columbian authorities, seeking to protect long isolated Amazonian tribes from germs and disruption of their unique lifestyles, intercepted two American evangelical missionaries. But similar efforts in Brazil of the American missionary organization Ethnos 360, formerly called New Tribes Mission, are finding support in the Bolsanaro government according to a March 2020 story in *The Guardian*. The story[15], headlined "The Isolated Tribes at Risk of Illness from Amazon Missionaries," reports the group's newly purchased helicopter will aid contact. It now sits beside a reserve with "the world's highest concentration of isolated indigenous groups, who have little resistance to common illnesses." Polish doctor Adam Mol, who has worked with these remote tribes, has blasted these missionary efforts. He cited the case of twenty-six year old John Chau who was killed[16] in November 2018 by the hunter-gathers he was trying to convert on North Sentinel Island in the Indian Ocean. "He literally accepted killing some of them with the excuse of bringing them God's word. That's literally how these people think," Mol said.

Those who are (choice #3) humbly unsure don't become such evangelists. They don't possess an attitude shaped by ethnocentrism, nor have committed to belief in an afterlife spent in heaven, hell, etc. Beliefs they have are often filled with doubt sufficient to preclude their vigorously promoting them in trying to convert others. But historically, powerful, more arrogant, less humble men shaped Christianity as we have seen. Our next section speculates as to how Christianity might have evolved had those teaching loving kindness above all us prevailed.

F. Christian Love / Stewardship Worldview

Notably absent from the Figure #7 list of some Christian preferences is the (choice #18) Golden Rule, Village Ethic of Mutual Help theme. What might have happened differently long ago that could have insured its inclusion? Imagine, at the Bishop's Ecumenical Council in Nicaea in 325 CE, the different choices that could have been made for the words of the Nicene Creed, and the books to include in the Christian *Bible New Testament*... What if the creed coming out of that meeting, drew heavily on the words in the book of *Matthew*:(25: 35-40)? "For I was hungry and you gave me food, I was thirsty and you gave me drink. I was a stranger and you welcomed me, I was naked and you clothed me, I was sick and you visited me, I was in prison and you came to me...Truly, I say to you, as you did it to one of the least of these my brothers, you did it to me."

What might have happened differently long ago that could have kept (choice #8) Religious Fundamentalism, (choice #13) apocalypticism, and (choice #18) Culture of Fear themes out of the Figure #7 list? Back at the Nicaea meeting, what if the gospel of *Thomas*, not the gospel of

John, had been included in the *New Testament*? What if today's Christians did not encounter the words *John* begins with, "In the beginning was the Word, and the Word was with God, and the Word was God,"—might far more people see the *Bible* as human words, not God's words? What if the final *New Testament* book of *Revelation* had been omitted and replaced with something more somber / less crazed, less violent / more peace-loving? Might there be far fewer people today fearing the "End Times" and preparing to face the Apocalypse with guns they've bought?

According to *Thomas*, Jesus said, "The kingdom of God is inside you...When you come to know yourselves ...you will see." But those words were suppressed long ago, thus hundreds of millions of today's Christians anticipate Jesus' triumphant return to rule over a future Kingdom of God on Earth and expect to meet God someday in Heaven. Had different choices been made at Nicaea, these folks might conceive of Heaven differently, and have a different choice #16 preference. They might not think of Heaven as an actual place in the sky where the souls of righteous people spend a peaceful eternity with God, but instead look within themselves for it. This could be a metaphorical look, or one in which they imagine some unseen higher dimensional part of themselves is connecting with God. And (choice #6) mystically connecting with everyone else, who is also connected in this way to God.

Enough imagining of what might have happened differently. Suppose, as a Christian, you're aware of what we've described above, and are uncomfortable with some of the Figure #7 list of preferences. How would you go about reworking it? You have many decisions to make.

What about (choice #5) Belief in a Personal God concerned with human beings—should you put your faith there, or in a distant God who does not interfere in the workings of the universe, per the Monotheistic Deism theme? You certainly wouldn't pray to the latter type of God—but you don't have any evidence to decide how to conceive of God. Except, sometimes during troubled times in your past, praying has made you feel better. Then you've conceived of God as like "a loving sky parent" who is always on your side, and who will somehow facilitate things working out for the best.

Let me interrupt here. While I generally want to steer people away from (choice #1) faith-based wishful thinking, what do I say to grieving people who reach out to a (choice #5) Personal God for comfort? I recently imagined that I listening in person—not to a April 23, 2021 "Climate Migrants Battle Flooding Again" *NPR* story—to a distraught "Mama Dee" describe the flooding ruining her home in an East Palo Alto low income neighborhood adjoining San Francisco Bay. And she asks me directly, "The last two floods over here, where was God?" What do I tell her? Certainly the (choice #8) secular humanist in me doesn't answer.

Rather I can imagine the (choice #6) mystic in me, my inner John Steinback saying something to her. Something like how Tom Joad, near the end of *The Grapes of Wrath*, answers Ma when she asks, "They might hurt you. How'm I gonna know?" Tom tells her, "Well maybe like Casy says, a fella ain't got a soul of his own, but only a piece of a big one...Then I'll be around in the dark. I'll be ever'where—wherever you look. Wherever they's a fight so hungry people can eat, I'll be there. Wherever there's a cop beatin' up a guy, I'll be there...I'll be in the way kids laugh when they're hungry an' they know supper's ready. And when our folks eat the stuff they raise, an' live in the houses they build—why I'll be there." I don't believe in a Personal God, and don't practice (choice #14 and choice #18) loving kindness and the Golden Rule as much as I should, but I like what Tom tells Ma. Hopefully I could say something like that to comfort Mama Dee.

Back to our Christian uncomfortable with Figure #7 list preferences. You certainly can't imagine praying with an image of Jesus nailed on the cross in the back of your mind. You're shaken by encounters with those holding a Christian Salvation dominated worldview You won't pray to a (choice #16) judgmental God who demands you believe Jesus died to save you from sin, and only by believing in Him can forgiveness be had.

People are often guilt ridden; worried about burning in Hell if they do bad things; miserable—given their conception of God, not as loving and kind, but rather as potentially vengeful and judgmental. And feeling, after each potential misstep, alienated—certainly not the feeling of belonging that you've cultivated. You decide that praying to the loving, comforting God you imagine can't hurt. And, even if it's all just another useful fiction, if it makes you feel better, you ask, "Why not?" So you hold on to Belief in a Personal God, but give Moralistic God the boot.

So, from the (choice #3) humble territory you've staked out, you weave these beliefs and others into your worldview because they have psychological advantages and make you a healthier, more together person. You're not unequivocally convinced they're part of the ultimate, true description of Reality. But, you're convinced, if others also believed them, the world would be a better place. If asked to define your worldview, you might do so with choices indicated in Figure #8.

Figure #8: The Christian Love / Stewardship Worldview

Choice #	Preferred theme	Choice #	Preferred theme
1	Positive Expectations	24	Culture of Tolerance
3	Humbly Unsure	25	Love As Family Glue
5	Belief in a Personal God	28	Celebrating Team Accomplishments
7	Magic	32	Service to Others
9	Vitalism	34	Liking Co-operation-Based Communities
14	Relaxed, Generous, Loving	40	Limits & Ethics
15	Conscientious, Efficient Stewardship	42	Sanctity & Dignity of Life
18	The Golden Rule, Village Ethic of Mutual Help	45	Enoughness
19	Gratitude & Forgiveness	49	Attitudinal Fix
22	The Self Restrained Person	50	Pacifism / Non-Violence

Other differences between your preferences and those of Figure #7 deserve comment. Given your tentativeness and humility, you aren't out there evangelizing. Given your choice #3 preference, You can't say, "I know what's best for you." Since you don't believe in (choice #17) evil demons, nor in a God whose (choice #8) supposed words are sacred, and don't fear a (choice #13) vengeful God, you're more relaxed. Less fearful of being harshly judged, you often refrain from judging others. You more frequently give people (choice #14) "the benefit of the doubt" and are (choice #24) more tolerant of them. You strive to be kind, have a loving heart and helping hands.

Politically, you are less of (choice #29) an authoritarian follower, more of a democrat. You don't think God keeps score and metes out justice, but rather think, as Manitonquat[17] has said, "God Is Love...Love is life believing in itself." Although conservative tendencies limit your social justice activism, you appreciate Cornel West's statement[18] "Justice is what love looks like in public." You express that in (choice #32) Service to Others terms.

Choices We Make in the Global Village

In looking over your Figure #8 preferences, you reflect on American history. You recall that nearly two hundred years ago French observer of American society Alexis de Tocqueville credited religion with playing a key role in shaping American ideals such as "all men are created equal." Taking a long view of human history, in *Democracy in America*, he wrote, "Christianity, which has rendered all men equal before God, will not be loathe to see all citizens equal before the law." You agree—this belief bolsters your (choice #24) preference for tolerance.

Speaking of Christianity and American democracy, nearly two centuries after de Tocqueville's observations, evangelicals were well represented among the protesters—call them terrorists many insist—who laid siege to the US Capitol on January 6, 2021. As reported by *Time* magazine[19], "The intruders displayed JESUS SAVES signs next to those calling for the hanging of Vice President Mike Pence." And, "once inside the building, thanked God for the opportunity to get rid of the communists, the globalists, and the traitors within the US government." You realize these folks did not possess a (Figure #8) Love / Stewardship Worldview—no signs proclaiming JESUS LOVES were seen.

The Capitol intruders distanced themselves most notably from Figure #7's authoritarian Salvation / Having Dominion Over Worldview with their demonstrated preference for (choice #17) Taking Charge➔ Violence. But, given the documented large number of (choice #38) QAnon conspiracy theory believers in this crowd, you suspect many shared one belief with Figure #7 worldview subscribers: that Evil is Out There. And they were acting on that belief: fighting the forces of evil— wanting to root out deep state forces, typically Democrats, embedded in the US government, Satan worshippers, and child-molesting pedophiles, some reportedly cannibals.

If you were in Washington DC on that day with your "Christian Love / Stewardship Worldview," besides JESUS LOVES signs, you might have held a banner urging, "Care for God's Creation." Environmentally, responsible (choice #15) stewardship, as in taking good care of creation, not potentially reckless "having dominion over" mandate, shapes other preferences that round out your worldview. You see the need for (choice #40) limits and regulations that rein in development. You like what Adam Daniel Finnerty wrote nearly fifty years ago in his book *No More Plastic Jesus*, "The world is urgently in need of a simple lifestyle." He added, "...if I am...to take Christ's teachings seriously, I must restrain my consumption of the world's resources."

So your lifestyle is rather simple. Indeed, your (choice #22) self-restraint, austerity, and appreciation of (choice #45) Enoughness, has led others to say "You'd have been a good medieval Christian monk." You greatly prefer (choice #34) co-operation to competition. You feel disdain for those whose ethics are not (choice #3) humble, (choice #18) Golden Rule based, but rather arrogant (choice #33) "Those who have the gold make the rules." That attitude has led others to compare you to Jesus throwing the money changers out of the Temple, or commenting on the difficulty rich people will have in entering the Kingdom of God.

You have not-quite-as strong preferences beyond the twenty listed in Figure #8. At times you think your Christian love / God is love conception extends to believing love connects all living things, and in something of a "Respect for Nature" (choice #41) feeling. This feeling would be behind tentative support you'd express for the assertion, "God sometimes hears and answers our prayers." As would something you'd pull from one of the choice #16 themes. While you want nothing to do with Salvation and Moralistic God, and don't know if you believe in reincarnation, you like the idea of connecting actions, including prayers, with "the moral arc of the universe somehow bends toward justice— perhaps in a spiritual version of action / reaction or cause / effect."[20]

G. Imagining "Opening the Muslim Mind"

The fundamentalist Islam worldview resembles the Christian Salvation / Having Dominion Over one with some key differences. One of those is a clear Islamic preference for (choice #11) Fatalism — based on the prevalence with which Muslims use the Arabic language expression "Inshallah"—meaning if Allah or God wills it. For many, fatalism brings with it passivity. In her 2010 book *Nomad*, Somali born Dutch-American activist Ayaan Hirsi Ali tells a story about puddles of water in an Ethiopian village serving as a breeding ground for mosquitoes / malaria. Her expressed concern was met by her stepmother's "shrugged... shoulders in charming helplessness. 'It is as Allah wills,' she said. 'The puddles will dry when it stops raining. Allah brings the rains and Allah makes the sun shine.'"

Many link belief in fatalism to living in poverty. They say poor people become resigned to poverty and feel, no matter what they do, since they were destined to be poor, they can't escape it. Some who've worked helping people get off welfare, claim a person's escape from poverty often begins with taking personal responsibility. Doing this attests to people believing "their actions...shape their destinies," and (choice #11) Free Will. In contrast, a stubbornly fatalistic person might claim, "No one ever acts freely, so taking personal responsibility is meaningless."

Taking personal responsibility is an important first step in Working for Change —the choice #31 theme paired with Valuing Traditions and Status Quo. Conservative, accomplished Muslim men may argue nothing needs to change. They point to surveys showing a great deal of life satisfaction due to feelings of oneness and connectedness to each other that Islam promotes. Liberal Muslims identify the place of women in Islamic society as most needing to change. They note an Islamic preference for (choice #23) not granting women the same rights as men, and keeping them in near Servitude conditions. Many Muslim women would challenge the "abhorrent" and "severely constrained" characterizations of their lives that this theme suggests. Many claim to be happy. Many of these women, and the men who dominate them, would put Allah's will squarely in the way of change.

In this regard consider Ali's description of her half sister's dress and life. "...Her black shroud extended beyond the tips of her fingers and trailed on the ground; she sought with every word and gesture to express her submission to Allah's will and to the authority of men. The Muslim veil, the different sorts of masks and beaks and burkas are all gradations of mental slavery. You must ask permission to leave the house, and when you go out you must always hide yourself behind the thick drapery. Ashamed of your body, suppressing your desires—what small space in your life can you call your own?"

Critics of fatalism argue believing in it is psychologically unhealthy. Not so, proponents claim—countering that such belief can considerably simplify lives. So can, they argue, belief in (choice #8) Religious Fundamentalism, which also does this by severely constraining behavior. Progressives feel that adopting a Free Will mindset is a key step in "Opening the Muslim Mind"—a phrase found in this section's title and as the title of chapter 14 of Ayaan Hirsi Ali's book.

Just as we earlier imagined new archaeological findings opening Christian eyes as to how the *New Testament* of the *Bible* was put together, Ayaan Hirsi Ali sees something similar of potential great importance for Islam. Going right to the heart of (choice #8) belief in holy books as "the unerring word of God," she cites "vital" ongoing work investigating the origins of the *Qu'ran*. "If the Muslim mind can be opened to the idea that the *Qu'ran* was written by a committee of men over the two hundred years that followed Muhammad's death," she says, "the read-only lock on the Holy Book can be opened. If Muslims can allow themselves to perceive the possibility that a holy book was needed to justify the Arabs' conquests, every kind of inquiry and cultural shift is possible...Tradition and habit are powerful forces. But behind the veils and beards would be minds asking questions."

Her book's chapter 14 subtitle is "An Enlightenment Project." She connects the needed cultural shift to Western Enlightenment values. But Moslems can look to their own history of intellectual accomplishment. American-Turkish physics professor and historian of science John Freely, in his 2009 book *Aladdin's Lamp*, chronicles Islamic scholars' quests for answers to all sorts of questions. Covering the millennium preceding the eighteenth century Western Enlightenment, he tells the stories of (choice #12) intellectually curious Islamic mathematicians, philosophers, astronomers, doctors, and engineers.

Muhammad ibn Musa al-Khwarzmi (780-850), generally credited with being the father of algebra, lived at the beginning of that millennium. Also famous for astronomical tables, around 820 he headed the "House of Wisdom" library in Baghdad. Nearby, his contemporary, theologist ibn Hisham was editing a biography of Muhammad written—from oral tradition— by ibn Ishaq at least fifty years earlier. Many believe the work of these two men, and other theologians, form the basis of the *Qu'ran* and the *Hadith*[21] as they exist today.

A copy of that biography made it to the library in Cordoba in Islamic Spain ·by 864. With a library eventually growing to number 400,000 volumes, Cordoba joined Baghdad and Cairo as important centers of learning in the Islamic Renaissance. At its mid-10th century peak, Cordoba is believed to have been the largest, most opulent, and most technically advanced city in the world. The medical school there became renowned throughout (Dark Ages?) Europe, as did treatises produced by its scholars on spherical trigonometry, water clocks, astronomical instruments, and astronomical tables.

The ninth and tenth centuries represent a golden age of Islamic astronomy. During that period most of the brighter stars visible in the night sky were tagged with Arabic names that today's Western astronomers still use. Among others, they have Hunayn ibn Ishaq (808-873) of Baghdad to thank. One of the Greek classic books he translated into Arabic was *The Great System of Astronomy* by Claudius Ptolemy (100-178 CE), who lived in Alexandria and spoke Greek. Even its 12th century translation into Latin retained its Arabic title, *Almagest*, although some star names were corrupted. By the early 11th century, al-Khwarzmi's astronomical tables had been improved, adapted to the Cordoba location, and were used by astronomers there in studying Ptolemy's planetary system. With its translation into Latin by Adelard of Bath (1080-1152), this work became accessible to Christian Europe.

Before Christians conquered Cordoba in 1236, the work of ibn Rushd (1126-1198) stands out. Besides rising to become personal physician to the caliphate —and discovering that the retina was the light sensitive part of the eye—he distinguished himself as a philosopher. His work—including commentaries on Aristotle—earned him the title "The Father of Rationalism," and influenced Jewish sage Maimonides and Catholic scholar Thomas Aquinas. Ibn Rushd was, John Freely claims, "the first writer in any language to complain about discrimination against women, which he felt was one of the most serious problems in Muslim society."

Before ibn Rushd's time, a visiting Saxon nun referred to Cordoba as "The Ornament of the World." Over ten centuries later this became the title of a 2002 book by Yale professor Maria Rosa Menocal (1953-2012.) She argues that—five hundred years before Ferdinand and Isabella funded Columbus' voyage and overcame the last Islamic stronghold at Granada in 1492— "...Muslims, Jews and Christians Created a Culture of Tolerance in Medieval Spain." Whereas "the most Catholic majesties" expelled Jews and brought Inquisition torture to non-believers, Menocal depicts earlier Islamic rulers as tolerant of minority religions. She also provides cultural and political examples of tolerance.[22]

(Choice #24) a culture of tolerance is not something we associate with (choice #8) religious fundamentalists, Islam or Christian. Might we add becoming more tolerant to our wished for list in imagining changes brought by a 21st century opening of the Muslim mind? Perhaps add it to a list which includes (choice #11) trading fatalism for freewill, taking personal responsibility, trading (choice #12) "groupthink" for asking questions," etc? How might such a worldview transformation, and return to Muslim greatness, begin? Educational reform provides one route.

Certainly the attempt Mustafa Kemal Ataturk (1881-1938) made to transform authoritarian, rigid Islamic Turkey into a secular state after World War I deserves attention in this regard. Valuing (choice #29) Education for Democracy and (choice #12) intellectual freedom themes, he realized the critical importance of education. Finding traditional fundamentalist Islamic religious schools (madrassas) abhorrent, Ataturk brought in American educational system thinker John Dewey to aid his reform effort. Eventually thousands of new schools were started. Primary education was made free and compulsory. His achievement was such that the United Nations declared 1981—the centennial of his birth—to be "The Ataturk Year in the World."

Sadly, given the increasingly authoritarian and theocratic direction in which Turkey has moved in the last two decades, what Ataturk envisioned has not come to pass. Throughout the Islamic world, madrassas stressing studying / memorizing the *Qu'ran* and promoting rote learning, not critical thinking skills, have not died out. Rather in places like Pakistan—where Saudi oil money has promoted extreme Wahhabi sect beliefs—they have made a strong comeback. Thus children spend hours memorizing verses like, "The true believers are those who feel a fear in their hearts (of the consequences of violating the commands of Allah) when Allah is mentioned. And when His Revelations are recited to them, they find their faith strengthened. They do their best and then put their trust in their Lord" (from the *Qur'an*, 8:2) And "This Book, there is no doubt in it, is a guide to those who keep their duty" (from the *Qur'an*, 2:2). That is, they learn to obey, not ask questions.

Traditional ways stubbornly persist. Ayaan Hirsi Ali faced "an education in subservience," had she not had a more progressive opportunity. Of that opportunity she writes, "Whenever I hear Westerners today say, "Education is the answer," I need only think back...The women of the neighborhood would get together and complain that school was corrupting young girls like me and making them more rebellious."

Ayaan Hirsi Ali's book ends with a "Letter to My Unborn Daughter." After acknowledging how painful her rejection of God was for her mother, she recalls that her father "could never understand my unbelief." But, transcending all that she says, "Our unconditional love for one another was so much more powerful than that belief. And the proof was the way we clutched each other's hands at the end" — her father's death. She then makes a graceful literary transition from dying to living and, in directly addressing her soon to be born daughter, ends on a hopeful note. "That earthy love is my faith. It is the love I shall always give you."

Her example inspires hope that Muslims—from a choice #25 perspective —might come to prefer unconditional love that binds families together, to the tough love that dictates submission to will of Allah, praying five times a day, etc. Hope, like what we've imagined for Christians, that they trade a rigid fundamentalist faith for something else. Trade a worldview preoccupied with fear, with behaving as supposedly prescribed by Allah to avoid hellfire, for (choice #14 and choice #18) one connecting Allah with love, valuing loving kindness, generosity, the Golden Rule, etc.

Islamic legal tradition offers another route to a more progressive Islam. That tradition distinguishes the independent reasoning associated with Ijtihad from the conformity of Taqlid.[23] Ijtihad requires one get expertise in several fields before being qualified to perform it. Just as few jurists might aspire to it, in broader educational settings many students might seek to refine critical thinking skills, and not be satisfied with instruction based on imitating / memorizing. Recollection and celebration of the (500-1500) era of Middle Eastern medicine as the most advanced in the world might inspire medical careers. Similar appreciation of Islamic tradition in math and astronomy could bring (choice #1) an evidence-based rekindling of (choice # 12) Islamic intellectual curiosity.

Ancient connection with the formal beginning of observational astronomy could provide Muslims with a reason for "Discovering the Sky" (chapter 5) that most Americans and Europeans don't have. Possible sources of such inspiration are 1) The poetry in the *Rubaiyat* of Omar Khayyam (1048-1131), dubbed "the Astronomer Poet of Persia"; 2) Sufi (choice #6) mysticism, where whirling Dervish dance has been seen as symbolizing planets orbiting the Sun; 3) long-ago Islamic (choice #4) skepticism of the details of Ptolemy's cumbersome Earth-centered system. Islamic astronomers' advances may have— directly (through undiscovered Latin version of Arabic text) or indirectly— influenced Copernicus and spurred his Sun-centered model for planetary orbits.

Speculations abound as to how Islam might become more progressive. But most agree widespread rekindling of Islamic intellectual curiosity must begin with cultural accommodations that allow more (choice #12) intellectual freedom. Reforming schools to move beyond the "education in subservience" Ayaan Hirsi Ali describes, is a critical first step. . Greg Mortenson's *Three Cups of Tea* book paints a sad, at times frightening, picture of both Pakistan's public schools and madrassas. Those private schools—numbering 32,000 enrolling 2.5 million students according to a 2019 survey —came under western scrutiny after the 9/11/2001 terrorist attacks. Many faulted the intolerant / jihadist inspired brand of Islam they were spreading. They charged many madrassa graduates had become fighters for the (now triumphant) Taliban in Afghanistan.

"One man's mission to fight terrorism… one school at a time" was the subtitle Mortenson's co-author / editor and the publisher initially gave the book in 2007:" Greg objected. Eventually it acquired the subtitle he preferred: "one man's mission to promote peace… one school at a time." He later explained his reasoning in what I see as choice #18 terms. "If you just fight terrorism, it's based on fear. If you promote peace, it's based on hope." Honored with a "Star of Pakistan" award in 2009, Mortenson was forced by controversy and poor health to retire from humanitarian work in 2015. By 2018, the elevation of Imran Khan to prime minister of Pakistan suggested change might be expected. In his first public address, he called on madrassas to provide a core curriculum that included instruction in math, science, and English.   Pakistan educators advised him to concentrate on first fixing the public schools.

H. Imagining More Change in Religious Landscapes

Earlier in this chapter we discussed the meanings of several words and terms—notably religion, faith, reason, hope, and considerations behind (choice #1) evidence-based vs. positive expectations / wishful thinking / useful fiction/ adopting healthy beliefs tradeoffs. We now consider meanings of five additional words and terms: spirituality, evangelical, new evangelism, humility and reverence. As we do this, we shall weave consideration of two more choices, #2 and #3, into the discussion.

We can use choice #2, between Mind Narrowly Focused and Mind Open, Vision Global preferences, to frame two definitions of spirituality. First, spirituality can be narrowly defined as "relating to matters pertaining to vital spirit or soul." This spirituality is problematic for science. Science —in the narrowly focused fashion that has led to technological marvels such as the smart phones lots of us depend on— finds no measurable evidence for souls and spirits. By contrast, a second definition of spirituality is very broad, open-ended, and full of possibility.

Those who value science, yet think of themselves as having a "spiritual" component, appreciate this alternate definition. So do those valuing global education. Here it is: "Spirituality is the domain at the intersection of what both our thinking heads and our feeling hearts tell us is fundamentally important." Using the words of Manish Mishra-Marezetti and Jennifer Nordsrom, this appreciation of spirituality can be extended into the joining and doing realms. In their 2018 book *Justice on Earth*, they write, "In spiritual circles, it is sometimes said that the biggest step one can take is from one's head to one's heart. In a similar matter, when it comes to justice-making, the biggest and most important step may be moving from one's head to embodied action."

We'll return to "justice-making." Let's first consider choice #2 with respect to beliefs per an open-minded vs. close-minded characterization of people. Despite often feeling that those in the latter group have beliefs set in concrete, we recognize beliefs can change—although this can be a slow process if it happens at all. New experiences and new knowledge can trigger abrupt changes in beliefs. And new evidence can dispel long-held faith in something. This can result in a (choice #4) true believer in a (choice #5) personal God becoming a non-believing (choice #8) secular humanist. It can result in an atheist embracing God.

We previously mentioned Valerie Tarico. She documented her transition from evangelical Christian religious fundamentalist into secular humanist psychologist in a 2010 book: *Trusting Doubt—A Former Evangelical Looks at Old Beliefs in a New Light*. Doubt can be linked to a term physicists can appreciate: uncertainty. Well- known author Deepak Chopra has expressed amazement at his evolution: from holding an evidence-based perspective in his1970s medical school days to being increasingly open to various New Age beliefs. One of Chopra's recent (2015) essays concerns what he calls The Law of Detachment—one of seven "Spiritual Laws of Success" he's formulated. It begins[24], "In detachment lies the wisdom of uncertainty…" Doubt and uncertainty are part of (choice #3) the Humbly Unsure theme. Its pairing with I Know What's Best For You can prompt humility and evangelism discussions.

Humility, according to Alan Morinis[25], involves "limiting oneself to an appropriate amount of space while leaving room for others." Weaving humility into relating to other people means valuing an orientation that proclaims, "I don't have all the answers and I want your contribution." In contrast, an evangelical feels he or she has answers they want to aggressively share. Aggressive, as in involving a militant or crusading zeal, characterizes some evangelical Christian efforts to convert others. According to Rick Warren in his 2002 *A Purpose-Driven Life* book, that was one of God's purposes in creating human life. In other words, God made these people so they could proclaim "I Know What's Best For You"—where the "what" is the proselytizer's brand of Christianity.

Within Christianity, some are taking a "new evangelism" direction. This activist movement broadens evangelicalism beyond salvation, pro-life and other issues important to the religious right, to also include pro-poor, (choice #27) pro-social justice issues important to the left. In terms of doing "the Lord's work" or "what really matters," this trend could conceivably move conservative Christians toward liberal UU folks—like the authors of *Justice on Earth*.

For many Christians this new social gospel brings with it a global perspective. In global education / broad definition of spirituality terms, the movement addresses what thinking heads and feeling hearts proclaim is fundamentally important. It has potential to bring people together and offer helping hands eager to take action. Certainly this requires "selfless leaders willing to helpfully step up and point the way forward," to again use words from the (choice #3) I Know What's Best For You theme.

Not to slight the other side of this choice, acting with humility, according to Gary Zukav[26], means embracing the "harmlessness of one who treasures and honors and reveres life in all its forms." This brings us to reverence. Defined as "profound respect mingled with love and awe," it requires humility argues UU minister Phillip Hewett (1925-2018). To feel reverent, he writes, necessitates that "you are humble enough to see yourself as a modest part of a greater whole, not the pivot around which it revolves." Certainly "reverence" has connotations that connect it to religion—one being the Rev. title reserved for ministers, pastors, etc.

Has anyone connected these words just mentioned—like reverence, love, and awe—in a science and religion context? The 1955 book *The Phenomenon of Man* by French, Jesuit priest, Catholic mystic, and paleontologist Teilhard de Chardin (1881-1955) brought all of them together. We'll discuss his ideas more in chapters 5 and 8. While we can't simply say that he equated God with love; suffice it to say that Teilhard assigned love with a key role in how he saw human evolution unfolding. He connected it with "the psychical convergence of the universe upon itself." With the statement quoted in chapter 1, Carl Sagan links all of them together except love. His vision is constrained compared to visions of (choice #10) scientists who are also (choice #6) mystics.

As David Lorimer describes it in the 1999 book *The Spirit of Science* that he edited, "The very first Mystics and Scientists conference was held in 1978, just two years after the publication of Fritjof Capra's *The Tao of Physics*, and the year before Gary Zukav's *The Dancing Wu Li Masters*. The idea of a confluence between mysticism and science was just being tentatively put forward and many were struck by the parallel language being used to speak about the underlying nature of reality." As philosopher Renee Weber described it in her 1985 book *Dialogues with Scientists and Sages*, "Science and mysticism—once separated by the scientific pursuit of mechanistic models—are drawing closer together in a new and necessary dialogue." She argues that the same principle drives them both: "the assumption that unity lies at the heart of our world."

In the years since, many physicists, philosophers and theologians have imagined a whole new science and spirituality movement. In chapter 8 we'll sketch related theoretical exploration. And what related imagined change in the religious landscape might bring about in terms of reverence, sacred ground, celebration and worship. Prior to that, we'll explore the intellectual territory of science in the next chapter. But first, we'll take our imagining change in religion into fundamental shift in consciousness territory, and consider the question, "How can Christians think of themselves as global citizens?"

I. Christians As Global Citizens?

The majority of religious Americans are Christians, with conservative brands dominating. Yes, religion has been called "the childlike condition of humanity." Typical Sunday morning services don't promote open-mindedness, nor the critical thinking associated with mature adults. But some pastors, ministers, and rabbis lead their congregations into global education territory. Out of enough such trips, global citizens can emerge.

In chapter 1 we linked global citizens to people who make "big responsible caring choices" — not "small stupid selfish ones." And to those who feel "we're all in this together"—where "all" refers to all life on Earth. In the last section of Chapter 2 we distinguished the adult choices global citizens make from those of children, with discussion touching on over a dozen formally numbered choices. Discussion at the end of chapter 3 similarly considered many such choices— focusing on how global citizen behavior plays out on the world's stage, and with respect to institutions operating there. We continue this discussion from a religious / spiritual perspective.

We previously provided lists (Figures #7, #8) of choices that define two of twelve generic worldviews: Christian Salvation /Having Dominion Over, and Christian Love / Stewardship. Many religious fundamentalist, moralistic (choice #16) Christians are narrowly concerned with saving their souls from burning in Hell and invest in "fire insurance." Global citizens have another "saving" concern. Their "save the planet" effort— and the (choice #44) sustainability-based ethical behavior they encourage —seeks to insure that future inhabitants don't inherit a hot, dead world.

As previously discussed, global citizen boundaries of concern extend far beyond those of ordinary citizens—beginning with their embracing the (choice #2) Mind Open, Vision Global theme. In putting together a global citizens generic worldview we begin by listing this theme. But, in continuing this effort, we see a problem. In characterizing each of the two Christian generic worldviews, providing twenty "most strongly" preferred themes seems adequate. But, based on our chapter 2 and 3 explorations, characterizing what it means to be a global citizen will require more. Thus we plan to make two lists of "most strongly" and just "strongly" preferred themes—totaling forty preferences altogether. We begin this effort to extend our list of themes global citizens like by considering the (Figure #8) Christian Love / Stewardship generic worldview themes for possible inclusion.

To instill current events relevance—and initially place it in an American context—we use what respected author, magazine editor, historian, and Christian Jon Meacham has written in recent years. We begin with his description —from the 2018 book *The Soul of America: The Battle for Our Better Angels* —of the dominant feature of the American soul. He writes, "the air we breathe, or to shift the metaphor, the controlling vision—is a belief in the proposition…that all men are created equal. It is therefore incumbent upon us, from generation to generation, to create a sphere in which we can live, live freely, and pursue happiness to the best of our abilities…we must do all we can to ensure equal opportunities."

The phrase "better angels," that he uses to name the battle his book is largely about, comes from America's (perhaps) greatest president, Abraham Lincoln. In a last chapter, about the duties of today's American citizens, Meacham poses a question. "How then, in an hour of anxiety about the future of the country at a time when a president of the United States appears determined to undermine the rule of law, a free press, and the sense of hope essential to American life, can those with deep concerns about the nation's future enlist on the side of the angels?"

Meacham seemingly answers this with a list of five section-heading titles that follow: "Enter the Arena; Resist Tribalism; Respect Facts / Deploy Reason; Find a Critical Balance; Keep History in Mind." As far as he goes, I basically like this list. I translate "Enter the Arena" into avoiding (choice #32) Cynicism in embracing Service to Others. I interpret "Resist Tribalism" as rejection of (choice #36) Proud Identification & Tribalism. "Respect Facts and Deploy Reason" I take to indicate something of a preference for (choice #1) the evidence-based theme. But, keeping in mind his "Find a Critical Balance" admonition, we need to give the theme it's paired with—Positive Expectations —and related ones some value. "Keep History in Mind" suggests disdain for (choice #2) Mind Narrowly Focused, and concurrence with our Mind Open, Vision Global preference. Given his Christian faith, this list is surprisingly secular and perhaps incomplete.

Meacham remedies this in a February 25, 2020 *New York Times* opinion piece: "Why Religion Is the Best Hope Against Trump." There, he vents frustration that "so many evangelicals have thrown in their lot with a relentlessly solipsistic American president who bullies, boosts and sneers [and] has used the National Prayer Breakfast to mock the *New Testament* injunction to love one's enemies." And expresses hope that Christianity "can become a force for good once more." Along with describing the Christian story as "about love, not loathing; about generosity not greed"—and invoking the Rev. Dr. Martin Luther King, Jr. and John Lewis—he says "faith can still offer hope for liberation and progress."

With respect to composing a longer list for global citizens, we build on his list of duties for American citizens, and include his human rights connection to the dominant feature of the American soul. Then, bolstered by his clear preference for our Christian Love / Stewardship generic worldview over the competing, darker one we've sketched, we add key themes from this generic worldview. For additional help, we turn to a second Meacham article, a November 23, 2020 "Recovery Act" essay in *Time* magazine. There, after noting his links to incoming USA president Joe Biden, he emphasizes this man's "pragmatic empathy." He describes the importance of Biden's Christian faith in shaping his worldview, writing, "From his Roman Catholic ethos, he sees life as a covenant...He will try to preach and embody the idea...that the country and the world is a neighborhood, not a war-torn wilderness." In short, it seems Meacham is saying Biden thinks of America as part of a global village.

From there, we move the hope for America Jon Meacham expresses in his book—that "from generation to generation" all can "pursue happiness" with "equal opportunities" —onto the global stage. There, it becomes a hope for all humanity. Certainly Jesus, were He with us today, would not preferentially wish this for Americans, but turn a blind eye to unhappiness, suffering, and injustice elsewhere in the world—right?

Jesus identified with poor people, and urged the rich to (choice #33) give away their wealth. Sadly today, many supposedly religious and spiritual-minded folks single-mindedly pursue wealth. Thus we have Christians attending "prosperity theology" inspired churches. Both they, and New Age enthusiasts for "expansion" thinking and "a community of abundance," prefer the first of the following (choice #45) two statements. #1: "I like having the freedom to generally have more!" #2: "I like the freedom to take personal responsibility and say, 'I have enough!'" Global citizens like Dana Meadows—whose Global Citizen columns provide many more examples to use in characterizing them—prefer the second statement associated with Enoughness.

Putting Jon Meacham's "from generation to generation" prescription in a global context reinforces our including (choice #44) Sustainability in the generic global citizen worldview. But his wanting Americans to be able to "live freely" must be constrained by factoring in global realities—and avoid encouraging (as previously described in chapter 2) "the freedom to make stupid choices." Thus the previously noted (choice #40) Limits and Ethics is a key part of our list. Politically, in freedom-loving America, promoting this theme will be difficult. Also fraught with challenge: selling Americans on the need for pricing carbon, which economists see as essential to tackling climate change—and an important component of the (choice #52) Environmental Economics theme.

Imagining Christians becoming global citizens would not be complete without consideration of (choice #42) abortion—perhaps the most hot button issue on the American political landscape. Narrow-minded, anti-abortion, single-issue voters formed a key part of Donald Trump's base. These "pro-life voters" prefer the "Sanctity and Dignity of Life" theme, and absolutely accept restricting the freedom a woman would otherwise have to control her own body. They typically cite moral and ethical reasons—including their desire to protect the smallest, most innocent and vulnerable of all people, the unborn— to justify their position.

The challenge of selling Christians on accepting the (choice #40) Limits and Ethics theme —based on growing population / global climate change / future disastrous impact concerns, —will involve encouraging pro-life individuals to broaden their perspective. Getting them to consider the future world babies will be brought into, and accordingly extend their ethical concerns. This certainly will be easier if they already embraced (choice #15) stewardship and "Caring for God's Creation," rather than asserting God has (choice #41) given humans dominion over nature.

We'll return to the abortion issue in the next section, but first let's put it in the bigger context of population control / family planning. The next section will take us from America to Pakistan. Before heading there, note Pakistan began 2020 with a population of roughly 220 million people. With a current growth rate of 2.0 %/yr, its population increases by over four million people every year. If this rate is maintained, its population will double in 36 years—reaching 440 million by 2056.

The above can be used to illustrate applying "the rule of 72." To roughly project an exponential growth pattern into the future, you simply divide the associated % per year increase into the number 72 to get the doubling time in years. Example: if Pakistan's population continues to grow at 2.0% / yr, 72 divided by 2.0 gives a doubling time = 36 years. So starting from a 220 million people in 2020, 36 years later in 2056 we can project it to be 220 million x 2 = 440 million.

That figure alarms many with (choice #44) sustainability and global climate change concerns. And those worried about (choice #47) the number of the world's poor Struggling With a Basic Need: Sustenance. To both groups it portends a scary future—but it could be worse. Were Pakistan's population growth to return to its highest (early 1980s) level of 3.6 % / yr and stay there, its population would double in a mere 20 years.[27] Conceivably that growth rate could also fall dramatically — as it has in other countries (like Japan and Russia) where population has ceased growing. Exactly what the future brings in terms of Pakistan's population will be determined by choices Pakistani people make.

What they choose may critically depend on education. In chapter 7 we'll cite many analyzes made by a group called Project Drawdown,[28] which has been especially focused on finding ways to prevent greenhouse gas emissions from causing unacceptable climate change. Citing evidence from poor countries like Pakistan, they ranked "Educating Girls" and "Family Planning" as the 6th and 7th most important of the 100 global climate impact solutions they assessed. Lumped together, they represent the single most important of the solutions they analyzed. Having established this importance, we turn to the story of a man who became famous building schools (with girls in mind) in Pakistan.

J. Global Citizen Worldview

As we pull together what it means to be a global citizen, consider the foreign school-building adventures of American Greg Mortenson. Recalling (chapter 1) my past enthusiasm for the "building bridges" metaphor, I like it that work on Greg's first school only began after a bridge was built across a river. And that didn't happen until Greg and the isolated mountain Pakistani villagers established a bond of caring, found ideological common ground / shared values, and built a bridge of trust.

Years ago, *Three Cups of Tea* and media accounts elevated Mortenson to (choice #32) serving others / good guy / near Christ-like status. But today, after other portrayals, Greg is now seen as an imperfect creature— human after all, and more like the rest of us. "What happened?" you ask.

After a 2011 *60 Minutes* takedown, he eventually apologized for mishandling charitable contributions and repaid around $ one million. Never charged with criminal conduct, a 2016 documentary *3000 Cups of Tea* by Jennifer Jordan dispelled many of the charges and somewhat restored Greg's reputation. While the earlier attack said he knowingly (choice #43) deceived and cheated, my appraisal suggests something different. I believe success overwhelmed Greg with demands. And he failed to exercise (choice #15) Conscientious, Efficient Stewardship — behaving in opposite (lax, irresponsible, disorderly, cavalier) fashion.

Having defended him, I turn to the scene that provides Greg's book with its title. It happens when the illiterate village chief—and Mortenson's much-loved surrogate father— takes him aside as he's frantically trying to get the first school built. He offers, in Greg's words, "The most important lesson I've ever learned in my life...Haji Ali taught me to share three cups of tea, to slow down and make building relationships as important as building projects. He taught me that I had more to learn from the people I work with than I could ever hope to teach them."

I have two comments related to this recollection. First, given my own (choice #3) struggle between humility and arrogance, I needed to hear this story. Second, given this book's "building bridges, not walls" theme, we can metaphorically connect building relationships with building bridges as trust grows. Of course there are many components of building relationships and now is not the time for that discussion. But unlike that typically slow trust-building process, upon finishing the *Three Cups of Tea* page-turner many are high and filled with an exciting realization. The book seemingly offers, as Tom Brokaw put it, "thrilling...proof that one ordinary person, with the right combination of character and determination, really can change the world."[29]

I attribute Greg's overcoming great obstacles and succeeding to three things: perseverance, patience, and tolerance. Upon finishing his book, I thought back to a time when I seemingly moved away from tolerance. As described in chapter 1, I'd backed away from a 1960s counter-cultural creed "No one judges anyone else" I'd briefly accepted. Greg's example had me wondering, "Was choosing a different path, and becoming more judgmental, a mistake?" I don't think so—but this book you're reading is built around the belief that life's choices are often not easy, not clear cut, and not black and white simple. The (choice #42) abortion issue, which we'll be returning to shortly, provides an example.

Inspired by Mortenson's incredible tolerance—and noting where he intolerantly draws the line—I asked myself, "Of the 104 worldview themes in the *Project Worldview* version 5.0 structure, which ones can I simply not tolerate?" I put this in a context of whether I could live in close proximity to a person who valued one of the detestable themes I'd identify, and might need to build a relationship with. In a metaphorical sense, which of the worldview themes did I feel stood for something so abhorrent that I wanted only to put a wall around it? To isolate both myself, and others, from it—not try any bridge-building at all.

I quickly found I could make peace with many themes I did not like. Suffice it to say I was able to find some redeeming value in ninety-eight of the 104 themes—enough to at least tolerate a person who greatly valued one or more of these. Most notably I put (choice #8) "Religious Fundamentalism" in this category. By not including it in my (Figure #9) list, I'm not giving extreme expressions of it a pass—although most such expressions would not stand alone but would typically require being bolstered by another one of the "dirty half-dozen" themes in my list.

Figure #9: Despicable WV Themes Global Citizens Can't Tolerate

choice #	Detested theme	choice #	Detested theme
17	Taking Charge➜Violence	24	Blaming / Scapegoating
19	Bitterness, Vengeance	32	Cynicism
23	Servitude— Suffering, Enabling or Enslaving	43	Spreading Disinformation / Tactical Deception

Cynicism is there since living with it is living without hope for humankind. Religious Fundamentalism by itself would be acceptable— but not if it was paired with valuing Jihadist (choice #17) violence, (choice #23) trampling human rights / enslaving women, or with (choice #43) propaganda /disinformation promoting (choice #19) Bitterness, Vengeance, and (choice #24) Blaming / Scapegoating. Mortenson came to a similar conclusion in regulating curricula in the schools his Central Asia Institute supported. He wouldn't let "schools preach the fiery brand of fundamentalist Islam taught in many of the country's madrassas."

Besides Greg Mortenson, Mohamedou Ould Salahi is another man who has shaped my thinking about unacceptable worldview themes, and finding common ground with religious true believers. Imprisoned by the US government for fourteen years in Guantanamo, he was never charged with a crime. Suspected for aiding the 9/11/2001 terrorists, the illegal, inhumane torture to which he was subjected is described in both his 2015 book *Guantanamo Bay Diaries* and the 2021 movie *The Mauritanian*.

If this grim movie has a hopeful message it comes with Salhi's statement at his first trial in 2009. Facing a (choice #19) bitter hatred for his captors or willingness to forgive them choice, his religious beliefs guided his decision. "I am trying to forgive. I want to forgive because that is what Allah, my God, wants. For this reason, I do not hold a grudge against those who abused me...In Arabic, the word for 'free' and the word for 'forgiveness' are the same word." Christians see this as Jesus urging those who suffer to forgive their abusers and turn the other cheek.

For choice #17, I use World War II to make sense of two themes I don't value. Specifically Hitler /Nazis were a secular manifestation of evil, and violence was needed to stop them. In fighting a war (or to survive?) I can find some redeeming value in the six detested themes. But I'm more of a (choice #50) pacifist than militarist. I associate war with hate triumphing —a failure I don't want to glorify. I picture it, not with hands reaching out, but with arms holding swords or guns drawn in conflict. Sadly many approach running a business—or political campaign—like it's a war. No wonder many feel competition brings out the worst in people. Figure #9 is the first of three lists we'll use to characterize responsible, caring global citizens. It can be used to exclude people like Donald Trump.

After looking over discussion in previous chapters, we now pull together results of past considerations of choices global citizens make, and construct the lists of Figures #10 and #11.

Figure #10: Strongest Preferences Global Citizens Worldview

Choice #	Preferred theme	Choice #	Preferred theme
2	Mind Open, Vision Global	24	Culture of Tolerance
7	Orderly & Explicable	29	Education for Democracy
11	Free Will	32	Service to Others
12	Imagination, Curiosity, Intellectual Freedom	36	Global Citizen
13	Complexity—In Our Hands: Dancing With Systems	40	Limits & Ethics
15	Conscientious, Efficient Stewardship	43	Valuing Honesty, Learning
18	The Golden Rule, Village Ethic of Mutual Help	44	Sustainability
19	Gratitude & Forgiveness	45	Enoughness
22	The Self Restrained Person	51	Ethical Globalization
23	Human Rights	52	Environmental Economics

Figure #10 contains choices global citizens easily make because of a very strong preference / strong dislike situation existing as they evaluate the two themes the choice pairs together. Figure #11 identifies choices where global citizens have a clear preference, but making the choice is more difficult since they also find some value in the less preferred theme.

Figure #11: Additional Preferences Global Citizens Worldview

Choice #	Preferred theme	Choice #	Preferred theme
1	Evidence-Based	28	Celebrating Team Accomplishments
3	Humbly Unsure	31	Working for Change
4	Skeptic	33	Ethical Orientation
6	Mysticism	34	Liking Co-operation-Based Communities
8	Secular Humanism	35	Social Welfare Statism
10	Scientific Method	41	Respect for Nature
14	Relaxed, Generous, Loving	42	Hands Off My Body
20	Dispassionate	46	The Small Producer
21	Healthy Orientation	48	Work, Play, Pay As You Go
27	Egalitarian Progressive	50	Pacifism / Non-Violence

Consistent with *Project Worldview* analysis tools, theme preference can be gauged on a 0 to 10 scale. Our generic global citizens would give a 10 to all themes listed in Figure #10, whereas the not preferred themes they're paired with would all receive a 0. Themes listed in Figure #11 would all receive scores of 8, whereas the less preferred themes they're paired with would all receive a 2. For example, for the (choice #42) abortion issue, note preference there for the Hands Off My Body theme. So our generic global citizen assigns a score of "8" to that theme, and a score of "2" to the Sanctity & Dignity of Life theme it's paired with. Many won't be satisfied with this assignment, so how was it made?

First, these scores indicate that our global citizen (whose views are unavoidably somewhat biased by my own) is not simply pro-abortion or anti-abortion. Personally, I find many abortions abhorrent —especially late in pregnancy. But I also find abhorrent political leaders (often elderly males) telling a young woman she has no control over her own body with respect to abortion related decision-making. To escape this dilemma, I encourage people take appropriate personal responsibility. So I strongly support efforts—like birth control, sex education, etc.— to prevent unwanted pregnancies. And hope these can successfully avoid the painful choice of whether to have, or not have, an abortion.

As for the language in the Sanctity & Dignity of Life theme description, I'm good with its first half, before the "Note"—but I'd insert "certain" before "medical, biotechnological…" I'm not opposed to gene therapy and genetic engineering, but feel we need to proceed with caution in considering particular applications. The life I worry about inflicting pain on is a "conscious, feeling" one. I don't believe just conceived, smaller than pinhead size human embryos fit into that category. I worry about inflicting pain in killing larger animals—so I don't eat beef, pork, etc. Likewise, I don't worry about killing tiny yeast cells when I bake bread.

Since I'm not a (choice #9) vitalist, nor do I believe in (choice #5) a personal God, I don't worry about souls, vital spirits, or about insulting God. But my non-zero score indicates I have some sympathy for Pro Life views. I believe that conscious, feeling human and animal life should be treated with dignity and respect. But I think one can do that and embrace the Hands Off My Body theme, which I accept as written. I especially like its ecologically inspired concluding "Note." In embracing "our crowded planet needs fewer people, not more," I go beyond many in the Pro Choice camp who lack a big picture perspective.[30]

The abortion issue is another one in which a background in science can inform, shape and bolster one's position. And it can help in formulating answers to underlying questions. Such as, 1) "What does it mean to say something is alive?" 2) "Is possession of a "vital spirit" required—yes or no?" 3) "What does it mean to say a creature possesses consciousness?" 4) "Does that possession mean the creature has a soul—yes or no?"

Given the neglect of science in their education a large segment of the American population would answer "Yes" to both of the above yes or no questions. Critics would say ignorance is behind their strong preference for (choice #9) Vitalism, and disdain for the Scientific Materialism alternative. Global citizens value science. They see it as a big part of the hope they have in the human future. But also valuing (choice #3) humility / doubt, and shying away from controversy, many feel the scientific materialism theme carries too much baggage. Thus it's not included in either Figure #10 or #11. Instead, strong support for the less controversial (choice #7) Orderly and Explicable warrants its Figure #10 inclusion. While wholistic, creative thinker global citizen types value (choice #10) Non-Rational Knowing, a more widespread preference for the Scientific Method lands it in the Figure #11 list.

Finally, consider the "in the beginning" arena in the science vs. religion conflict. First, good news: an August 24, 2021 story by Matthew Rozsa from salon.com headlines "Science quietly wins one of the right's longstanding culture wars." It reports on a new study published in *Public Understanding of Science* that documents the trend behind the growing acceptance of evolution among Americans. Yet segments of the population remain unconvinced. Whereas a 2014 Associated Press-Gfk survey recorded 60% of Americans were confident Earth is roughly 4.5 billion years old, it also reported 51% questioned the settled scientific fact that "the universe began 13.8 billion years ago with a Big Bang."

Another result from this survey is also disturbing to those with a (choice #2) Mind Open, Vision Global preference. 72% expressed confidence in the statement, "The universe is so complex, there must be a Supreme Being guiding its creation." Evolutionary biologists are disturbed that lots of people believe "humans have always existed in their present form since the beginning of time." A February 2019 Pew Research poll found 66% of white evangelical Protestants agreed with that statement.

Astronomers and geologists are distressed that most Americans think of heaven and hell as actual physical places. According to a 2014 Pew Religious Landscape Study, 72% of Americans believe in (choice #16) heaven "defined as a place where people who have led good lives are externally rewarded." And 58% believe in hell as "a place where people who have led bad lives and die without being sorry are eternally punished." Of course the *Bible* and Sunday Christian church services have shaped—some would say brainwashed—American positions on many questions for which science provides different answers.

These results underscore the challenge facing those interested in building a bridge between religion and science. Our next chapter aims to build scientific literacy, for which we provided a definition from the American National Academy of Sciences in chapter 1. An international educators' flavored OECD / PISA definition is "the ability to engage with science-related issues, and with the ideas of science, as a reflective citizen."

Notes

1 Mortenson, Greg and Relin, David, *Three Cups of Tea — One Man's Mission to Promote Peace...One School at a Time* Penguin Books, New York 2007
2 A documentary film *3000 Cups of Tea* and website 3000cupsoftea.org address allegations against Mortenson.
3 In the 1980s, old-fashioned phone party lines still existed in rural America.
4 Over a lifetime I've lifted such buckets thousands of times—unlike most

(choice #21) physically fit Americans who confine such lifting to gyms.

5 Recalling Angie Schmitt's story (in chapter 2) about truck drivers fomenting conflict, perhaps this guy hated the Prius I was driving?

6 Fowler, James W. *Stages of Faith: The Psychology of Faith Development* Harper Collins, New York 1995

7 Schultz, William F. "Our Faith" in *The Unitarian Universalist Pocket Guide* Skinner House Books, Boston 1999

8 Buehrens, John A. "Preface" in *The Unitarian Universalist Pocket Guide* Skinner House Books, Boston 1999

9 Tarico, Valerie "Six Reasons Religion May Do More Harm Than Good" posted on salon.com November 17, 2014

10 Miller, Lisa "Belief Watch: Harvard's Fuss Over Faith" in *Newsweek* 1/22/17

11 I made this climb in March 2020 before Israel shut down given the pandemic.

12 described in the apocryphal book *Acts of John ,* see Ehrman *Lost Scriptures.* Michael Howard, Queen of Heaven Gnostic Church Portland, OR, describes the Round Dance ritual as "the ego discovers a realm beyond its own..."

13 Troyat, Henri *Tolstoy* Dell Publishing, New York 1967

14 Ganna, Andrea *etal* research article and article "The Genetics of Sexual Orientation" in *Science* August 30 2019 issue

15 Conroy, J. Oliver "The Life and Death of John Chau, the man who tried to convert his killers" *The Guardian* February 3 2019

16 Phillips, Dom "The Isolated Tribes at Risk of Illness from Amazon Missionaries" *The Guardian* March 23 2020

17 Spiritual elder of the Assonet band / Wampanoag Nation and Rainbow Gatherings participant, he died in 2018.

18 Professor of Philosophy at Union Theological Seminary Princeton University

19 Luscombe, Brenda "Conservative Christian Russell Moore has a message for believers who also worship Trump" *Time* magazine February 1 2021

20 Theodore Parker (1810-1860) first talked about the moral arc of the universe being long and bending toward justice. The Rev. Dr. Martin Luther King, Jr. later paraphrased his words and made them famous in the 1950s and 1960s.

21 stories about the prophet Mohammad and his sayings

22 Darlo Fernandez-Morera disputes her characterization in his 2016 book *The Myth of the Andalusian Paradise*, saying tolerance was not that prevalent.

23 Taqlid has one passively conforming to another's teaching; Ijtihad involves actively engaging in physical or mental effort in a legal sense.

24 a May 21 2015 post in the meditation category found on chopra.com

25 a Canadian anthropologist, filmmaker, author of *Everyday Holiness*, and leader in reviving a Jewish ethical Musar movement

26 Zukav, Gary *The Seat of the Soul*, Simon and Schuster New York 1990

27 Applying the rule of 72, 72 divided by 3.6 equals 20.

28 Hawken, Paul ed. *Drawdown: The Most Comprehensive Plan Ever Proposed to Reverse Global Warming*, Penguin Books, New York 2017

29 He said this before Mortenson's downfall and 2014 apology on *Today Show.*

30 see discussion of China's population control efforts at end of chapter 6.

Chapter 5: Science: Sky, Earth, Life
A. Science—What is it?

Consider three statements as to why science is relevant. 1) "Who are we? The answer to this question is not only one of the tasks of science but THE task of science." (Erwin Schrodinger); 2) "By emphasizing and explaining the dependency of living things on each other and on the physical environment, science fosters the kind of intelligent respect for nature that should inform decisions on the uses of technology." (*Science for All Americans*, by F. J. Rutherford & Andrew Ahlgren); 3) "Science alerts us to the perils introduced by our world-altering technologies, especially to the global environment on which our lives depend. Science provides an essential early warning system"[1] (Carl Sagan).

As the above quotes suggest, science is critically important to our understanding (as a species) who we are, where we're going, and the impact of the technology we're using to get there. Its power to shape that future inspires both hopes and fears. Human history is a story of people fearing what they don't understand. If promoting science literacy begins with a good definition, we're in trouble: science is difficult to define. Consider three definitions: 1) the study of matter, energy, nature, and natural phenomena focused on finding order and universal laws; 2) a body of knowledge ultimately based on observation obtained by application of the scientific method; 3) a methodical effort to provide a map or conceptual framework for understanding Reality.

The first definition is a narrow one, but it recalls the beginnings of science. In the 6th century BCE Thales, a Greek thinker living in Miletus on the Ionian peninsula in modern day Turkey, spurred belief that the world was (choice #7) "Orderly and Explicable." Its order, organization, and functioning are based on a small number of natural laws. These laws can conceivably be uncovered and understood by humans. The second definition might be shortened to *The Knowledge Machine,* which is also the title of a 2020 book by NYU Philosophy Professor Michael Strevens. In doing this, "machine" stands in for "the scientific method." But there's a problem—besides my not so high opinion of this book, which I'll share later. Unlike a machine which operates the same way each time you run it, there's no universally agreed on way that scientific investigation proceeds. I prefer the third definition. With respect to how the scientific conceptual framework it alludes to develops, I offer a description presented by Harvard physical chemist E. Bright Wilson in his 1952 classic, *An Introduction to Scientific Research.*[2]

"Science begins with observation of selected parts of nature. Although the scientist uses his mind to imagine ways in which the world might be constructed, he knows that only by looking at reality can he find out whether any of these ways correspond with reality. He rejects *authority* as an ultimate basis for truth. Though he is compelled by practical necessity to use facts and statements put forward by others, he reserves for himself the decision as to whether these other workers are reputable, whether their methods are good, and whether in any particular case the alleged facts are credible. He further considers it his privilege and sometimes his duty to repeat and test the work of others wherever he feels that this is desirable. The collective judgment of scientists, in so far as there is substantial agreement, constitutes the body of science. The fact that there are very large areas of agreement, in spite of the individualistic, antiauthoritarian nature of science, is partial evidence for the validity of scientific methods."

Science also begins with (choice #12) intellectual curiosity: someone is puzzled by something they observe. He or she decides to investigate. What characterizes an investigation as scientific is the method it employs. The (choice #10) scientific method has been characterized as humankind's greatest invention. It is systematic. It generally involves gathering data, evaluating it with respect to some hypothesis and to a conceptual framework in unbiased fashion, making refinements and drawing conclusions as appropriate.

While generally speaking the above sketch is accurate—with testing hypotheses / feedback playing a key role in its implementation—not all scientists do things the same way. The order in which steps are performed can vary with the application. Experimental scientists do things differently from theoretical scientists—or from those working in branches of science where experiments aren't possible (astronomy for example.) A representative version of the method is illustrated in Figure #12 for an experimental investigation.

An experiment is conducted—which means the scientist interferes with nature and creates conditions or events that favor making a particular observation or establishing a particular hypothesis. The results of this experiment are compared with the results expected (or predicted) based on the hypothesis—this is the "testing" part of the method. If the fit between the actual and predicted results is a good one—as judged by observational, statistical, or other tests—then the hypothesis is accepted. If the fit is not good, the hypothesis and/or experiment will be modified, and the testing will be repeated. The investigator(s) may spend months, even years, stuck in this feedback loop part of the scientific method— forming new hypotheses, gathering data, testing, etc. only to emerge from it with a hypothesis that demonstratively fits the data.

Figure #12: One Representation of the Scientific Method

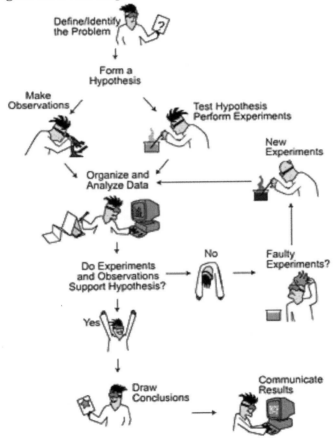

Eventually they will publish their findings for others to verify—and provide more feedback: "Yes, we can reproduce your results!" or "No, you guys failed to control X. If we control X, we find that your hypothesis is not established!" —or whatever. In short, the feedback built into the scientific method serves as a self-correcting mechanism that weeds out findings based on shoddy experimental design, questionable observations, someone's (choice #1) wishful thinking, bias, fraud or whatever. This prevents the faulty conclusions of such flawed work from becoming part of the body of scientific knowledge.

Theories help structure this knowledge. A theory is a general principle, or set of principles, based on well-tested hypotheses put forward to characterize and explain a collection of facts and observations associated with some area of investigation. A particularly good theory can spawn many predictions. If these are verified, investigators place greater confidence in the theory. Those not verified can help refine it, or replace it with something better. Science, its theories, and the framework they fit into, is tentative.

This last observation brings me to the first of four distinctions I want to make. Many years ago Judge William Overton, in an Arkansas case pitting teaching evolution vs. teaching creationism, did a nice job of distinguishing science and religion. He wrote, "A scientific theory must be tentative and always subject to revision or abandonment in light of facts that are inconsistent with, or falsify the theory. A theory that is, by its own terms, dogmatic, absolutist and never subject to revision is not a scientific theory." Religious structures are rigid, and typically built more on (choice #1 and choice #4) wishful thinking and faith, than evidence. Scientific frameworks are flexible, dynamic, ideally evolving so that the fit between their description of Reality and Reality itself, as gauged by predictions they make, steadily improves.

Second, as a way of thinking, a problem solving or making future predictions tool, science is to be distinguished from other procedures that don't work. To paraphrase Carl Sagan, "Science is what works. If there was something that worked better, I'd be for it." Third, science and technology, while related, are different things. Whereas science involves understanding nature, (choice #49) technology involves controlling it. Whereas technology initially developed in trial and error fashion, by the 20th century, technological advances were increasingly based on scientific understanding (applied science.)

And fourth, while science and (choice #29) democracy have things in common they have a key difference. The origins of both can be traced to ancient Greece. Both are human endeavors. Both require social environments valuing (choice #43) honesty, reason, debate, and (choice #12) free inquiry. One science writer (Watson Davis) went so far as proclaiming "the scientific way is the democratic way!" Yet while science and democracy have feedback loops as key parts—one involving hypothesis testing, the other people voting—there is a big difference. In evaluating the testing of a scientific hypothesis or interpreting the evidence for or against some proposed theoretical framework, decisions are not democracy-based. They are not based on polls where all votes count equally. They are based on the best available evidence and most careful methods of interpretation—with the verdict determined by those best qualified to judge.

Who are these judges? Initially, they are the investigators themselves, and people they consult if they get help interpreting their own data. Later they are other scientists working in the same field. Some serve on peer review boards that screen papers submitted to specialized journals for publication. Some do their work after publication in attempting to verify what is reported—that is, to get reproducible results. While they are human, they are highly trained in rigorous, objective methods. What if they fail? What if subjective biases creep in, or someone doesn't apply the right statistical test, or simply makes a mistake? Failures will eventually be fixed. Science has a built-in, self-correcting mechanism that depends on (choice #4) healthy skepticism to weed out what is not true. When properly functioning, erroneous judgments will be rare, and when they are made they will soon be fixed.

I've been describing what science is—let me pause and describe what science is not with two main points. First, science—especially to the extent that it involves quantitative data gathered by instruments that extend the human senses—should not involve subjective judgments. Second, in searching for fundamental laws behind Reality, what science concludes should be based on reason and relevant data—not outcomes of battles involving cultural issues, personalities, emotions, etc. So I take issue with CUNY sociologist Stanley Aronowitz, who has written[3], "Science legitimates itself by linking its discoveries with power, a connection which determines what counts as reliable knowledge...The strongest team decrees what counts as truth." Perhaps this is true to some extent in the social sciences, or when politicians are lobbying for funding some science-based technology and anticipating related building in their districts. But let me repeat, ideally verdicts establishing science-based truth are based on relevant data and rendered by those best qualified to judge in an arena in which emotions stay on the sidelines. Relative power enters in only to the extent that truth has power behind it and lies do not.

I suspect Aronowitz' and similar opinions have been influenced by philosopher Thomas Kuhn's 1962 book *The Structure of Scientific Revolutions*. Rather than focusing on science developing in a gradual, cumulative process, Kuhn emphasized the importance of revolutionary periods of paradigm shifts. He argued that those on opposite sides of one of these shifts couldn't communicate because of fundamental differences in worldviews—which could reflect cultural differences. And that with those differences come different ways of doing science—with the implication that different truths could result.

"Not so!" say many critics. Thomas Kuhn's book—in the words of his graduate student Errol Morris—has contributed to "the debasement of science and the debasement of truth." Kuhn's thesis benefited from soon being embraced by those seeing the development of civilization through a cultural relativism filter. Anthropologists—especially Franz Boas—helped popularize use of that filter. In 1887, Boas wrote, "civilization is not something absolute, but...is relative, and ...our ideas and conceptions are true only so far as our civilization goes." While the term cultural relativism wasn't used until thirty years later, it became popular after Boas' death in 1942.

Kuhn promoted the idea that scientific theories are incommensurable if they are embedded in very different conceptual frameworks. German physicist turned philosopher Paul Hoyningen-Huene has been a leading interpreter of his work. British philosopher Alexander Bird summarized Hoyningen-Huene's interpretation of Kuhn as follows. "We cannot possibly find out whether a theory is true for that requires that we are able to compare the theory and reality, which in turn requires having an independent grasp on what reality is like. And that is precisely what we do not have—and if we did have it, we would not need the theory..."

This view—suggesting that testing of scientific theories is impossible—hits at the heart of what science is all about: the testing of hypotheses. For a hypothesis to be considered scientific, it must be written so that it can tested and shown to be wrong. For example, the speculation "The universe is pervaded by an immaterial, undetectable quintessence" does not represent a testable hypothesis. Since the imagined quintessence is undetectable there is no point in looking for it and no way to test whether it exists. Critics say Kuhn introduced subjectivity, cultural relativism, and irrationality into science that typically isn't there. Yes scientists use ordinary language in their descriptions[4], and different languages can introduce a cultural differences dimension into science. Thus they prefer using numbers /mathematical equations to remove cultural ambiguities. This universal language also facilitates statistical testing of hypotheses.

With this in mind, let's examine a statement in Michael Strevens' book: "...in their thinking about the connection between theory and data, scientists seem scarcely to follow any rules at all." Were the author of this ridiculous statement here, I would patiently pull several books out of my library to convince him of his folly. I'd begin with Bright's book. I'd show him the mathematical details of the 150 pages spanning four chapters with titles, "Classification, Sampling, and Measurement," "The Analysis of Experimental Data," "Errors of Measurement," and "Probability, Randomness, and Logic." I'd point out that scientists were trained with books like this seventy years ago. And that today—with improved techniques for statistical analysis of data—they're undoubtedly getting even better equipped to <u>not</u> do what Strevens implies some are doing: getting away with cheating. Strevens' 350 page book has exactly three paragraphs related to statistical analysis. Such techniques, he says "can be gamed to illuminate the data from the most favorable (or publishable) angle." I say he's unfairly and (choice #32) cynically connecting scientists with a professional (choice #33) ethics failing.

I will renew my criticism of Strevens' comments linking science with irrational subjectivity with specific examples of where he gets it wrong, but first let's describe the biggest of all the scientific revolutions—the one that ushered in modern science. It began with Copernicus (1473-1543) and culminated with Issac Newton (1642-1727.) In section E I'll describe Johann Kepler's (1571-1630) contribution to this effort—as he struggled to turn his back on (choice #1) wishful thinking, (choice #6) mysticism, (choice #7) pseudoscientific magic, (choice #10) Non-Rational knowing, etc, and embrace the scientific method. Newton is generally thought of as the father of modern physical science. He was undoubtedly thinking of Kepler— and others such Copernicus, Tycho Brahe, and Galileo—when he said, "If I have seen farther than others, it was by standing on the shoulders of giants."

The so-called classical physics Newton laid down—including his theory of gravity in his 1687 book *Mathematical Principles of Physics* — survived unchallenged for two centuries. Only in the first two decades of the twentieth century was its absolute picture of space and time, and deterministic treatment of physical events replaced by theories of relativity and quantum mechanics, respectively. Relativity, worked out by Einstein (1879-1955) in 1905-1915, is needed to understand the motion of objects moving at speeds comparable to that of light or in strong gravitational fields. Experimental tests have confirmed it to a high degree of precision. Quantum mechanics has been similarly validated, despite Einstein's dislike of its probabilistic nature and belief it would eventually be replaced by (choice #11) a deterministic theory.

Einstein became famous after a team led by Sir Arthur Eddington seemingly confirmed his prediction that starlight passing near the Sun would be bent a slightly greater amount than Newton's theory predicted. Michael Strevens' book blasts Eddington for subjectivity in analyzing the data gathered during a total solar eclipse in 1919. He even reproduces a table from the expedition's scientific report showing deflection amounts for eighteen stars, and accuses Eddington of unethically throwing data out when it didn't give the result he supposedly wanted.

Non-scientists often don't understand that all measurements have some associated error or uncertainty. I took one look at the data for those eighteen stars, put it in a spreadsheet, and calculated a standard deviation measure of that uncertainty. And I saw why Eddington justifiably threw it out: that associated error or uncertainty was very large. The average deflection was 0.86 arcseconds— but the uncertainty was plus or minus 0.47. Strevens says nothing about uncertainties associated with the measurements. Eddington decided the poor data was a result of the telescope mirror getting too hot and expanding— blurring the star images on the plates, making them difficult to measure. As someone who has spent hours measuring star positions on such plates, I can appreciate Eddington's decision to throw out the data.

In contrast, physicist Clifford Will—in his 1986 book *Was Einstein Right? —Putting General Relativity to the Test*, presents measurement uncertainties. He reports the two independently obtained data sets Eddington used as follows: one based on eight photographic plates gave average deflection value of 1.98 arcseconds with plus or minus 0.12 uncertainty; the other based on just two plates gave 1.61 arcseconds with plus or minus 0.31. These uncertainties are much smaller—especially for the first data set—indicative of much better data. Averaging the two values gives a result rather close to Einstein's prediction of 1.75 arcseconds deflection. Does it conclusively prove the theory behind Einstein's prediction was right? No. But it did not prove it is wrong.

Elsewhere, Strevens, goes after 1923 Physics Nobel Prize winner Robert Millikan for omitting "many measurements that did not 'look right'" He questions Millikan's handling of data in his famous oil drop experiment, from which he derived the charge on the electron. I've spent hours with students in physics labs doing a version of Millikan's experiment—and watching a Caltech produced video[5] account of Millikan's data handling. And decades dealing with problematic data gathered by instrumental setups, either compromised in some way, or operating with low signal to noise ratios. Again, I have no problem with what Millikan did.

When a theory or model makes predictions that repeatedly and verifiably come true, people take it seriously. But scientific understanding sufficient to make good predictions is lacking in many areas. The future may bring significant changes to the (choice #7) scientific conceptual framework as it evolves to incorporate phenomena that currently don't fit—like UFOs, and other poorly observed, even paranormal phenomena. It may bring good predictions of earthquakes, better climate models, etc. All this depends on testable hypotheses being formulated and verified.

Big changes in the framework will require new theories. Creating them will depend on people having (choice #12) Imagination, Curiosity, Intellectual Freedom. And, based on a few history of scientific discovery episodes, conceivably insight gleaned from "Non-Rational Knowing" might help. For example, the 1865 discovery of the chemical structure of the benzene ring was inspired by a lucid dream.[6] Recall this choice #10 counterpart of the "Scientific Method" — which, besides valuing imagination, appreciates "what can't be measured." Speaking of measurements, advances in data-gathering (choice #49) technology / techniques and instrumentation have historically led to scientific advance. As this happens, uncertainties in measured quantities become smaller, and a finer probing of Reality becomes possible.

B. Thinking like a Scientist—my Personal Connection

An interest in baseball played a key role in my cognitive development. Not content just playing ball with bat and glove, by age eight I was playing it in an abstract world. In a burst of creative thinking, I invented what today would be called "fantasy baseball" games—played by throwing dice. I kept records, computed batting averages, pitchers' earned run averages, team's winning percentages, etc. Thousands of hours doing this helped wire my brain for manipulating numbers.

By age thirteen I'd lost interest in fantasy baseball, but my need to play with numbers and keep records persisted. About that time I acquired a telescope and got involved in making observations of variable stars—a "citizen science" activity I still pursue. Before returning to a story I began in chapter 2—in particular how my Christmas 2020 celebration gave way to nighttime observation of an eclipsing variable star—I note my early mastery of a particular skill. Sometime in early teenage years I began doing what physicists call "back of the envelope calculations." They typically involve plugging numbers into a formula. I made many such calculations to predict future eclipses of variable stars.

But I didn't appreciate the full power of back of the envelope calculations until a few years later. Besides simple precise answers, for more complicated problems they can provide quick estimates. Working closely with common sense, they can involve putting numbers into formulas in rounded off form, so as to avoid getting bogged down carrying too many digits. They often call on skill in doing unit conversions, and use of scientific notation—although this may not be necessary if you're dealing with problems daily lives present. They can also involve the ability to use proportional reasoning. For example knowing that something varies directly with something else, tells you that if one of the quantities doubles in size, the other one does also, etc. Beyond providing a (choice #45) recycling / reusing of junk mail envelopes, such quantitative activity is a key part of (choice #10) one's training as a scientist. Simple examples appear in chapter 7 in "What If...?" energy use contexts. Spoiler alert: I end this section by sketching a bit more complicated one (separated from rest of text for non-science types to skip if they find it too tedious!)

Back to my Christmas night 2020 activity. Unlike many stars whose light output changes due to some instability in their makeup, eclipsing variables' brightness changes are due to chance alignment. Consider, for example, what happens when light from a hot, bright smaller star is completely or partially blocked by bigger, fainter star orbiting it. Monitoring of the combined light from this binary pair records dimming, as the bigger, fainter star covers the hotter, brighter one, and subsequent brightening back up again as the orbital motion continues.

Orbital periods of binary stars—how long it takes one of them to completely revolve around the other—are needed to figure out how massive the individual stars are. Knowing a star's mass is the single most important thing to know about it, since a star's life history depends on its mass. For example, stars more massive than our Sun can die in catastrophic explosions. If this happened to a relatively nearby star, a worst case scenario could result in mass extinction of life, as Earth is bathed in dangerous radiation. Changes in the periods of these binary stars also provide information about how the two stars interact.

Before that 2020 Christmas night, I'd last documented an eclipse of the variable star AP Andromeda in 1997. Prior to that, the orbital period of this system was listed in catalogs as 1.587292 days. My 1997 observations, and those of other astronomers—both amateur and professional—helped refine its period to 1.587291156 days. On Christmas night 2020, using my small telescope, CCD imaging camera, and computer processing three hours of images, I confirmed that this new orbital period—a mere 0.073 seconds shorter than the older value—was a good one. The eclipse's mid-point—consistent with AP Andromeda's mid eclipse faintest moment—came essentially on schedule as expected to the nearest minute.

Why I am sharing this in some detail? We'll use this story to help contrast the worldviews of two different people. Recalling Figure #3 in chapter 2, call them person A and person B. We previously linked them (respectively) with (choice #2) Mind Narrowly Focused and Mind Open, Vision Global perspectives. Here we saddle them with choice #7, choice #10, and choice #13 beliefs. In particular, Person A prefers Magic, Non-Rational Knowing, and Simply in God's Hands: Apocalypticism themes. Person B likes their Orderly and Explicable, Scientific Method, and Complexity—In Our Hands: Dancing With Systems counterparts.

My observation of eclipsing binary star story is set in the highly predictable physical world of inanimate matter—that of the Orderly and Explicable theme Person B is comfortable with. In many respects, this is a simple world. Predicting future events in it, using physical laws / scientific methods, can be relatively easy. And typically can be done much more accurately than predictions in the world of living things—

especially human society. That's the complicated world of social systems, computer models and even—something science-based assessment tries to avoid—value judgments. Person B can deal with such complexity, Person A can not.

Person A types live in a world of accepting that inexplicable things occur. In his 1962 book, *Profiles of the Future*, Arthur C. Clarke said, "Any sufficiently advanced technology is indistinguishable from magic." If a Person A from 1962 could somehow wake up in today's world, he or she would simply accept the capabilities of smart phones without wondering how they work. But that also describes Person A types living in 2021. Many such people depend on this and other magical black boxes they use with no appreciation of how they work, or their science and technology heritage.

Person A types don't worry about such things. They insist on seeing the world in black and white terms, whereas Person B uses many shades of gray. In that way Person A's world is much simpler than Person B's. Person A types shun analysis. They often trust (choice #10) gut feelings and intuitive insights—without regard to the wisdom or origin of such things. They readily believe in things they don't understand. They like simple explanations—including those offered by pseudoscientific quacks. They may accept statements like "Disinfectants kill germs and viruses—so injecting disinfectant into our bodies can stop the Covid-19 pandemic, right?" or "Plants need carbon dioxide to grow. Burning more coal puts more of this in the air, encouraging plant growth. This is good. Those trying to shut down coal mines, and scare us with this global warming silliness, don't want you to know this."[7]

Person B types can appreciate that, compared to predicting the next eclipse of well-studied binary star system far out in space, predicting human behavior is laughably imprecise. And appreciate predictions suggesting certain nearby massive stars conceivably pose threats to life on Earth. Person A types can not. If my observational astronomy efforts were aimed at detecting unknown large rocks out in space that might some day catastrophically hit Earth, I'd have an easier time explaining the value of this work to Person A types. But many simple minds would connect (choice #13 and choice #11) this potential apocalypse with God's will, or His displeasure. While accepting the reality of magic that person B types would dispute, Person A types are nonetheless disturbed by thinking things happen by random chance.

My conception of probability began with those childhood rolling the dice baseball games. Given stories I've shared, you know me well enough to firmly place me with Person B types, right? Alas, characterizing worldviews based on black and white distinctions is often too simple. As is stereotypically putting people in boxes. Reality is more complicated. Thus, with respect to choice #7 and choice #10, while my worldview greatly values the two science-based themes, I nonetheless see some value in the themes they're paired with.

I'll illustrate that with stories in the next section. And in chapter 8 I'll more fully address how paranormal and other mysterious happenings may someday fit into the scientific conceptual framework. But first, consider the following example of thinking like a scientist or engineer.

For several days in the middle of February 2021, several people suffered due to unexpected bone-chilling cold weather. In the past such weather might have inspired jokes from climate change deniers such as "Where's Al Gore when we need him?" Increasingly people appreciate that the climate crisis should more properly be thought of as one of "global climate change" not just "global warming." And as *Time* magazine put it in a recent issue[8], "a growing body of research links climate change with the occurrence of the so-called polar vortex…[where] warming in the Arctic…weakening the jet stream…[which] allows freezing air to drift down to lower latitudes." Given lots of climate change deniers' (choice #1) positive expectations / wishful thinking—and (choice #40) freedom-loving hostility to regulations that would have required appropriate energy-grid protecting winterization—Texans paid the price for their failure to be firmly grounded in changing climate reality.

During this time I wondered, "What if such cold crippled utility service in my Arizona mountain town—could I stay warm without power company electricity and natural gas for heat?" In chapter 7, I'll fully describe my solar-assisted zone heating approach to staying warm in winter. While it includes a small solar-charged battery bank that can power supplemental heaters, most notably it features a massively insulated loft to which I sometimes retreat. I call this my "Boutique Capsule" (BC.) Thinking of it, I added a second question: "Under the most extreme imaginable conditions, could I stay warm in my BC?" I did a (choice #10 and choice #49 relevant) back of the envelope engineering heat loss calculation to find out.

Before presenting this, I offer comments in the form of definitions. First it—and much of chapter 7—involves energy. Energy can be defined as the ability to do work—meaning a force acts to move matter through some distance. The energy I use in lifting my 154 pound body up five feet to get into my BC loft is 154 pounds x 5 feet = 770 foot pounds—which is roughly 1 BTU. The latter is a heat energy unit—defined as the heat needed to increase the temperature of one pound of water 1°F. Climbing into my BC provides an example of energy being transformed: the chemical energy stored in food I've eaten is transformed into mechanical energy my muscles use in providing a lifting force. One important thing about energy: you don't create it or destroy it—but you often change its form. The watts alluded to in the following calculation are units of power. This refers to the rate at which energy is used, where one watt = 3.41 BTU per hour. ***********************************

I did the calculation in two parts. A typical winter night provided design parameters for the first part: 23 °F outside, 48 °F inside the rest of my house, and 73 °F inside my BC. My calculation is based on heat transfer equations, and—among other things—surface areas of the sides of the BC and corresponding R-values measuring resistance to heat loss. It says the BC will lose 78 watts of heat by conduction, and 6 watts by convection = 84 watts total. (I assumed heat loss from radiation would be small enough to neglect.) Given that heat loss from adult male resting bodies has been estimated to be in the 100 to 120 watts range, the calculation suggests that my body heat alone should be able to keep it warm. Actual experience supports this conclusion.

But what heat would be needed during a night that's as cold as I can conceive of during most extreme polar vortex chill? Second part design parameters: -27 °F outside[9], 48 °F inside the rest of my house, and 73 °F inside my BC. Since heat loss is directly proportional to temperature difference, on the 23 °F outside night, the inside minus outside difference is 50 °F, whereas it has doubled to 100 °F in this extreme cold scenario. So heat loss might be expected to double, from 84 watts to 168 watts. But, not so fast…there's a complication. The temperature difference I mentioned above doesn't double for all six surfaces of my BC. It does so only for the two of them exposed to the outside ambient temperature. So I can't take this proportional reasoning shortcut.

And to make a truly worst case, let's assume there's no natural gas heat to maintain my inside the house temperature at its thermostat setting of 48 °F. Revised second part design parameters: -27 °F outside, 30 °F inside the rest of my house, and 73 °F inside my BC. New calculation gives 140 watts of heat loss from conduction and 11 watts from convection, or 151 watts total. To make up the roughly 50 watts of heat needed beyond my body's waste heat, in a worst sunless scenario, my battery bank would need to provide 400 watts 1/8 of the time (50 / 400) or 7.5 minutes every hour. Assuming it was fully-charged when it was called on to do this, more than 16 hours such demand would deep cycle the battery bank below an 80% discharge emergency level and compromise its life expectancy. In practice long before that could happen, I'd allow the temperature inside the BC to begin falling below the nice toasty 73 °F design parameter. Hopefully the validity of this calculation is never put to the test.

C. Non-Rational Knowing—My Personal Connection

Just as I operate more in the (choice #14) Cautious Processing mode than in a relaxed, nonjudgmental, loving kindness one, I'm much more comfortable functioning on (choice #1) safer, evidence-based ground, than in faith-based terrain. While I won't entirely write off (choice #10) non-rational knowledge obtained through intuition, gut feeling, instinct —nor totally dismiss what dreams and synchronicity type experiences seem to be communicating—I'm generally (choice #4) something of a skeptic. As for problem solving, I trust (choice #10) the scientific method far more than non-rational approaches like consulting a psychic or an oracle. Yet I admit finding psychics entertaining, and to having designed an oracle where random worldview themes provide "guidance."[10]

Certainly imagination and creativity can be inspired by Non-Rational knowing experiences—but there are dangers associated with making intuitive leaps. One danger involves (choice #1): making choices based on wishful thinking, not evidence. Rather than acting on gut feeling with a snap judgment, a safer, (choice #20) rational / dispassionate approach, is to step back and ask a "What if?" question. This treats the Non-Rationally acquired contemplated action as a hypothesis in need of testing. The testing will first be done mentally.

For example, imagine, after a lucid dream adventure with a charismatic person you've never seen before, you seemingly actually encounter this person. Feeling "This is Mr. Right" or "This is Ms. Right," you could throw caution to the wind, trust your dream, and be instantly receptive to this person's romantic advances. But slowly getting to know the person would be a safer approach. This can be done in the virtual world looking for this person's "digital footprints." And in real world interaction, looking for red flag behavior or with character tests you devise.

I have stories to share involving my own (choice #10) Non-Rational knowing experiences. The first involves something that psychologist Karl Jung helped popularize: synchronicity. Synchronicity refers to events that occur either simultaneously or nearly so, but yet have no evident cause and effect connection. Often the person experiencing the synchronicity attaches special meaning to it. For example, as a twenty-nine year old back in 1980 I'd been dreaming about watching the USA vs. Soviet Union hockey game on television. As the game wound down and tension built up, the scoreboard clock assumed an increasingly prominent place in my dream. Just as the winning goal in my dream was scored and the clock read 00:00, something else happened: my alarm clock went off! I awoke convinced I'd predicted when the alarm would ring long before it happened.

About five years ago I had another demonstration of what might be called pre-cognitive ability. One Sunday morning I was sitting near the back of a UU Church next to Rev. Sue, an elderly former Presbyterian minister I'd just met. She turned to me, asked, "Did you say your name is Gary?" I didn't answer since I saw Sue discover my name tag, and noted the worship assistant was asking for introductions of visitors. Then, within ten seconds of Sue calling me "Gary," someone introduced himself—you guessed it—as Gary! Coincidence? As you might expect, I couldn't help feeling I'd been involved in predicting a future event.

Still, the skeptic in me demanded assessing the probability that the next male name we'd hear would be Gary. With roughly 20,000 such names, one might say the odds were 1 in 20,000—but some names are more popular than others. Going online, I found Gary was the 560th most popular name for baby boys in 2014, which suggests this probability is roughly 1 in 560. But, the average age of folks inside the church that morning was rather high, and perhaps Gary was once a more popular name? Aha, in 1954, around the time our typical member was born, Gary was the ninth most popular name. So perhaps the seemingly wildly improbable name match was not really so improbable?

Something more bizarre happened to me in June, 2014. Ending months of house hunting, I moved to an Arizona mountain town where I knew no one. While cleaning the kitchen of the house I'd just bought, I discovered something on top of a cabinet. Using a chair to stand on, I pulled the object down, wiped dust off, and looked at it. What I saw was a shock: a plastic-wrapped, unopened three DVD music/video set, copyright 2003, titled "The Rolling Stones, 1962—present." Shocking because I think of myself as one of the world's biggest Stones' fans. I'll spare you evidence that bolsters this claim except one item: on July 16, 2012, in honoring the band's 50th anniversary, I posted on my *Worldview Watch* blog, "The Worldview Behind the Rolling Stones' Music." Like the hockey game dream of 1980, this discovery shook my worldview.

If nothing else, it renewed my interest in exploring what Arthur Koestler[11] called (in the title of a 1967 book) *The Roots of Coincidence*. While I'm pretty much of (choice #1) an evidence-based skeptic, I am not immune to positive expectations. As previously described, I'll believe in something—"useful fiction" I call it—if the associated belief hypothesis can not be demonstrated to be false, and if that something is psychologically healthy. Example: In my late twenties I had a transcending peak experience spurred by the rock music infused climax on a big screen movie. (More on that in chapter 8.) I came away from this mystical encounter thinking that I'd seen behind the illusion of separateness. I'd seemingly experienced a (choice #6) transcendent unity / mystical fundamental oneness. The experience raised questions.

Should I revise my worldview to accommodate this supposed insight? Should I begin believing, for example, that human beings are all connected to each other in an unseen way? Clearly in the three dimensional world perceived by our ordinary senses human beings are separate, unconnected entities. But the possibility exists that humans are linked in other ways: in higher spatial dimensions, in a spiritual realm, by each being connected to God, etc—right? If, after investigating pro and con evidence related to this belief, I was still undecided as to its ultimate truth, I might adopt it and offer two reasons. First, if "I'm convinced that if everyone believed this, the world would be a better place." And second, if "I'm convinced this belief will enhance my psychological health." (I wouldn't feel so alone, so alienated, etc)

I might weave this belief and others into my worldview because they offer psychological advantages and are worthy of belief—not because

I'm unequivocally convinced they're part of the ultimate, true description of Reality. Similarly I don't adopt beliefs, where evidence pro or con is lacking, if I think they're potentially unhealthy. Thus a friend, with impressive academic credentials in religious studies, has not succeeded in getting me to invest in believing as she does.

For all I know, this woman may be one of the world's experts on the West African religion known as Santeria. This (choice #6) polytheistic religion involves worship of deities known as oricha. Offerings to both oricha and spirits of the dead /ancestors are supposedly facilitated by spirit mediums. Thus every year on her "religious birthday," she celebrates by putting offerings on an elaborate altar she's constructed in her living room. What happens to the offerings—fruit being a common one? She gives them away to friends at those birthday celebrations.

Just as I feel a bit drawn to a connectedness / feeling of oneness based on my handful of (choice #6) mystical moment experiences, my friend's experience has led her to a different belief. Not sensing distinct gods or deities, in rare perfect moments I feel union with an undifferentiated whole. In contrast, she senses distinct deities having their own personality traits, needs, desires, etc. I'm not clear as to the extent to which she gives these gods additional powers / supernatural attributes—if any at all?

I am clear in feeling that, in one key respect, (choice #5) monotheism represented an important advance for humanity over the pagan, polytheistic, animistic beliefs it largely replaced. I say that—not out of firm belief in "God is love," "we're all connected through God," or in an impersonal monotheistic deism in which God leaves us alone after creating natural laws—but rather for psychological health reasons. I'm convinced that people feeling connected through some unified whole—and believing that the universe is (choice #7) largely orderly and explicable—is something healthy to believe in.

It's healthy for individuals and for society, and it fits right in with what I'd like to see become a mantra for global citizens: "We're all in this together!" Having connected global education, religion and science with the above stories, we move on to more formally consider science. This will (hopefully) first, reintroduce it in a non-threatening manner, and second, bring certain aspects of it down to earth in more ways than one.

D. Science and Religion in Conflict; What is Life?

If you think science's search for an ultimate description of Reality moves it into religious territory, and potential conflict, you're right. Perhaps history's most famous clash between science-based and religious-based worldviews involved Galileo and the powerful Catholic Church. In choice #1 and choice #2 terms, like modern scientists Galileo preferred Evidence-Based and Mind Open, Global Vision themes. This got him in trouble with Church authorities—they clung to dogma, Positive Expectations and Mind Narrowly Focused themes. We can imagine a modern enthusiast for their viewpoint saying, "I find comfort in <u>not</u> seeking out facts—or exposing myself to beliefs, and values—that would necessitate some revising of my associated worldview framework …" And that's exactly what happened in 1610 in Venice in Italy, during Galileo's demonstration of celestial sights visible with his newly created telescope. Some Catholic priests simply refused to look.

Today, what students learn in churches or from religiously dogmatic parents can destroy their motivation to fully explore aspects of biology, geology, and astronomy that involve evolution. In some schools, evolution is simply not taught in high school biology classes given administrators' desires to avoid controversy and placate religious fundamentalist (choice #8) parents. Sadly, nearly 400 years after Galileo got into trouble with Church authorities for teaching the Earth orbits the Sun, in some places religious orthodoxy is still an obstacle to (choice #12) free inquiry. While not as well publicized, scientific materialist atheistic parents can likewise stifle young people's spiritual exploration. Consider how well known skeptic Paul Kurtz addresses the possibility of science and religion finding common ground. "Science and religion are compatible, but only if religion is reinterpreted primarily as a form of existential poetry, dramatizing the fragility and contingency of the human condition in an impersonal universe and recognizing with awe and wonder the vastness and mystery of the cosmic scene."[12]

Rather than being obstacles, parents can aid their children's full pursuit of intellectual freedom. As James D. Moran describes it[13], "Adults can encourage creativity by emphasizing the generation and expression of ideas in a non-evaluative framework and by concentrating on both divergent and convergent thinking." He adds, "[they] can also try to ensure that children have the opportunity and confidence to take risks, challenge assumptions, and see things in a new way." If those adults embrace the broader definition of spirituality presented in the last chapter, building a bridge between science and religion will be easier. We'll return to this effort in chapter 8.

Finding common ground in answering certain (choice #9) questions— like "Do souls / vital spirits leave the body upon death? — may be impossible. Scientific materialist skeptics say that many assumptions (choice #4) true believers make are not necessary. These include postulating 1) the existence of God, 2) the universe had a Creator, 3) an intelligent design or meaning behind creation, 4) that (choice #5) a Personal God and His agents can work miracles, and 5) vital spirits and souls are associated with living things. Thus they make no use of these assumptions in formulating the Big Bang Theory—nor in their accounts of over nine billion years of physical evolution that preceded formation of the Earth 4.5 billion years ago, nor in theories of the origin of terrestrial life nearly four billion years ago and its subsequent evolution producing such diversity of living things.

Biological evolution is the process by which the individual members of a species, and species themselves, slowly change due to changes in genetic makeup, environmental circumstances, etc. We understand the process, first detailed by Charles Darwin (1809-1882), as having three basic components: 1) there are many variations of a basic form (often produced by mutations which can be random); 2) the variant of the form best adapted to the environment ("the fittest") is selected by that environment in a process called natural selection; 3) the most fit form lives on as it is promoted by a hereditary mechanism. Thus it survives and reproduces, whereas the less fit forms die out.

In collecting data from which his theory of evolution emerged, Darwin was especially interested in beetles. Entomologists have now described over 350,000 different beetle species, and many more are believed to exist. Why so many? Those who understand key concepts behind evolution, notably random mutations, natural selection, and geological time, have little difficulty providing an explanation. But why would God make so many of them? For centuries, scientists have looked for signs of intelligent design / proof of God's hands at work. While they recognize their framework is still evolving, as Nobel Prize winning physicist Leon Lederman put it, "The space available for God seems to be shrinking."

Biological scientists face challenges answering critics of evolution. They're asked, "How can natural selection and random variation produce a complex structure like an eye?" Physicist and Anglican priest John Polkinghorne asks, "How many steps would take us from a slightly light sensitive cell to a fully formed insect eye...and ...[what] number of generations [would be] required for the necessary mutations to occur?"

Biologist Richard Dawkins answers in his 1996 book *Climbing Mount Improbable* using a "climbing a tall mountain" example. He likens those who find it inconceivable that mindless processes could produce a structure like the eye, to those who think the mountain must be climbed all at once— by directly scaling the imposing cliff. He contrasts this to taking the other route: going around to the back where a path gently, but steadily, winds its way to the top. Dawkins feels ordinary peoples' inability to grasp the long (millions of years) time spans involved—and the very slow pace at which very slight change occurs—is a big part of the problem. Their deficiency can be discussed in (choice #2) lack of global vision terms.

Biologists also struggle to provide a detailed, complete account of the origin of life. Lacking that, how can they, (choice #9) vitalists ask, be sure that production of complex living structures doesn't require a Creator's purpose-driven vital impulse? They subscribe to teleology— the idea that there is a design or purpose inherent in everything. And that events unfold toward some divinely specified ultimate end, or that everything strives to fulfill some purpose. Richard Dawkins, in his 1986 book *The Blind Watchmaker*, answers that the evidence behind evolutionary theory supports "a universe without design."

Other choices are often behind acceptance or rejection of biological evolution. (Choice #8) religious fundamentalists typically reject it, and embrace a belief shaped by religious sacred texts: creationism. This typically claims that all life, and most notably the human species, resulted from a specific act of creation performed by a Personal God (choice #5.) This Creator, they say, acted with a definite purpose— something that those who prefer the Monotheistic Deism theme alternative dispute.

(Choice #9) scientific materialists and vitalists fundamentally differ over what life is. Even among scientists, given its diversity, defining life is challenging. Most such definitions agree that living things need to 1) be able to make copies of themselves (replication), 2) use matter and energy to regulate and sustain themselves (homeostasis and metabolism), and

3) repair errors that may arise in their genetic or metabolic related structures. But, to illustrate what else is involved, consider viruses—like the SARS-COV-2 virus behind the Covid-19 pandemic.

Old school biologists feel that viruses are not truly living organisms. Their definitions require living things be made of cells, and be able to reproduce and metabolize on their own—not through the hijacking of some other organism's cellular machinery as viruses do. In contrast, those with a less restrictive definition may believe viruses are alive. To the horror of vitalists, some molecular biologists downplay the issue of what is alive, and what isn't. They're increasingly thinking there's no fixed dividing line between what's alive, and what isn't. They're focusing on double helix shaped DNA molecules—typically chains of one nanometer (=one-billionth of a meter) radius—recognizing them as repositories of critical information. Some are working on creating life.

The ingredients they use are specified by a language that employs letters A, C, G, T— referring to nucleobase compounds adenine, cytosine, guanine, thymine. These come from the fundamental DNA constituents of the genetic code. They often work with these building blocks of DNA in powder form, an instruction set they design (specifying complicated sequence based on A, C, G, T,) and a DNA sequencer machine, to make genes. Genes can be thought of as the basic physical and functional units of heredity that are transmitted from one generation of living things to the next. More than any other factor, our genes determine what we become—shaping everything from what we look like to how we behave. Located on chromosomes residing in the nuclei of cells, genes are segments of DNA coded to provide instructions for making those 3D molecular structures known as proteins. Besides giving structure to cells, proteins provide vital functions like catalyzing reactions. Functioning like keys, their unique shapes determine their properties and activity.

Some biologists are working on synthesizing a gel-like container (an enclosed volume with a manmade cell membrane) from non-living organic molecules to hold the genes they make. At Harvard, they've built a model of what they think the first cell was like. Many feel that creating life in the lab from non-living components is doable. Others point out that life is more than just parts—it's a set of processes. And that getting these going from scratch is the challenge. (Choice #9) vitalists express (choice #4) skepticism saying that without the life force, injection of vital spirit, divine spark, or God blowing "breath of life," they can't succeed.

Scientists have looked for a spiritual component to life: comparing the weight of living things and dead corpses, investigating such things as out of body experiences, near death experiences, reports of auras around faith healers, séances in which mediums make contact with the dead, and a wide range of paranormal experiences. The consensus is no convincing evidence for it exists. Most feel human spirituality exists only in the mind. They say near death experiences are just electrical surges in dying brains,[14] and note researchers have triggered intense feelings of spiritual transcendence using electrodes to stimulate certain regions in the brain.

Figure #13: Is This Really What Life is All About?

Table of Standard Genetic Code

	T	C	A	G
T	TTT Phe (F) TTC * TTA Leu (L) TTG *	TCT Ser (S) TCC * TCA * TCG *	TAT Tyr (Y) TAC TAA Ter TAG Ter	TGT Cys (C) TGC TGA Ter TGG Trp (W)
C	CTT Leu (L) CTC * CTA * CTG *	CCT Pro (P) CCC * CCA * CCG *	CAT His (H) CAC * CAA Gln (Q) CAG *	CGT Arg (R) CGC * CGA * CGG *
A	ATT Ile (I) ATC * ATA * ATG Met (M)	ACT Thr (T) ACC * ACA * ACG *	AAT Asn (N) AAC * AAA Lys (K) AAG *	AGT Ser (S) AGC * AGA Arg (R) AGG *
G	GTT Val (V) GTC * GTA * GTG *	GCT Ala (A) GCC * GCA * GCG *	GAT Asp (D) GAC * GAA Glu (E) GAG *	GGT Gly (G) GGC * GGA * GGG *

The above is a map connecting tri-nucleotide sequences called codons and amino acids. Every triplet of nucleobase letters A, C, G, T in a DNA sequence specifies a single amino acid, with amino acids the building blocks of proteins.

Just as scientists struggle to define life, vitalists have different conceptions of what spirit is. Some conceive of it in a way that is potentially measurable: as an animating principle or vital force that gives life to organisms. It accounts for the difference between a living being and a corpse. While spirit is sometimes considered synonymous with soul, for many this latter term implies having an immortal existence— something not necessarily attributed to spirits. Many connect spirit with apparitions, ghosts, demons, sprites, or supernatural beings— with God falling in this last category. It should be noted some conceptions of spirituality—particularly those of (choice #6) mystics— imagine all individual spirits interconnecting to form Cosmic Mind, God, etc.

In rebutting scientific materialists like Leon Lederman, John Polkinghorne suggests, "God may act in subtle ways that are hidden from physical science." Agreeing with him, vitalists— and some who value (choice #10) "Non-Rational Knowing" —put down scientists who say something doesn't exist if it can't be measured. It's not surprising, they say, that scientists haven't found evidence of spirits since they are the "non-physical, non-quantifiable substance or energy present in living things." Scientists point out that defining spirits in that way makes their existence not testable—and science considers only testable hypotheses.

There's something of a middle ground between extreme scientific materialist and extreme vitalist positions. The "Notes" at the end of the choice #9 related theme descriptions suggest this. Putting both together, we offer a statement someone in this middle (choice #13 information / systems-based?) camp might make. "I'd like to move beyond vital spirits, ghosts, and non-physical, non-quantifiable conceptions of life. I link life with a creative/ organizing principle. I see it as emerging from the collective behavior of a complex system, and as something more than the sum of its parts. I connect life with this system interacting with the environment to get information, and structurally coupling with it."

The origins of this view can perhaps be traced to paleontologist and priest Teilhard de Chardin. His ideas on evolution, considered more in chapter 8, were influenced by Henri Bergson. In his 1907 book *Creative Evolution,* Bergson postulates a vital impetus ("élan vital") in addressing self-organization in the evolution of increasingly complex matter. He links it to consciousness. Bergson's conception goes beyond the simple 19th century vitalist ones; Teilhard, while doing without the élan vital, takes it into entirely new territory. His book *The Phenomenon of Man* was translated into English and published in 1959. British biologist Sir Peter Medawar was a prominent critic of book, and felt "the greater part of it is nonsense." He nonetheless connected Teilhard's radial (spiritual?) energy with the information content of messages. He pointed out that communication engineers readily quantify information content transfers.

As Teilhard was developing his ideas, the new field of cybernetics was broadening the conception of life. Norbert Wiener was fascinated by systems where "causes produce effects that are necessary for their own causation." To paraphrase Nobel Chemistry Prize winner Ilya Prigogine, in referring to a key genetic code mechanism, "nucleobases code for proteins, which in turn code for nucleobases." By the early 1970s in Chile, biologists Varela and Maturna were using the term autopoiesis to characterize the self-maintaining chemistry of living cells. And for life's complex adaptive systems—noting that the key to life was "the product of its operation is its own organization." Along with this pattern of organization, they said that living things are embodied in a dissipative structure that couples with the environment. Just as Prigogine, whose dissipative structures concept they borrowed, liked to stress the dynamic, spontaneous aspect of life by emphasizing its "becoming" rather than its "being," Varela and Maturna have said that "to live is to know." [15]

Nearly fifty years later, while getting renewed interest from researchers working on the origin of life, in artificial intelligence, and in astrobiology, critics point out that autopoiesis is seldom used in definitions of life. In recent years Chilean theoretical biologist and systems thinker Pablo Razeto-Barry has clarified its status and addressed complaints with a paper[16]: "Autopoiesis 40 Years Later. A Review and Reformulation." Physicist and author Fritjof Capra is a long-time cheerleader for this approach to characterizing life—what he calls "The Santiago Theory of Cognition (STC)"

Capra, psychologists, neuroscientists and others see the famous mind / body problem differently from traditional vitalists. The key question here is, "How do our thoughts, beliefs, desires and other intangibles in our mind interact with our bodies, and trigger the actions and behaviors that are so real and tangible—and have so dramatically reshaped the natural world?" Capra writes[17], "In my view, the STC is the first scientific theory that overcomes the Cartesian division of mind and matter, and will thus have far-reaching implications. Mind and matter no longer appear to belong to two separate categories, but can be seen to represent two complementary processes of the phenomenon of life—process and structure. At all levels of life, beginning with the simplest cell, mind and matter, process and structure are inseparably connected."

Theories of the mind have evolved, from being built around the longtime vitalist conception of the soul, to involve substance and behavior. So late 20th century scientific thinking emphasized interpreting the mind according to what it does, not what it is. New understanding of how the brain works, and theoretical insights spurred by efforts to create artificial intelligence, has increasingly shaped 21st century thinking. One popular theory—the computational theory of the mind—goes beyond behaviorism in asserting, "The mind is what the brain does."

In psychology, what was once considered the "study of the soul" is now the nearly exclusive domain of scientific materialists. A great, unsolved, related problem involves providing a detailed account of what human consciousness is, and the mechanism by which it functions. Until they can do this, vitalists and some New Age spirituality enthusiasts ask, how can scientists be so sure consciousness is not what it has long been thought to be: "a process not a thing, held by religious tradition to reside in the soul or spirit, and identified with self awareness?"

An overwhelming scientific consensus is behind the scientific materialist view. Their true believer critics say overwhelming anecdotal evidence exists for a real spiritual presence in human beings. They point to all sorts of phenomena and events that cannot be explained using the scientific conceptual framework. Stories of prophetic dreams, the presence of ghosts, angels and super-natural beings, and legends of miracles, abound throughout history. More recently, reports of thousands of people—many declared clinically dead—that survived a near death experience (NED) show an impressive consistency that cuts across cultural and religious boundaries.

Scientists point to how easily human senses can be fooled, and say paranormal phenomena are either not real, or not what believers claim they are. They explain bizarre, seemingly psychic, links / synchronicities in terms of very low probability coincidences—which, statistically, will happen given enough trials. As for NED, neuroscientists argue they stem from what people have been conditioned to believe. They say that what some claim are encounters with an external spiritual dimension, are but neural activity processes internal to the brain. They may find explaining a great deal of evidence for (choice #16) reincarnation— decades' worth of data— from the University of Virginia a bit more challenging.[18]

New Age spirituality enthusiasts claim some are gifted with perception not restricted to what the five ordinary senses reveal. And claim those who rely on an (choice #10) intuitive sense are simply connecting with their spiritual essence. As Gary Zukav puts it, "When a multisensory personality looks inside itself, it...comes to experience the energy of its soul." Most scientists scoff at this. They point out belief in such "energy" is not (choice #1) evidence-based, but wishful thinking—just like believing in life after death, "God is Love," and reincarnation, etc. Their critics turn the tables and accuse scientific materialists of being (choice #2) closed-minded. We'll return to this "matter only" or "matter and spirit" discussion in chapter 8.

We complete our exploration of what life is with mention of what some conceptions of God include. Many in the religious community like the pseudoscientific argument for the existence of God known as Intelligent Design. Since the (choice #5) Monotheistic Deism theme description does not depict God as a Creator with a purpose, it will not draw the hostility of scientific consensus opinion as belief in an Intelligent Designer has. Foes of Intelligent Design are disturbed that so many Americans apparently believe in it, despite absence of (choice #1) supporting scientific evidence.[19]

Physicists are distressed that so many people believe in a God who "will intervene on behalf of worshippers (performing miracles, etc)" to borrow words from the (choice #5) Belief in a Personal God theme. Such belief sells books like *Sun Stand Still—What Happens When You Dare to Ask God for the Impossible* by Steven Furtick. Astronomers—especially the cynics among them—suspect that millions of American adults' understanding of celestial motions is so poor that what the *Old Testament* God did as described in the book of *Joshua* was to stop the Sun in its orbit around the Earth. Whereas a more scientifically literate Christian would ponder whether the God they believe in would have really stopped the Earth from rotating on its axis.

Looking for answers to questions like "What's below us under the Earth's surface? and "How can we make sense of what we see in the sky?" —we turn our attention to these realms in the next two sections. As we do so, we recall longtime radio DJ Casey Kasem's message, "Keep your feet on the ground and keep reaching for the stars."

E. Discovering the Sky

As a global education effort built around "Choices We Make," this book invites you to say "Yes!" to the chance it provides in these next two sections to most fundamentally reconnect with Earth and Sky realms. Basic understanding of what happens beneath the Earth and up in the sky is important—not just in scientific literacy terms, but in one's search to find meaning in life. That search often enters the realm of spirituality.

Recall (from chapter 4) this book promotes metaphorically looking at spirituality—as the domain at the intersection of what both our heads and our hearts tell us is fundamentally important.

The human saga has included Earth and Sky-centered exploration informing human spirituality in two important ways. First, metaphorically speaking, both our Earth and Sky parents, taught us to appreciate natural cycles. They gave us (choice #2) global vision to not only read the pages of Earth history written in the layers of rock, but to see through space and time. And to eventually discover a hundreds of millions of years long rock cycle. Second, Earth is our platform for observing celestial objects. By inspiring us to explore the question, "Why do we see what we see?" our Sky parent, taught us there's (choice #7) order in how the world works.   And that we <u>can</u> understand its functioning.

The International Year of Astronomy (IYA) in 2009 celebrated the 400th anniversary of Galileo's first telescopic observations and Johannes Kepler's publication of his first two Laws of Planetary Motion. The logo for the IYA featured a parent holding a child's hand with both looking up into a starry sky under the banner: "The Universe—Yours to Discover. " How might that discovery process systematically proceed? Consider the following ten basic observational exercises.

Basic Observational Exercises
#1 The Sun's Energy. (CAUTION: Don't stare directly at the Sun!)
The Sun provides heat and warmth. Young children discover this by standing in the shade on a cold winter day, then moving into the sunshine. This energy makes life on Earth possible. Older children learn that the Sun's brilliance makes it impossible to see any other stars while it's above the horizon. Those stars are still there—we just can't see them until the Sun settles below the horizon, and night begins.

Unlike ancient or primitive peoples, we recognize stars as large, hot glowing balls of gas that energy is pouring out of. Like the Sun, they typically shine by converting hydrogen into helium via nuclear fusion reactions. Unlike the Sun, they are tremendously far away. While the Sun is a mere 93 million miles away, the nearest star beyond the Sun is four light years or 25 trillion miles distant. So even the nearest star is about 270,000 times farther away than the Sun is— which is why the stars look very faint compared to the Sun.

#2 The Sun's Apparent Motion.
The Sun appears to move as the day goes on. You can watch it rise in the east, and climb to a high point (called its culmination) around noontime to the south. If you continue watching, you'll see it settle down— technically we refer to its losing altitude—and eventually set in the west. "So," you say, "It looks like the Sun moves around us here on the Earth as the day goes on." While this is a reasonable conclusion, actually, something else is happening. Suppose you're saying this to a child while holding a large ball. You continue, "Imagine you're an ant living on this ball looking at the Sun. Imagine the ball is spinning this way toward the east, what do you see the Sun do? You see it appears to move to the west. It turns out this is the most basic of motion of the Earth: it spins or rotates on its axis once a day." You can point out that it's only been in the last four hundred years this was generally accepted. Before that, everyone thought the Earth stayed put, and the Sun, Moon, planets and stars—all celestial objects—moved around it.

#3 The Sun at High Noon Throughout the Year
"Why do we have seasons?" This question once famously stumped some Harvard students[20], who incorrectly explained Earth is closer to the Sun in summer making it hotter. They grew up not paying attention to where the Sun is in the sky around noon throughout the year. Not so for hundreds of earlier generations of kids growing up working in fields—or for the builders of Stonehenge 5000 years ago. Some 3500 years later, Roman agriculture writer Palladius, in *The Work of Farming*, presented tables showing lengths of noon-time shadows (cast by vertical mounted sticks) — shortening from their longest in December to their shortest in June. This work was still being used a 1000 years later by medieval British farmers and monks[21], who saw the predictability of such shadows as evidence of an (choice #7) "Orderly and Explicable" universe.

Rather than shadow lengths, the following exercise for (northern hemisphere observers) gauges the Sun's noontime position above the southern horizon on four dates: Mar 21, Jun 21, Sep 21, Dec 21. You're to measure its altitude by holding your hand out at arm's length—with fingers parallel to the horizon, tightly touching each other, and thumb pointing up. Assume your four fingers block out 5° of sky. If the space between horizon and Sun requires six four fingered hands, you'd report a 6 x 5 = 30° altitude. This might be a reasonable December 21 value, depending on location. Repeating the measurement on June 21 will yield a much greater value—specifically 47° more, or 30 ° + 47 ° = 77 ° altitude would be expected.

In other words, in summer the Sun is higher in the sky at mid-day. So it sends energy in more direct fashion, not spreading out as much when it hits the ground as it does in winter, heating more effectively making it hotter. In winter—most prominently on December 21— it's lower in the sky. So its rays hit the ground in a glancing fashion. That, combined with shorter days in winter—meaning the Sun is not above the horizon as long to send us energy—results in colder winter-time temperatures. From an observer's point of view, that's why we have seasons.

"But why," you ask, "Does the Sun change position in the mid-day sky throughout the year?" Answer: "It's because the Earth's axis (an imaginary line drawn from south pole, through the center, to the north pole) is tilted 23.5 ° with respect to its orbit plane. The northward extension of that axis tilts Earth most strongly toward the Sun on June 21, putting the sun highest in the sky at noon. On December 21 the tilt is most prominently away from the Sun, putting the Sun lowest in the sky at noon. Those extremes are twice the tilt angle, or 2 x 23.5° = 47°.

#4 The Stars Move As the Night Progresses.
Just as the Sun appears to move as the Earth spins on its axis, so do stars. You can verify this by going outdoors after dark and facing east—the direction opposite to where the Sun has set. Pick out a bright star that's relatively low in the sky. Note its position and the time. Repeat observation of the star every thirty minutes, noting it's rising and gaining altitude (as Figure #14 depicts for a star rising due east.)

Figure #14: The Apparent Path of a Star On the Celestial Sphere

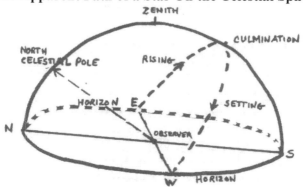

#5 The Stars Don't Move Relative to Each Other

Prior to this exercise, you'll need to go online and print out a star map. Over the course of several nights, we want you to spot as many of the brightest (first magnitude) stars as you can. Make a list. Note: the brightest celestial objects you see, besides the Sun and Moon, may actually be planets (see exercise #10.) They may not be plotted on your star map because their locations change. Pay attention to directions it includes as to how to orient your star map. If you're having trouble identifying anything, one strategy is to look for bright stars or planets near the Moon.[22] (Since the Moon takes roughly four weeks to circle the Earth, its position in the sky changes from night to night.)

As for actual stars, the ancients recognized that— as far as people could tell during their lifetimes— they stay fixed relative to each other. This— and a bit of imagination—connects them in characteristic patterns. Long-ago people in various cultures named these groupings of stars, called constellations, after animals, mythological figures, etc. Thus— using names officially recognized—the constellation Ursa Major is the big bear, Orion symbolizes a hunter, Scorpius a scorpion, Lyra a harp, Cygnus a swan, Pegasus a winged horse, and so on. The International Astronomical Union today recognizes eighty-eight constellations, and hundreds of star names. Identify and list as many of the brighter constellations as you can. If you're doing this from a light polluted urban area where only a few bright stars are visible, this may be easy.

#6 The Stars in a Dark Sky

On a clear moonless night, from a dark location far away from city lights, you can see roughly 2000 stars. Astronomers have devised a magnitude scale to gauge the brightness of objects. Remember that the smaller the number, the brighter the object, and that the scale is not linear. Thus a star of magnitude one is about 2.5 times brighter than one of second magnitude. Roughly twenty-five bright stars are considered to be first magnitude stars. The unaided eye can see stars to sixth magnitude from a dark sky location; telescopes reveal trillions more.

This exercise highlights the difference between big city night sky observations, and what a trip to the countryside reveals. In particular it asks you to pick a well-defined region of the sky—such as within the Great Square of Pegasus (defined by its four second magnitude stars). Count number of stars you can see within its boundaries from light polluted and dark sky locations, and compare. (Note: the song featured in Figure #17 celebrates dark skies.)

#7 The North Star Doesn't Appear to Move as the Night Goes On.
One of the first star patterns northern hemisphere observers learn to spot is known as The Big Dipper, formed by the seven brightest stars of the constellation Ursa Major. And they learn to use the two stars in the Dipper's bowl—known as the Pointers—to direct them to the second magnitude star Polaris, also known as "The North Star." This star—as far as the unaided eye can discern—stays put as the night goes on. Why? Because, coincidentally, looking in the direction of Polaris also has us looking in nearly the same direction in space that the Earth's axis points to. So, as the night progresses and the Earth spins on that axis, Polaris stays put and other stars appear to move around it.

You can verify this by watching the motion of one of the brighter northern sky constellations—either Ursa Major or Cassiopeia are good choices—over a few hours. For example, early in the evening in late summer suppose you spot the center of the prominent "W" (or upside down "M") formed by the stars of Cassiopeia. Imagine you see it some angular distance X to the right (due east) of Polaris. But, six hours later—with Earth spinning on its axis through one-quarter revolution— the center of Cassiopeia will have moved a quarter of the way in its circular path. So, after moving through arc length of 90° around Polaris, it's now seen that same angular distance X above Polaris. (Note X is around 30°.)

There are two practically important lessons associated with the above. First, if you're lost at night in the northern hemisphere, if you can find Polaris you'll know that moving toward it is heading north. Second, you can gauge the relative passage of time by watching stars—like those of the Big Dipper or Cassiopeia—circle Polaris.

A final note: if you're really lost—say you have no idea where on Earth you are—the altitude of Polaris provides key information. Namely the altitude of Polaris = the latitude of your observing location. So if you're in Portland, Oregon USA at latitude 45°, you'll look halfway between horizon and overhead to see it at altitude 45°. If you're at the north pole (latitude 90°) Polaris is overhead; if you're at the equator Polaris is on the horizon (altitude zero). Of course you can't see it from the southern hemisphere. (The southern hemisphere lacks a prominent, bright pole star. There, a bright star pattern known as "the Southern Cross" can help you find the direction south.)

#8 The Stars Appear to Move—both as the night goes on and as the year progresses.

Select a bright star high in the sky and watch its motion over the course of a single night. Decide when its altitude is greatest, and note the day and time. Then repeat the exercise one month later. An ideal example involves the bright star Vega in the constellation of Lyra. Watching Vega on the night of July 1, you determine its altitude steadily increases as the night progresses until it's greatest at midnight (when it's nearly overhead). Repeating this exercise on August 1, you find its altitude is greatest at 10 PM—two hours earlier.

You've uncovered something important to know with respect to the changing appearance of the night sky: one month (thirty days) later, stars will appear at the same spot in the sky two hours earlier. From night to night, there's about a four minute difference—meaning that a star seen at one location (say overhead) one night at 10:00 PM, will be at that same location four minutes earlier—at 9:56 PM—the next night. The same thing applies to when stars first rise above the eastern horizon, or set below the western horizon.

What's going on? Recall all celestial objects appear to move in the sky due to the Earth's rotation. But besides rotating once a day, the Earth—which we think of as our observing platform for these exercises—has a second motion: it revolves around the Sun once a year. This motion also affects where we look to see stars in the sky—but it takes many days, not hours, to noticeably show up. This motion explains that roughly four minutes per day change discovered in the last exercise. It's what brings new stars slowly into view after dark, as the weeks and months go on. If you add up a whole year's worth of four-minute lags—365.4 x 4 minutes—you get 1440 minutes or roughly twenty-four hours. This means that, as for the directions we look to see stars, a year's worth of Earth revolving around the Sun has the same effect as twenty-four hours or one day's worth of Earth rotating on its axis.

#9 Observations of Stars Tell Us Earth is Round

Let's return to exercise #2's small ant on large ball analogy. Imagine you're the ant looking in the direction of a very very far away star and you see that star just visible on your horizon. Imagine you crawl toward the direction of the star, how does your view of that star change? Answer: the star appears to get higher in the sky—that is, its altitude increases. From observations of bright stars (like Canopus) near the horizon in a due south direction, as observed from different locations in Europe and the Middle East over 2,000 years ago, a few people figured out that they lived on a huge sphere. Not only that, they deduced roughly how big spherical Earth is. Here's a modern day version of what they did.

Observational Method:
From 35° latitude locations (like Albuquerque, NM or Flagstaff, AZ), at times when it's highest in sky, Canopus is seen at 2° above the southern horizon (Figure #15a). Similarly from a more southerly location 32° latitude (like Anthony, NM or Sahuarita, AZ) Canopus is seen at 5° altitude (Figure #15b), or 3° higher. Note 3 ° is 1/120 of going all the way around a sphere—that is, through all 360°. So to roughly get the circumference of Earth, we simply multiply the distance between Albuquerque & Anthony, NM —or Flagstaff & Sahuarita, AZ—by 120.

Figure #15: Canopus As Seen From Different Latitudes
a) Canopus from 35° latitude   b) Canopus from 32° latitude

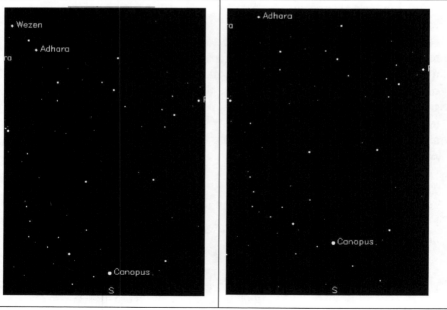

#10 The Apparent Motion of Planets

Long ago, careful sky watchers distinguished two types of celestial objects: lots and lots of "fixed" stars, but a select few bright objects that move with respect to them. These objects are the Moon, and planets—in fact, to the Greeks, "planet" meant literally a "wandering star." Brilliant Venus—easy to spot in the western evening sky soon after sunset, or in the eastern sky before sunrise, is often the first planet many identify. But for this exercise, documenting so-called retrograde motion, we recommend observing one of the outer planets—Mars, Jupiter, or Saturn.

Imagine you watch reddish Mars, which normally moves very slowly eastward against the background of fixed stars over the course of several weeks. Sometimes Mars can be seen to depart from its usual eastward motion and move westward, before again resuming its usual eastward motion. To view this, we recommend watching Mars (or Jupiter or Saturn)— for a few weeks both before and after their times of opposition. That refers to when they appear in the opposite direction from where you look to see the Sun. Ideally you should chart the position of one of these outer planets, with respect to the stars of the (zodiac[23]) constellation it's in, over the course of a couple of months. To understand the strange motion you'll detect, consider Figure #16 below.

It uses a sun-centered representation (heliocentric model), to show why retrograde motion occurs. The apparent motion of a planet with respect to those fixed, background stars is due to a combination of the Earth's motion and the planet's own motion around the Sun. Retrograde motion of a planet like Mars happens when the Earth overtakes Mars—between times 3 and 4 in the figure—and the planet appears to move backwards (westward.) Once ancient astronomers documented such phenomena, simple models of planetary motion—such Mars simply circling the Earth, like the Moon does— were seen to be impossible.

Figure #16: The Retrograde Motion of Mars

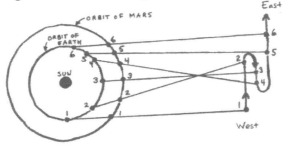

Nicolai Copernicus's 1543 book presented a new model. It removed the Earth from its previous stationary position at the center of the universe. Copernicus's model had the Earth in an annual circular orbit around the Sun., and all other planets likewise circling the Sun. He also gave it a daily spin on its axis. This model had a big advantage over the long accepted, but complicated, geocentric model of Claudius Ptolemy. It offered a simple explanation of retrograde motion. But it didn't offer any real advantage in predicting future planetary positions —say of a planet like Mars—given its use of circular orbits.

Johannes Kepler, a man seemingly with feet in both ancient and modern worlds, began his analysis of Tycho Brahe's twenty years of carefully observed positions of Mars in 1600. He struggled for many years to find a model to fit the data. This involved applying the (choice #10) scientific method and painstakingly testing various hypothesized orbital paths, starting with a circular one. When that didn't work, he began testing other shapes. He eventually found Mars moved around the Sun in an elliptical path. His work illustrates that important scientific advances often require both methodical tenacity and (choice #12) imagination.

If asked to summarize roughly four thousand years in the human "Discovering the Sky" story with a single sentence I'd reply, "Curiosity, careful observation, analysis, more observation, imagination and more analysis, etc. characterized the quest to understand and answer the question 'Why do we see what we see?'" By 1700, a few years after the publication of the classic book *Principia*, in which Issac Newton provided his theory of gravity and the basis for understanding motion in general, many were celebrating. Not only had nice progress been made in answering that question, but those who sought an (choice #7) Orderly and Explicable universe were pleased. Yet this new understanding spurred revisiting old questions.

"Where do we come from?" has long been at the center of my expanding worldviews efforts as an astronomy teacher—both indoors in the lecture hall, and outdoors under the night sky. In the former setting, students can sit back and watch my slide show chronicling the history of, and evidence supporting, the Big Bang theory. It begins with 1) astronomers in the 1920s using the big telescopes on Mount Wilson in southern California. They established that those numerous fuzzy "nebulae" were not nearby gas clouds inside our Milky Way Galaxy, but were whole galaxies, each containing billions of stars, far away and outside it. It moves to 2) the 1930 announcement of the discovery of strong evidence (provided by Doppler-shifted galaxy spectra) that the universe is expanding; and to 3) the unexpected 1965 discovery of the ever present cosmic background radiation, a relic dating to the formation of the universe's first stable atoms, 380,000 years after the Big Bang creation event 13.8 billion years ago. The first stars came 300 million years later.

Outside with students, I continue "The Great Cosmic Story." A product of (choice #2) minds open and possessing global vision, this tale is both a (choice #41) Respect for Nature, and recycling story. It spans nearly fourteen billion years of evolution, and ends with us gazing at the stars in wonder. With everyone assembled, I say, "Folks, as the sky gets really dark, let's begin by getting oriented." After a few minutes of noting individual prominent stars and constellations, I ask eyes to scan the galaxy we live in. We see the Milky Way as a faint, but beautiful, band of light stretching across part of the sky. Once thought to be at the center of the universe, we now know the Earth lies in the outskirts of this galaxy— in one of its spiral arms. Within this band of light, I point to a dark region —where dust obscures our view. And note that new stars form inside clouds of gas and dust.

From inside, we can't see the whole Milky Way as someone outside would see it. But we can view other galaxies believed to resemble our own. We do that by turning the telescope to the Andromeda Galaxy. As they stare at this large, relatively nearby galaxy, I tell them, "The light you're seeing—traveling at 186,000 miles per second—left 2.5 million years ago when people were little more than animals! Like our Milky Way, this galaxy also has around 200 billion stars. And our largest telescopes, in every direction, generally detect as many galaxies, out to over 10 billion light years distant, as they do stars in the Milky Way. This means we have evidence of over 200 billion galaxies out there!"

Telescopic views of the Andromeda Galaxy find me asking students to imagine our Milky Way galaxy nearly five billion years ago. And imagine, inside it, a giant cloud of gas and dust, roughly 99% hydrogen and helium, 1% heavier elements. To aid imaginations, we view the wispy, dusty clouds of the Orion Nebula and describe the birth of the Sun as part of the cloud collapses. After appreciating how dependable and stable the Sun is, we consider how the Orion Nebula might look a few million years from now. "It will look like this," I tell them, as eyes peer through the telescope and scan the cluster of young stars known as the

Pleiades. We then consider stellar energy crises. "After billions of years turning hydrogen into helium," I say, "a star runs low on nuclear fuel—and nears death."

By now we're examining the aging red supergiant star Betelgeuse. I sing a silly song (sung to the tune of "Edelweiss") about it eventually exploding as a supernova. I mention the new star Chinese astronomers saw in 1054, and speculate that Native American petroglyph drawings also depict it. We soon turn the telescope to the remnant of that event, the Crab Nebula, and note the explosion enriched the interstellar medium. The cycle of stellar evolution / cosmic ecology lesson ends with the birth of the next generation of stars—as the now enriched gas and dust of the interstellar medium again is pulled together by gravity. I tell them "We are the ash of stellar alchemy ...The iron bound up in hemoglobin giving our blood its red color originated in the nuclear furnace of an old star, was dispersed when the star exploded, and became part of the collapsing cloud that spawned Sun and Earth over 4.5 billion years ago."

After everyone gets a good look at the Crab Nebula, we form a circle around the telescope, and sing a song (with lyrics shown in Figure #17) to commemorate what we've learned this evening.

Figure #17: Song: "Dark Sky Night"

lyrics by S. Cook sung to the tune of "Silent Night," trad. religious	
Dark sky night, holy night All is calm, all is right There's Polaris' steady starlight Stars turn round it, circling all night Watch the celestial show, Watch the predictable show	Dark sky night, holy night Milky Way oh what a sight In Sagittarius shining bright Galactic Center hidden from sight In its arms stars are born In its arms stars are born
Dark sky night, holy night Evening star so very bright Planet Venus reflecting sunlight Morning star so very bright Watch it move round the Sun Watch it move round the Sun	Find tonight, telescope sight Crab Nebula what a delight Long ago once super bright Exploding star lit up the night What a story to tell What a story to tell

The story from there shifts from sky to Earth. It is one of how — as wholistic thinker and astronomy educator Brian Swimme[24] puts it — "Earth, once molten rock, now sings opera." Opera originated in Italy as the Copernican worldview revolution was beginning. That revolution moved the Earth out of its important position at the center of the universe. But alas, many people today are stuck in pre-Copernican days. They're ignorant of all we're learned about where we come from, and how insignificant we are. They prefer the first of the two themes which make up choice #41. That is, they prefer the Human-Centered.theme in which everything revolves around assigning fundamental importance to humans and their needs. They discount Respect for Nature, which asserts, "Humans are part of nature, not its rulers."

F. Discovering the Earth

In transitioning from "Discovering the Sky" to "Discovering the Earth"—from astronomy to geology—you might imagine this section proceeding as the last one did. That is, teacher and students assemble to survey evidence acquired to answer a question. Here we're interested in, "How did the surface of our Earth come to look the way that it does?" After classroom lecture and slides telling the story of three centuries of geologists' efforts in this regard—culminating around 1970— we move outdoors with a field geology trip.

Imagine toward the end of trip—after connecting the geologically revealing site we've stopped at, with the framework for understanding the Earth's surface known as plate tectonics—we pause to celebrate. We put down rock hammers, stand together facing the canyon, mountain, fault, or whatever has drawn us there, and sing a song (with lyrics shown in Figure #18) to commemorate what we've learned.   But, alas, we're getting ahead of ourselves...Let's go back and trace the history of how what our song celebrates came to be.

By the end of the 17th century, physics and astronomy had shed ancient misconceptions and were on their way to becoming the sciences we know them as today. Only by the end of the 18th century were chemistry and geology also doing this. The former was saddled with an ancient misconception. Think of it as the wrong answer— "earth, water, air, and fire" — to the question, "What is everything made of?" The 1789 publication in France of LaVoissier's *Elements of Chemistry*, answered this question differently. It correctly identified twenty-three substances that can't be broken down into simpler substances by chemical means— what we recognize as chemical elements. "Earth" and air are not among them. The former is a mixture of many things with highly variable composition; the latter, while also a mixture, typically consists of roughly 20% oxygen, just under 80% of (relatively inert) nitrogen, and roughly 1% water vapor, carbon dioxide, etc. Fire is linked with a combustion process involving some fuel rapidly combining with oxygen.

Figure #18: Song: Digging Into Planet Earth

lyrics by S. Cook
sung to the tune of "Angels We Have Heard On High" trad. religious

Digging into Planet Earth
Geologists gather data
Building theory of great worth
Making sense of all the strata
Plaaaaaa.............te tectonics.
   In excelis Gaia.
Plaaaaaa.............te tectonics.
   In excelis Gaia

Continents drifting slow
Floating on the rigid crust
Driven by heat from below
Forward with a mighty thrust
Plaaaaaa.............te tectonics.
   In excelis Gaia.
Plaaaaaa.............te tectonics.
   In excelis Gaia

Plates hung up something must move
As they lurch we get the shakes
San Andreas fault big groove
Rock and roll and strong earthquakes

Plaaaaaa.........te tectonics.
   In excelis Gaia.
Plaaaaaa... ... te tectonics.
   In excelis Gaia

A plate slowly slides beneath
Taking eons man it's slow
All the while the heat it grows
One day the volcano blows
Plaaaaaa.........te tectonics.
   In excelis Gaia.
Plaaaaaa...... te tectonics.
   In excelis Gaia

India plate what a crash
Into Asia rocks don't lie
For planet Earth something rash
Himalayas thrust up high
Plaaaaaa......... te tectonics.
   In excelis Gaia.
Plaaaaaa......... te tectonics.
   In excelis Gaia

Geology was held down by religious dogma. And by the pronouncement of influential Irish Bishop James Ussher—based on careful reading of the *Bible*—that God created and populated the Earth in a six-day process that began at 9:00 AM on Monday, October 23rd in the year 4004 BC. So by the time William Smith in England began digging canals, and James Hutton in Scotland published his book *The Theory of the Earth* in 1795, the consensus worldview pegged Earth to be less than 6000 years old. While Smith and Hutton did much to convince others that Earth was far older, exactly how much older they couldn't say. Only with the early 20th century development of radioactive dating techniques did providing exact absolute dates (in years before the present) for geological events in Earth history become possible. By the middle of the 20th century these dates put the oldest such event—the Earth's formation—as occurring roughly 4.5 billion years ago.

Smith and Hutton—who seemingly compete in today's reckoning for the title "Father of Modern Geology"— recognized that surface rocks are subject to weathering and other forces. These ultimately break them up and deposit the debris in rivers, lakes, and the ocean. Thus sediments, which typically also include organic matter, build up. Cemented together by chemicals and by crystallization, these sediments become sedimentary rocks. Both men similarly had exciting "Aha!" moments while studying sedimentary rock layers.

Smith first noticed a succession of rock and fossil types underground in a coal mine at Mearns Pit in Somerset, England; Hutton's speculations were inspired by his views of exposed layers at Siccar Point in Berwickshire, Scotland. Out of these early attempts at reading Earth's history as recorded in the rock record came appreciation that, at particular locations, some pages in this metaphorical book are missing. These are called unconformities. Properly explaining them requires going back to first principles—geological principles.

Smith and Hutton helped develop what are called relative geological dating techniques—based on establishing which of two geologic events happened first. They can be used to delineate much interesting past geological history. They employ a few basic laws and relationships to read the record rock layers provide. This record may tell a story of sediments being eroded or deposited; of uplift above sea level or submergence under water; of rocks being squeezed or stretched causing folding or faulting; of hot molten rock known as magma intruding, etc. Geologists see these phenomena happening today and reason that they have always happened. This provides the basis for a principle first stated by Hutton:

1) **The Principle of Uniformitarianism**: the processes that have shaped Earth throughout geologic time are the same ones observable today. Interpreting the cutaway rock profiles of Figure #19—views some call "layer-cake geology" —requires two other fundamental laws of geology:

2) **The Law of Horizontal Originality**: sediments deposited in water are laid down in horizontal layers.

3) **The Law of Superposition**: in undisturbed layers of sedimentary rock, the layer at the bottom is older than the layer at the top.

Thus in Figure #19A, layer 1 was deposited first and is the oldest. Then layer 2, layer 3, and, most recently, the youngest layer, layer 4 was deposited. When layers are horizontal applying The Law of Superposition is straightforward, but faulting (Figure #19B) or folding (Figure #19C and #19D) can lead to tilted layers. Even then, superposition can be used by following the layers back to places where they remain horizontal. Also, layers can sometimes be unambiguously matched up across fault lines.

Figures #19B—#19D show sedimentary layers disturbed by forces, which break them to create faults or fold them. Figure #19E shows what can happen when intense heat melts rock and magma flows. Igneous rocks form when that magma (whose origin may be far below in Earth's interior) solidifies. They come with a wide variety of chemical compositions and textures— the latter determined by the rate of cooling. Granite, a common igneous rock, forms when magma cools and crystallizes slowly— giving it a coarse-grained texture.

Where igneous rocks intrude, as in Fig. #19E, relationships can become complicated. Here, another basic principle can be applied:

4) **The Law of Crosscutting Relations**: any rock unit (or fault) that cuts across other rock units is younger than the rock units through which it cuts.

Thus the igneous intrusion of Figure #19E (where it reaches the surface it becomes an extrusion) is younger than all the layers shown. Figures #19C and #19D depict folds termed anticlines and synclines. Inspection of these figures—and imagining a time of horizontal layers before folding—leads to the following relationships:

5) **For Anticlines**: the oldest rock layer will be exposed at the center of the fold, parts of the same rock layer—a younger layer-—will be exposed on each side of the center fold (given typical erosion.)

Figure #19: What Geological Cross-Sections Can Tell Us

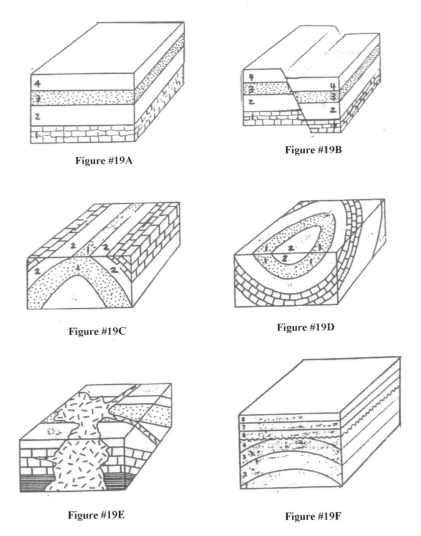

Figure #19A

Figure #19B

Figure #19C

Figure #19D

Figure #19E

Figure #19F

6) **For Synclines**: the youngest rock layer will be exposed at the center of the fold, parts of the same rock layer—an older layer—will be exposed on each side of the center fold (given typical erosion.)

Thus, in Figure #19C, layer 1 is older than layer 2, and in Fig. #19D, layer 2 is younger than layer 1.

Finally, we recognize that the rock record may have gaps in it due to erosion or non-deposition. Layers, which might otherwise document millions of years of geologic time, may simply have been eroded away—they're gone. Or were never deposited in the first place. Of course, rates of deposition of sediments can vary greatly, so a layer's thickness and the passage of time can't generally be correlated.

Breaks in the rock record are called unconformities. The break they note hints at a time of uplift, when layers were above sea level long enough to be eroded or for sedimentation to halt. Consider the events that led to the unconformity in Figure #19F—the wavy line erosion surface between layers 4 and 6:

1st: layers 1,2,3,4 and perhaps others were deposited
2nd: uplift and folding occurred with an anticline forming
3rd: erosion occurred (of layer 4 and perhaps others above sea level)
4th: submergence occurred
5th: layer 6 deposited with unconformity developing
6th: layers 7 and 8 deposited

In general, a representative cross-sectional rock record for the ground beneath a particular region is called a stratigraphic column. Figure #20 shows a much-simplified one for a place in the Grand Canyon, charting the layers in the exposed canyon walls. With additional information, including what absolute dating techniques provide, we can describe the fascinating region represented there as follows.

The upper layers are all sedimentary, varying in thickness and depositional environment. The Coconino Sandstone, the youngest, can be traced to a desert sand dune / winds blowing small rock particles environment of 275 million years ago. Only with the oldest rocks at the bottom—the Vishnu group —were metamorphic processes involved. Such metamorphic rocks result when heat, great pressure, and / or chemically active fluids (like water) act on rocks over a long period of time to transform them—both in texture and composition. Limestone is thus changed into marble; granite becomes gneiss. These lowest (basement) rocks are truly ancient—dating to between (at the top of the Vishnu Group) 1.68 billion = 1680 million years ago and (at the bottom) 1.84 billion = 1840 million years ago.

Note the Tapeats sandstone, originally formed from marine deposits laid down 525 million years ago, is shown sitting on top of Vishnu Group rocks. Elsewhere in the Grand Canyon, tilted sedimentary rocks known as the Grand Canyon Supergroup, sit in between the Tapeats sandstone and the Vishnu Group—but not in the place whose stratigraphic column we're considering. There, these rock layers—and others —are missing. We connect gaps in the rock record with unconformities. This part of the Grand Canyon showcases a most impressive one. Where Tapeats Sandstone sits directly on Vishnu Group rocks, we have 1680 – 525 = 1155 million years = 1.155 billion years of rock record missing—like pages torn out of a book.

Figure #20: A Geological Cross-Section of the Grand Canyon

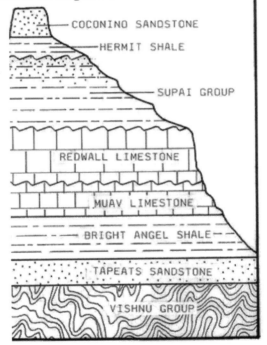

Note the youngest rocks exposed at the surface, Coconino Sandstone, are still 275 million years old. Why don't we see younger rocks? Perhaps this region, which today sits at roughly 7000 feet in elevation, has been above sea level for a long time and no sedimentary layers have been deposited? Or perhaps such layers that were once there have since been eroded away?

Not far from Grand Canyon we find much younger igneous rocks—the result of fairly recent volcanic activity. Indeed the cinder cone at Sunset Crater National Monument was created less than a thousand years ago—a mere blimp of time when you consider that the oldest rocks exposed at the bottom of the Grand Canyon are 1.84 billion years old. And what of the magnificent Grand Canyon itself—when did the erosive forces provided by the water of the Colorado and ancestral rivers begin cutting that through those 1.84 billion years of rock layers? Geologists think that began around five or six million years ago, as the river began to carve its way downward. Erosion created by streams flowing into the big river led to the canyon's widening.

Many realize that a river like the Colorado flowing into an ocean—which it once did before human water needs dried it up before reaching its longtime destination in the Pacific—is part of a water cycle in which seawater evaporates. Driven by solar energy, this process lifts seawater back into clouds, from which it eventually— pulled by gravity— falls downward as rain. Of course some of that rainwater soaks into the ground replenishing aquifers, nurturing life, etc. And some runs off into rivers, and so on. The whole cycle— mostly quietly, but sometimes noisily with thunder and rain—endlessly repeats year in, and year out.

Fewer realize that the erosion created by streams—and that due to other agents most notably weathering—is also part of a cycle that operates with an extraordinarily long period: hundreds of millions of years. This rock cycle connects processes that happen above and beneath Earth's surface. Weathering, transport, deposition, uplift, etc. fit in the former category; submergence, compaction, metamorphism, melting, magma generation, crystallization, etc. fit into the latter. The theory behind this rock cycle explains how these processes relate to the three rock types— sedimentary, metamorphic, and igneous. It also explains how one of those rock types can slowly transform into another. The development of this theory—plate tectonics—stalled over failure to answer the question, "What drives this cycle?

Consider the first bit of evidence in what eventually came together in a definitive theory 350 years later. In 1620, Francis Bacon, perhaps the first to write extensively about the promise of employing (choice #10) scientific methods to gather knowledge, noted that the coastlines of South America and Africa roughly fit together like puzzle pieces. While early maps were admittedly crude, it was suggested that conceivably these two continents were once joined together. And that they broke apart and somehow moved to their current locations separated by the Atlantic Ocean. "There's no fit and that didn't happen," Comte deBuffon essentially argued in 1749. He suggested the Atlantic ocean formed when the supposed ancient continent of Atlantis sunk. He promoted a "catastrophic" origin of features on the Earth's surface. James Hutton's arguing for "uniformitarianism" in this regard was still decades in the future.

By 1910 Alfred Wegener revived old ideas of continental drift —pulling together lots of geological evidence in postulating the existence of a single super-continent he called Pangaea. This, he argued, began to break apart around 200 million years ago. Unfortunately geophysicists— limited by what they then knew about the properties of the Earth's crust—could not conceive of how this crust moved laterally. So they ridiculed Wegener's ideas. But new data decades later—during the 1957-1958 International Geophysical Year, which also saw the launching of the first Earth orbiting artificial satellites—spurred a reevaluation.

This reevaluation led to significant tearing down and rebuilding of the Earth science-related conceptual framework. To underscore how fast this happened, consider passages from books published a mere seven years apart. In 1963, in his *A Planet Called Earth*, George Gamov wrote, "...the possibility that the continents are drifting along the Earth's surface still remains an unsolved problem..." Fast forward to November 1970 to what the authors of the MIT Press / Open University Book *Understanding the Earth* wrote in its preface. "During the last decade, there has been a revolution in the Earth sciences, largely due to the fruitful researches of the oceanographic geophysicists, which has led to the wide acceptance that continents drift about the face of the Earth and that sea floor spreads, continually being created and destroyed. Finally, in the last two to three years, it has culminated in a theory known as 'plate tectonics'."

According to plate tectonics, the Earth's surface is broken up into seven or eight large crustal plates, and many minor ones. The plates—some carrying continents, others oceanic crustal units—can be thought of as floating on partially molten rock beneath. Heat from the Earth's interior drives their movement. What happens at plate boundaries (colliding, diverging, sliding by or under, etc) results in mountain building, formation of new crust, destruction of old crust, earthquakes, volcanoes, etc. Plate movement is very slow. One analogy suggests they move at about the same rate as your fingernails grow: around an inch per year. So significant regional changes can take millions of years. For example, it took roughly 40 million years (between 70 and 30 million years ago) for what we see today as the high and relatively flat Colorado Plateau in the Four Corners region of the southwestern USA to be uplifted.

Plate movement provides for ultimate recycling of rocks and thereby drives the rock cycle. Plate tectonics has provided a wildly successful framework for understanding the Earth's surface, just as the theory of biological evolution has in accounting for the history of life on that surface. Are these theoretical frameworks now permanently fixed in place, never to be modified? Since they are evidence-based, of course not. Like all such products of science, they're subject to revision if new evidence suggests a need. But those who challenge the structure of evidence-based frameworks that successfully make sense of so much, must have good supporting evidence, and good reason to press their challenge. And, even then, as we've seen with continental drift / plate tectonics, they should expect to be engaged in a long battle.

As we turn attention toward humans living on the Earth's surface—and the associated technology— we note this topic holds more than its share of mysteries and unresolved questions. But before venturing into that territory, we begin with reviewing some basic understanding.

G. Living on Earth—as Human Technology Develops

Energy from the Sun makes life on Earth possible. Most notably it drives a photosynthesis process in which plants pull carbon dioxide from the air, and water from the ground, to form carbohydrates and release oxygen. The chemical reaction associated with this biomass building, with reactants written on the left and products on the right, is:

$$6CO_2 + 12H_2O + energy \rightarrow C_6H_{12}O_6 + 6H_2O + 6O_2$$

In contrast, animals "burn" carbohydrates —that is, these serve as fuel, which combines with oxygen pulled from the air in breathing. Known as respiration, in breaking down biomass, it releases carbon dioxide, water and, most importantly, the energy animals need to function:

$$C_6H_{12}O_6 + 6O_2 \rightarrow 6CO_2 + 6H_2O + energy$$

These chemical reactions are associated with a key turning point in human evolutionary history: the beginning of agriculture. While we trace the origins of this path from humans' steady divergence from apes and chimpanzees 5 to 10 million years ago—it was only 12,000 or so years ago that we initiated a significantly different relationship with these chemical reactions. Put another way: we began establishing and tending fields of green solar collectors—plants— to produce the food and deliver the energy needed for our (choice # 47) sustenance. This didn't happen all at once, but took roughly 5,000 years to get going over a wide region.

Preceding this, an important milestone in our hunter-gatherer existence came with learning to use combustion. Today's archaeological investigations suggest that sporadic efforts to use fire began over 500,000 years ago. Eventually our distant ancestors learned to control it: with dead wood they gathered serving as fuel, and the heat energy released facilitating staying warm and cooking.

Much more recently—around 250 years ago—we entered a new phase in our long relationship with utilizing the energy released in combustion of hydrocarbons. As the Industrial Revolution surged in England in the latter 18th century, so did digging below the Earth's surface to extract fossil fuel. Where to dig for the coal that powered it initially motivated William Smith's map-making efforts.

In the century before Smith, Robert Hooke—a contemporary and sometime antagonist of Issac Newton's—argued that fossil-rich rocks like coal represented the remains of once living creatures. Only with interest spurred by Charles Darwin's publication of *The Origin of Species* nearly two centuries later did people realize he was right. Such rocks are often found in layers termed "carboniferous"—a name that applies to a whole (generally very warm) era in geologic time roughly 300 million years ago.

Smith observed coal seams typically sandwiching layers of sandstone, siltstone, and mudstone, which itself was sandwiched between non-marine fossil bivalve layers. Coal's origin can be traced to colossal Carboniferous era trees, and large amounts of biomass in swampy jungle ecosystems of ferns, clubmosses, horsetails, dragonflies, other huge insects, and amphibians of all sizes. All of this life was eventually drowned with rising sea level, and packed in what geologists today call a marine transgression. Sand and particles of varying sizes were laid down on top of the dead vegetation, becoming heavier, hotter, and applying more pressure as time passed. Eventually—after millions of years— the decaying organic matter had been transformed into coal.

The seasonal flooding of English coal mines—making digging impossible until the water was removed— was a mining problem that pre-dated William Smith. Horses were initially employed to do this lifting job. They were soon replaced by a new, fossil fuel-powered (choice #49) technology: steam engines. Trading horses for pumps driven by steam engines perfected by James Watt, revolutionized coal mining; trading horse-drawn carriages for gasoline-powered internal combustion engine automobiles revolutionized transportation over a century later.

We'll continue this march of technology-driven account of human history in the next two chapters. There we'll jump ahead in (choice #2) global vision fashion to imagine future (choice #49) technological fixes. But now, let's again look back. Back to the transition people made in trading the hunter-gatherer lifestyle for agriculture and domesticated livestock. We consider, to begin with, the archaeological site at Catal Huyuk in southeastern Turkey. It provides a fascinating look at a place and time this transition was occurring. The site, though occupied for nearly 2000 years, flourished around 9000 years ago when perhaps 7,000 people lived there. Besides killing wild game and gathering fruit / nuts from trees, these folks ate wheat, barley, peas, etc. grown from seeds they'd previously planted. They kept flocks of sheep, and were beginning to domesticate cattle. (Horses wouldn't be put to use—nor would the wheel—for another 2500 years or so.)

Archaeological investigation of housing, along with numerous female statues and figurine finds, suggest that the society at Catal Huyuk was one of (choice #6 and choice #27) relative gender and economic equality. Some reputable investigators—notably Marija Gimbutas (1921-1994) — have used evidence found at this site, and others, to conclude that Neolithic western Eurasia was a peaceful, matriarchal society that worshipped a "Mother Goddess." In describing this, Richard Rudgley, in his 1998 book *The Lost Civilizations of the Stone Age*, writes, "The earth was revered as the embodiment of the goddess and death seen as a return to the womb of the earth/goddess."

He goes on to sketch the (choice #17) violent end Gimbutas concluded it suffered. "The holistic ideology of Old Europe was challenged and eventually overrun by the forefathers of the Indo-Europeans …horse-riding warriors armed with lethal weapons, brought into Europe with an ideology based on patriarchy, hierarchy, and military prowess. Their pantheon of gods was male-dominated and headed by a sky god. The Earth Goddess and other female deities were...reduced in status to become merely the wives of the gods."

Alas, in the nearly three decades since Gimbutas' last book, more evidence has led many to challenge her conclusions —although ecofeminists claim some of the challenge is male orchestrated backlash. Certainly, as Cathy Gere puts it[25], "archaeology can easily slip into reflecting what people want to see, rather than teaching people about an unfamiliar past." Sadly many archaeological enthusiasts have fallen into this trap and, to varying extent, left (choice #1) evidence-based scientific methodology behind. (More on these pseudoarchaeologists in chapter 8.)

The many early human archaeological sites found in Europe prior to 1975 led to a "Europe first" chauvinistic view. Namely, many asserted that it was in Europe that our Homo Sapiens species made the first tools indicative of abstract and symbolic thought. And in Europe where, roughly 50,000 years ago, they began (choice #47) creatively expressing themselves / behaving like modern humans. Doing things like burying the dead, decorating their bodies, engaging in artistic activities, showing signs of interest in spiritual matters, etc. But the last forty-five years of discovery and excavation of numerous sites in Africa suggests some of this happened long before Homo Sapiens arrived in Europe. Indeed, recent evidence suggests that anatomically modern humans (AMH) / Homo Sapiens may have been doing some of those things in Africa as far back as 300,000 years ago.[26] And, as artifacts found at one site in Kenya suggest, just a bit later they were engaged in long distance trade, making pigments, and projectile points. Another African site—dating to 100,000 years ago—indicates AMH technology had extended to include mining.

At some point evidence of early human activity begins documenting complex behavior—something meeting (choice #47) psychological, spiritual, and creative expression needs, more than sustenance / physical needs. Why certain artifacts, that suggest advanced cultural evolutionary development, were made may never be known. But, retrieving (from chapter 2) speculation by Jo Marchant with (choice #41) belonging to nature implications, we imagine something important preceded that. As she put it, "humans mentally separated themselves from nature, and it became conceivable to manipulate and dominate the natural world."

Today, we may be hundreds of thousands of years removed from that era, but we're only roughly 10,000 years removed from living very close to nature. And what a contrast exists between modern metropolitan environments—brightly lit, noisy, concrete jungles—and the natural world. Thus, Sigurd Olsen, in an essay[27] "The Spiritual Aspects of Wilderness" written over fifty years ago speculates as follows. "Here perhaps is a clue to our predicament: the world has changed too swiftly for modern man so recently out of the primeval. He still moves to ancient rhythms, and his spiritual needs are the same. Though he is far removed from the past, it is not far enough for him to forget. Still part of his background, the song of the wilderness is clear and strong."

Many of the ancient rhythms he refers to have an astronomical / day / night / Earth / Sun / Moon origin we discussed earlier in this chapter. Many city dwellers, upon escaping urban chaos —even for a weekend— and experiencing the quiet tranquility and celestial sights of remote dark sky locations, are undoubtedly soothed and comforted. With longer stays, some feel drawn into the vastness of the natural world above and around them, and (choice #6 and choice #41) momentarily lose their sense of separateness. As Olsen put it in arguing for preserving wilderness, "What we are trying to conserve is not scenery as much as the human spirit itself...the intangible values of wilderness are what really matter, the opportunity of knowing again what simplicity really means, the importance of the natural and the sense of oneness with the earth that inevitably comes...These are spiritual values."

In experiencing wilderness, people can recapture the feeling of belonging to nature. With this comes humility— totally unlike the arrogance behind using our technology to exploit and dominate nature. Where that attitude leads, Bill McKibben names in the tile of his 1989 book: *The End of Nature*. He hopes we can instead "bow down and humble ourselves."

H. Technology and a Big Beautiful Tomorrow?

A scant twenty-five years before McKibben's grim book, technology seemingly pointed the way to a wonderful future. In 1964, the song "There's a Great Big Beautiful Tomorrow" celebrated Walt Disney's techno-optimism as part of the General Electric sponsored "The Carousel of Progress" exhibit. This opened at the New York World's Fair and later moved to TomorrowLand in Disneyland. One of its verses begins, "Man has a dream and that's the start..."

Choices We Make in the Global Village   page 219

TomorrowLand was but partially completed when I first visited in 1955, but most expected the bigger road ahead for society would be paved with the technological realization of dreams. By the mid-1950s nuclear power enthusiasts were promising electricity "too cheap to meter." At the televised opening of Disneyland, Walt Disney touted TomorrowLand by saying, "Tomorrow offers new frontiers in science, adventure, and ideals. The Atomic Age, the challenge of Outer Space, and the hope for a peaceful, unified world." By the mid-1970s NASA had scored dramatic space exploration successes, and even the Americans and Soviets were peacefully co-existing. But by 1975 many of us were convinced that nuclear was the wrong technology to bet on. Neither did we like what fueled 20th century growth: oil. We liked solar energy—and silicon-based technology seemed a promising way to harness it.

The previous twenty-five years fueled that enthusiasm. We'd seen the realization of someone's dream of replacing big, unreliable, power hungry vacuum tubes with tiny, efficient, cheap solid state electronic components. By 1959 inexpensive transistor radios were everywhere. The next dozen years saw slide rules and bulky unreliable mechanical desktop calculators replaced with hand-held electronic calculators (some eventually priced at $1)— offering proof that someone's dream of putting many electronic components on a single silicon chip to make an integrated circuit (IC) had been realized. By the late 1970s a related solar photovoltaic technology that could produce pollution free electricity for homes seemed poised for explosive growth.

But alas, while the cost of electronic calculators dropped by a factor of 100 in a decade—as did those of ICs—solar panel prices remained high. Why? I suspect the problem was political more than technological. In May, 1975 I'd authored a paper "Nuclear Vs. Solar Energy—An Environmental and Economic Comparison" for a UCLA engineering class. There I quoted from a Jet Propulsion Lab / National Science Foundation November 1974 plan to drop the price of solar power. "The primary goal of this program is to develop by 1985 the technological and industrial capability to produce silicon solar photovoltaic arrays at a rate of more than 500 MW per year and at a cost of less than $0.50 per peak watt." After the election of Ronald Reagan in 1980 this went nowhere.

Since 1975, silicon-based integrated circuit / microchip technology has facilitated dramatic technological advances such as in reading genetic code. In 1976, after ten years work, a Belgium lab succeeded in reading all 3,569 letters of the MS2 (RNA type) virus. To illustrate the stunning advance in (choice #49) medical technology know-how since then, consider what happened forty-four years later. In early 2020 Chinese researchers, after a few weeks of work, published the genome of a virus causing illness in Wuhan. This virus— responsible for the Covid-19 pandemic— has a much larger genome: 29,903 base pairs. In the year that followed, this sequencing has been repeated by labs throughout the world roughly one million times, in a (choice #21) public health / vaccine development effort to find dangerous variants of it.

One can say that the silicon chips which made this possible—along with development of computers, internet, smart phones, electric / self-driving vehicles, etc. — are "the new oil." But only in the last decade have solar photovoltaic panel prices plummeted and production soared—vastly exceeding the long-ago hoped for JPL / NSF goals. Meanwhile, US production of microchips, dropped from essentially 100 % in 1965 to 37% in 1990 to but 12% in 2020, as production shifted to Taiwan (50%), China (24%) and South Korea. Photovoltaic solar panels experienced a similar shift to overseas manufacture, with dramatic cost declines.

While solar is surging, nuclear power is struggling. On January 26, 2021 the American Nuclear Society reported "New York Sues NRC over Indian Point Decommissioning." Indian Point refers to the 2000 MW (megawatts) nuclear power plant twenty-four miles from New York City. The plant was shut down on April 30, 2021. While it never suffered the catastrophic accident that many of us feared, its five decades of operation left behind radioactive contamination in need of expensive cleanup that we predicted. How expensive? The report notes $2.1 billion is now set aside for the first phase of the cleanup—not including the thousands of years baby-sitting to isolate the dangerous mess from human health dangers it will long pose. At current $0.33 per peak watt solar panel prices, $2.1 billion dollars could buy 6.3 billion = 6300 MW of solar.

Sadly, when the state of New York or others wish to purchase solar photovoltaic panels they'll find the few American manufacturers of them don't have competitive prices. As a September 14, 2020 *Bloomberg News* report headlines, "The Solar-Powered Future is Being Assembled in China." This has happened after four years of Trump administration promotion of coal and a continuing little-regulated boom fracking natural gas. This, and global climate change concerns, suggest America has backed the wrong energy technologies and needs to change course.

What does this account of what happened to the promise of a "Great Big Beautiful Tomorrow" say about that promise in coming decades? Certainly the Sun is big and bright—and a future powered by it holds great promise. But it's not clear that humanity can transition to that future fast enough to meet the "existential threat" global climate change poses. And, we ask, "Beautiful for whom?" Many see the growing gap between "haves" and "have nots" as also having reached the crisis level.

Most will agree free market forces were slow to spur the development of cheap solar photovoltaic electricity—the key technology America is looking to if it is to do its share addressing climate concerns. And that those forces are failing to provide widespread affordable housing. Perhaps, as the next chapter will explore, big government needs to step in and (choice #52) implement Environmental Economics measures—not let Big Business operate as usual. Likewise it needs to facilitate (choice #27) egalitarian progressive outcomes and reverse trends in which new homes are getting bigger and more expensive.[28] Some hope one promising technology can help individuals, corporations, and government officials make better choices: artificial intelligence (AI.)

Like nuclear power, promise and peril are associated with this new technology. With the internet—and appliances increasingly connected to it—smart phones, smart homes, self-driving cars and more sophisticated (choice #13) hardware and software for modeling real world problems, humanity has clearly entered the intelligence demonstrated by machines / AI era. Signs that this can guide people to better choices are everywhere —recognition holding great promise. Beyond less (choice #37) privacy, the most concerning peril[29] comes from what's called strong AI—in particular from machines as smart or smarter than humans that are fully conscious like we are. With respect to this last stipulation, the relevant question to ask is: "Is this possible?" The answer is an unknown mystery.

Behind this mystery is our current inability to fully understand human consciousness. Two leading explanations are 1) Global Neuronal Workspace (GNW) by which peculiar architectural features in the human brain give rise to consciousness, and 2) Integrated Information Theory (IIT), by which varying amounts of self awareness / consciousness exist—measured by a variable denoted Φ, which varies from zero to one. With respect to AI, GNW seems to indicate a "Yes" answer to the last paragraph's key question is possible, whereas IIT, according to neuroscientist Christof Koch, suggests[30], AI computers "will remain only super sophisticated machinery, ghost-like empty shells, devoid of what we value most: the feeling of life itself."

In looking to the future, the long-time quest of trying to explain what we don't understand will undoubtedly continue. It seems reasonable to think the future promises science-based explanations of modern day natural world mysteries. It may even bring big revisions in—and additions to— the existing scientific conceptual framework. Recall our account of development of plate tectonics provided an example of this. A recent example of clearing up a long-time mystery involves bird navigation. More specifically, the ability of birds to navigate— in some cases they can return to the same place after flying thousands of miles—has long made one wonder, "How do they do it?"

A key breakthrough in understanding this came in 2018 with the discovery of a particular protein in birds' eyes that helps provide them with an internal compass. It acts as a sort of filter and enables birds to literally see the Earth's magnetic field. We'll save the more recently uncovered quantum biology details for chapter 8—but we can connect this ability of birds to something bigger. Just as the day-night cycle that's such a key part of our lives depends on Earth's spinning on its axis, so too does the magnetic field based navigation that birds employ. "How so?" you wonder. Geophysicists tell us that a planet's magnetic field depends on the movement of molten iron deep inside the planet— something aided by the planet's rotation. This may essentially account for why Earth's nearby sister planet Venus—with nearly the same size and mass as Earth—has no magnetic field. Earth spins on its axis once a day, whereas Venus takes 243 days to do so.

This example—of starting with birds finding their way and ending up talking about the Earth's hot interior and slow-turning Venus—illustrates what John Muir (1838-1914) meant when he said, "When we try to pick out anything by itself, we find it hitched to everything else in the Universe." He said this over a century ago. Since then, both the number of, and our ability to make new connections have steadily increased. But there are undoubtedly all sorts of connections we haven't made, and mysteries remaining for (choice #12) curious minds to unravel.

For example, modern astrophysicists can't get too (choice #3) "know it all" arrogant since academics in competing disciplines can rightly point out the following. If the whole universe is their subject matter, astrophysicists only know something about the 5% of it that is ordinary matter. The remaining vast bulk of it—thought to consist of dark matter and dark energy—remains unknown. And another: New Age enthusiasts ask a question few scientists take seriously, "Is the Earth itself alive?"

Earlier in this chapter, we discussed (choice #9) "What does it mean to say something is alive?" We mentioned homeostasis. This refers to the normal steady state condition of a living organism in which a balanced internal environment is maintained. At both cellular and tissue levels, energy and mass transfers occur, metabolic activities are regulated, and various control mechanisms function. Typically many organ systems work together to maintain internal temperature, pressure, nutrient concentrations, waste products, etc. within normal ranges. When external stresses overwhelm the organism's ability to do this, the result can be malfunction, disease, and—if the damage cannot be repaired and homeostasis restored—death.

From this modern science-based viewpoint, one can argue that Earth maintains homeostasis. Some nonscientists go far beyond this. Many New Age enthusiasts—recalling (choice #9) vitalists—claim Earth is alive and possesses the vital spirit that they associate with living things. The difference in these viewpoints can be illustrated by considering The Gaia Hypothesis. Popularized in the 1970s and early 1980s, it builds on the work of scientists James Lovelock and later Lynn Margulis. And gets its name from the ancient Greek earth goddess. Its scientific conception posits that Earth effectively functions as a single self-regulating entity in maintaining homeostasis with global feedback mechanisms. A New Age vitalistic conception imagines the whole Earth is in some sense alive and possesses unified spiritual essence. (Note: some New Agers embracing (choice #6) an extreme animism think everything is alive!)

Could we effectively make Earth come alive through our technology—alive in a human-provided artificial intelligence sense? This could involve giving humanity a conscience, typically a global environmental one. While environmentally-concerned (choice #36) global citizens may build a whole Earth perspective into their own consciences, (choice #13) systems thinkers and futurists have imagined a collective consciousness / global brain. One, they imagine, that automatically makes individuals aware of planetary well-being and encourages them to factor it into the choices they make. The *Coming of Age...* book provided an example of this (called GAIA.) The worldwide web and smart phones—which didn't exist when I imagined and described this global brain over three decades ago—can be seen as steps in its realization. To those who value (choice #37) privacy, future global brain dreams are the stuff of nightmares.

Besides those idealistically (or naively?) imagining (choice #43) human cultural evolution soaring in this direction, others have more basely (and deceptively?) moved in to profit. A Colorado-based company called Gaia, Inc.— heavily promoting a wide range of fringe alternative nonscientific beliefs, (choice #7) magic, (choice #38) conspiracy theories, etc. —has steadily grown in the three decades since its founding in 1988. By late 2018, reportedly over half a million people had paid subscriptions to its video streaming service. Its content includes some of what we take a (choice #4) skeptical look at in chapter 8. Besides taking "skeptical looks," we'll also take moments there to celebrate mystery.

But first we need to more fully consider the increasing stress that people making a living puts on their planet Earth home. Whereas so many beliefs are faith and (choice #1) wishful thinking based, the economics and environment territory to which we turn to in the next chapter is full of data. Data upon which (choice #13) models of how economies might function better can be based—models from which evidence-based solutions to both livelihood and environmental problems can be found. Science needs to play a key role in these efforts. And in the effort to make tomorrow great, beautiful, and meaningful—not just for a handful of wealthy people in affluent countries, but for everyone worldwide.

Notes

1 Sagan, C. and Druyan, A. *The Demon Haunted World—Science as a Candle in the Dark* Ballantine Books, New York 1996
2 I offer apologies for male gender bias in this book, so typical of the earlier era.
3 Aronowitz, Stanley *Science As Power—Discourse and Ideology in Modern Society* Palgrave MacMillan London 1988
4 For a cute exercise in how difficult it is to describe anything, see an attempt to describe a man named George in the Appendix of Michael Crichton's autobiographical book *Travels* published by Alfred A. Knopf, New York 1988
5 You can watch this on *You Tube*, episode 12 *The Mechanical Universe* series
6 For a nice account of this, see chapter 14 "Kekule: Molecular Architecture from Dreams" in *Serendipity: Accidental Discoveries in Science* by Royston M. Roberts John Wiley, New York 1989
7 see Harvey, C. and Waldman, S. "Climate Skeptics Want More CO_2" posted on scientificamerican.com Oct 17, 2017 for a debunking of this argument.

8 Worland, J. "Texas Blackouts Raise Climate Warning" *Time* March 1 2021

9 The coldest recorded temperature for my town is –21°F 85 years ago.

10 see "The TFJD Oracle: An Oracle for the 21st Century" in *The Worldview Theme Songbook* Parthenon Books 2015 (available from *Project Worldview*)

11 Koestler, writer and journalist, had an amazing life. His 1959 book *The Sleepwalkers* inspired my interest in the history of science. Seems he dabbled in many things I've been interested in. Coincidentally my first destination in Europe was Budapest, where he was born.

12 Kurtz, Paul ed. *Science and Religion –Are They Compatible?* Prometheus Books Amherst, NY 2003

13 Moran, James D. "Creativity in Young Children" *ERIC Digest* 306088 1988

14 Morelle, Rebecca "Near Death Experiences are Electrical Surge in Dying Brain" report from *The BBC News* Aug 12 2013

15 This paragraph is adapted from Cook, Stephen P. "Imagining a Theory of Everything for Complex Adaptive Systems" in *Origin(s) of Design in Nature*, Springer Science Dordrecht 2012

16 in *Origins of Life and Evolution of Biospheres* v 42 #6 Springer Nature 2012

17 Capra, Fritjof. *The Hidden Connections*, Doubleday New York 2002

18 University of Virginia, School of Medicine, Division of Perceptual Studies / Study of Reincarnation

19 Recall end of chapter 4 survey data.

20 see "A Private Universe" film from Pyramid Film and Video

21 see Falk, Seb *The Light Ages—The Surprising Story of Medieval Science* Norton, New York 2020

22 The daily McDonald Observatory program *Stardate* (carried by most *NPR* stations) often helpfully points out such proximity.

23 the band of twelve constellations the Sun appears to move through as Earth moves around the Sun

24 Brian Swimme (1950-) writer, professor at California Institute of Integral Studies in San Francisco, founder of Center for the Story of the Universe

25 Gere, Cathy *Knossos and the Prophets of Modernism* University of Chicago Press 2009

26 Gibbons, A "World's Oldest Homo Sapiens fossils found..." in *Science* June 7 2017

27 in Schwarz, William ed. *Voices for the Wilderness* Ballantine Books New York 1969

28 USA median home price in November 1974 was $30,953—or $156,551 in 2021 dollars. By December 2020 that price was $300,987 roughly twice the cost in inflation-adjusted dollars (from data at dqydj.com)

29 science fiction fans can enjoyably ponder both the promise and perils of strong artificial intelligence in reading Douglas Preston's novel *The Kraken Project* Forge Books, New York 2014

30 Koch, Christof "Consciousness: Proust Among the Machines" *Scientific American* December 2019 pp. 46-49

Chapter 6: Economics, Ecology, Ecosharing
A. Introduction

I turned seven years old in May 1958. Whether behavior I was exhibiting should be termed "oppositional defiance" or skepticism wasn't clear. At the dinner table I ignored my mother's plea, "Steve, eat your vegetables. People are starving in China." At Sunday school, I rejected the notion that God knew everything, even of the fall of a tiny sparrow.

"1958, wasting food, China, and falling sparrows? How can you justify beginning a chapter titled 'Economics, Ecology, Ecosharing' like this?" you ask. Answer: In 1958 the Chinese Communist Party launched its 'Great Leap Forward''—which turned out to be a disaster, especially for food production and birds. But it set the stage for more to come.

The words economics, ecology, and ecosharing have the same root: the Greek word oikos from "eco" meaning home or household. We get "economics" by adding "nomos" — referring to law or custom. And speculate that economics originally meant following traditional customs—which had the force of law—to insure one's household functioned smoothly. While the scope of economics broadened from households, to extended families, to tribes, to city-states, to nations, and eventually to the entire world, we note its literal meaning connection to one of our choice #31 themes: Valuing Traditions / Status Quo.

So we aren't surprised that tradition headed economic historian Robert Heilbroner's (1919-2005) list of three arrangements that have worked in the long history of protecting society against calamitous breakdown. And we find what he lists second—religion—as too closely related to tradition and custom to inspire our interest. Rather in this chapter we'll dwell on the third arrangement Heilbroner identifies—what he referred to as "the astonishing game" known as the market system.

Only recently have I warmed to the "astonishing game" tag Heilbroner put on capitalism. Games should be fun. Yes, I've lived most of my life a step ahead of the "life and death struggle" / stress that billions of people experience given economic realities, but my participation has necessarily been based on luck and frugality. But now, no longer needing to make super-efficient use of available funds given their adequacy, I realize I no longer need to play this "game" the same way. But I mostly do anyways. Seems behaving differently doesn't feel right, and it's no fun throwing money at buying things neither I, nor the planet need, or paying someone else to do a job I could do myself. What is fun? The challenge of making money-related choices consistent with what I've long valued—especially (choice #45) Enoughness, and (choice #41) Respect for Nature. And living in a way that promotes (choice #21) health and good relationships with others. And in (choice #32) giving money or time to worthy causes.

As described in chapter 4, Greg Mortenson recognized building relationships was as important as building projects. Likewise these were an important part of Chinese sage Confucius' (551-479 BCE) teaching / (choice #33) ethical system / agnostic practical philosophy. Its key teachings include: 1) ultimately the happiness of society rests on (choice #12) sincere investigation that produces relevant knowledge; 2) happy societies are built on a foundation of (choice #22 and choice #25) disciplined individuals in disciplined families; 3) respect for and fidelity to natural obligations, most notably to parents and family, is essential; 4) the right relationship between individuals is important, one based on (choice #18) sympathetic "fellow feeling," treating those subordinate to you as you would like to be treated if you were the subordinate–ideas which provide the basis for a Confucian Golden Rule; and 5) avoiding extremes and embracing moderation, and finding a Golden Mean

Confucius said nothing about God, so in that sense his philosophy can be termed (choice #8) "humanistic." With respect to the (choice #27) Hierarchical Rigidity associated with traditional power structures, Confucius said, "In teaching, there should be no distinction of classes." Out of this grew a system of meritocracy in China, where people had to prove themselves worthy of holding certain positions by passing examinations. While the respect for authority, atheistic and classless aspects of Confucianism appealed to Chinese Communist Party leaders, much of the rest of this tradition presented challenges—one being extending family loyalty to Party loyalty.[1]

Against this traditional backdrop, many of the (choice #31) Working for Change efforts Party leaders had made in the ten years following their taking power in 1949 were radical. Their (choice #38) socialism brought the abolition of private property. Rural households were forced to join state-run agricultural communes, and private farming was prohibited. An economic and social campaign launched with great promise, the Great Leap Forward of 1958-1962 was a step backwards. Its policies led to a shrinking economy, and to the Great Chinese Famine—with an estimated 15 to 55 million Chinese dying of starvation between 1959-1961.

China's economy boomed only after its tight central economic planning loosened. Beginning in 1978 under Deng Xiaoping's[2] leadership, reforms were instituted that increasingly tied China's economy to market system, private ownership, and capitalist economies. And perhaps Chinese Communist Party leaders became determined to avoid the fate of the socialist, centrally-planned economy of the Soviet Union, which collapsed in 1991. Whatever lessons they learned, the economic results have been spectacular. China's economic growth lifted hundreds of millions of people out of poverty. For the period spanning 1989-2020, China's economy grew at a staggering rate of 9.21 % / year[3].

But China made big environmental mistakes. These began with an embarrassing basic ecology failure of the Great Leap Forward, known as the Four Pests campaign. In an effort to increase rice production, rats, flies, mosquitoes and sparrows were to be eliminated. The government claimed "birds are the public animals of capitalism," and that sparrows in particular each ate four pounds of grain per year. They organized millions of people to exterminate them.[4] People with basic knowledge of ecology might have predicted what happened as a result. Without sparrows to eat them, insects destroyed crops. The Great Chinese Famine can be partly traced to failure to understand how ecosystems work.

Ecology is a branch of biology involving the study of living things, their interrelationship with each other and the environment. Ecosystems are self-sustaining, interacting natural communities of animals, plants, and their physical environment. While matter cycles through such systems, energy moves in one-way (linear) fashion through the associated food chain. This latter process begins with plants capturing solar energy, and ends with decomposers—the long unknown and then unappreciated microorganisms—eating remains of everything. By that time, all of the energy that initially flowed into the system will have flowed back out as waste heat. The former process involves plants being eaten by animals (herbivores and omnivores), which in turn are eaten by other animals (carnivores and omnivores.). Each living component has a continuing, dynamic relationship with the others. If numbers of species A fall, numbers of species B, which preys upon A, will similarly fall. With less predation of A its numbers begin climbing, and likewise numbers of species B will grow as well.

Decades later, the Chinese sparrow population has recovered. But it's unclear whether planet Earth will similarly recover from China's turn toward market-based capitalism, and the environmental effects of the global 1990-2020 economic boom that it led. But...Hey—we can't blame them—they just sought the prosperity those of us in rich countries have had, right? And followed a similar path to get there. Before turning to environmentally-concerning data behind this boom, let's review the history of an earlier capitalist-led economic expansion.

Chapter 3 in Robert Heilbroner's 1972 book *The Worldly Philosophers* is titled "The Wonderful World of Adam Smith." Many date the beginning of (choice #34) capitalist economics from the 1776 publication of Smith's *The Wealth of Nations*. The book appeared as the Industrial Revolution, discussed in the previous chapter, was underway in the British Isles. As Heilbroner describes, Adam Smith wasn't worried about something which troubles economists today: the rich getting richer as their capital accumulates, but the poor failing to benefit as that increasing wealth is hoarded. Not shared, not reinvested in manufacturing to make more profits, and pay more workers' wages. Smith wasn't worried. He had abiding faith that, rather than accumulating, capital would be used to buy more and more machines. And this would multiply human productive energy to the benefit of the common good.

Imagining machines spurring human productivity is nothing new. Human history is one of (choice #49) technological fixes steadily bringing nature under its control, and increasing human comfort. Human technology began with using stones and bones as tools, using pieces of wood as levers, using them in constructing shelter and in harnessing fire. Later, agriculture began, animals were put to work, and smelting metal was mastered—producing stronger tools, water and wind-driven mills, etc.

But until the coal-powered Industrial Revolution, technology had been renewable (ultimately solar) energy powered. As such, human environmental impact (choice #40, choice #41, choice #44, choice #45) was limited. (Choice #48) ecological debts were minimal. But massively utilizing fossil fuel—essentially drawing on solar energy captured by countless plants that lived long ago, died and accumulated for millions of years—changed that. Limits were removed; debts were incurred.

Today, all of the carbon dioxide released from fossil fuel combustion associated with generating electricity, heating buildings, powering transportation, growing food, etc. is causing big problems. Seemingly, nature is fighting back. Fortunately, more nature-friendly technological fixes have been developed. They include using the sun to make electricity via photovoltaic conversion, using the wind to turn electrical generators, powering cars with batteries charged by electricity produced in this fashion, etc. Many feel implementing them fast enough to stave off unacceptable climate change depends on (choice #22) exercising self-restraint, and weaning humanity off its fossil fuel addiction.

If fossil fuel use ceases late in the 21st century, the 300-year fossil fuel era could eventually represent a tiny blip in human history. Its energy use transition to it, and then abandonment, could be largely forgotten—except to remember a significant milestone. Fossil fuel use didn't end because supplies ran out. It ended because humanity agreed (choice #52) that depending on it was too dangerous, too threatening to its prospects for a (choice #44) sustainable long-term future. And it wisely chose to keep remaining fossil fuel reserves in the ground—in a perhaps significant / "childhood's end" / coming of age milestone. (Chapter 7 will make the case for this and discuss needed technological fixes.)

About the time (February 1972) Heilbroner was writing a new preface for the fourth edition of his book, another book, *The Limits to Growth*[5] was exploding onto the scene. Roughly seven million copies of it were sold. Simply put, it argued that continued long-term pursuit of (choice #44) economic growth in a (choice #52) big business as usual manner, would lead to catastrophic collapse of human society. This was what the Club of Rome backed MIT team's (choice #13) computer models forecast. A member of that team, and one of the book's authors, Donella ("Dana") Meadows, inspired and contributed to my 1990 book *Coming of Age in the Global Village*.

In that book, I offered what can be seen as a common sense guided, ethically inspired prescription for living. Later (in section C) I'll connect this effort with the "Steve, eat your vegetables" of my childhood. And with working to revamp capitalism related lessons we all should learn as we grow up. For now, I'll simply identify that book's prescription as ecosharing—where the "eco" refers to home as in our planetary home. And note the "sharing" comes from a key component of how global citizens ideally might behave. Recall these are folks who've received a global education, and value "People, Planet, Prosperity."

From a global humanitarian (choice #51) perspective, one can argue we need more individuals earning a livelihood by doing things that promote the common good. A list of such activities would include being primary producers of what meets basic human needs—like growing food or building affordable housing—and working as recycling or ecosystem services maintenance specialists, educators, health or social workers, etc. And conclude we need fewer people in (choice #33) greedy pursuit of wealth. Others say not so fast. To convince them, we turn to evidence suggesting market-based capitalism needs a makeover.

B. The Market System in Crisis

19th century German economist and social revolutionary thinker Karl Marx felt that (choice #34) capitalism was inherently unstable. He argued that it would be socially impossible for governments in such societies to right wrongs, for that would require the (choice #27 and choice #33) powerful upper class to act in something other than its own economic self-interest. As a result he felt that capital would accumulate and wealth become concentrated in fewer and fewer hands. Viewing this as a dangerously unstable, intolerable situation, he predicted apocalyptic collapse of the capitalist system. Replacing it, he said, would be a (choice #38) classless socialist society, with production centralized in the machinery of the state. Some initially considered the early Soviet Union (established in 1917 with the overthrow of the Russian Tsar) as the fulfillment of what Marx predicted, and as a test of his ideas.

Modern economic history suggests that Marx failed to appreciate the social adaptability of capitalism. One example: Western economies moving away from pure capitalism and toward (choice #35) social welfare states in building (choice #27) social justice into their systems. But its critics—notably French economist Thomas Piketty in his 2014 book *Capital in the Twenty-First Century*—argue "there is no natural, spontaneous process to prevent destabilizing, inegalitarian forces from prevailing permanently."

In America, critics of capitalism note the supposed panacea of (choice #44) economic growth as "rising tide that lifts all boats" has not worked. Yachts have cruised; dinghies have sunk. The gap between "haves" and "have nots" has widened. One measure of such inequality is the ratio of (choice #35) corporate CEO pay to that of the average worker pay. Based on the Institute for Policy Studies[6] data, this is steadily increasing. In 1990 it was 100 to 1, in 2005 it was 411 to 1, and in 2019 it was 1586 to 1. Thus in 2019 a typical worker at one of the top fifty (in terms of pay gaps) publicly traded American companies would have to work over

1500 years to earn what the company's CEO earned in one year. Average annual CEO pay at these firms was $15.9 million, whereas that same year median worker pay was $10,027. By the end of 2020, in this land of colossal wealth, roughly one in eight families were experiencing food insecurity: suffering chronic hunger, depending on food from government and private programs, etc.[7] And efforts to raise the minimum wage to a more livable $15 / hour had stalled.

Even if the American economic system is failing to share the wealth, can the market system be universally indicted for a similar global failure? At first glance, the combating global poverty data does not similarly fault the market system, rather it shows great progress in the last three decades. World Bank figures suggest the percentage of (now nearly eight billion humans occupying our planet) living in extreme poverty (on less than the equivalent of $1.90 per day) fell from 36% in 1990 to but 8% as 2020 began. But closer examination shows that a significant portion of this can be attributed to China's extraordinary success at growing its economy in the last three decades at an average of 9.21% / year.

And inequality is growing. According to investment bank Credit Suisse, the fraction of global household wealth controlled by the richest 1% of humanity grew from 42.5% in 2008 to 47.2% in 2018. Likewise Oxfam[8] estimated that, whereas in 2010 388 billionaires held as much wealth as the bottom half of humanity, by 2019 that wealth was concentrated in just twenty-six very rich individuals. They held as much wealth as the world's poorest half—nearly four billion people. Thomas Piketty's pointing to a flaw in capitalism that promotes inequality must be taken seriously in light of such data. So too must something a multinational corporate leader said, given recent global climate concerns.

In looking back on the 1991 unraveling of the Soviet Union, former Exxon executive Oystein Dahle said, (choice #38) "Socialism collapsed because it did not allow the market to tell the economic truth." And in looking ahead he suggested (choice #34), "Capitalism may collapse because it does not allow the market to tell the ecological truth." Along with what Marx pointed to, and Adam Smith didn't worry about, behind capitalism are four big problematic (choice #52) environment and quality of life related economic realities.

First, unlike (choice #38) pure socialist / communist systems, capitalism is built on private property. Fans of this say that's not the problem, rather the problem arises with what is <u>not</u> owned by anyone. It's been given a name: the tragedy of the commons. This term, popularized by Garrett Hardin in a 1968 article[9], refers to users of a common resource—like air, the oceans, grazing land, etc. —selfishly polluting, overusing it, and degrading its capability to serve the common good. As Hardin saw it, since no one owns the common resource, no one feels a corresponding responsibility to protect it. And even if nearly all could be persuaded to exercise (choice #22) restraint and (choice #15) good stewardship, a small number of exploiters could ruin the commons for everyone else.

Second, modern economics focuses on capital and ignores what has been called natural capital. Capital refers to accumulated goods and resources (or their value) devoted to the production of other goods, or set aside to produce income. Capital can take the form of money, raw materials, buildings, equipment, inventories, etc. Natural capital, in contrast, refers to natural resources (air, water, soil, forests, minerals, fossil fuels, fish, etc,) the biodiversity of natural living ecosystems (grasslands, wetlands, ocean coral reefs, etc,) and ecosystem services. In quantitatively valuing products and services, conventional economics ignores what nature provides. For example, wetlands provide the ecosystem service of natural water regulation—something with flood control and other values. Economists don't quantitatively recognize this in land use planning.

Third, in trying to gauge economic well-being, use of the gross domestic product (GDP) indicator is inappropriate. This refers to the annual market value of a country's total domestic economic output, including all end goods and services purchased. Based on 2019 World Bank figures, total global GDP is around $87.6 trillion—led by the USA at $21.4 trillion and China with $14.3 trillion. GDP accounting not only fails to rightly appreciate many signs of health and well-being, it wrongly counts what is bad as if it were good.

In summarizing the problem, Paul Hawken[10] writes, "…Economists count most industrial, environmental and social waste as GDP…all expenditures regardless of whether society benefits or loses. This includes the cost of emergency room services, prisons, toxic cleanups, homeless shelters, lawsuits, cancer treatments, divorces, and every piece of liter…Instead of counting decay as economic growth, we need to subtract decline from revenue to see if we are getting ahead or falling behind." Critics have labeled GDP as the "grossly distorted picture index." Proposed alternatives include the human development index, the genuine progress indicator, and the happy planet index.

Fourth, consider what market prices typically don't include: social and environment costs. For example, suppose you see two pairs of jeans that look identical, but one is priced at $25 and the other $35. As fashion industry author Elizabeth Cline describes it[11], "The apparel industry churns out about 5 billion pairs of jeans each year in a resource-intensive process; making a single pair requires at least 800 gallons of water and is responsible for the release of 20 kilograms of CO_2 equivalents...Add to that about a third of a cup of chemicals to achieve the colors and distressed look consumers have come to expect. " And that much clothing is made in third-world sweatshops paying near starvation wages.

Suppose the lower-priced jeans in our example are produced in this unethical, wasteful way, whereas the others are produced in a more sustainable manner in a factory paying living wages. Given environmental and social costs not paid by the corporation making them, its cheaper priced products offer both incentive for (choice #46) consumer purchase and additional profit for producers. Those costs are paid by everyone— as resources are depleted, pollution mounts, social tensions rise—and society moves closer to catastrophic collapse. Later in this chapter we'll describe how this problem can be fixed, but this is a market mechanism tweak. What of big picture evidence of the market's failure to tell the ecological truth?

Do bad global environmental consequences data suggest humanity must escape the fantasy land in which all economic growth is good and must continue? Yes. Recall China's extraordinary climb out of poverty. Remember its 1990-2020 economic growth, and those hopeful signs in the global battle against extreme poverty? This economic progress came at a high environmental cost. One global environment indicator trend during this period suggests a coming environmental train wreck, falling off a cliff, apocalypse or however you care to refer to it. Simply put, the world's fossil fuel energy use—and related emission of carbon dioxide pollution as a byproduct—grew dangerously during this period.

According to Carbon Budget Project figures and Institute for European Environmental Policy (ieep.eu) provided graph (Figure #21), human activity has put roughly 1600 gigatons of carbon dioxide (= 440 gigatons of carbon) in the atmosphere since the industrial revolution started roughly 270 years ago. What's startling? **Over half of that has been emitted in the last thirty years**. This colossal greenhouse gas emission suggests no one was calling for curtailing fossil fuel use back in 1990, when in fact a great many were. (Note one gigaton = one billion tons.)

As the graph of annual global carbon dioxide emissions shows, more carbon dioxide was emitted in those 30 years than in all the rest of human industrial era history. Given current environmental impacts (see chapter 7 for a summary) if the trend this graph shows continues—the Business as Usual theme in choice #52— the scientific consensus is that future climate disaster looms.

Figure #21

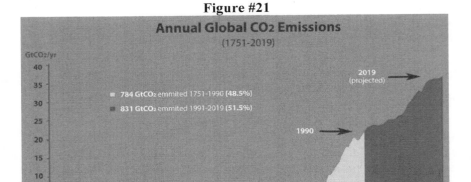

C. Rebuilding An Economy Based on Simple Lessons

In chapter two, a list of lessons from kindergarten ended with, "Play fair," "Share everything," and "Clean up your own mess." To that I add four related observations: 1) parents of young children provide dinner table instruction about the importance of not wasting food; 2) parents reckon children, old enough to do household chores in exchange for a weekly allowance, are ready to learn the importance of money, connect it with work, and that you don't get something for nothing; 3) college students learn how to budget, not waste, both time and money; 4) young people similarly learn to budget money and some financial literacy basics. One such basic: in the long run, you can't spend more money than you earn –or money out can't exceed money coming in.

Perhaps I'm simple-minded, but I took all of the above to heart. By the time I was twenty-four, I'd seen enough of the urban rat race to want to escape it. I began to imagine a simpler life—and began thinking of what it would be based on. I soon learned others had both traveled and reported on this path. In particular I discovered the 1954 book by Helen and Scott Nearing, *Living the Good Life*. Subtitled "How to Live Sanely and Simply in a Troubled World," the book's second paragraph begins, "During the deepest part of the Great Depression in 1932, we moved from New York City to a farm in the Green Mountains."

People today continue to follow in the Nearings' footsteps—Elizabeth Thames even ended up in Vermont. As the cover jacket to her 2018 book *Meet the Frugalwoods* describes, she and husband Nate "abandoned a successful career in the city and embraced extreme frugality in order to create a more purpose-driven life and retire to a homestead in the woods at age thirty-two." She writes, "frugality isn't about what you're giving up, but about what you stand to gain through the freedom of a financially secure lifestyle." Helen and Scott Nearing said, "We came to regard our valley in Vermont as a laboratory in which we were testing out certain principles and procedures of more general application and concern." They were thirty-two and fifty years old when they made their move.

I bought twenty-two acres in the Arkansas Ozarks at age twenty-five, intent on following in their footsteps. I called what I was working out ecosharing. My 1990 *Coming of Age...* book reported what I'd learned, and placed it in a global education context others could learn from. It presented thirteen "Ecosharing Objectives" in three groups: 1) six "sharing objectives," 2) three "efficiency objectives," and 3) four "responsible decision-making" objectives. These fleshed out the details of an (choice #45) enoughness-based, environmental, respect for nature (choice #33, choice #40, choice #41) ethic to live by: your impact on Earth's biosphere should be limited to no more than your fair ecoshare.

It described how "an ecoshare" was to be determined: by assessment of human impact on the biosphere, (choice #13) computer models of its condition, and necessary limits imposed by (choice #44) sustainability criteria. And sought to quantify it in terms of average world per capita income, energy use, and other indicators. Of course it did this without those choice #s, which this book uses. But it did outline "An Ecosharing Co-operate / Defect Choice," cited the role of individuals "choosing between yes and no," and said "human history is the aggregate of quadrillions of individual 'yeses' and 'nos.'" It envisioned a future built around (choice #34) co-operation rather than competition.

It's been just over thirty years since the publication of the *Coming of Age*...book. With thirty years of history bolstering its global environmental crisis based case—and growing disparity between rich and poor—I can argue the need for humanity making good choices is more urgent than ever. I'll have more big picture and economic simple lessons related comments shortly, but first I offer some small picture ones. I mean small as in my lifestyle and financial choices.

With respect to my current lifestyle, I've just finished quantitatively checking its compliance with the Ecosharing Objectives. The results appear in the Appendix C, along with notes on my carbon footprint analysis. With respect to my entire adult life working for wages, I've added up the $ value for all wages I received for the last fifty-three years. In current (year earned) dollar amounts, the total is $665,846. Dividing by fifty-three years, my working wages income has averaged $12,563 per year. (For comparison, the average median value of US single family homes was $120,000 during that period, from dqydj.com.) Looking at that pitifully low income figure—and realizing some of this money was needed to help put two children through expensive colleges[12]—one might conclude that I've struggled and am still struggling to get by.

In fact, I've prospered—and not because I've benefited from inheritance, lucky stock market investments, etc. I've made my own way. Valuing the (alternative hedonism) freedom that having time brings—and given my frugal lifestyle— I retired from the work force after turning fifty-two. Since then, except for one year when I took a job to help my new wife recover from divorce-related legal expenses, I have not worked full-time for wages. My only such part-time work has been for short stretches during five of those last eighteen years, at jobs I enjoyed doing / was glad to help out with. Currently, I live comfortably on roughly 36% of my retirement account / investment income, and save or give away the rest. I have no debts. My net worth is nearly $ one million. My biggest financial problem is, "What shall I do with the social security income I'm about to start receiving upon turning seventy-years old?"

Skeptics might look at my total of $665,846 earned for a lifetime of work and say there's no way—without gifts or improbable windfalls—this guy's net worth is what he claims. In fact, two things are missing from my reported income: 1) the value of my own labor in "sweat equity" in building homes I've lived in, my do-it-yourself work, etc, and 2) interest income from savings / bond's earnings: Since mid-2003 when I retired from the full-time work force, this has totally roughly $350,000.

This last figure comes from a lifetime of budgeting and abiding by two principles: (choice #48) The Pay as You Go Approach and (choice #45) Enoughness. The lessons they embody are basically 1) don't get on the wrong side of debt: you want to be earning interest on your investments and savings—not paying interest charges on debt, 2) don't buy things you don't need, [13] and 3) inspired by *Three Cups of Tea* and Confucius' wisdom, maintain the right relationship with people. One unexpected benefit of helping people: they've given me things they didn't want that I've put to good use—thus eliminating the need to buy it.

Many dreams of financial independence begin with lessons in financial literacy. According to the *National Endowment for Financial Education*, this is "the ability to read, analyze, manage, and communicate about the personal financial conditions that affect material well-being. Financial literacy includes the ability to discern financial choices, discuss money and financial issues without (or despite) discomfort, plan for the future, and respond competently to life events that affect everyday financial decisions, including events in the general economy." Financial literacy workshops often start with discussion of "analyze, manage" with budgeting, and caution not to live beyond your means.

The American economy depends on people ignoring this advice. Helped in this regard by corporate advertising "pushers," they have become "prisoners" of (choice #46) consumerism. The "Pushers and Prisoners" chapter in the *Coming of Age...* book is every bit as relevant today as it was thirty years ago. Total USA advertising expenditures have grown from $133 billion in 1990 ($530 per person per year), to $243 billion in 2020 ($735 per person per year.)[14] With all these voices saying (choice #3) "I Know What's Best for You," many Americans have lost sight of who they are, and what they want. As Elizabeth Thames puts it, "It was only after I stopped buying that I actually appreciated my own unique character, me on my own, divorced from the trappings of consumerism."

During pre-Christmas-time in America, both poor, spending money they don't have, and more affluent supposedly financially sophisticated individuals, become "shop 'til you drop" super consumers. Many in the latter group seemingly have brains hard-wired with both (choice #48) a Borrowing Mentality and a (choice #45) More is Better Mentality. They value their increasing ability to borrow money—in economic terms the leverage they possess and assets they can control—and their steadily increasing debt, as status symbols. Given that such folks often become leaders of economic institutions—and are heavily tapped to staff government administrations—national governments typically run large budget deficits. And measure success by economic growth based on % GDP change / year.

Someone who promotes alternatives for managing household finances is viewed as a nonconformist. So is someone who values a (choice #48) Work, Play, Pay As You Go approach and (choice #45) Enoughness — meaning you live within your means, refuse to be held hostage by obligation to pay off freedom-crushing debt, and recognize you don't need increasingly more of everything / status symbols to be happy. If he or she also values (choice #40) Limits and Ethics and (choice #41) Respect for Nature—alternatives to saying / buying / doing whatever you damn well please with your mouth / money / property / screwing the environment—other descriptions may be used to describe you: radical environmentalist, dangerous threat to our free enterprise system, etc.

In fact, such behavior is conservative and based on simple lessons: enjoy what you have and share it; don't lust over something else; clean up your messes. Taking to heart such advice has great potential (choice #31) to change the world, and give all the world's children a better future. From a (choice #2) Mind Open, Vision Global perspective, a living simply as a responsible global citizen orientation can be truly revolutionary.

Revolutionary as in everyone does what they were taught in kindergarten —to tell the truth—not one in which all of us live with the consequences of a few problem children's (choice #43) Spreading Disinformation / Tactical Deception. Revolutionary as in not an (choice #30) elitist world in which (choice #33) "Those Who Have the Gold Make the Rules," but one where sharing is valued, an uplifting world of "The People—Yes!" Revolutionary in that hard work and continuing education are rewarded. Revolutionary as in working to close the (choice #27) huge gap between the few rich and many poor—and eliminate the dangerous explosive potential that carries for chaotic instability. Revolutionary as in not creating superfund toxic waste sites needing cleanup since (choice #48) ecological debts are not incurred.

In a world where (choice #18) a Culture of Fear promoted by a powerful few sowing division to further their own agenda no longer reigns powerful, a Golden Rule-based revolution might sweep away the guns of the old order. This could usher in a (choice #36) global village feeling of connectedness and "we're all in this together." We can continue this idealistic imagining with contrasting the world we have, with the one we want. Consider this in terms of men and women. As Ervin Laszlo, in his 1989 book *The Inner Limits of Mankind*, sees it, "Our patriarchal society in which an unhealthy imbalance towards masculine qualities is enshrined has led our civilization to exhibit 'manly qualities' such as war, aggression and greed, that...we can correct [with] much needed feminine qualities of gentleness, care, and service."

We might bring other worthy themes into this discussion, such as (choice #23) Human Rights, (choice #24) Culture of Tolerance, (choice #27) egalitarian progressive, (choice #44) Sustainability, (choice #51) Ethical Globalization, and (choice #52) Environmental Economics. And—like John Lennon— imagine a world without the most dangerous excesses of religion: themes like (choice #8) Religious Fundamentalism, (choice #13) Simply In God's Hands: Apocalypticism, and (choice #16) Salvation and Moralistic God.

Alas, we live in a real world of imperfect human beings. In some places (choice #29) authoritarian regimes, or (choice #47) extreme poverty, limit choices. My experience has been in areas where relatively affluent participants— largely free to choose (Milton Friedman's phrase) — have driven human society. Since I wrote the earlier book, experience suggests revising my assessment of change that's realistically achievable.

For example, my involvement with a local co-housing community has dampened enthusiasm I once felt for the (choice #34) Liking Co-operation Based Communities theme—although I've certainly met good people and witnessed people co-operating triumphs. But I've also seen personality / issue conflicts and depressingly long, tedious procedures needed to get relatively simple things done. And I've developed a grudging new respect for the market system—especially its built-in feedback loop and the "wisdom" associated with its operation. But along with this I recognize the absolute necessity for government regulators to occasionally step in and break up monopolies and promote competition. In simple lessons terms, they represent the adults in the room telling those who want all the marbles to share with others, and play fair.

The four themes covered by choices #34 and #35 can be distinguished in competition vs. co-operation terms—recognizing there is value in both of these. Ideally, more competition means more choices for consumers and lower prices. The extreme expression of this—The Competitive Capitalism theme of individuals and small businesses—can also be associated with entrepreneurs' innovation and pursuit of dreams. And valuing co-operation can mean valuing the common good—with Social Welfare Statism its extreme expression—and discouraging greedy individual impulses. But co-operation can be bad if one-time competitors join forces in becoming bigger corporations, or engage in price-fixing. Either way, the resulting monopolies or interference with prices set by supply and demand factors, typically lead to concentrating wealth and increasing inequality. Suffice it to say that a revamped capitalism will value all four of the choices #34 and #35 themes. All should have a role in building the much-needed sustainable and ethical global economy.

(Choice #18) fear is also behind my decreased hostility toward the (choice #35) corporate sector. Sadly, here in supposedly democracy-loving America, I now fear (choice #29) authoritarian forces and those (choice #43) Spreading Disinformation / Tactical Deception. My (again naïve and too idealistic?) self even imagines more progressive CEOs as allies in some political battles, perhaps even in pushing for revamping capitalism. Yet I continue to think that starting from simple lessons is a good way to reach people. Pushing for common sense government policies should make the "communicating to the general public" job of political activists (choice #31) working for change easier, right?

For example, it seems a "no brainer" that we don't want governments subsidizing what is not good for people and our planet—such as smoking cigarettes or fossil fuel. And we do want them taxing certain behaviors / products we want to discourage—making them so expensive that people have an economic incentive to stop or find an alternative product. Accordingly we should steeply ramp up taxes on packs of cigarettes, and put a steadily increasing tax on carbon.   Massive (choice #29) educational campaigns should precede doing this.

And there's a connection here: ignorant people who get hooked on tobacco at a young age are unlikely to value reining in pollution associated with burning fossil fuel—since they are polluting their own bodies / cutting short their own lives with their (choice #22) smoking addiction. Education can help them appreciate illogical behavior. In that regard I've met a few crusaders for climate action who smoke cigarettes. Sadly, these people —working to end humanity's fossil fuel addiction and associated planet threatening pollution—are unable to personally end polluting their own bodies with their nicotine habit.

Besides (choice #31) working as activists, individuals have power in at least three other ways. First, they have the "power of the pocket book." That is, they should not buy products, or give business to companies, they don't approve of. They can magnify that power by telling friends of their (choice #46) consumer choices, and by letting affected companies know exactly why they aren't buying. (If they wish to cross the line into political activism, they can organize boycotts.) Second, they can support non-profit organizations or causes they believe in—either with (choice #32) financial contributions or volunteer work. Third, they can model the product choices / lifestyle behaviors, etc they wish other people would adopt. What follows are examples of my political activist and simple living adventures. (The *Coming of Age...*book and *Updates* have more.)

D. Stories of Making a Livelihood /Working for Change

As you might expect over a seventy-year lifetime, I've interacted with my share of famous people. One of these was Bill Clinton. Soon after my 1977 move to Arkansas, the local Democratic Party County Chairman told me that many people expected great things from the state's attorney general. He fully expected Clinton to someday be US President. During young, idealistic Bill's first (1979-1981) term as Governor, and later, Annie and I encountered him on a few occasions.

Bill especially got attention from women. I remember coming back from a meeting in Little Rock between Bill's "whiz kid" staffers in the new Arkansas Energy Department and us anti-nuclear activists. Bill had unexpectedly made an appearance—and the four women (including Annie) I was traveling with kept talking about Bill's good looks and blue eyes. Sometime after this, Annie gave me a verbal "honey do" list of jobs needing my attention. After completing one tough task I joked about compensation saying, "I'll send you a bill!" Whereupon she turned to me, batted her eyelashes, and said, "Can I have Governor Bill?"[15]

During this time my environmental activist adventures included chatting with (best selling baby book author and political activist) Dr. Benjamin Spock at a small dinner gathering, and a phone conversation with (Washington University professor, author, and Citizens Party presidential candidate) Dr. Barry Commoner. During our talk, he'd tentatively agreed to be the keynote speaker at a statewide event I was helping organize. (He latter cancelled). I recall telling him how his 1971 book *The Closing Circle* broadened my thinking about environmental problems.

Fast forward to the January 2021 issue of *Sierra* (the Sierra Club magazine,) and an article by Elizabeth L. Cline titled, "Will the Circular Economy Save the Planet?" There she credits economist Kenneth Boulding with first advancing "the idea of a modern society built around nature's circular systems" in a 1966 essay.[16] Yes, but I'd say it was Commoner's book that brought widespread attention to this idea—that "industrial activities most like natural processes [with] matter recycling in closed systems should be promoted" to borrow words from the (choice #52) Environmental Economics theme.

In the fifty years since Commoner's book was published, the wasteful, throw away, what can be called linear economy has moved forward— little affected by environmentalists' outcries. As Cline describes it, "Our entire economy is built on an inefficient and dangerous system of resource extraction. In 2017, the world passed a grim new annual record of 110 billion tons of resources consumed—from gravel and cement to fossil fuels, metal ores, and timber—an 8 percent increase from just two years before. According to the consultancy Circle Economy, a scant 8.6% of materials used are reused."

My own last fifty years has been characterized by activity unusual for (choice #46) American consumers. I've fought being brainwashed with the (choice #45) More is Better Mentality, and embraced Enoughness. Again to borrow words from a theme description, "I like the 5 R's: reusing, repairing, recycling, refusing to buy what I don't need, and reducing waste..." Thus I have never bought a new car—typically managing with small, used good gas mileage vehicles. While significant resources are extracted and go into building a typical car—most significantly around one ton of steel—roughly 80 to 90 percent of automobile environmental impact can be traced to their fossil fuel use and associated greenhouse gas production.

From my first purchase in 1970 to my most recent, vehicles I've driven accounting for 90% of my lifetime gasoline use have averaged 35 to 80 miles / gallon. I will more completely address energy use aspects of my lifestyle in the next chapter. While my next story involves a fossil fuel using automobile, it illustrates the tenacity (choice #45) I often apply to fixing things myself —instead of paying someone else for repair, or simply discarding the broken whatever and buying something new.

During one difficult period, after Annie crashed our (50 miles / gallon) VW Rabbit and before I bought a Honda Civic, getting between my Ozarks home and Arkansas River Valley university workplace sixty-five miles away was especially challenging. I negotiated a three ten hours a day = 30 hours per week work schedule, and spending two nights in a college dorm room, to limit my weekly commute to one trip. But for a few months my only options for making this trip were using either a (80 miles / gallon) 125 cc motorcycle, or a big Jeep Wagoneer.

I logged 17,000 motorcycle miles that year, but sometimes had to use the Jeep. One evening, on a long stretch of highway through national forest devoid of houses, I slowed in rounding a bend and then pushed the accelerator pedal to speed up. Upon doing this, my foot felt a strange giving way sensation. The big vehicle immediately slowed as if it wasn't getting gas. After coasting to a stop, I reached down and came up holding half of the pedal, which had broken off. Looking in the back of the Jeep, I found a rope we'd previously used to restraint goats, and both a hammer and large nail in the vehicle's toolbox. I proceeded to knock a hole between driver and engine areas, hook one end of the rope to carburetor throttle linkage, and feed the other end through the hole. A few minutes later I was back on the road. Pulling the rope gave the vehicle gas; my hand was quite sore when I finally got home. (I later went to a junkyard and got a replacement accelerator pedal.)

More recently —in the stationary setting of my Arizona home—I've had a problem with tree roots clogging the sewer line. I've attacked the problem with a few days of manual digging work. I began by locating clay sewer pipe section joints where roots typically entered, then unclogging them and repairing damage. Upon finding vulnerable to being severed gas and phone lines occupying the same trench as the sewer line, I was glad I hadn't hired someone with a machine to do this digging. I later learned I'd also avoided paying licensed and bonded professionals — the only ones allowed to work where private sewer lines connect to the city sewage system—large sums over $5000. I dealt with the clogs and kept my sewer line open with only slight inconvenience.

The latter brought positive changes to my lifestyle. First, on days I couldn't pee in the toilet, I captured urine in a plastic gallon milk jug, top partly cut to make a bigger opening, with handle preserved. After a (choice #49) attitudinal fix overcoming the "yuck factor," I'd empty urine into compost piles. I hadn't thought about the potential for using this resource. Suffice to say after learning of its benefits, I got hooked on "peecycling." One person's urine provides enough nitrogen and phosphorus to fertilize 6300 tomato plants per year enabling harvest of up to two tons of tomatoes! Scrounging wood ashes from campground fire pits, and saving spoiled milk, can rectify urine's deficiencies in potassium and calcium that some plants also need.

A second benefit came after washing my clothes by hand during the clogged sewer line period. Realizing how much water my washing machine used, I soon (choice #46) rerouted that drain water for garden use. Just above the garden I installed a 325 gallon metal tank —bought used for $20, repaired, and painted. It also catches rainwater off the roof. This, and other tweaks, has reduced my water consumption to an annual average of 10 to 15 gallons per day—roughly one-seventh of the 88 gal / day the EPA (in 2018) estimated an average American uses at home. I've learned not to use chlorine or boron containing laundry detergents, and that gray water benefits garden fertility by adding phosphorus.

Besides fixing cast off items, and producing food in backyard garden or on a small farm, a whole range of activities fit under the umbrella The Small Producer theme promotes as alternatives to typical consumer behavior. While many make their livelihood here, others do it as a sideline for economic / environmental reasons. Many enjoy (choice #47) expressing themselves by working with their hands and small tools— and, given the effort involved, getting some (choice #21) healthy exercise as an added benefit. Unlike some do it yourselfers, I often shy away from installing labor-saving devices. For example, I could install drip irrigation, but I like the exercise I get from—two or three times a day in hot weather—using a watering can to feed thirsty garden plants.

The *Coming of Age...*book described my extensive organic gardening and food production (raising goats, chickens, making tofu and bread from bulk sacks of soybeans and wheat berries, etc.) during my years living on a large, naturally fertile mountain bench in a well-watered (fifty inches of average annual rainfall) Arkansas Ozarks region. Here in small mountain town Arizona, where I have but a 7000 sq ft residential lot, mountain soil with no organic matter, and less than twenty inches of average annual rainfall, I'd struggled to move my gardening out of the soil-building, still learning and building infrastructure phase. The latter has included creating a (surprisingly aesthetically pleasing) eight-foot x ten-foot greenhouse built out of cast-off materials for $160.

Within are two compost piles—nicely housed in a separately insulated (cast-off) metal bathtub—which benefit from my peecycling. In addition to its fertilizer benefits, recent research[17] suggests urine can overcome a problem with composting wood. Wood lacks nutrients needed to sustain microorganisms working to break it down and release energy. Urine has them, and as one report noted, "...experiments suggest compost-heaps of wood fed suitable nutrients can sustain internal temperatures of 40-55 °C for long periods. That is useful for heating buildings..." Given my five decades' experience building compost piles, and wood chips freely available where I live, I've begun experimenting adding urine to them in an effort to help heat my greenhouse in winter.

Beyond just occasionally using cast-off materials, I've long felt that one could (choice #47) make do "living off the trash of an affluent society." Now, I also try to help others in their creatively making do. The free section on *Craigslist*, and my now living close to one of the world's best thrift stores, aids such recycling. To those who feel some stigma is attached to their second-hand store shopping, I say (choice #28), "Celebrate the fact you're part of co-operative 'win win' effort." And that your (choice #45) recycling is not adding to those 110 billion tons of Earth's resources annually consumed.

Equally important to me as practicing enoughness, is (choice #21) Healthy Orientation behavior. Other than paying for health insurance[18], my life has been characterized by having essentially zero health care treatment expenses. I do have preventive health expenses—for annual checkups, healthy food, etc.—but they are wise investments. I've also invested time in developing skills so I can be self-reliant—meaning I do jobs most employ others to do (like auto maintenance / simple repairs, household repairs, tax returns, investment portfolio managing, etc.) Using these skills to help others is especially nice. Combining these things with little energy use (see chapter 7)—and aggressive "getting the best price" shopping for typically just "needs" not "wants," —my (choice #22) self-restraint based lifestyle expenses are minimal. And there are health, "feel good," and other rewards.

I'm (choice #19) grateful for my financial success, and no doubt some luck has been involved. But, as described, good choices I've made are mostly responsible. My choice #48 "Work, Play, Pay As You Go" commitment heads that list. Other than a brief eighteen-month period after my first marriage broke up, I have not had mortgage payments. Other than a six month period, as I started working at Arkansas Tech University and temporarily relocated close to campus, since I moved to land I owned, I have not paid rent. Nor have I had income from significant real estate appreciation due to changing market conditions.

Gains I realized upon sale of the five houses that I (choice #46) either built or occupied / maintained, during the 1977-2013 period were from sweat equity. I'm referring to (choice #48) work I invested in building /making improvements compensated at roughly an average minimum wage. During that time span, I built three houses and numerous small outbuildings, doing roughly 95% of the work myself.[19] The first of these houses—a unique passive solar, earth-tempered structure—was described in the *Coming of Age* book. Sale of that property in 1991 basically returned nothing beyond $ invested in original land purchase price, in improvements like building an access road and water tanks, etc, and the cost of house-building materials. As with all my building, it was done in (choice #48) Pay As You Go fashion.

The second house—an 1100 square foot passive solar one in the southern New Mexico mountains—was built during summers 1999-2003 under the watchful eye of building inspectors. It was built to the same code standards as required of houses erected in cities like Albuquerque. Other than employing one ready mix truck to bring concrete that was poured into forms I'd built for foundation footings, I did all of the work myself. Building materials not delivered were hauled in my 1990 Ford Festiva— including a few tons of sand, gravel, cement, masonry blocks, and one 20 foot long, 700 pound power pole—with all seats except the drivers' removed. By the time the last inspector left and I moved in, I'd spent around $20 per square foot. This can be compared to the $100 per square foot that people typically paid building contractors in the area at the time.

Besides providing a place to live (rent and mortgage free) for ten years, upon selling it I realized financial gain equivalent to a wage of around $20 / hour for the labor invested. That may not sound impressive, but by doing the work myself I avoided paying the extra roughly $80 per square foot that employing a building contractor would have necessitated. This made (choice #48) avoiding a mortgage—with its interest charges, red tape, etc.—possible. It also got me plenty of (choice #21) healthy exercise. I would typically start the summer building season weighing around 160 pounds and, when I quit ten weeks later, end up weighing 148 pounds. This occurred despite my consuming all the calories I could to keep up the rigorous activity the project demanded.

While that second house benefited from reasonable and helpful building inspectors, the third house in rural west central New Mexico, with one exception, did not. One guy, inspecting my hand dug trenches and salvaged wood forms / tied rebar prior to pouring the footing work, scornfully put down my effort. After signing off on it, he pointed out how much easier using a backhoe and ready-made foam forms would have been. Perhaps, I answered, but that the cost of doing that would have been substantially more. I also pointed out that the resulting footings would have been much wider than needed. And that such over-engineered footings would require more expensive ready mix concrete. The electrical inspector was much harder to deal with.

I had dealt with him months earlier with the power pole service hookup inspection, and knew he was a stickler. Interestingly enough, I finished the rough in house plumbing and electrical work about the same time in July 2013. I've long felt I'm (choice #46) a better amateur electrician than plumber, so was relieved when—while under the house looking up at pipes— the plumbing inspector started his comments. "Steve, this is every bit as good as what the professionals have me look it." I was surprised, but recovered to say, "Great. I wish my wife could hear you say that!" After signing off, I was pleased that he told her just that.

Alas, when the electrical inspector showed up he found sixteen things supposedly wrong, when, if truth be known, little if anything was really wrong. Not used to inspecting owner-builders' work, this guy cited me for some incredibly nit-picking things, and for things where he turned out to be simply wrong. I concluded this after letters and conversation with both my former electrical inspector in southern New Mexico and this guy's boss in Albuquerque. Why am I sharing a small part of a much more complicated story here? Two reasons.

First, I think regulatory hurdles —and occasional unhelpful inspectors and outright corruption—have added a scary, time-consuming, often expensive dimension to owner-builder projects. While I support common sense building regulations—especially as related to energy efficiency—I feel some are excessive and don't like aspects of the "one size fits all" approach. Given shortage of small, affordable housing—and right-wing frustration with what they see as (choice #40) freedom encroaching regulations in general—I feel building officials need to back off. Rather than engaging in heavy-handed, by the book policing, they need to be educating, accommodating, and helpful to owner-builders— while at the same time making sure serious safety-related corners are not cut.

Second, caught between an unreasonable electrical inspector and an unreasonable wife, I decided to end both my building project involvement and my nearly eight-year relationship with this woman. Again, after initial pain brought on by sadness that this woman I'd loved did not really respect me or trust my construction-related judgment, I have largely thrived. This flourishing was facilitated by a 2014 decision to purchase an unconventional home in a central Arizona mountain town. My choice came down to selecting between two real estate offerings.

One was a very conventional, fairly new 3 BR 2 BA 1200 sq. ft. house with attached garage on a 5200 sq.ft. lot in a suburban neighborhood full of similar looking houses and manicured lawns. After weeks of searching I had essentially settled on it, and saw the $130,000 cash I'd pay as an outstanding investment. But just before closing the deal, I chanced on another property: a twenty-three year old manufactured home (MH) 2 BR 2 BA 900 sq. ft of living space on a permanent foundation. While it lacked a garage, the neighborhood it sat in possessed character. And I much preferred its location—within walking or easy biking distance from places I would be going. It was listed for $79,000.

I have no doubt that nine out of ten Americans faced with this choice would have picked the conventional suburban house. Certainly (choice #27) status-conscious folks would not live in a MH given "trailer trash" and other associations that have given the species a bad name. And for this particular dwelling there was another yuck factor: trash in the form of old carpet, dry wall pieces, plastic visqueen, etc littering one part of the property. After making needed (choice #49) attitudinal fix adjustments, I began a critical appraisal of technological fixes I'd need to make before I could move in. Critically its roof—a contributing factor to MH poor reputation—was relatively new and of the type typically found on site built homes. Its directional orientation—with long axis and windows oriented to let in sunshine in winter—was outstanding, with one big shade tree strategically located to keep sun out in summer.

The conventional house had a beautiful stucco exterior— a niceness that doesn't welcome do-it-yourselfers punching holes for additions or various projects. Its interior living space was bigger than I was seeking, and exterior land was equally divided between front and back yards. Imagining prying, judgmental neighbors seeing and frowning upon anything this aging hippie would do, I decided the front yard would be pretty useless. In back, it was hard to imagine tearing up the nice lawn to put in a garden. The more I thought about the very limited "technological fix" possibilities of this property, the more I soured on it.

Suffice it to say my $72,000 cash offer for the MH was accepted. It's proved to be a quiet, extremely convenient, friendly neighborhood great place to live. (Yes, the roots of that otherwise wonderful shade tree provided one of the few challenges.) The view I have of a prominent mountain landmark from the clothesline I installed soon after moving in, is outstanding. Likewise I love feeling the sun as I hang clothes out in the thin air of the 5300 ft elevation location. In the seven years I've lived here my (choice #46) Small Producer type projects have included adding a solar photovoltaic system / energy saving features (described in the next chapter), installing an air conditioner for a neighbor, building several garden beds, adjoining compost bins, wood plank walkways, and two wonderfully functional outbuildings. Besides the greenhouse, I built an astronomical observatory "warm room" to complement the telescope platform I built. Keeping their size small—under 120 sq.ft— has helped me avoid building permits, inspectors, and regulatory heavy-handedness.

Were I to run for local political office—which I have no plans to do— (choice #31) working for change related to building would be a top priority. I would promote small affordable housing. In an area with limited water and a last, beautiful free flowing river threatened by ground-water sucking development, I would work to limit big corporate developers' plans. I would severely restrict (choice #33) greedy folks from being able to subdivide large acreage and put in many—in some cases thousands—of large, expensive houses. I would (choice #40 and choice #41) limit their ability to tear up land / disrespect nature, deplete groundwater, and make out like bandits—with other people doing the real work. In this part of the world, those other people are typically (choice #36) Latinos / immigrants who are (choice #19) grateful for jobs, even though they involve hard manual labor. A neighbor who'd watched me dig trenches and built the foundation for that third house I mentioned in west central New Mexico offered one of the best compliments I've ever received. "Steve," he said, "You work like a f——-ing Mexican!"

Some may find what I've written above offensive, but no disrespect is intended. Nor do I want to promote stereotypes, nor add to prejudice in favor of the able-bodied—able-bodyism—something that can figure in discussions of (choice #26) the Physically Challenged →Independent Living theme. I'm just (choice #19) grateful to have had a body that has worked and enabled me to do many things. As you might expect from someone who has embraced the nickname "The Human Backhoe," I have (choice #46 and choice #47) enjoyed using it. I'm very motivated to (choice #21) continue taking care of it. (Note: I've managed to lobby for both sides of choice #21 here: health and pleasure.) I often encourage (choice #26) elderly folks doing things that would not challenge a younger person—like climbing stairs—by saying, "The more you do that, the longer you'll be able to keep doing it as you get old."

I realize my body will eventually break down. Thinking about that inspired my song (see chapter 8 Dispatch #4) "Caring Respect"—to be sung to the tune of "Seventy-six Trombones." While many escape the psychological challenged / low self-esteem territory of choice #26, unless you die suddenly in an accident, everyone eventually finds themselves in the physically challenged realm. With respect to both pursuit of independent living as a physically challenged person or in (choice # 31) working for change, I like Theodore Roosevelt's advice: "Do what you can, with what you have, where you are."

I also like another bit of lifestyle-related philosophy, a quote sometimes attributed to Mahatma Gandhi (1869-1948), "Be the change you want to see in the world." While I've shared many livelihood-related stories of my modeling such behavior, I realize its (choice #31) working for change potential is limited. No doubt you can influence more people by joining with others in working for (choice #27) progressive change, (choice #41) respect for nature, and (choice #44) sustainable development.

Thus in recent years I've served on the boards of two local community groups organized in response to concerns about water issues in the mountains in southern New Mexico where I lived. And here in Arizona, I similarly serve a local Sierra Club group and local climate action group.

After serving as a volunteer firefighter for ten years in New Mexico, in Arizona I've worked with progressive political action and church groups in other giving back type / (choice #32) Service to Others activities. And, I idealistically view my teaching, writing / *Project Worldview* efforts as similarly fitting into the (choice #31) working for change category.

I've concluded this section mentioning giving back, progressive activist aspects of my life. But, regarding its economic impact implications one can ask, "What about the (choice #33) ethics of this lifestyle? Wouldn't the American economy as we know it collapse if everyone quit being super-consumers?" Yes, perhaps—and that's the point! Our current throw-away wasteful economy is (choice #44) unsustainable. It needs to gradually change if catastrophic collapse is to be avoided. Workers need to be retrained to fill roles that are part of the solution, not the problem.

Those who dream of life's small pleasures, and of a simple lessons and ethics-based sustainable economy, have liked the illustrative examples from my life experience this book provides. But the fun is in steering your lifestyle in this direction in your own (choice #47) creative, unique way. And in the unexpected surprises you have along the way.

Growing zucchini has provided me with one. This has been unexpected in that squash bugs plagued my Ozarks' garden experience. But it seems those critters can't survive our dry Arizona mountain climate. In 2018, I grew 85 lbs of zukes; my 2021 harvest (currently 90 lbs) should exceed 100 lbs.I love its taste, all the creative culinary things you can do with it—pickles and pepperoni for pizza are my latest discoveries— and many nutritional benefits: rich in fiber, folate, anti-oxidants, vitamins, etc.

While (choice #32) cynics will scoff at what any one person can do, those small individual contributions to a better world add up. Certainly if lots of people today make big, responsible, caring choices—and inspire other people with their (choice #36) global citizen behavior—prospects for tomorrow's global village brighten.

No doubt many will read of my lifestyle, my activist pursuits, my idealistic practices and the philosophy they're based on, and say "Get real!" Or, "You're living in Fantasy Land if you think others will change their ways and follow you." How do I reply? I tell them I'm (choice #19) grateful for the good life I've had. I mention my desire to give something back and help people see an alternative way of life they may want to choose. After this humility, I make a stronger statement. I say, "You're the one in Fantasy Land if you think your consumerist, throw away lifestyle based on continually having more is sustainable, ethical, and something you'll be comfortable defending many years from now." I again point out I don't pretend to have all the answers, but hope that their encounter with me will spur their own thinking about Tomorrow Land.

E. Pointing the Market System in the Right Direction

Economist John Maynard Keynes' 1930 book *Economic Possibilities for Our Grandchildren* inspired an effort seventy-five years later. In his 2005 book *The End of Poverty*, economist Jeffrey Sachs pointed to global success (choice #47) combating poverty in industrial countries in the years since 1930. He wrote, "Keynes wondered how the society of his grandchildren would use its wealth and unprecedented freedom from the age-old struggle for daily survival." Sachs then turned that long-ago question into a choice for us, still relevant today, "Will we have the good judgment to use our wealth wisely, to heal a divided planet, to end the suffering of those still trapped by poverty, and to forge a common bond of security, and shared purpose across cultures and regions?"

We'll more fully address the ending poverty aspects of this question later in this chapter. Here we consider its connection with environmentally sustainable development—the focus of the center with that name at Columbia University's Earth Institute, which Sachs directs. In particular, we consider three important (choice #41, choice #44 and choice #52) related books published since 1990. First, published in 1999, we note *Natural Capitalism* by Paul Hawken, Amory Lovins, and Hunter Lovins. This book begins with a dedication: "to Dana, David, Herman, and Ray." And ends with the statement, "Natural capitalism is about the choices we can make that can start to tip economic and social outcomes in positive directions. [This] is already occurring—because it is necessary, possible, and practical." This last sentence is truer today than when it was written.

Second, in 2002, Michael Braungart and William McDonough collaborated to give us *Cradle to Grave: Remaking the Way We Make Things*. There they say, "If humans are truly going to prosper, we have to learn to imitate nature's highly effective cradle-to-cradle system of nutrient flow and metabolism, in which the very concept of waste does not exist." They imagine that making and consuming products can help regenerate ecosystems, instead of harming them. Braungart is a German chemist who co-founded the chemistry section of Greenpeace. He's also an (choice #31) activist who once lived in a tree as a protest. Many think of McDonough as the father of the circular economy concept.

Third, in 2017, University of Oxford economist Kate Raworth offered *Doughnut Economics*. Its name comes from the diagram—reproduced in Figure #22—she presented in 2012 while working for Oxfam: "A Safe and Just Space for Humanity." That names the diagram's doughnut shaped green zone, which lies between inner and outer rings. The inner ring lists (choice #27 and choice #35) twelve social foundation essentials—based on Sustainable Development Goals of the United Nations. These are essentials that no one in society should have in insufficient amounts. The outer ring identifies nine (choice #40, choice #41, and choice #44) ecological limits[20] that humanity must not exceed if its relationship with Earth's life-supporting biosphere is to be respected. If all people are to live within the "safe and just" zone the diagram defines, two big global problems must be successfully confronted:
1) (choice #47) extreme poverty due to unequal distribution of wealth, and 2) (choice #41) excessive use of the Earth's resources and fossil fuel based energy threatening biodiversity and the global climate.

Figure #22 Doughnut Economics

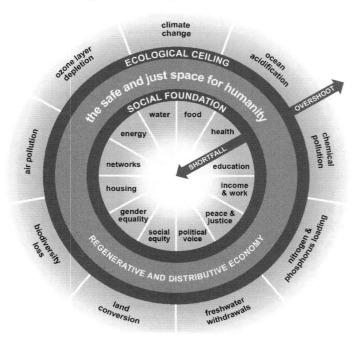

I see these three books as pointing the way to a sustainable future with a "regenerative and distributive economy" —another label applied to the Figure #22 doughnut ring. Or, more simply, to get us to ecosharing. I prefer this term to the labels Kate Raworth uses. But whereas my earlier book defined the ecosharing zone using numerical limits and mathematical expressions (in a "The Sharing Objectives" figure,) her doughnut diagram elegantly places it an environmental and social justice context. Thank you, Kate.

In this book we seek to understand ecosharing—and its natural capitalism, circular economics, and doughnut economics components — and make it part of a down to earth, global education, *Choices We Make* framework. Continuing our analysis of its fifty-two choices spread over "thinking, feeling, joining, and doing," we stake out "think globally, but act locally" territory as related to humanity's continuing environmental and social justice challenges.

These two challenges are most closely linked to *Project Worldview* meta themes, on ace of spades and ace of clubs cards, namely (choice #40) Limits and Ethics, and (choice #27) Egalitarian Progressive themes. Runnerups in relevance here on king of spades and king of clubs cards, are (choice #41) Respect for Nature and (choice #28) Celebrating Team Accomplishments. We qualify these latter preferences by noting Respect for Nature practically means advocating (choice #52) Environmental Economics. And that being the ultimate team player—as in "We're all in this together"—means celebrating (choice #36) global citizenship.

While those choices are critically important, meeting specific challenges will point us to preferred themes from many choices. From the lowest level and for world's poorest individuals, the challenge to succeed often involves (choice #47) Struggling With a Basic Need: Sustenance. At the global planning (top) level, the challenge is to succeed in (choice #44) sustainable development, and on the (choice #51) Ethical Globalization playing field. That is, for billions of individuals to pursue livelihoods and live together so that global society functioning is sustainable, and ensuing activity does not lead to catastrophic breakdown.

Given current crises with pandemic, growing poverty / inequality, environmental health concerns, it's not clear how we avoid catastrophic suffering, and get to a healthy world of ecosharing. We note that roughly fifty years have passed since the publication of *The Limits to Growth* without significant overhaul of the capitalist system. Some feel, as the world recovers from upheaval brought by the Covid-19 pandemic, only to face the growing climate crisis, the time is right to push for change.

F. Top Down and Bottom Up: A Tale of Two Kates

The work of Kate Raworth and Kate Soper has inspired this section's title. If asked to name a British "Kate," these two women would qualify. But given their relative anonymity, many would name Kate Middleton, the Duchess of Cambridge. Given her aristocratic ties, that Kate represents the "old order," whereas this section celebrates the vision of these two other Kates. It's a vision of a new direction society might head in. We've already introduced Kate Raworth and her (Figure #22) diagram. I believe this captures the essence of a top down vision for humanity: everyone living in that "just and safe space." Kate Soper, an emerita professor of philosophy at London Metropolitan University, offers the bottom up vision. We'll describe it shortly.

Ideally a bottom up approach of billions of individuals making good choices could reshape the world into a fairer, healthier, more stable place. But making this possible—or jump-starting it—will be easier if national, and (choice #51) international, leadership can put a top down framework in place that facilitates those individual good choices. Jeffrey Sachs has been one of many people working to do that. Thus a framework, consisting of eight goals with 2015 target date, was put in place in 2000 with the UN Millennium Development Goals. It served as the basis for the (choice #27 and choice #44) Sustainable Development Goals, which succeeded it. The seventeen interlinked goals / topic areas (see Figure #23) of this framework were created with the world of 2030 in mind. Each of them typically has eight to twelve targets, and one to four indicators to gauge progress toward the smaller target goal.

This UN effort inspired the twelve social foundation essentials of Kate Raworth's diagram, to which she added nine ecological limits. Together they identify the challenging, but more manageable, parts of a bigger problem. Separated into its social and ecological components, we cast the need to fit everyone into the Safe and Just Space for Humanity she diagrams as a two part question. "How do we organize society so that, first, people are happy, healthy, and given roughly equal opportunities to prosper and grow, and second, their growth and prosperity does not strain the Earth's ability to support life indefinitely in a healthy sustainable manner, and cause calamitous breakdown?"

Figure #23: UN Sustainable Development Goals / Topic Areas		
#1 No Poverty		#2 Zero Hunger
#3 Good Health & Well-being	#4 Quality Education	#5 Gender Equality
#6 Clean Water & Sanitation	#7 Affordable & Clean Energy	#8 Decent Work and Economic Growth
#9 Industry, Innovation, Infrastructure	#10 Reducing Inequality	#11 Sustainable Cities & Communities
#12 Responsible Production & Consumption	#13 Climate Action	#14 Life Below Water
#15 Life on Land	#16 Peace, Justice, Strong Institutions	#17 Partnerships for Goals

Beyond putting our (choice #10) scientific methodology to work in addressing this problem, something else is needed: a method that guides our planning and directs our technological tools in a (choice #2) global vision fashion. The (choice #13) Complexity—In Our Hands: Dancing With Systems theme provides this. You can read its complete description in Appendix A; here we offer Dana Meadows' (from her "Dancing With Systems" essay) observation:[21] "The future can't be predicted, but it can be envisioned and lovingly brought into being." And sketch her "seeing the future" (choice #40) exercise that points to a pitfall.

In an example detailed in *Natural Capitalism*, Meadows employs four different generic (color-coded) worldviews. These are ones held by mainstream free marketers (blues,) those with an ecosystem perspective (greens), those seeing social problems in terms of exploitation of labor (socialists—reds), and hopeful, rational, progressive optimists she calls synthesists (whites.) She then asks, "What would we see if we were willing to approach the question of human population growth and planetary limits purely scientifically?" Based on her analysis from all four of these perspectives she concludes, "All sides are partly right and mostly incomplete. Each is focusing on one piece of a very complex system. Each is seeing its piece correctly. But because no side is seeing the whole, no side is coming to wholly supportable conclusions."

From Meadows' example, authors Hawken, Lovins, and Lovins conclude, "A successful business in the new era of natural capitalism will respect and understand all four views. It will realize that solutions lie in understanding the interconnectedness of problems, not in confronting them in isolation." So, we seek the best tools in seeing the big problem we've outlined from multiple perspectives, and moving ahead

Thus we combine both (choice #10) scientific method and (choice #13) systems thinking approaches. Thus our (choice #1) evidence-based, data driven approach is steered by a vision of the (choice #27, choice #41, and choice #44) socially just, nature-respecting, environmentally sustainable world we're trying to bring into being. For me, imagining real people — (choice #47) struggling for a place in the abstract space Kate Raworth's diagram defines —captures that vision. Having this can be critical in evaluating both input and output in terms of what's important and what can't be quantified. The *Choices We Make* way of characterizing worldviews can help decision-makers see the whole picture.

This work—in manageable pieces— has been going on for decades. In the patchwork world of planning / research, and technological advances as related to truly global problems, keeping track of findings and recognizing how to move forward can be difficult. Sometimes actually implementing recommendations on a global scale may be impossible, given economic and political realities. The public health battle against tobacco use, the Trump era USA effort to limit greenhouse gas emissions per international accords, the ozone hole scare, and the battle against the Covid-19 pandemic provide relevant case studies. The first two battles share a common history: even when overwhelming scientific consensus existed as to the needed action, (choice #43) doubt manufactured by those with a vested interest in no action stalled moving ahead.

Of course individuals can take matters into their own hands in a bottom up way. They can (choice # 31) "be the change." They can live in a way that models how they want the world to be. They can work to build a groundswell of public enthusiasm for action that forces leaders to reform the capitalist market-based system, with key institutions operating under new rules. Among other things, concerned individuals can demand (choice #52) society get off the current Big Business Pushes Global Limits path, and instead go in an Environmental Economics direction. They can do this while at the same time working to (choice #45) minimize their own environmental impact / carbon footprint.

An April 3, 2021 need for climate action related article in *The Economist* begins, "Politics, Otto von Bismarck is supposed to have said, is the art of the possible. And one of the most depressing features of discussions about global warming is their tendency to take place in a fantasy land of the politically impossible." Or, I'll add, the personally very unpalatable. Selling people on lifestyle changes involving sacrificing, or giving up things, fits into the impractical realm. Kate Soper has a different vision.

In approaching it we ask, "Of all the imagined mental landscape defined by *Project Worldview's* 104 worldview themes, where would you most like to dwell?" Before anyone answers we qualify the question with, "Forget all the consequences of time you spend there, other tradeoffs, etc." I argue most people, without having to worry about those consequences and tradeoffs, would prefer feeling good (choice #21) Hedonism. And they'd also want this for others.

But this is fantasy land, right? There are bad consequences. Tradeoffs are such that you won't want to live in a world of hedonists, right? Not so fast...What if someone defined and elaborately sketched out how to recast hedonism (into alternative hedonism) to remove these difficulties? Surprise! Kate Soper has—in her November 22 2017 short book length article "A New Hedonism: A Post-Consumerism Vision."[22]

Her put down of (choice #46) The Consumerist lifestyle begins with John Maynard Keynes condemning its basis: "the pathology of monetary greed...[but] is now regarded as an essential driver of national well-being. Its effect is to subordinate everyone to a time economy and work ethic that sees free time as a threat to human prosperity rather than a form in which it can be realized." She describes "the central failing of consumerist provision: it seeks to gratify psychological and aesthetic needs by purely materialist means." And notes, "The tendency ...of consumer culture is to remove both the spiritual dimension from the satisfaction of our more purely physical needs, and to materialize the ways in which we meet the more intangible and spiritual needs..." To those who value (choice #40) freedom from limits, she says, "Time scarcity must also be seen as a major constraint on personal liberty."

She advocates "the transition to a more sustainable and more sensually, spiritually, and aesthetically rewarding way of living." She argues "for an 'alternative hedonist' approach to thinking about human well-being, consumption, and the politics of prosperity." Its "essential focus," she writes, " ...is on enjoyment rather than frugality, on the rewards of a socially just and eco-benign consumption rather than on the restrictions that will need to be placed on the older way of living." She argues, "the consumerist way of living offers too little in the way of joy and fulfillment, rather than too much." She wants "a reduction of the working week and a slower pace of living," and notes, for fans of (choice #29) democracy, this "would release time for civic engagement."

She urges "green and fair trade purchasing…green taxation… regulation of advertising." And notes in promoting "spiritual consumption" she isn't advocating "an overtly religious, mystical, or ascetic way of living." To this I add other "feel good things" that can be done responsibly: helping people, giving back, teaching, celebrating with friends / music, enjoying nature, hiking, holding hands, and love-making. Alternative hedonists, with time to stop and smell the flowers, have more freedom, and more time for family. They don't measure success by how much money you have, the size of your house, the car you drive, a prestigious job title, etc. They don't equate money and property with happiness and well-being.

G. Putting Environmental and Social Costs into Prices

In the (choice #34) market world of transactions, consider buying zucchini. Imagine a (choice #35) corporate (fossil-fueled) agribusiness offering, along with a higher priced locally grown organic zucchini one. This choice can be seen as between two approaches: #1: a cutting corners one that maximizes short-term benefits, vs. #2: a more conscientious effort to produce (or maintain) something to maximize its long run service (or health). From buying cars or making lifestyle choices, we know that long run costs are less if we initially invest in quality or, in health matters, avoid short-term (choice #21) hedonistic pleasure opting instead for preventative, long-term maintenance. So we expect overall lifetime costs associated with organic zucchini to be less. So why is it priced higher? Answer: just as in the earlier example involving jeans, environmental, health, and social costs are not included in the prices.

The purchaser of agribusiness zucchini doesn't initially pay them: he/she and society pays later. Examples: costs of pesticide-related cancer, fossil fuel use, cleaning up water pollution, etc. If prices reflected real costs, organic zucchini would be lower priced and thus preferred. Efforts to put hidden costs into prices represent one (choice #52) environmental economics mechanism for fixing market system holes. Some cities are trying to make this happen now. A "Doughnut City" story in *Time* magazine's February 1, 2021 issue begins with describing new price tags in Amsterdam. "The label by the [agribusiness] zucchini said they cost a little more than normal: 6 cents extra per kilogram for their carbon footprint, 5 cents for the toll farming takes on the land, and 4 cents to fairly pay workers...these are extra costs to our daily life that normally no one would pay for, or even be aware of...The so-called true price initiative is one Amsterdamers have introduced in recent months as they reassess the impact of the existing economic system." These eco-friendly encouraging ethical consumption tweaks can work with top down ones.

Governments putting a (choice #52) price on carbon can motivate consumers to reduce their greenhouse gas-related impact. Carbon footprints gauge carbon dioxide CO_2 equivalents released into the atmosphere per year due to one's purchases, resource consumption, fossil fuel energy use, etc. They include both direct (e.g. gasoline powered auto travel) and indirect (e.g. electricity use from coal-fired power plants) contributions. Per capita emissions based annual carbon footprints in affluent countries (in metric tons CO_2/ yr person) include[23]: 16.92 for Australia, 16.56 for the USA, 15.32 for Canada, 9.13 for Japan, 9.12 for Germany, 7.05 for China, 5.62 for England, and 5.19 for France. Another measure—broader, more difficult to quantify— is termed ecological footprint. This gauges one's overall impact on Earth's life-supporting ecosystems due to one's purchases, resource consumption, fossil fuel energy use, land use and other relevant environmental impacts.

Imagine—as the USA's Citizens Climate Lobby (CCL) has in proposed 2021 (revenue neutral) carbon fee and dividend legislation[24]—carbon is initially priced at $15 per metric ton of CO_2 equivalent, with a $10 per ton increase every year. Initially a typical American family of four with 80 tons / yr carbon footprint would pay $1200 extra per year. Ten years later, with carbon priced at $115 / ton, that same carbon footprint would cost them an extra $9200 per year. While rebates might return nearly half of that amount, unless they've reduced their carbon use, they'll be out a good chunk of money. But, this American family would have quite an incentive to cut its carbon footprint. If, by year ten, they'd cut that footprint from 20 metric tons CO_2/ yr to 6 metric tons CO_2/ yr, the extra $2760 / year they'd pay in a carbon fee, would be more than offset by a $4410 rebate. Every year they'd save $4410 - $2760 = $1650.

I'd love to see American politicians find courage, throw off their (choice #12) Group Think Imperative strait-jacket, and buck the party-line orthodoxy that George Washington warned against in his Farewell Address. I'd love to see them get beyond simplistic "no new taxes" thinking and vote for some sort of a carbon fee and dividend plan. This could show the world that America can make responsible choices. That America can do its part to combat global climate change, and now recognizes, "We're all in this together."

Economists agree carbon pricing is the best way to immediately address climate change concerns. Both fans of (choice #34) capitalism and (choice #52) environmental economics like this market-based tweak. But, naysayers object. "You're adding a tax, and asking me to pay for something I'm not paying for now," they say. Carbon pricing fans reply, "You're paying for it now, and you'll really pay for it in the future unless we do something now!" Those fans note you pay for climate change impacts in many ways—including higher insurance rates, higher product prices, and through higher taxes. Environmentalists have long claimed the taxpayer-funded US Defense budget is bloated by the need to protect US access to cheap Mideast oil.

You similarly pay another "hidden cost" associated with burning fossil fuel: government subsidies to this industry. According to a June 15 2019 *Forbes* magazine report on a International Monetary Fund (IMF) study, the world spent $5.2 trillion in 2017 (representing 6.5% of that year's GDP) on subsidies to the coal, oil, and natural gas industry. The US figure of $649 billion represented an expenditure of roughly ten times more than what it spent on education. The IMF also concluded that reducing such subsidies "to create efficient fossil fuel pricing...would have lowered global carbon emissions by 28% and fossil fuel air pollution deaths by 46% and increased government revenue by 3.8% of GDP" based on 2015 data. Speaking of fossil fuel air pollution, a collaboration of Harvard University, University of Birmingham, University of Leicester, and University College London scientists found this to be responsible for a staggering 8.7 million people globally dying in 2018—more deaths than from smoking and malaria combined.

Continuing to ignore tragedies of the commons, ignore depletion of natural capital, value ecosystem services at zero, use GDP to gauge economic prosperity, make no attempt to break down market prices so consumers can see environmental and social costs, ignore costs of damages associated with climate change impact, and continuing to massively promote fossil fuel use through government subsidies, all represent (choice #52) big business as usual behavior. To that we add ignoring inequality growing to outrageous levels and bring choice #27 into the discussion. While fans of Environmental Economics and Egalitarian Progressive themes recognize the long-standing economic arrangement is ultimately (choice #44) unsustainable, what do powers that be say? What do those at the top of the Hierarchical Rigidity power structure think about changes suggested above?

With respect to carbon pricing, eight of the world's ten largest economies currently price carbon—only the US (as a whole) and India do not. By March 2021, the US business community appeared to be moving to support carbon pricing—with the US Chamber of Commerce, the Business Roundtable, the Electric Power Supply Association, and the American Petroleum Institute on board. Many small businesses and large corporations—including Exxon-Mobil, and Royal Shell oil companies— also (suposedly?) pledged support. What of wealthy power broker support for the ecosharing / doughnut economics alternative?

One reviewer of Kate Raworth's book said that for doughnut economics to catch on in a big way would require people to "magically" become "indifferent to how well we do compared to others, and not really care about wealth and income." That grim assessment may be true. Most business careers are seemingly driven by (choice #33) pursuit of wealth and power. Don't hold your breath waiting for droves of business school applicants valuing an Ethical Orientation — where things like right and wrong, sharing, and consideration for others matter.

Recall Chapter 3—Sociology: People, Trust, Institutions—began with describing a splashy ad for an MBA program that proclaimed, "Learn to be CEO of Mars, Inc." This contrasts with the humble announcement of an Arizona State University one-day workshop leading to an "Executive Certificate in the Ethical Circular Economy." This "includes mapping exercises on take-make-waste linear economy adapting to a circular economy model, and identifying additional stakeholders, gatekeepers, policies, and strategies." To me what stands out here is not just contrast between the two economics—the conventional wasteful linear and the efficient, sustainable circular—but words ethical and stakeholders. Two words we need to hear more often in doing business discussions.

H. Reworking the Market System to Fight Inequality

From an average person income perspective, global economic well-being trends are moving in the right direction. Per capita income has increased from roughly $4000 / yr per person in purchasing power parity (PPP) terms in 1990, to a 2020 $18,500 / yr per person PPP. And there have been gains at the very bottom, with as noted, the % living in (choice #47) extreme poverty falling from 36% to 8%. But (choice #33) very rich individual incomes are growing much more rapidly. According to Oxfam, during 2018 the wealth of the world's 2200 billionaires increased by 12 % (or $900 billion,) while that of the world's poorest half fell by 11%. By the end of 2019, their data suggested those billionaires had more wealth than the world's poorest 60% or 4.6 billion people. Simple division suggests each billionaire, on average, has over two million times as much as the average poor person. Not surprisingly, (choice #27) "Reducing Inequality" is UN Sustainable Development Goal #10.

This battle is being fought in many arenas, including in international organization-sponsored policy forums, multinational corporate boardrooms, American state legislatures, etc. The latter has been a battleground in the fight to raise the minimum wage to $15 / hour; likewise growing inequality in America has been widely discussed. Data documenting this include rising ratio of corporate CEO pay to average American worker pay (cited earlier,) and gini coefficient (described in chapter 3) increasing from 0.45 to a record 0.49 (according to US Census Bureau data) in the last decade.

Inequality is a worldwide problem—plaguing not just western democracies, but Russia with its kleptocrats stealing from ordinary people, and even China. A February 11 2021 *Foreign Affairs* article headlines "China's Inequality Will Lead it to a Stark Choice." Along with citing a gini coefficient in China of 0.47, it claims inequality has become "the Chinese system's Achilles heel, belying the government's nominally socialist tenets and undermining the implicit contrast between the rulers and the ruled." Xi Jingping and China's leaders will have to choose between "the trust that Confucius thought even more essential for good government than food" and the hypocrisy behind inequality.

Working to boost poor folks' income is the focus of many battling inequality. Here let's step back and probe its origin. Let's return to Adam Smith's and Karl Marx's question: "Will capital accumulate and wealth become concentrated in fewer and fewer hands?" French economist Thomas Piketty's 2014 book *Capital in the Twenty-First Century* gives this question a fresh look. His analysis involves a variable designated "g"— standing for rate of <u>growth</u> of income and economic output. China's extremely high 9.21 % / year growth in the last three decades provides an example.

For comparison, USA GDP grew at average rate of 3.1 % / year between 1948 and 2020. A sustained 9.21% / yr growth rate would lead to a doubling of (choice #44) economic output in less than eight years— something China's economy has repeatedly done in recent decades. The global pandemic recently brought China's streak of a hundred quarters + of consecutive growth to a halt in the first quarter of 2020. Globally, the pandemic has thrown hundreds of millions into poverty. Minorities and the have nots—the losers in the increasingly "winner take all" economy —have suffered the most. The United Nations estimates that it will push between 240 million and 490 million people into (choice #47) "multidimensional poverty"— lacking basic shelter, going hungry, etc.

Back to Thomas Piketty's "g" variable. Toward the end of his massive book, he identifies "The Central Contradiction of Capitalism" as "r > g" —meaning generally the value of variable r is greater than the value of variable g. Variable r is the private rate of return on capital. For example, according to *Investopedia*, data based on average annual rate of return for an investment in the USA stock market S&P 500 index for the 1957-2018 period, puts r at 8 % / yr. This is also high—data for the first two decades of the 21st century suggests values of r more typically are averaging 4 to 5 % / yr. But, these levels of return on capital are typically quite higher than—more than double—values of g, the rate at which incomes and economic outputs are growing. Those are more typically averaging 2% / yr at best (when it's not declining as in pandemic times.)

That r > g has big, troubling consequences. As Piketty puts it, "The inequality r > g implies...the entrepreneur...tends to become...more and more dominant over those who own nothing but their own labor. Once constituted, capital reproduces itself faster than output increases. The past devours the future. The consequences for the long-term dynamics of wealth distribution are potentially terrifying, especially when one adds that the return on capital varies directly with the size of the initial stake and that the divergence in wealth is occurring on a global scale."

Looking back to China's sustained g = 9.21 % / yr value, perhaps you're thinking that value of g is greater than most values of r, so that's the solution—have economies growing like China's has—right? Not so fast. That growth rate leads to environmental problems as we've seen. From his European Union perspective, Piketty writes, "The problem is enormous, and there is no simple solution. Growth can of course be encouraged by investing in education, knowledge, and non-polluting technologies. But none of these will raise the growth rate to 4 or 5 percent a year. History shows only countries that are catching up to advanced economies—such as Europe in the three decades after World War II or China or other emerging countries today can grow at such rates...there is ample reason to believe the growth rate will not exceed 1 – 1.5 percent in the long run no matter what policies are adopted."

Does Picketty hold out hope for any way around this problem? Yes, he says, (choice #27) "The right solution is a progressive annual tax on capital." Back in 2005 Jeffrey Sachs explained[25] how this might work: "A 5 percent income tax surcharge on incomes above $200,000, directed toward the U.S. contribution to end global poverty...That surcharge would be paid as a tax to support U.S. government efforts, or it could be directed by the taxpayer to a qualifying charity or philanthropy that has registered programs in support of Millennium Development Goals." A decade later Picketty noted, "The difficulty is that [implementing a] progressive tax on capital, requires a high level of international co-operation and regional political integration." That is (choice #51) Ethical Globalization theme territory.

Let's continue cloaking Piketty's analysis in *Choices We Make* framework terms. To fans of (choice #34) Competitive Capitalism he says, "Pure and perfect competition cannot alter the inequality $r > g$, which is not the consequence of any market imperfection." To those idealistic fans of (choice #29) Education for Democracy as noted he promotes investing in education / knowledge. And—despite identifying uncertainty and risk— he says to small European countries, "We must bet everything on democracy." He thinks larger countries like the USA and China have more options—with China firmly in the Authoritarian Followers camp. Overall his prescription seems to be one of reigning in rate of return on capital through a policy that fans of (choice #27) Egalitarian Progressivism will like, rather than the (choice #44) pushing for more economic growth as many politically right-leaning folks— including (choice #39) libertarians—would prefer.

How can this $r > g$ situation can this be rectified? One could simply tax capital income heavily and intentionally reduce r to no more than g. But—as Piketty cautions— indiscriminate / heavy-handed taxation runs "the risk of killing the motor of accumulation…" (i.e. killing the (choice #33) goose that lays the golden eggs.) The progressive taxation he urges is a less extreme solution. As are closing tax loopholes and shutting down offshore tax shelters. "To curb profit shifting overseas" to lower tax jurisdictions, as reported by *The New York Times* on May 20, 2021, "The Biden administration proposed a global tax on multinational corporations of at least 15% in the latest round of international tax negotiations." (This was advanced at a G-7 meeting of wealthy nations.)

Putting increased tax revenue to work by creating jobs in areas where work needs to be done is essential. In its January 20, 2020 report as the (choice # 30 and choice #33) world's wealthy elite were headed to their annual gathering in Davos, Switzerland, Oxfam said, "Getting the richest one percent to pay just 0.5 percent extra tax on their wealth over the next ten years would equal the investment needed to create 117 million jobs in sectors such as elderly and childcare, education and health."

Another strategy is to encourage (choice #22) restraint and voluntary adoption of ecosharing type limits. Billionaires Bill Gates, Melinda Gates, Warren Buffet, McKenzie Scott and others have pledged to give away nearly all of their wealth before or at death. [26] Worthy causes and recipients for (choice #32) large voluntary gifts are everywhere. Ideally (choice #12) peer pressure from other billionaires might trigger a wave of wealthy folks parting company with excessive income, and prominent CEOs setting examples to facilitate production of what people and the planet need—not what brings the most profit. Many hoped Elon Musk's announcement that he was "selling all physical possessions"—including a $37.5 million California home— and moving into a "kinda awesome" 400 sq. ft. prefab house would spur a tiny house movement away from McMansions. And wealthy folks' "corporate do goodism" support would kickstart a (Choice #35) corporate responsibility movement.

While some promote giving everyone a basic minimum income, American right-wingers railing against (choice #35) Social Welfare Statism would never vote for this, given their abhorrence of handouts and "free lunch." Instead, within a market-based capitalist system, the government could help that "invisible hand" reduce the gap between haves and have-nots by returning to aggressive past (choice #27) progressive taxation. The first figure in Piketty's book graphically identifies the 1948—1980 era in the USA as having the lowest level of income inequality for the 1910—2010 period. Not coincidentally this era was marked by taxing those with higher incomes at higher rates than earlier or later periods. The graph shows steadily rising American income inequality beginning in 1980—with the election of Ronald Reagan boosting the (choice #33) "greed is good" mentality.

Ideally, progressive taxation would transfer wealth from those most able to pay to those (choice #47) most needing help. Undoubtedly loopholes through which rich folks wiggle out of paying taxes will also need to be closed. Those on the political left prefer the Social Welfare Statism to the Corporate Capitalism half of the choice #35 pair. Others might echo the last sentence in this latter theme: "I'm optimistic management will move beyond seeking short-term profits for share-holders and steadily become more sensitive to stakeholders —including workers, the community, the environment, etc."

I. Steering Markets Toward Respecting Nature
What individuals can do to address a potentially looming environmental catastrophe is discussed in the next chapter. Here, we focus on reworking the market system into something environmentally much better in the long run. We previously mentioned Barry Commoner's *The Closing Circle* connection with the history of the circular economy. What would such an economy look like? And what might spur transitioning to it? The (choice #52) Environmental Economics theme identifies three key ingredients. Each has its own additional motivating factors for making the transition to the mimicking of natural processes.

First, it would be renewable energy based. Here job creation is a motivating factor. Given research suggesting investments in solar, wind, energy-efficiency, etc. employ more people than those in oil & gas / fossil fuel, this is an important way to put more people to work in that new economy. One study put the figure at three times as many.[27] Second, work is needed to build environmental costs into prices—starting most basically with putting a tax or fee on carbon emissions and other environmentally disastrous practices, such as excessive water use in arid regions. Third, the new economy should promote social stability by reducing inequality. Even without (choice #27) social injustice reasons for wanting to close the huge gap between rich and poor, from a (choice #44) Sustainability perspective this dangerous instability must be fixed. It carries with it the potential for violent social upheaval. One hopes the power elite realize their reign could end unless they restrain greed?

What about the organizational size scale behind a future circular economy? Those (choice #34) Liking Cooperation Based Communities favor community-based, decentralized organization, and politically correct thinking touts environmental benefits of local economic arrangements. But, some data suggest there can be both economic and environmentally important advantages to (choice #35) large, centralized corporations operating in a globalization context. Consider two examples—one energy-related, the other food-related.

First, I doubt that the dramatic decrease in the price of photovoltaic (PV) solar panels—which made thoughts of transitioning to a renewable energy based economy more than pie in the sky dreams —would have occurred in a world dominated by small businesses and local co-ops. My own experience in this regard tells some of the story: the PV panels I bought in 1980 cost $9.50 / watt, whereas those purchased in 2014 cost $0.65 / watt. Applying a 2.87 factor to account the difference in value of 1980 dollars compared to 2014 dollars (due to inflation) suggests a price decrease by factor of forty-two. (Since then prices have dropped more.)

Second, consider the belief that locally grown food is always to be preferred to food grown far away and shipped in. Not so, argues the 2012 book *The Localvores' Dilemma: In Praise of the 10,000 mile Diet* by Pierre Desrochers and Hiroko Shimizu. Two research investigations it describes involve providing tomatoes and apples to consumers in the UK. The first concluded that growing tomatoes in warmer, sunnier Spain and transporting them to the UK resulted in 630 kilograms of carbon dioxide emitted per ton of tomatoes, compared to 2394 kilograms of carbon dioxide emitted per ton of tomatoes grown locally in heated British greenhouses. The second compared locally grown apples stored an average of six months, with shipping freshly picked apples grown in New Zealand. Given that the shipped in apples were linked to 60 kilograms of carbon dioxide emitted per ton of apples, compared with 85 kilograms of carbon dioxide emitted per ton of apples for the local apples, they conclude, "avoid cold storage as much as possible and purchase products grown in different latitudes instead."

Economists talk of nations possessing a comparative advantage if they can produce and export goods at relatively lower costs than other nations. Market pricing could be tweaked to reflect a version of this after (choice #52) environmental costs such as carbon dioxide emitted have been factored in. But local, smaller scale economic ventures can play a role in a new circular economy in how people earn a livelihood.

Renewable energy installation or energy efficiency treatment related jobs are typically more decentralized / local business oriented than fossil fuel economy based ones, which are at often at centralized multi-national corporation energy installations. Ideally energy input for production in the new economy will have a renewable (ultimately) solar energy origin such that solar input equals waste heat escaping back into space. Some would argue that if certain envisioned products can't be made in some way mimicking nature's cycles, they should never make it off drawing boards and enter production. Likewise prices incorporating fees, taxes, or credit mechanisms, along with priority to reuse / recycle, can help limit the production of ecologically unsound products.

If we are ever to transition to a circular economy, both industrial scale production and consumer mindsets need to change. The (choice #45) Enoughness theme needs promoting, its More is Better Mentality counterpart discouraging. The latter theme can be linked to unhealthy excess, obesity, etc, the former one with lessening ones' dependence on "energy slaves." My formal energy education began in 1974 with learning that Americans essentially had ninety slaves working for them, computed from energy use beyond meeting basic metabolic needs.

Today's USA energy use data (see chapter 7) suggests that an average American is served by sixty-eight fossil fuel energy slaves. Accomplishing tasks with human muscle power could be connected to getting exercise needed to (choice #21) stay fit and trim. If they can do so in environmentally responsible ways, people should be encouraged to become (choice #46) small producers—especially to grow food or build small, energy-efficient houses. Eating less (or zero) meat and minimizing consumption of protein produced in wasteful, inefficient fashion should be similarly welcomed. Ideally, the market would eventually incorporate environmental and health factors into food prices.

People need to be better informed as to the environmental costs of products available for purchase, and the freedom to make smart, responsible choices needs to be encouraged. Likewise people need education that instills (choice #41) Respect for Nature feeling—not man apart (to use poet Robinson Jeffers' phrase.) If prices can be set so that the market tells the ecological truth, this will provide people with a strong incentive to choose wisely. Given centralized economies run by (choice #29) authoritarians or (choice #38) socialists typically have nonexistent or inadequate feedback loops, market based economies seemingly have an inherent advantage. So, rather than "throwing the baby out with the bath water," hopefully capitalism can be tweaked with several mechanisms to make Adam Smith's invisible hand and Barry Commoner's the closing circle economic realities.

Can national governments get out in front and help lead institutions, businesses, and individuals in the needed direction? Sir Partha Dasgupta, has recently finished an exhaustive study[28] on the economics of (choice #41 Respect for Nature) biodiversity commissioned by the UK Treasury Department. Unlike past economic analysis, it incorporates natural environmental factors into its production function, which more typically relates inputs (like labor and capital) to production output leaving them out. It concludes that failure to account for the rapid depletion of natural capital—which plunged in value by 40% per capita between 1992 and 2014 —puts the world at "extreme risk." It estimates that demands global economic activity puts on Earth's carrying capacity exceed (choice #44) sustainable levels by 60%. In identifying food production as the biggest destroyer of biodiversity, it reports national governments are globally (choice #52) subsidizing agricultural practices which damage nature to the tune of a staggering $4 trillion to $6 trillion per year.

Among its key recommendations: 1) national governments replace GDP with an economic indicator that includes natural capital and enables charting of depletion of national resources, 2) addressing population growth by expanding women's access to education and (choice #42) family planning, 3) paying national governments to protect huge areas whose ecosystems provide global benefits, such as the Amazon rain forest, 4) requiring those who exploit global commons such as the oceans pay for their use, 5) using (choice #49) less damaging farming practices, such as agricultural precision and new genetic techniques, and decreasing beef consumption, 6) increasing the efficiency with which humans transform natural capital into GDP, from a current 3.5% / year to at least 10% / year, to stop its decline, and 7) (choice #29) "education systems should introduce nature studies from the earliest stages of our lives, and revisit them in secondary and tertiary education."

In covering the report in its February 6, 2021 issue, *The Economist* notes, "Professor Dasgupta argues that economists should acknowledge that there are in fact limits to growth...a striking admission from an economist." And, after citing the professor's appeal to the "sacredness" of nature, ends by saying, "Clear thinking about nature can benefit from framing it in economic terms...Building the political will to prevent irreparable harm to the environment, though, may require an appeal to values that are beyond the purview of economics." This also provides choice #40 and choice #41 food for thought.

J. Choices: Health, Education, and Natural Security

Over our last fifty years as a species, clearly we've gotten lots smarter as measured by our increasing knowledge and technological capability. But in terms of your typical person's ability to make good choices, progress (if any?) has been much slower. In chapter 2 we considered "The Freedom to Make Stupid Choices," and presented examples of individual choices with significant bad economic, environmental, or health consequences. Bad choices including (choice #22) addiction, which many commercial businesses service. Thus America, according to the National Association of Convenience Stores, has over 150,000 such establishments, of which 80% are places Americans can satisfy their craving for gasoline to fuel their cars. Virtually all of them are places people can get fixes for addictions: to tobacco, alcohol, sugary soft drinks, junk food, coffee, and even gambling (by buying lottery tickets).

In contrast, 25 million Americans live in "food deserts"—meaning they live a significant distance away from supermarkets or places where they can buy fresh / natural food including fruits and vegetables. There, food often comes from convenience stores. It's typically highly processed, and high in sugar and fat—what health professionals say drives the nation's epidemic of obesity. In the last five years, two of these have sprung up within a mile of where I live. One, eying student business, was built in a vacant lot close to a high school; the other was built after a perfectly serviceable building—previously occupied by a Hastings video / book / music store that went out of business—was completely demolished. As I write, it prominently displays a "Lower Price on Cigarettes" banner.

Imagine Mark Zuckerberg[29] steering Facebook away from, as Salesforce CEO Marc Benioff puts it, being "the new cigarettes—it's addictive, bad for us, and our kids are being drawn in." Imagine, as Elon Musk has, America transitioning away from fossil fuel. Imagine a new chain of filling station equipped convenience stores—one called "Totally Total." You can go there to get your EV charged from renewable electricity, or get fresh, natural food. Many provide a place to sit and eat a meal while you wait; none sell cigarettes, beer, or junk food. Imagine an America, perhaps inclusively spurred initially by government incentives, in which people choose to start and operate businesses to meet real needs in healthy fashion—not just to make lots of money. Imagine—perhaps a bit further in the future as America transitions to a zero population growth, sustainable, no wasteful growth, service and maintenance economy—a non-profit chain offering a service called "Passing it on." It pairs old people— lacking needy relatives and about to die— with young adults in need of housing and what goes with it. People both worthy of help and physically capable of helping the elderly meet end of life challenges.

Nations can also make poor choices. Many question the wisdom of the US spending (choice #50) $13 billion each on nuclear-powered aircraft carriers to replace its aging ones. Some claim these ships could be easily destroyed with cheap surface to air missiles in a war with China. Rather than supposedly boosting national security by spending $130 billion to buy ten of these, some suggest using it to boost students' (choice #29) educational capabilities. That money could be used to increase teacher salaries to attract more capable people into the profession. Assuming 10% annual turnover in the nation's 3.3 million public school teacher population, that $130 billion could pay for $40,000 bonuses offered to all new teachers hired over a ten-year period. Or—as Joe Biden has proposed—spending $109 billion to make two years of community college free to students who live in states where it still is not free.

Democracies investing in education can equip their citizens to (choice #29) choose better leaders and make better choices. Governments can also fight (choice #43) misinformation. Suggestions have been offered to fight "the weaponizing of disinformation and parallel dismantling of trust in media." —what political consultant Mark McKinnon identifies as "the greatest consequence of the Trump presidency."[30] One idea: reforming section 230 of the Communications Decency Act, which shields online companies from liability based on what others post on their platforms. Tightening (choice #12 and choice #23) American free speech laws, and shifting the debate over its abuse, from First Amendment territory issues to protecting public health concerns, is another possibility.

Make those convicted of knowingly posting false information harmful to public health ineligible to vote? "Not necessary," others say. They argue the existing legal system can deal with such problems—pointing to multi

$ billion (choice #17) lawsuits brought by voting machine manufacturers. These were directed at those (including Fox News) who falsely associated their equipment with (choice #38) conspiracy theories regarding perpetrating election fraud. Libel laws could be important in this battle. Many feel it may be easier to sue someone on the back end for damage, rather go after them on the front end, where restricting freedom of speech may be alleged. Attention, lawyers: here's a do goodism opportunity to be part of the solution—not the money-grabbing problem.

Not all suggestions are new. Since the 2010 *Citizens United* USA Supreme Court decision, efforts have been underway to limit donations to political campaigns—so that money can't unduly magnify a wealthy person's influence in elections for selecting leaders. Those who value USA (Choice #29) democracy should realize that action is needed to strengthen it. If authoritarian followers and "the freedom to make stupid choices" folks prevail, democracy and a market-based capitalist economy could become a thing of the past. People should be taught to celebrate the (choice #40) freedom to take personal responsibility and make good choices, not to complain if they can't do whatever they damn well please. Attention, First Amendment lovers: promoting and exercising freedom to make stupid choices could eventually end freedom as we know it.

In his 2021 inaugural address President Joe Biden said, "Each of us has a duty and responsibility, as citizens, as Americans, and especially as leaders...to defend the truth and defeat the lies." Without access to good objective information, citizens will struggle to do this. Laws could prohibit an individual or corporation from posting online or dispensing by television information they (choice #43) know to be false. Given the key role online media platforms and television news outlets have communicating information in shaping people's beliefs, America's Federal Communications Commission (FCC)[31] could lead efforts to reform the information landscape.

The FCC could reintroduce, in modernized form, what it adopted in 1949 and eliminated during the Reagan years in 1987: the Fairness Doctrine. This law required those who held broadcast licenses cover controversial issues of public importance in a way that was fair, honest, and balanced. Balanced to the extent that contrasting viewpoints were at least presented, if not allotted equal time. Many feel that rescinding this policy contributed to current USA polarization and culture war. In the doctrine's new incarnation, online platforms would be covered, and with respect to issues of public importance, viewpoints based on lies silenced. Laws going beyond limiting speech that presents "a clear and present danger" and (as later interpreted) where the speaker intends to incite "imminent lawless action" should be thoroughly debated.

These could prohibit knowingly dispensing misinformation that would compromise citizens' basic knowledge with respect to civic, consumer, financial, health, scientific, and technological literacy. The existence and enforcement of such a doctrine would increase the value of knowledge, and make education more important. Ideally (choice #29) education (to a certain level) should be free—with increased funding from (choice #27) progressive taxation aiding this revamping of societal priorities. As folks encounter penalties for ignorance, society could elevate teaching into a valued, better-paid profession. Better-educated citizens with critical thinking skills could greatly boost democracy and business productivity.

Both governments and the private sector have leverage short of outlawing individual freedom to make stupid choices. Government can raise taxes to make certain stupid choices too expensive for most to casually select. Private corporations can raise prices to certain groups, like cost of health insurance to smokers. But they should proceed carefully, and distinguish matters where people have a choice, from those where they really don't. For example, if you're hopelessly (choice #22) addicted to nicotine, doing without it may not be a choice.

More poignant examples are provided by those profoundly (choice #37) uncomfortable with an assigned gender role. This is especially troubling when one feels the wrong body parts have been provided at birth. The general problem of discomfort with gender can likewise be discussed using (choice #49) Attitudinal Fix and Technological Fix themes. Merely changing gender roles—as in "living as a man" instead of "living as a woman"—can fit squarely in the attitudinal fix realm. In contrast, medical procedures such as hormone treatments and sex reassignment surgery are clearly technological fix interventions. Often physical body surgery changes are irreversible.

In all of the hoopla surrounding transgender issues it seems one fact is overlooked. Only in the last few decades has modern medical technology provided an alternative to simply being stuck in the gender that nature seemingly wrongly assigned you. In chapter 1, a related (choice #37) decision for a gay or trans person to publicly acknowledge their sexual identity, instead of keeping it private, was linked to finding courage. Clearly an informed decision by a person so uncomfortable in a gender role that they seek a modern technology fix requires even more courage.

The above example—and futuristic technology-facilitated body additions (some already in use such as hearing aids) to enhance human senses—suggests that a long-time definition of (choice #41 and choice #49) technology needs modification as follows. Seems we need to rewrite, "Technology is what humans do to gain control over nature in shaping the environment to its liking," to read, "Technology is what humans do to gain control over nature in shaping the environment and themselves to be more to their liking." But, while technological fixes will undoubtedly be important in building a desired future we can envision, they won't be enough—attitudinal fixes will also be needed.

Stopping the Covid-19 pandemic provides one problem-solving example of how attitudinal and technological fixes are often both needed. It illustrates how, even if human ingenuity finds a technology-based, scientific consensus validated good solution such as a vaccine, attitudes may preclude its successful implementation. An early 2021 survey of health care workers in nursing homes—where the Covid-19 has claimed a disproportionately large share of victims—found that 62% did not plan on getting vaccinated, typically due to lack of trust in its safety.

From a global public health perspective, despite all the death associated with it, the world has potentially benefited from the Covid 19 pandemic. It has helped to drive home "we're all in this together," and "if any are at risk, all are at risk" lessons. Besides the pandemic, there are many issues that demand nations work together. Perhaps most needed are joint efforts to avoid catastrophes that could be brought on by nuclear war, climate change, and overpopulation. In this regard, the world is looking to two nations—the USA and China—to lead and behave responsibly.

.

Can the USA and China avoid making the stupid (choice #50) choice of fighting a war? As the world's two largest carbon dioxide emitters, might they instead act maturely and work together to limit their own greenhouse emissions, and spur other nations to do so? Might they ramp down their (choice #36) national security concerns based on (choice #18) fear of each other, and co-operatively join together with the rest of the world in working for natural security? Most basically, security involves feeling safe and free from danger. Natural security is feeling this way about the integrity of the natural world, its living things, and life support systems. Working to instill (choice #41) Respect for Nature feelings promotes natural security.

Trading both (choice #2) narrow focus and (choice #41) human-centered orientation, for a global vision inspired nurturing and protecting nature stance, can come with recognizing the origin of a big threat. Robert Carlson's essay "From National Security to Natural Security" ends by describing that threat and the appropriate response. It concludes, "Human security requires natural security; perversely, the greatest threat to natural security stems from human action. If humans are to continue to thrive, we must determine how to become nature's greatest hope." This 2013 essay appears on *The Bulletin of the Atomic Scientists* website. The group, famous for maintaining a "doomsday clock,"formed in response to the need to educate people about the danger of nuclear weapons that ended World War II in 1945. Four decades later, scientists like Carl Sagan came to realize that even a limited nuclear exchange could wreak havoc in the form of a planet-wide "nuclear winter." Urging all nations to choose (choice #50) peace has always been central to their mission. But in recent decades increasing appreciation of the (choice #44) fragility of Earth's climate, and its vulnerability with respect to human greenhouse gas emissions, has led the group to climate action activism.

Besides that, Carlson's essay identifies another threat. He writes, "Our increasing numbers impose a load that is now impacting nature's capacity to support human societies." Roughly two years after Carlson's essay appeared, China announced it was replacing its (choice #42) notorious one-child-policy with a two child one. Introduced in 1978, the Chinese Communist Party claims it prevented a staggering 400 million births.[32] While those on the (choice #40) Freedom from Limits bandwagon frown on any such limits, others applaud. From a global public health and (choice #25) family perspective, they say, "In raising a family considerations, quality rather than quantity of children should be emphasized given the environmental impacts associated with more people." They urge couples to have no more than two kids of their own, and to adopt kids lacking parents if they want more.

If we're to survive, humanity will need to debate and establish ideal target levels for long-term (choice #44) sustainable levels of its numbers on Earth—perhaps three billion people? And likewise find target levels for carbon dioxide and other atmospheric greenhouse gases—say 350 parts per million (ppm)[33] for CO_2? First we must (choice #40) stop those levels from growing. By 2020 seven of the ten leading economies had pledged to be carbon neutral by 2050. With China pledged to do so by 2060, and the USA rejoining the 2015 Paris Climate Accord, only India needs encouragement to move in this direction. In thinking of action to stabilize population, it's helpful to recall more history.

In 1968 the rate of growth of the human population peaked at 2.09% / year—a pace which if maintained leads to a doubling in around 34 years. The same year, with Earth populated by 3.6 billion people, Stanford University professor Paul Ehrlich's book *The Population Bomb* was published by Sierra Club / Ballantine Books. While selling over two million copies, the book was attacked for its alarmist tone. Even within the environmental community some took issue with its identifying population growth as the biggest environmental problem. The book nonetheless alerted people to dangers of unchecked population growth. Encouragingly by 2018, in a world with over four billion more people than it had in 1968, the rate of growth of the human population had fallen to 1.09% / year. But even that rate, if maintained, would lead to a doubling in around 70 years—a possibility few welcome.

Each additional person—especially in affluent countries—adds to the cumulative ecological footprint of humanity. Globally, the (choice #31) traditional Catholic Church remains a big source of opposition to (choice #42) family planning. Critics charge that both they, and those on the Protestant evangelical religious right, are more concerned about (choice #16) saving souls from eternal damnation than they are about saving the planet from human activity triggered ecological catastrophe.

Obviously differences of opinion and many other obstacles exist as the human community attempts to move forward together in addressing numerous global challenges. In chapter 4—using the words of a conservative Christian leader—we previously identified cynicism as one such obstacle, Obviously this is not confined to religious matters—(choice #49) attitudes associated with it can paralyze efforts to tackle problems throughout society. Members of liberal (choice #27) progressive religious groups typically are not cynics. In this regard I especially like how the Unitarian Universalists (UU) (using hand gestures) characterize themselves: "This is the church of open mind. This is the church of the loving heart. This is the church of the helping hands."

Ecological handprints represent the flip side of the ecological footprint perspective. Unlike footprints, which register often unintentional negative impacts, ecological handprints refer to what we intentionally give—positive and tangible action we take out of environmental concern. This also drives certain citizen science efforts, which technology in the form of smart phone apps increasingly helps to gather ecological data.[34]. This has revolutionized counting birds. Beyond that, iNaturalist—run jointly by the California Academy of Sciences /National Geographic Society—has received 66 million observations of over 300,000 species.

This is one way those with helping hands who care about biodiversity work to preserve ecosystem integrity. The next chapter addresses ecological handprints one can leave in a world facing a climate crisis. Beginning with lofty pie-in-the-sky expressions of (choice #25) love, it gets down to earth with helpful, practical suggestions of climate action that individuals can pursue. And it identifies associated tough love choices both individuals and society can make.

Notes

1 In 2013, Chinese leader Xi Jinping visited Confucius' cemetery at Qufu and called for "new and positive roles" for his teachings. Now—as reported by *The Economist* (May 22 2021)—the master's classical teaching and character-building lessons are rapidly returning to Chinese schools. It says, "In neglected Confucian morals, educators see a set of values that may be a solution to modern social ills, just as some in the West turn to traditional Christian values."

2 Deng made a restaurant in Beijing famous for the Peking Duck that it offered. I sought out this difficult to find place during a December 2012 visit and got lost. I was helped by a Chinese man I encountered on a deserted street. I'll never forget his smile when he finally understood the Chinese name of the restaurant that I was trying to say. And his enthusiastic motioning / pointing.

3 based on data on the tradingeconomics.com website accessed March 2021

4 "Red China: Death to Sparrows" *Time* magazine May 5, 1958 issue

5 Meadows, Donella H., Meadows, Dennis L. Meadows, Randers, Jorgen, Behrens, William W. *The Limits to Growth*, Potomac Associates / Universe Books Falls Church, VA 1972

6 an American progressive think tank founded in 1963 in Washington, DC.

7 "America at Hunger's Edge" *New York Times* September 2 2020

8 Founded in Oxford, UK in 1942 and named for famine relief, it's now a confederation of twenty humanitarian charities headquartered in Kenya

9 Hardin, Garrett, "The Tragedy of the Commons" *Science*, vol. 62 pp.1243-1248 1969

10 Hawken, Paul "Natural Capitalism" *Mother Jones*, March 1997

11 Cline, E. "Will the Circular Economy Save the Planet?" *Sierra* Jan 2021

12 Done with helping pay for Dayton's and Ruth's college education, I retired and started living off interest income. Given that my real, full time work career only spanned the nineteen year mid 1985 to mid 2003 era, and even then I was working as a (lower rung) university or high school teacher, my being able to do this amazes many people. I did benefit from bequests of around $25,000 —but paid out a similar amount in divorce settlements.

13 and only buy something new at full price if there is no other option.

14 based on figures from statista.com accessed in April, 2021.

15 For the record, I don't think she ever did.

16 Boulding, Kenneth "The Economics of the Coming Spaceship Earth" first presented at the Sixth Resources for the Future Forum on Environmental Quality in a Growing Economy in Washington, DC March 8, 1966

17 "Recycling: From Clochemerle to Compost Heap" *The Economist* Jan 2 2021

18 Insurance companies have done well taking my money.

19 I left the last one as interior finish work loomed and my third marriage ended.

20 from the 2009 work of an international group led by Johan Rockstrom

21 you can find this in the Donella Meadows Archives at donellameadows.org

22 You can go to thenextsystem.org website and download / read / soak up her vision of a 21st century global cultural revolution.

23 from the Union of Concerned Scientists, 2018 figures (ucsusa.org)

24 This is based on the CCL "Energy Innovation & Carbon Dividend Act" proposal – go to citizensclimatelobby.org for details.

25 Sachs, Jeffrey *The End of Poverty: Economic Possibilities for Our Time* Penguin Books, New York 2005

26 The Giving Pledge is "a commitment by the world's wealthiest individuals and families to dedicate the majority of their wealth to giving back." A list of who has pledged can be found at givingpledge.org. When accessed in April 2021, it listed 220 individuals and families.

27 Garrett-Peltier, Heidi "Green Versus Brown: comparing the employment impacts..." *Economic Modeling* vol. 61 pp439-447 February 2017

28 "Final Report —The Economics of Biodiversity: The Dasgupta Review" February 2, 2021 610 pages download at www,gov.uk

29 Mark was at Harvard when my daughter and son-in-law were there. My April 2018 *Worldview Watch #56* suggested where he might lead Facebook. The quote from Benioff is from his October 16, 2019 tweet.

30 Russonello, G. "Trump Isn't the Only One on Trial—The Conservative Media is Too" *The New York Times* February 8, 2021

31 I know the FCC once had a "good guy" as a commissioner. His name was Nicholas Johnson. Many years after I read his 1972 book *Test Pattern for Living,* I wrote to thank him for this book and received a nice letter in reply.

32 Results of China's census released in May 2021, suggest its 1.4 billion population is on the brink of decline. This has prompted a three child policy.

33 concentration of 1 ppm is like one drop of water in a ten gallon aquarium

34 using an internet connected smart phones with appropriate app, one can point to a plant to both identify the species and send a record to a regional database

Chapter 7: Choices in a Time of Climate Crisis

A. Introduction

One day in the fall of 2019, I joined millions of people—at 620 plus locations throughout America and countless more worldwide—in rallying for climate action. Excited by the 400 people I marched with, sobered by messages on signs they carried, I felt both crisis and love. The (choice #14) love grew out of compassion for energized young people I saw—most with signs putting their small individual hopes and pleas out there that we can meet this very big collective challenge. How big? As then sixteen-year-old Greta Thunberg put it, "This is an existential crisis that is going to affect our whole civilization, the biggest crisis humanity has ever faced." The previous year she had become concerned about climate change and began a school strike in Sweden. Protests she started, over leaders' failure to act, spread around the world —leading to her *Time* 2019 Person of the Year selection

I felt connected to the people I marched with. They silently told me I'm part of something much bigger than myself. One guy's sign showed Earth from space with message: "We're all in this together!" Signs picturing children made me think of my own grandkids—who embody the love I feel and hope I have for the (choice #44) sustainable future I want everyone to choose with their actions.

When I began drafting this chapter I had fond memories of a morning I spent with my two grandkids and my son earlier that spring in 2019. So, just as I'd begun my 1990 *Coming of Age...* book with a letter to my own two young children, I penned a letter to my two grandkids. Despite big disruptive events and changes affecting my family and the world, I've decided to keep this letter as I wrote it and present it in the next section. Perhaps my grandkids—or your children—will read it at some future time when they're ready.

The disruptive events that shook both America and the world in 2020 included still more unprecedented weather-related disasters, more widening of gap between rich and poor, a global pandemic that killed millions of people with no end in sight, a video of a policeman's outrageous (choice #17 and choice #24) cruel killing of a black man in Minneapolis, and the culmination—actually on January 6 2021 with a siege of the US Capitol—of a (choice #43) disinformation campaign led by an American president that posed an existential threat to democracy.

For my extended family, the year began with my daughter's New Year's Eve announcement (at my son's house) that she was pregnant with her first child. Days later, she and my son-in-law were slammed by a (suspiciously Covid-19 like) illness. Her unrelated diagnosis as having a chronic, potentially life-threatening illness followed. I next saw her—in masked, socially distant fashion—in mid March 2020. The day before she had saved me $2000 in using frequent flyer miles to get me out of a Covid-19.spooked, rapidly shutting down Europe. By mid-June we were celebrating two things: 1) the drug (choice #10) modern medical science had created that would apparently make it possible for her to live a full life, and 2) the birth of my third grand daughter.

In the letter directed to my two grandkids that follows, I recall a walk with them through downtown San Francisco and a panoramic look we had of the whole area. It recalls our view that morning of the Golden Gate Bridge—and past views I'd had of it. Little did I know when I wrote the letter, that on September 9, 2020—a day when Californians might otherwise be celebrating the 170th anniversary of their state's admission to the union—California was on fire like never before. It seemed the dreaded future of global warming had arrived ahead of schedule. Normally chilly San Francisco had been sweltering in triple digit record heat. To its south, on September 6th, the city of San Luis Obispo—just a few miles from the Pacific Ocean, recorded a mind-bogglingly hot 120 °F temperature. The heat, drought, and fierce winds spawned fires and smoke so bad that on September 9th the sky seen around the Golden Gate was an unreal orange color. And little did I know that the 2021 California fire season would be even worse.

My letter imagines taking the kids to "my progressive …church one Sunday morning." Again, unbeknownst to me when I wrote it, I later outlined a program for a church service with theme "Love in a Time of Global Crisis." It's built around songs I've written in recent years—typically to be sung to the tune of well-known popular songs. I can imagine some day putting this program on during a time when all three of my (much older) grandchildren are visiting and can listen. (The program outline and song lyrics appear in Appendix B.)

This chapter metaphorically transitions from that letter and initial (choice #25) pie-in-the sky unconditional Love as Family Glue global family perspective addressing concerns related to key global crises, to focusing on one in particular: climate change. It then offers a big picture look at the global climate change problem, followed by a more down to earth, practical Tough Love orientation. This is specially directed at what people can do—both as individuals and in joining with others—to help combat climate change. It concludes with stories related to my own climate action related lifestyle changes providing illustrative examples.

Before reading the letter—which metaphorically attempts to lead the unknowledgeable and sheltered, who I nonetheless feel a bond with, from fantasy land to tomorrow land—think about why certain people you know would be unreceptive to its message as you look at Figure #24.

Figure #24: Choices <u>Not</u> to Make in a Time of Climate Crisis
* To deny there is a problem
comment: those who do this are ignorant (This book should remedy that.)
* To adopt a cynical attitude toward efforts to deal with the problem
comment: this choice #32 preference kills hope ➔ ethically unacceptable
* To hide behind God
comment: choice #13 Apocalypticism preference= ethically unacceptable
* To be a defector when co-operator actions are needed
comment: defecting with last move is good end game strategy, but here if
the game ends, everyone loses (see *Coming of Age...* book for more)
* To be part of the tragedy of the commons problem
comment: you are failing to take responsibility, free-loading off others
*Doing what you know is part of the problem when alternatives exist
comment: where practically possible, pursue alternatives as you can
* To let down those depending on you, and suffering psychologically
comment: letting down family or loved ones can cause guilt; letting
down humanity suggests you're alienated and don't belong = not healthy.

B. "Love in a Time of Climate Crisis" Family Letter
Dear Children:
I suspect you'll grow up in an affluent America with love all around you and where stories have happy endings. Shielded from the world where that is not so, eventually you'll be ready to see something more than what your narrow view from fantasy land shows. This letter—and the big picture it paints to correct your distorted view—is for that eventuality...

Remember a spring 2019 morning when, guided by your Daddy, we walked together, in downtown San Francisco? You were ages six and almost four. We ended up near the top of the city's tallest skyscraper—the Salesforce Tower, at 1073 feet tall, where your Daddy sometimes works— with a stunning view. On the way, walking through city streets, I recall worrying we'd have a view you weren't ready for: of homeless people begging. In wanting to avoid that particular "teachable moment," I recall thinking, "You aren't ready for certain grim realities."

You know nothing of climate change wrought by just 1.2° C of global warming from pre-industrial times. Approaching our destination, I wondered, "What will the world be like when you're old like me? By century's end with 3 °C warming as many computer models project— or even more (reputable models say 6° C under certain assumptions)? I recalled a report[1] on projected sea level rise in coastal areas as polar ice melts and seawater expands. If current trends continue, it suggests the lowest levels of this building could be underwater by the turn of the century.[2] Riding the elevator I imagined someday using a blanket analogy (Figure #25) to help you understand how greenhouse gases like carbon dioxide (CO_2) warm our planet.

The panoramic view from the top undoubtedly expanded your mental map of nearby space. My seeing the Golden Gate Bridge triggered memories and got me thinking, "You girls have little idea of—not only the big picture state of the world—but of your own roots." I later worked out a genetic heritage / big picture in space & time lesson.

Your great great great great great grandfather Neverson Cook was born in 1785 in Laurens County, South Carolina at a time when the human population was less than one billion.[3] The industrial revolution—fueled by burning coal with CO_2 gas emission—had yet to get going to the extent where carbon dioxide atmospheric concentration had risen much, so it stood at 280 parts per million (ppm.) Neverson's wife Margaret, born in 1788, always wore a hat since, as an infant, she was (choice #17) scalped by Indians and left to die in a massacre of her parents.

She lived to be eighty-five years old. Between the time her Daddy was born—around 1750—and 1900, when my grandfather Edgar Neverson Cook was seventeen, human fossil fuel burning added 44 billion tons of carbon dioxide to the atmosphere (Figure #21.) About this time Edgar got restless and dreamed of moving to California. He did this in 1904, after first stopping at the World's Fair in St. Louis. By 1939 he was working as (choice #18) "The Golden Rule Plumber," as a business card I see years later proclaims. Since 1912 he'd been married to my grandmother Mary, in what reportedly was "a really good marriage with lots of love." My father Edgar Neverson Cook Jr. was the middle one of their three children. He was twenty-four years old in 1939 and working in Hollywood at the Walt Disney studio.

My father—your great grandfather— first saw the Golden Gate Bridge in 1939. He and I saw it together when I was around your age. A few years after my father died in 2007, I had another close look at this bridge while staring out a window during a break in my visit to the Walt Disney Family Museum. As I ate my lunch that day I saw a picture on the cover of a brochure I'd picked up earlier. It shows two people and the famous multi-plane camera. Not unexpectedly the man prominently featured in the center is Walt Disney. But I'm shocked when I realize the other one is the man I called Daddy. As I look, all the (choice #25) love I felt for him comes rushing back. Tears soon cloud my view.

As we looked at the Golden Gate Bridge that morning, I pointed in the direction of Santa Rosa. Your mommy grew up there, and my cousin Gary and his wife live nearby. Two years ago something scary happened to them: they barely escaped a really big, fast moving fire that burned thousands of homes. What made it so bad? Record heat[4] and drought made worse by global warming. Last year, a bit farther north and east, an even worse fire destroyed Paradise, California—a city of 30,000 people. As I write, millions of California utility customers are without power— given intentional, days long blackouts triggered by fear that sparks from power lines will start new fires.

The last five years, the hottest ever since record-keeping began in the 1880s, have brought extreme drought and mega fires. But global warming—more properly called global climate change— also brings heavier rains, more powerful and longer lasting storms /hurricanes, and extreme temperatures (mostly hotter but sometimes bitter cold). In the last thirty years, seawater has become 30% more acidic[5], Arctic ice is melting at a rate of 13% per decade over the last four decades, and some of the oldest and thickest ice has declined by 95%.[6]

In the last three years, the list of related USA catastrophic weather events includes: 1) 4.5 feet of rain that fell around Houston, Texas during Hurricane Harvey in 2017 is a two day continental USA record; 2) weeks of mid 2019 rain produces unprecedented flooding in the USA Midwest; 3) Hurricane Dorian hits the Bahamas in fall 2019—with storm surge of twenty-six feet, average winds of 185 mph sitting over it for twenty-four hours with gusts to 220 mph. All this prompts 11,000 scientists to publish a letter (in a November 2019 issue of *BioScience*,) declaring a "climate emergency." As 2020 begins, a reported nearly 30 million acres in Australia are burning—with up to one billion animals feared dead! [8]

Scientists overwhelmingly link climate change to burning fossil fuels / resulting CO_2 pollution. In the 120 years beginning in 1900, this has added 1577 billion tons of carbon dioxide to the atmosphere. You'd expect these additions to be decreasing based on recent steps we've taken to address the problem, right? Tragically, human burning of fossil fuels in 2018 put an all time record 37 billion tons of carbon dioxide into the atmosphere (up 2.7 % from the previous year, and up from 25 billion tons in 1990.) Each day this traps heat equal to that released by 500,000 Hiroshima size atom bombs. CO_2 atmospheric concentration is at 415 ppm and steadily growing. Worse, this gas lasts around 1000 years in the atmosphere, so even if we quit burning fossil fuel—and cutting trees (which absorb it) — those levels will not decrease any time soon.

The numbers I've mentioned indicate dramatic increases in carbon dioxide added to the atmosphere, as Figure #21 shows. While 44 billion tons were added in the 150 years from 1750 to 1900, that soared to 1577 billion tons in the just 120 years from 1900 to 2020. Population grew from less than 1 billion people in 1785 to 7.7 billion in 2020. This is exponential growth—quite different from linear growth. The latter involves something growing by the same amount each year, the former by adding a steadily increasing amount each year — since it's based on adding a fixed percentage of the whole. For example, 70,000 years ago, during a trying time when we faced extinction[7], the (Homo Sapiens) human population was perhaps less than a thousand people. We might imagine it's since grown linearly, adding roughly one billion plus people every 10,000 years to get to the current seven billion plus number. In actually it has grown exponentially, taking some 69,780 years to add the first billion, but a mere 220 years to add 6.7 billion more!

The Limits to Growth book provides another example of exponential growth. "Suppose you own a pond on which a lily plant is growing. The lily plant doubles in size each day. If the lily were allowed to grow unchecked, it would completely cover the pond in thirty days, choking off the other forms of life in the water. For a long time the lily plant seems small, and you decide not to worry about cutting it back until it covers half the pond." When will that be? On the 29th day: you have one day to save your pond!

This brings us to choice #44, between Economic Growth and Sustainability themes. To parents who love their children this choice seems like a total no brainer. Simply put, if we really love our kids, we want each new generation of them to inherit "at least as much wealth per capita" as the previous generation (where "wealth includes both manmade and natural capital.") In short we want economic development to proceed in a sustainable fashion. Those who choose differently might tell you that an economy is healthy when it's growing at 3% / year. This is exponential growth and there's a problem.

Those who like 3% / year (or greater) growth rates might also claim (choice #40) "I'm free to do whatever I want with my property— including land I own." But they're ignoring an inherent limit given Earth is only so big. At 3% growth / year a quantity doubles in roughly 24 years.[9]   Such doubling cannot continue forever. This is what Greta Thunberg means by "fairy tales of eternal economic growth." Anyone who appreciates the lily pond example—and can see that, metaphorically with our population and pollution growth, for humanity the 29th day has started— will choose the "Limits and Ethics" theme in choice #40.

Ethics—it's a complicated subject that basically boils down to doing what is right. I never really got to know my grandfather, but I have two reasons to believe he valued treating others right. First, he used (choice #18) "The Golden Rule" on his business card. Second, his son, my father, was well-behaved. I never saw this other-oriented, (choice #24) very tolerant man—who often said skin color doesn't matter, people are people, good and bad—act unethically. His behavior modeled those three principles cited in (choice #33) "Ethical Orientation." After a few minor adolescent missteps nearly all of us make, I too embraced them.

"Thinking of others before you act" is quite different from the aggressive self-interested stance of those "Seeking Wealth and Power" — the theme on the flip side of the choice #33 card. Sadly, in a greedy quest for wealth and power, many behave badly and do things—lying, cheating, and stealing—they teach you **not** to do in kindergarten. Besides being (choice #43) honestly grounded and lacking in deceit, my lifestyle— quite different from most —builds on two more things I learned in kindergarten: "Play Fair!" and "Clean Up Your Own Mess!" They're at the heart of an approach to life called "Ecosharing" based on an environmental ethic I outlined long ago.

You should know that your Daddy was born in the middle of a ten-year attempt at self-sufficient living. I later documented this "Ecosharing Experiment" in the *Coming of Age...* book. It provided an example of a lifestyle roughly characterized by world average per person income, energy use, etc. Suffice it to say that by the time your Daddy—my son Dayton—was five he'd consumed lots of home grown garden produce, milk and eggs from our goats and chickens. He'd lived his whole life in a house with wood and solar heat, electricity from solar cells and wind generator, water from a spring coming out of a bluff, hot water from either wood or solar heat, a compost toileting[10] equipped bathroom, etc.

The experiment ended when the time and money demands of raising two children—to say nothing of stresses brought on by semi-wilderness Arkansas Ozark living— precluded it continuing. During these years I learned more about being a (choice #46) "Small Producer" than consumer. One lesson: it's hard work producing a significant amount of your own food, using little more than human muscle power, living more like people did over a hundred years earlier. Food produced by modern agribusiness yields ten times more per acre of land than food grown in 1900. Why? The (fossil fuel) energy used (by machinery, in irrigation, in farm fertilizer and chemicals etc.) to grow it is roughly ninety times greater. The best we did on the Ozark homestead was to meet around 40% of our food needs—this from a garden / small livestock operation in an area blessed with rich soil and fairly regular, often abundant rainfall.

Years spent trying to grow food in the arid mountain western USA confirm that I probably won't be striving for food self sufficiency again. But perhaps I'll attain energy independence —given all the sunshine and the dramatic fall in the price of solar cells. While a modified Ecosharing approach may intrigue some as the basis for a practically flexible, ethically / environmentally superior lifestyle, I'm not pushing it. Instead, I direct your attention to a worthy goal (choice #45):

excerpt from Enoughness theme

"I aim to maximize well-being, while minimizing consumption and ecological footprint. I like the five "R"s: reusing, repairing, recycling, refusing to buy what I don't need, and reducing waste. I like voluntary simplicity…" (Note: I think of enoughness as Dana Meadows' word.)

I can provide countless examples of how I do this every day. In contrast, consider two examples of what many Americans choose instead of Enoughness —the More is Better Mentality. First, growing over the last half century or so, we've had average size of new homes doubling from 1300 to 2600 sq. ft. (Note: buildings are responsible for almost 40% of greenhouse gas emissions—including everything from the materials (cement, steel, etc.) in constructing them, to energy use related to the thermal comfort of those inhabiting them.) Despite record-setting drought and looming water shortages, three western cities top the list of increase in average new home size: Las Vegas, San Diego and Phoenix. Second, US per capita food consumption and obesity have soared. Simply put, in 1960 only 13% of adults were too fat, now over 40% are.

There are other choices involved here besides choice #45. With respect to our second example —since maintaining normal body weight is so important to one's health—it must be folks are increasingly not choosing (Choice #21) the Healthy Orientation. Note its words, "You only get one body. How well you care for it…makes a big difference." I got those words from my Dad. Besides eating a healthy, no red meat, mostly plant / natural food diet, I exercise and purposely live a labor-intensive life. I also try to eat a diverse diet—one rich in anti-oxidants and compounds known to be capable of repairing (cancer-concerning) cell damage.[11] Staying healthy is easier if you also value (choice #22) self restraint.

Speaking of restraint, there are a few hate-filled, gun-toting crazy people out there who at times break down, abandon restraint, seek (choice #19) vengeance and kill innocent people. Sometimes schools are targeted and students are killed. Guns in the wrong hands in America are a real problem. Sometimes the wrong hands belong to children—who decide to play with a gun parents fail to secure in unloaded, locked up fashion. Sadly, many gun owners are caught in a "Culture of Fear" (choice #18). While some own guns to (choice #17) intimidate / threaten others should the need arise, I know many buy them with protecting their family in mind. Many of them no doubt think of themselves as Christians.

It greatly saddens me that so many people who think of themselves as Christians own so many guns, and so many of them don't practice what Christianity is supposed to be about: loving kind-heartedness and Enoughness. To help you understand this sad reality, I imagine taking you girls to my progressive (choice #27) church one Sunday morning—

where you join other children in religious education activity. When we get back together you express surprise, saying, "You know, Grandpa, friends tell me Sunday School is all about Jesus this, Jesus that, and how, and, if you don't do what He and God want, you'll burn in Hell when you die. But I didn't hear any of that this morning. Don't people here believe that?" "No, generally speaking," I say. But before I can continue you ask, "What do you think of Jesus?"

Recalling choice #19, I say, "Jesus taught us when you feel victimized to "turn the other cheek." To not give in to Bitterness, Vengeance—to not seek revenge with "an eye for an eye, a tooth for a tooth," but instead to forgive those who wrong you. He taught us to value Gratitude, Forgiveness (the other choice #19 theme.) This can be difficult to do in practice—as is something else he taught: that we should (choice #14) love our neighbors. But certainly the world would be more peaceful if more of us did this."

I point out Jesus didn't think much of (choice #33) people pursuing and holding onto great wealth. I (choice #32) add, "Rather than cynically railing against billionaires who selfishly flaunt and hold onto their wealth, I now prefer to celebrate the good that some of them do. Some of them use their wealth to make the world a better place[12]; some give most of it away." Wanting to say more about enoughness, I pull the *Coming of Age...* book from my backpack, and read what follows.

"This growing awareness that we are part of a global system—a global village...—is a tremendously revolutionary concept...Its implications are vast; it provides a basic understanding and simple set of ethical principles capable of remaking our entire planet. We...recognize that the world is urgently in need of a simple lifestyle...We are one world and the resources of the earth are limited. What I consume relates directly to what is available for others; if I consume more than my fair share, I am literally taking food from the mouths of others, clothes from their bodies. Therefore if I am...to take Christ's teachings seriously, I must restrain my consumption of the world's resources."

I won't continue our imagined trip to church. The above quote is from a 1977 book called *No More Plastic Jesus* by Adam Daniel Finnerty. It offers wisdom bearing on choice #36. Here my choice differs from that of most Americans. They like singing the national anthem and "God Bless America," whereas I prefer John Lennon's song "Imagine." And, while I love America, I think of myself first as a Global Citizen and an American second. My dislike for the Proud Identification and Tribalism alternative they prefer is increasing. I'm saddened that our leaders seemingly can't get beyond thinking of themselves as members of the tribes known as Republicans and Democrats, rather than as Americans.

I think political leaders everywhere need to be team players. This belief solidified after I reconsidered choice #28. Whereas I once preferred Individual Glory, now I like Celebrating Team Accomplishments. In resolving conflicts, I believe we all need to seek "Win, Win" solutions— avoiding "I win, you lose" outcomes since these can lead to renewed conflict. I think if enough caring people who prefer Service to Others over Cynicism in choice #32, also get firmly behind love and the (choice #36) global citizens team, we all can eventually win, although it will be a long battle. By all I mean all humans and all life on our planetary home. The latter should generally thrive once Earth's most destructive species (us) commits to it being a healthy place.

We can do that by embracing the love associated with a feeling of belonging to something bigger than ourselves—and overcoming the alienation that has too long separated us from nature. With a Not Man Apart attitude we can reverse previous collectively poor choices dominating and disrespecting nature (choice #41.) In battling climate change we should pursue (choice #49) either attitudinal or technological fixes, or both depending on which holds the greatest promise of success.

So my efforts (choice #31) Working for Change as an environmental activist in this battle involve pushing for technological fixes—using energy efficiently and more renewable (solar, wind, etc.) energy where possible, rather than using fossil fuel and needlessly wasting energy. And I pursue attitudinal fixes and seek to change minds. Among the latter I encourage people to think like global citizens of a small planet who value (choice #21) health (their own, their children's, their planet's, etc), appreciate (choice #40) limits, and (choice #45) enoughness.

Thus I urge people to make related lifestyle choices both out of love and practical considerations—realizing that those tiny contributions to a sustainable future can add to something big. It can similarly involve convincing young people—especially those talented in math and science —that their help is needed. Career choices they make can put them in the thick of the battle for a better future, seeing action on either (choice #49) technological (as engineers) or attitudinal (as teachers) fronts.

Yet, while things individuals do to decrease carbon footprint are important, perhaps more important are things we do to change "the system." It needs to move <u>toward</u> (choice #41) respect for nature, (choice #44) sustainably valuing human well-being and long-term biosphere integrity, and <u>away from</u> valuing short-term economic growth and concentrating wealth in the hands of the well-connected rich and powerful few. Changes driven by (choice #33) ethics can reduce corruption; those driven by (choice #27) compassion (for those living in heart-breaking poverty) can reduce (dangerously unstable) inequality. A less emotionally charged, but equally important, needed change involves fixing the market system with (choice #52) Environmental Economics.

Basically this starts with factoring environmental impacts (pollution, resource depletion, etc.) into the prices we pay. Implementing this safe, renewable energy promoting choice, would end fossil fuel subsidies, and put a fee on greenhouse gases emitted in producing or using products or services we purchase. Note choice #52 is the last one. I fear its Big Business Pushes Limits alternative as an existential threat, and as (choice #1) wishful thinking. We pretend there's no problem; we continue to do little or nothing, leading to widespread, catastrophic, unacceptable climate impacts that demand action. Then, having delayed, we could act hastily in the form of expensive geoengineering schemes, that, due to our limited knowledge, don't work how they're supposed to.[13] Many disastrous futures (including an ice age!) could result. Scary!

You girls'— and all children's — future is in <u>our</u> hands today. So, our (choice #10) science –based, (choice #13) …Dancing With Systems needs to be inspired by love, use (choice #2) global vision and draw on the 70,000 years of wisdom gained since we last faced extinction. This is what (choice #1) an evidence-based approach demands. It's also what both the Relaxed, Generous Loving and Cautious Processing themes of choice #14 call for. So people everywhere: Let's go for it together!
        Love, Grandpa, writing in a time of climate crisis.

C. A Big Picture Look at the Global Climate Crisis
A Summary of the current environmental impact
In terms of weather-related disasters, as bad as those recounted for 2017-2019 years were, 2020 was worse. Although it merely tied 2016 for

being the globally warmest on record, given a natural (eastern Pacific La Nina) cooling oscillation, 2020 wasn't supposed to be so warm. As such, it was 1.25 °C above the pre-industrial average value—and the last six years have been the warmest on record. 2020 began with record wildfires in Australia (burning an area larger than Pennsylvania) and California. There, 4.25 million acres burned with 9,917 fires destroying 10,488 structures killing 33 people. The Atlantic 2020 hurricane season saw a record thirty named storms, twelve of which made landfall in the US. Hurricane Iota hitting Nicaragua in mid-November was notable for two reasons: 1) it was only the second category five hurricane to occur in the North Atlantic in November, and 2) just thirteen days earlier category four hurricane Eta had struck basically the same part of central America.

Based on National Oceanic and Atmospheric Administration (NOAA) data, US weather and climate related disasters costing over $1 billion in damages and related charges are increasing—a trend reflecting growing impact of climate change. In the years spanning the 1980—2020 period, a total of 285 such disasters cost $1.875 trillion (in constant 2020 dollars.) If you divide the 285 disasters by the forty-one years spanned, you get roughly seven such disasters per year. But the annual average for the most recent (2016-2020) period is much higher—over sixteen such disastrous events. And ominously, the twenty-two billion dollar plus disasters in 2020 is the highest number for any of these forty-one years.

Weather-related flood disasters in India and China caused $40 billion in damages in 2020. In the Arctic, sea ice cover shrank to the second lowest amount on record, and temperatures were typically 3°C (=5.4°F) above normal—with some regions registering 6°C warmer. With a Siberian heat-wave—described as "almost impossible without climate change" and "600 times more likely" because of it[14]— came wildfires, loss of permafrost and invasion of pests (Siberian silk moths.) In Greenland, where loss of ice set a record in 2019, scientists feared irreversible sea level rise as temperatures continue to rise and the ice sheet continues to decline. A January 25, 2021 NOAA report highlighted the large uncertainty in global sea level rise predictions for the year 2100, depending on future greenhouse gas (GHG) emissions: one foot if GHG emissions are low, as much as 8.2 feet if they're high.

2021 brought record heat to the Pacific Northwest causing hundreds of deaths. In late June, Lytton, British Columbia measured 121.3 °F—a planet Earth record for locations above 50° N latitude. Two days later a wildfire destroyed the town. At 116 °F, the record high temperature in Portland, Oregon was a stunning 9 °F hotter than the previous record! Days later, saltwater intrusion weakening concrete was suspected as the cause of a Surfside, FL building collapse, killing 98 people. Since its completion, sea level had risen eight inches. Many saw this disaster as a scary prelude of things to come in south Florida. July brought the worse flooding in 500 years to parts of Europe, and in 1000 years to parts of China—and huge fires in Siberia. Both Turkey (in July) and Europe, on August 11, measured highest ever temperatures of 120°F. Two days earlier a UN issued climate report sounded a "code red for humanity."

The Basic Science Behind Global Climate Change
According to NASA's "Earth Observatory" web page, the solar energy received by the Earth's surface (land and water) annually averages out to a steady rate of 240 watts per square meter. If, on average, Earth radiated that same amount of energy back into space, its temperature would stay constant. But in the last two hundred years since the beginning of the Industrial Revolution humans have increasingly disturbed the Earth—Sun energy balance by most notably adding greenhouse gases (GHG)—chiefly carbon dioxide CO_2—to the atmosphere. Like a thicker blanket, this traps extra radiant heat energy—so with less heat escaping to space, Earth's temperature increases as Figure #25 (from the USFS) illustrates.

Figure #25A	Figure #25B
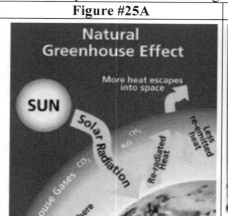	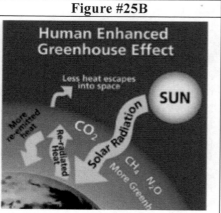

Analogy: Think of greenhouse gases as a blanket. The natural effect (shown in Figure #25A) warms Earth by around 60° F (or 33°C). Greenhouse gas emissions (carbon dioxide CO_2, methane CH_4, nitrous oxide N_2O, etc) make the blanket thicker, enhancing the greenhouse effect (Figure #25B). Concentration of CO_2 is 420 ppm, of CH_4 is 1.9 ppm— up 50% and 250% from pre-industrial levels.

Although concentrations of these gases are feeble— the 420 ppm for CO_2 = just over one-twenty-fifth of one percent—their steady increase can have disastrous consequences. Likewise global warming of average $2.0°C$ (=3.6° F) doesn't sound like much, but in places like the Arctic the increase has been considerably more. And in a natural world whose ecosystems have been fine-tuned and typically adapt to changes on a 1000 year or more time scale, such small temperature increases can wreak havoc. As they can to human infrastructure—where worldwide replacement costs could easily run into the $ trillions over a few years.

Globally greenhouse gas annual impacts are staggering: from emissions of 10 billion metric tons of carbon = 38 billion tons CO_2 eq + 5 billion from deforestation = 43 billion metric tons CO_2 eq / yr.[15] Dividing that number by the planet's 7.7 billion people gives roughly a 5.5 metric ton CO_2 equivalent impact per person per year. Average values for people in rich countries are a lot more: with around 14% of total impact, USA annual per capita impact is around 18 to 20 metric tons.[16]

Researchers like Thomas Piketty point out such national averages can be computed based on the country where the GHGs are produced, or where the consumer end products associated with them are consumed. He notes that rich Europeans, Americans and Chinese increasingly emit the most CO_2, while the emissions from the world's poorest citizens are falling. His figures say the richest 1% of Americans, Europeans, Singaporeans and Saudis emit more than 200 tons of CO_2 equiv per person per year: 2,000 times more than the poorest in Honduras, Rwanda or Malawi. A 2015 Oxfam study likewise found the richest 1% of the world's people population emit 175 times more carbon than the bottom 10% do.

Figure #26A (based on *IPCC* 2014)   **Figure #26B** (statista.com 2020 data)

Global GHG emissions by economic sector	% of global greenhouse gas impact	GHG from fossil fuels by economic sector	% of global greenhouse gas impact
Electricity and heat production	25	Power	44.3
Agriculture, forestry, other land use	24	Industry	22.4
Industry	21	Surface Transport	20.6
Transportation	14	Homes	5.6
Other Energy	10	Buildings	4.2
Buildings	6	Aviation	2.8

Regarding Figure #26: While the biggest source of GHGs from human activity is CO_2 from burning fossil fuel, other sources like deforestation (since trees absorb CO_2) are important. Note Figure #26A is based on old data: for emissions in 2010. In his 2021 book *How to Avoid a Climate Disaster*, Bill Gates presents a similar chart showing 31% coming from what he calls "Making things, like cement, steel, and plastic"—much higher than values in the "Industry" sector in the above charts.

"Climate Tipping Points — Too Risky to Bet Against"
summary of climate scientists report in *Nature* November 27 2019
If we emit more than 500 gigatons CO_{2eq} we'll exceed the $1.5°$ C global warming threshold beyond which changes may be irreversible. At the current 43 gigatons per year rate, humanity has 500 / 43 = 11.6 years to cut emissions to zero.[17] Given current realities, many expect the best we can do is limit warming to $3°C$. This is dangerous: it greatly increases chances that feedback /tipping points— leading to large discontinuities in the climate system—will be triggered.

Tipping point areas and concerns are: a) Amazon deforestation leads to lack of moisture to feed rain clouds /forest dieback /frequent droughts, b) Arctic sea ice loss, c) boreal forest—more fires and pests, d) coral reef die offs, e) Greenland ice sheet melting, f) permafrost thaw releases carbon, g) Antarctic ice unstable h) Atlantic circulation slowdown, and i) north polar vortex weakening. (Note: this list could be incomplete.)

Melting Greenland and West Antarctic ice, raising sea level by 10 meters=32 feet, could take 10,000 years if warming is limited to $1.5°C$, above $2.0°C$ it could take less than 1000 years. At $2.0°C$ warming 99% of coral reefs could be lost. Permafrost emissions—not including methane from deep tundra or undersea hydrates—could release 100 gigatons carbon, Amazon forest die-off could add another 90 gigatons. Note the effects of a weakened Gulf Stream and north polar vortex will be predominately felt by increasing frequency of winter cold snaps. Some evidence exists both are already happening, although more data is needed to confirm a link to climate change.

A sobering comment from the report: "Atmospheric CO_2 is already at levels last seen around 4 million years ago, in the Pliocene epoch. It is rapidly heading towards levels last seen some 50 million years ago — in the Eocene — when temperatures were up to $14°C$ higher than they were in pre-industrial times. It is challenging for climate models to simulate such past 'hothouse' Earth states. A possible explanation is that the models have been missing a key tipping point: a cloud-resolving model published this year suggests that the abrupt break-up of stratocumulus cloud above about 1,200 parts per million of CO_2 could have resulted in roughly 8°C of global warming." If CO_2 rises by 1% / year, we'd hit 1200 ppm (from current 400+ ppm) in just 115 years.

It seems (choice #52) business as usual can't continue—people must become convinced of a possible pending climate disaster and change their ways. The key question is, "When?" Sense of urgency can depend on the tipping point involved and its perceived impacts. Thus, given the role it plays in keeping Europe warmer in the winter than its high latitude suggests, scientists in Denmark are studying the Gulf Stream / Atlantic circulation.[18] Groups hoping to prevent future global environmental disasters are lobbying for international laws on ecocide like those on genocide that can be enforced through the International Criminal Court.

D. Choices: Tough Love in a Time of Climate Crisis

The letter / "Love in a Time of Climate Crisis" essay suggests (choice #25) love can be the glue that holds the human family together and motivates its members to sustainably preserve the environmental health of its planetary home for future generations. But, just as freedom doesn't mean you're free to do anything, love is not granted unconditionally. Those receiving it must increasingly take personal responsibility as they grow and learn. Thus tough love (choice #25) is part of the above title.

The climate crisis is an existential threat. Meeting the challenge it poses will demand sacrifice and require that both individuals and society make tough lifestyle choices. What choices? "What can citizens concerned about climate change actually do?" What follows is a list (with bold print highlighting important points) and discussion in ten areas. We've already provided some background to help with respect to the first thing you can do in this regard: **1) Educate yourself as to the problem**.

We introduce the next thing with the headline of a report on a Yale University study published in *The Proceedings of the National Academy of Sciences* in June, 2019. Designed to get your attention it reads, "The most important thing you can do right now to fight climate change, according to science." What is it? Perhaps surprisingly it is:
2) Talk about the problem and solutions with family, friends, neighbors, social groups you belong to, etc.

Awareness of the problem is needed. You should a) fully educate yourself on basics and issues, b) discuss with others this question "The climate is changing—Why aren't we?" and c) tell them, in locally relevant fashion, how you've changed your lifestyle in response to the climate crisis, and what benefits you've gained from this action.[19]

3) Join others to politically advocate for climate action. Be a climate conscious voter and urge others to vote for politicians concerned about the climate crisis and policies that effectively address it. Figure #27 lists the important (choice #52) environmental economic and related policies.

Figure #27 Climate Action Policies to Support

a) **Put a price on carbon.** While there are various ways of doing this, a "fee and dividend" approach is preferred by many. This would involve putting a "fee" (not to be called a "tax") on carbon and periodically returning a rebate or "dividend" to offset higher utility costs.[20]
b) **Stop building coal-fired power plants**, stop leaks of natural gas (which is ~ 96% methane CH_4.), rapidly phase out support for fossil fuel (coal, oil, natural gas) by ending subsidies, tax write offs, loans, etc.
c) **Support renewable energy** (especially solar and wind) and energy efficiency technologies, with target dates for achieving certain goals*, tax credits, subsidies, research dollars, and other incentives * examples: carbon neutral or 100% renewable energy powered by 2050.
d) **Support market incentives, regulatory changes, etc.** to expand energy efficient and renewable energy choices for consumers[21]
e) **Support the transportation sector makeover**, with high fuel efficiency standards to help rapidly transition to renewable energy and prohibiting sale of internal combustion engines after a target date (2035?)
f) **Vastly increase support for public transportation**
g) **Push the job-creating potential of solar, wind, energy efficiency**
h) **Support research** into better ways to capture energy from intermittent sources like solar and wind more efficiently and store it for later use; support finding ways to cut GHG emissions associated with making key industrial products like cement, steel, aluminum, etc..
i) **Support farming that builds carbon in soil and reduces erosion.** Reducing plowing with no till planting, growing cover crops, and interspersing plants with deep roots in between row crops can do this. Recognize farmers who both grow food and sequester carbon in soil.
j) **Recognize that infrastructure for supplying natural gas (currently methane) is valuable** and someday could deliver "green" hydrogen.[22]
k) **Allow current nuclear power plants to operate** since they are carbon emission free, but don't permit new ones to be built.

4) Individually take steps to understand and do simple carbon footprint / energy cost savings calculations. Recognize that this can aid individual efforts to minimize the fossil fuel use that can be quantitatively documented with energy bills. And that encouraging such skills promotes decision-making that can benefit society.

Carbon footprint calculators can be found online, but knowing how to do your own calculations provides certain advantages. Appendix C —which includes a worksheet (Figure #40) —will help you do this. This begins with figuring out how many kWh (kilowatt hours) of electrical energy, therms of natural gas, and gallons of liquid fuel (gasoline, fuel oil, propane) you're consuming. Appendix C provides an example detailing the calculation of my carbon footprint, summarized below.

Summary of My Carbon Footprint for the last year

Following Appendix C procedures, it is the sum of three parts: $C_H + C_N + C_L$ = 2.02 + 2.22 — 0.75 = 3.49 metric tons of carbon dioxide equivalents.[23] For comparison, the USA per capita value (based on 2019 EIA data) is 15.7 metric tons of carbon dioxide eq per person-year; the world per capita value is 4.8 metric tons. C_H is a measure of carbon dioxide emissions I've been directly responsible for based on actual use of fossil fuel in residential and transportation as shown in Figure #28.

Figure #28 My Carbon Footprint Analysis (Apr 2020 — Mar 2021)

Source / units	my amount	Unit / MBTU	my MBTUs	1bs of CO_2/MBTU	my 1bs of CO_2
Natural gas / cubic feet	9700	975	9.9	117	1158
Electricity / kWh	1197	95	12.6	88	1109
Gasoline, gallons	110	8	13.8	157	2167
Air travel	0		0		
Bus travel	0		0		
total			36.3		4434

C_H = 4434 lbs x (1 metric ton / 2200 lbs) = 2.02 metric tons of carbon dioxide
Note: one BTU is about equal to heat from burning a 3" long wooden match, or more precisely the heat needed to raise temperature of 1 lb of water by 1 °F. The MBTU unit = one million BTUs. BTU is short for British Thermal Unit.

C_N is a rough estimate of carbon dioxide emissions that I indirectly add to the atmosphere through my participation in the US economy. My value is 2.22 metric tons. This is based on average USA per capita combustion of fossil-fuel related impact in sectors excluding residential and transportation, corrected by factors based on my income and the energy intensiveness of my lifestyle. C_L is a correction for two factors not accounted in C_N that are important: diet and pet ownership. My negative 0.75 value for C_L—due to my essentially vegetarian diet and lack of pets— corrects an assumption inherent in the C_N calculation: that I'm a typical American.

Study of Appendix C suggests a typical American uses 271 MBTU / person –year of fossil fuel energy. Since roughly 4 MBTU / person –year of energy from food is needed to supply human basic metabolic needs, dividing 271 MBTU by 4 MBTU suggests typical Americans benefit from roughly 68 fossil fuel energy slaves. My own corresponding fossil fuel usage—a value associated with all three $C_H + C_N + C_L$ contributions to my carbon footprint is around 74 MBTU / person –year. Dividing that number by 4 MBTU indicates, in the last year, I managed to get by with just 18.5 fossil fuel energy slaves working for me.

Estimating energy and cost savings from making lifestyle changes in "what if" calculations is handy. In this regard consider the two examples provided in Figure #29. These examples illustrate that legislative efforts to mandate tougher fuel efficiency standards or prohibit sale of incandescent bulbs perhaps aren't (choice #30) an elitist / environmental extremist / liberal plot! Contrary to that characterization by some on the extreme political right, they can save (choice # 46 and choice #48) hard-working ordinary people not insignificant amounts of hard won cash.

They also illustrate how important fostering simple problem solving skills taught by education that focuses on promoting critical thinking can be. Not just important to individuals in making consumer choices, but to the operation of our (choice #29) democratic system in an age when voters are increasingly called on to vote on issues with a technology-based component.

Recall section B "Thinking Like a Scientist..." in chapter 5 provided an example of how a "what if" calculation can address a home heating energy problem. It sketched how heat transfer can be calculated with equations that are rather simple to use if you're not scared off by use of math—which sadly many people are. Also, see question 18) in the Appendix C "Questions & Projects" section for another example.

Figure #29 Two Examples: Energy-Saving "What If?" Calculations

Example: What if you replace your 20 mi / gal truck with a 50 mi / gal fuel efficient hybrid vehicle—how much money and energy is saved, and GHG avoided?

> Driving 10,000 miles per year requires 10,000 miles divided by 20 mi / gal = 500 gal gasoline.
> Driving 10,000 miles per year requires 10,000 miles divided by 50 mi / gal = 200 gal gasoline
> 500 − 200 = 300 gal of gasoline saved per year and
> 300 gal x 19.6 lbs CO_2= 5880 lbs x (1 metric ton / 2200 lbs)
> = 2.67 tons CO_2 emission avoided.

(Note if gasoline costs $3.33 /gallon x 300 gal = $1000 saved per year.)

critical thinking related question: a gallon of gasoline weighs 6.3 pounds, so how can burning it produce 19.6 pounds of carbon dioxide? Answer: most of the weight of the carbon dioxide doesn't come from the carbon in the gasoline, but rather from the oxygen pulled out of the air. High school chemistry students should be able to provide the details.

Example: What if you replace incandescent light bulbs with LED bulbs—how much money and energy is saved, and GHG avoided?
Imagine you replace thirty incandescent 100 watt 1300 lumen light bulbs, assumed to be on an average 2.74 hours per day, with thirty 13 watt LED bulbs, each providing the same 1300 lumens light output.
Using electrical energy (in watt hours) = power (in watts) x time (in hours),
Each incandescent bulb uses 100 watts x 2.74 hours = 274 watt hours per day
Each LED bulb uses 13 watts x 2.74 hours = 35.6 watt hours per day
So each replacement saves 274 − 35.6 = 238.4 watt hours per day
Multiplying by 30 bulbs and 365 days / year = 2610480 watt hours saved / year
Converting to kWh, 2610480 watt hours x (1 kWh /1000 watt hours)=2610 kWh
Multiplying 0.92 lbs of CO_2 avoided per kWh x 2610 kWh = 2401 lbs of CO_2/yr
2401 lbs x (1 metric ton / 2200 lbs) = 1.09 tons CO_2 emission avoided
(Note if electrical energy costs $.13 per kWh, multiplying this by 2610 kWh shows you save $339 per year.)

5) Take steps to minimize the part of your individual carbon footprint that can be quantitatively assessed based on reputable studies of the effect on greenhouse gas emissions of certain lifestyle changes.
For example: a study reported in the prestigious journal *Science* in July 2017, in which researchers looked at thirty-nine peer-reviewed papers, government reports, and web-based programs, assessed how (choice #45) lifestyle choices might shrink personal share of GHG emissions. Savings for choices considered appear in Figure #30.

Choices We Make in the Global Village
Figure #30

The top ways to reduce your carbon footprint

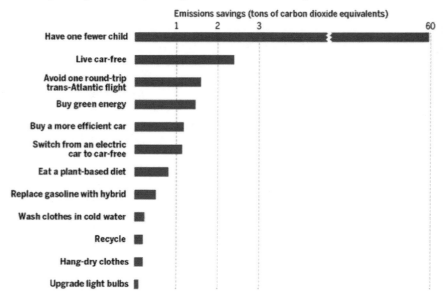

Emissions savings (tons of carbon dioxide equivalents)

CREDITS: (GRAPHIC) J. YOU/*SCIENCE*; (DATA) SETH WYNES AND KIMBERLY A NICHOLAS, *ENVIRONMENTAL RESEARC LETTERS* (201

While the study found that four such choices stood out, far ahead of all else was the decision to (choice #40 and choice #42) <u>not</u> bring an additional child into the (affluent nation) world.[24] As for the other three choices—(choice #21) becoming a vegetarian, reducing air travel, or not owning a car—report author Sid Perkins writes, "Eating no meat cuts an individual's carbon footprint by 820 kilograms of carbon dioxide (CO_2) each year [.82 metric tons / year]…in large part, from the large amounts of energy needed to grow, harvest, and process feed crops. Foregoing one round-trip transatlantic flight each year would cut a person's emissions of CO_2 by 1600 kilograms [this is 1.6 metric tons / year] Getting rid of their car would cut emissions by 2400 kilograms, or 2.4 metric tons / year."

6) Consider making lifestyle changes involving transportation.

Note five of the twelve "top ways to reduce your carbon footprint" in the Figure #30 chart involve transportation. Beyond those, consider additional GHG emission reducing transportation related suggestions presented in Figure #31.

Figure #31 Transportation Climate Action Suggestions

a) Get (choice #21) healthy exercise, and reduce CO_2 footprint, by walking where appropriate, and biking to destinations too far to walk
b) Where distance or hills preclude biking, use an electric motor assist equipped bike. While such E bikes purchased new can be expensive and electricity used to charge their batteries may be fossil fuel derived, (choice #46) do it yourselfers (DIY) can overcome that.[25]
c) If you can't walk or bike, maximize miles per person per energy consumed by using public transportation (buses, subways, trains) instead of driving.
d) Foster reduced CO_2 footprint in getting to work or school: 1) arrange to live near to where you work or attend school, 2) consider car pooling, 3) take advantage of online courses schools often offer, or 4) encourage employers to allow telecommuting /working by ZOOM / telepresence. With this, frequent overseas business travelers can vastly reduce the large GHG emissions associated with air travel.
e) If you must drive a car: 1) maintain it to increase fuel efficiency (regular tune-ups, keep proper pressure in tires, stay streamlined, etc.), and 2) drive at a reduced speed (<65mph on highways), employ "hyper-mileing techniques" where practical.
f) If you must fly, consider buying "carbon credits" to offset associated GHG emissions.[26]

7) Consider making lifestyle changes involving food.
Depending on how sectors are delineated, animal agriculture / the livestock sector is often cited as the second leading contributor to greenhouse gas emissions. Based on UN FAO and other estimates, GHG emissions here may be around 7 billion tons / year of CO_2 eq (representing roughly 18 to 20% of all GHG emissions.) However, fossil fuel industry and livestock / food sectors overlap—given that much of our food system is powered by fossil fuel: powering tractors and other farm machinery, fishing boats, food transportation trucks, etc, food processing, chemical / fertilizer manufacture, refrigeration, kitchens, distribution centers, etc. So, according to the 2017 book *Drawdown—The Most Comprehensive Plan Ever Proposed to Combat Global Warming* edited by Paul Hawken— "if you add livestock [emissions]] to all other food related emissions—from farming to deforestation to food waste— what we eat turns out to be the number one cause of global warming."

With respect to reducing food-related GHG emissions, here are some suggestions:

a) **Don't eat beef**— get protein from other sources.

Example: Here's a (choice #46) do-it-yourself tasty falafel burger patty alternative to hamburger beef patty or expensive, highly processed meatless burger. Open a 15.5 oz can (I paid 62 cents) of garbanzo beans (chick peas.) Mash them in bowl (or pulverize in blender.) Stir in an egg, 2 Tbsp of sesame butter (tahini), ½ cup corn meal, two tsp spices (cumin, coriander) Add enough water to make workable; form into four patties. Fry in 2 Tbsp of olive oil. Based on Walmart Grocery prices, total cost per patty is 30 cents, or $1.20 per lb (roughly 1/3 price of beef). Compare to (meatless) Impossible Burger at $7.95/lb or Boca Burger at $5.15/lb.

As Figure #32 suggests, cattle are by far the biggest source of GHG emissions from animal agriculture, with one recent study (*Environ. Sci. Technol.* 2016, vol. 50, # 15, pp. 8164-8168) showing that in an average American diet, beef consumption creates 1,984 lbs CO_2 $_{eq}$ / person annually. Replacing beef with plants would reduce that by ninety-six percent, bringing it down to just 73 lbs of CO_2 $_{eq}$ / person. Of course the term "plants" here is rather vague. And plants generally aren't associated with protein, nor (for some appetites) with good taste. Figure #32 presents alternative ways to get protein and associated CO_2 impacts. Note: *Drawdown* ranked "Plant Rich Diet" the 4th most important of the hundred global climate impact solutions it assessed.

Figure #32A		Figure #32B	
Protein source, kilograms of CO_2 associated w/ 50 grams protein from it		**AMERICAN DIETS** metric tons CO_2 per person per year	
Beef= 17.7*	Lamb=9.9	MEAT LOVER=3.3	
Crustaceans (farmed) =9.1		AVERAGE=2.5	
Cheese=5.4	Pork=3.8	NO BEEF=1.9	
Fish (farmed)=3.0	Poultry=2.9	VEGETARIAN=1.7	
Eggs=2.1**	Tofu=1.0	VEGAN=1.5	
Beans=0.4	Nuts=0.1		
*from 0.43 lbs beef ** from 8 eggs from report published in *Science* by Poore and Nemecek		from ERS /USDA, various LCA, EIO-LCA data	

Noting that it's missing from Figure #32, "What about cow's milk?" you ask. Studies find its carbon footprint (and those of yogurt, cottage cheese, and cream cheese typically made from it) is smaller than pork, poultry, and eggs. (Since it takes around 10 lbs of milk to make a pound of cheese, cheese has a bigger climate impact than milk.) The chart in Figure #33 offers more on milk and plant alternatives.

Figure #33: Environmental Impacts associated with a liter of "milk"

"milk" type	kg $CO_{2\,eq}$ emissions	Land Use, m^2	Water use, liters
cow	3.2	9.0	628
rice	1.2	0.3	270
soy	1.0	0.7	28
oat	0.9	0.8	48
almond	0.7	0.5	371

Source: report published in *Science* by Poore and Nemecek

b) **Don't waste food.** According to *Drawdown* "a third of the food raised or prepared" never makes it from farm to household to be eaten, and in its production, processing, transport, etc. this wasted food is globally linked to 4.4 billion tons / year of GHG emissions. The waste occurs mostly in high income countries where "up to 35% of food …is thrown out by consumers," whereas in low income countries "relatively little is wasted at the household level." Note: *Drawdown* ranked "Reduced Food Waste" as the third most important of the 100 global climate impact solutions it assessed.

c) **Consider not drinking coffee** (Coffee lovers, can I interest you in a cup of sun-brewed herbal tea?")
After oil, coffee is the world's second most important traded (and transported) commodity. And it's a substance with zero nutritional value. Nikko Mills' study[27]—posted on theecoguide.org website in March 2016—showed how each cup of coffee consumed can be associated with roughly 0.275 lbs of CO_2 emissions. Multiplying that by the reported 2.25 billion cups of coffee globally consumed every day by 365 days per year and converting to metric tons gives a staggering roughly 100 million tons of annual CO_2 emission (=0.27% of all global GHG emission.). As for USA annual coffee expenditures, estimates vary widely. One leading provider of marketing and consumer data (statista.com) put them at $82.4 billion for 2019 or around $250 per capita; another group estimated an average American spends $1100/year related to drinking coffee.

d) (Choice #46) **grow your own food.** Do this responsibly. Organic and regenerative agriculture techniques are preferred; watering using captured rainwater or gray water is advised in arid regions. And **support local organic farmers / growers with your food expenditures.** Note: *Drawdown* ranked "Regenerative Agriculture the 11th most important of 100 global climate impact solutions it assessed.

e) **Build soil by composting** and thereby avoid related greenhouse gas (methane) landfill emissions. One can argue that future (choice #44) sustainability of the human experience depends on preserving and building good soil. Adding compost can help. According to *Drawdown*, in 2015 the USA composted 38% of all food waste; the European Union achieved 57%; lower income countries much less. And "if all lower income countries reached the US rate, and all higher income countries achieved the EU rate, composting could avoid methane emissions from landfills equivalent to 2.3 billion tons of CO_2 equivalent by 2050." Thus "Composting" ranked the 60th most important of 100 global climate impact solutions *Drawdown* researchers assessed.

f) Build soil fertility with "**pee cycling**." Recall the story and discussion in chapter 6 regarding the benefits of using, instead of wasting, human urine. As to yuck factor, do an (choice #49) attitude fix: "get over it!"

8) Consider making lifestyle choices to save energy and reduce GHG emissions associated with the building you live in. If you have a choice, live (choice #45) in a smaller house, since in general unwanted heat transfer increases with exposed surface area. If planning a new house in a cold climate, opt for a small, energy efficient passive solar house. Where summertime cooling is the biggest thermal comfort concern, plan one with earth climate tempering features. Figure #34 provides suggestions to consider for where you currently live.

9) Take financial and other investment related steps at least partly based on climate change concerns.
a) Don't invest in —or pull any existing investments out of —fossil fuel companies. Obvious targets in this regard would be oil companies like Exxon-Mobil, Chevron, Shell, BP, etc. Many banks—which some environmentalists have called on to boycott—are heavily involved in financing fossil fuel projects according to "Banking on Climate Change 2019," a report endorsed by 160 organizations including the Sierra Club.

In this regard, the latter summarizes the report by noting that, in the three years since the Paris Climate Accord was reached at the end of 2015, thirty-three banks lent $1.9 trillion for such projects. It goes on to say, "$600 billion went to 100 companies that are most aggressively expanding fossil fuels. Alarmingly, these findings reveal that the business practices of the world's major banks continue to be aligned with climate disaster." At the time (choice #35) the four biggest backers of

Figure #34 Residential Building Climate Action Suggestions

a) Consider adding more insulation to under-insulated (first) ceilings, (next) walls, (last) floors, and installing storm windows and storm doors.
b) Consider weatherizing your house to plug cracks (especially around doors and windows), and using caulking and weather stripping to cut unwanted air movement.
c) Rather than heating your whole house in winter, including unoccupied rooms, consider using zone heating in which just the areas people use are heated. This can be done with "smart" household energy technology systems, or with an approach keeping whole house thermostat temperature low and using small, low wattage electric space heaters to target work-spaces. Such spaces can also be warmed by sun streaming in through windows—solar assisted zone heating.
d) In winter, open south window drapes to let sun in; on cold nights, close drapes or blinds to help keep heat in, or better use moveable insulation—perhaps of (choice #46) DIY construction, made from pieces of rigid board insulation, foam, etc.
e) In summer, close drapes or blinds to keep sun out. Note: this can be especially important for west facing windows in late afternoon.
f) If possible, avoid summertime air conditioner use, but instead encourage natural ventilation. In summer, take cool air in low and, since hot air rises, give it a path to rise and escape out a peak vent or through a high up, shaded window or door.
g) Wrap your hot water heater tank with an insulating blanket to cut heat loss. (Note: take care to avoid the fire hazard from gas pilot lights!)
h) Consider building and using (choice #46) a do-it-yourself (DIY) batch solar water pre-heater.[28]
i) Consider building and attaching a (choice #46) do-it-yourself (DIY) solar warm air heater to the south wall of your house, or putting one on a south-facing roof for winter temperature boosts.[29]
j) Save energy in other ways: turn off lights, TV, computers, appliances, etc. when not in use; replace incandescent lights with LEDs; turn thermostats down in winter and up in summer or use smart thermostats programmed accordingly. Avoid using an electric or gas clothes dryer but instead let the sun dry your clothes by hanging them on a clothesline. Wash clothes with cold water; install flow restrictors on showerheads to cut down hot water use, take shorter showers, etc.
k) Use solar photovoltaic electricity. Lease or buy photovoltaic panels and use in electric utility interactive fashion, or off grid with battery storage; use in more cost effective DIY ways as suggested toward the end of this chapter.

such projects were all US banks: JP Morgan Chase, Wells Fargo, Citi, and Bank of America. (Note: by March, 2021 those banks "have vowed to align their lending portfolios with the goals of the Paris Agreement.")

b) Invest in tree planting. Most trees absorb CO_2 using a rather inefficient photosynthesis carbon fixation process to sequester it, but a select few use an evolutionary more advanced (C4 carbon fixation) one. Thus an article by Emily Chasan (posted on the *Bloomberg* website on August 3, 2019) proclaims "We Already Have the World's Most Efficient Carbon Capture Technology." This is the fast growing Empress Splendor tree. Whereas most trees absorb just 1.1 to 9.5 metric tons of CO_2 per acre per year, Empress Splendor trees reportedly pull in 103![30] (Note: some, like Mark Benioff, are behind a planting one trillion trees goal for humanity.)

c) Don't use bitcoin or other cryptocurrencies. A Cambridge University study released in February, 2021 reported that Bitcoin / cryptocurrency mining was consuming 121.36 billion kwH of electricity per year—more than Argentina uses—with release of roughly 60 million tons of CO_2.

d) Fight putting data centers[31]—with powerful computers needing water for cooling—in arid regions. One proposed for Mesa, AZ would use 1.25 million gallons a day, and create few jobs despite $800 million invested.

10) Other Lifestyle Changes to Consider Making
a) Consider not owning pets. Besides ethical reasons for choosing this— such as extending a (choice #42) Sanctity and Dignity of Life belief to grant an animal rights / freedom from (choice #23) servitude—the ecological cost of a pet may outweigh the benefits. A 2017 study by UCLA professor Gregory Okin found that growing, processing, and transporting food—often highly processed meat—eaten by 160 million American dogs and cats annually contributes a whopping 64 million tons of CO_2 equivalent to the atmosphere. Simple division gives an average of 0.40 tons of carbon dioxide equivalent / year per pet. That, he notes, has roughly the same climate impact as a year's worth of driving from 13.6 million typical American cars. Household pet environmental impacts do not stop there: Okin figures American dogs produce about 5.1 million tons of feces every year—as much as 90 million Americans.

A study "The Ecological Paw Print of Companion Dogs and Cats" published in June 2019 in *Bioscience* by researchers in the Netherlands, China, and Japan found the average size dog associated with 0.773 tons of carbon dioxide equivalent / year. Similarly the average size cat had 0.185 tons of carbon dioxide equivalent / year. Without considering their relative numbers, a simple average gives 0.479 tons of carbon dioxide equivalent / year per pet—just a bit higher than the UCLA study.

Other studies[32] have found American feral and domestic cats kill billions of birds every year, and songbird populations continue to decline. Small mammal populations also suffer. Many would argue from a (choice #27) social justice point of view, that the roughly $75 billion per year (based on American Pet Products Association figures) that Americans spend on pets—mostly for food and vet bills—could be better spent elsewhere. Example: $75 billion per year could fund 150 million annual donations of $500 to charities like Save the Children, UNICEF, etc. This could give each of the world's roughly 750 million chronically hungry people a nearly $100 annual allowance (a bit less after administrative costs.)

b) If you (choice #21) must use marijuana or cannabis, consider (choice #46) growing your own outdoors. A Colorado State University study released in March, 2021 found that GHG / CO_2 equivalent emissions of between 143 to 324 pounds were associated with every ounce of dried cannabis (chiefly due to electricity use in commercial greenhouses.)

c) Practice (choice #45) the five "Rs": recycle, reuse, repair, reduce waste, and refuse to buy what you don't need. Doing this will distinguish you from typical American consumers and the associated throw away, affluenza afflicted society. And, rather than fitting into a (choice #46) consumerist lifestyle based on buying the often expensive, often heavily advertised, environmentally questionable products of multinational corporations, consider the alternative of becoming something of a small producer. In this regard many do it yourselfers (DIY) find they can put the trash of an affluent society to (choice #47) creative good use in environmentally responsible fashion.

Two examples from my lifestyle: First, I have a total of just $100 invested in all of the furniture / appliances in my living room / dining room. Couch (really nice!), coffee table, two lounge chairs, three entertainment units, end table, dining table, and television were free for the hauling; piano keyboard, nice desk, four chairs, two file cabinets round out the inventory. Second, while I have and use six computers, all of them are either unwanted castoffs from friends or relatives, or second-

hand store purchased. Not counting consumables like printer toner
cartridges, I have a total of less than $100 invested in all of them.

d) Factor (choice #27) social and environmental justice concerns into the
choices you make. It seems that (choice #44) sustainability requires
this—since a world with lots of have nots and a few haves, or with lots of
pissed off people who feel unjustly treated, is not a world with good
prospects for peace, stability, and widespread feeling of well-being.

e) Magnify the impact of your climate action lifestyle choices. Here are
three ways to do that and (choice #31) reach a wider audience. First, talk
to others about what's behind those choices—this can include teaching
classes or facilitating "Climate Dialogues" sessions. You can find help at
climatecommunication.yale.edu regarding employing the psychology of
climate change communication.

Second, serve as a role model by not only "talking the talk, but walking
the walk." Demonstrate for others to see —with activities you engage in,
political action, consumer choices, etc. —the lifestyle choices and
behavior consistent with values you'd like others to emulate. Third,
publicize your own successful—perhaps even innovative—solar /
energy-saving applications or (choice #46) do it yourself projects. This
can start with simply showing them off when friends come to visit.

E. Environmental Transgressions and Showcases
Before taking you on a literary "showing off" tour of the energy aspects
of my supposedly environmentally responsible lifestyle, I have a
confession. I am guilty of many past environmental transgressions. I like
to think that, from a "live and learn" perspective, the frequency and
severity of such behavior has lessened as I've gotten older. Alas, given
my steadily increasing financial means, this may not be strictly true.

Most notably in the last dozen years, I confess to transportation sector
transgressions with a) numerous greenhouse gas producing overseas
airline flights, and b) failure to own an electric vehicle. In the (choice
#46) building sector, I confess to being part of a disturbing trend. The
wood frame, passive solar, energy-efficient houses I started in 1978,
2000, and 2011 used increasingly more (carbon intensive) concrete and
new (non-recycled) materials. My internal wishful thinker suggests I've
atoned for these by a) investing with World Tree (www.worldtree.info)

in planting an acre of carbon absorbing trees, and b) finally settling in town—not in some remote outpost far from the rest of civilization.

Despite these, and other environmentally less than desirable activities, I feel I've learned a great deal. I'll start sharing that (wisdom?) with four general observations. First, you mustn't fool yourself into believing what you're doing has environmental benefits that it really doesn't have. And you shouldn't do such things solely for their feel good / lessening guilt / "greenwashing" value. Things done for "PR" value can explode into public relations nightmares if their supposed benefits are nonexistent. In this regard filmmaker Michael Moore in his 2020 film *Planet of the Humans* has (mostly rightly?) attacked certain utilization of biomass energy projects. (See the next section for what he got seriously wrong.)

Second, (choice #49) technology-related tradeoffs are everywhere. In building construction, wood grown in sustainable forests is generally much preferred to concrete and steel—but structures built out of it must be protected from fire. In food production, (choice #46) growing your own is generally laudable—unless you're doing it in an arid region, using lots of groundwater, and contributing to depleting an aquifer. In transportation, driving an electric car is supposedly environmentally responsible—unless you're charging it with electricity generated from burning fossil fuel. Or using it for short trips you'd otherwise make by walking or bicycling. The latter is great—just don't get hit by a car. And using your own muscle power instead of labor-saving fossil fuel powered conveniences is great— unless your life, like so many, is dominated by an inconvenient truth: you often don't have time to meet demands in the most environmentally responsible fashion.

Third, generally (choice #45) small is beautiful. Certainly small buildings and cars need fewer resources to build, and less energy to operate. But, obviously this prescription isn't a good one when more of something is needed to get the job done. Thus using more—not less— insulation is nearly always recommended to cut unwanted heat energy transfer in buildings (and save money.) And even E. F. Schumacher likes using many otherwise unemployed people to manually do some job that one fossil fuel burning machine could otherwise do. Yet that seemingly humane, environmentally responsible decision may not be wise if the job presents health and safety dangers. And your small is beautiful solutions may not be appropriate when someone else has already opted for More is Better. Thus trying to meet a large family's transportation or privacy needs with a small car or small house may be impractical.

Fourth, energy conservation or wise energy use / ecological responsibility doesn't have to mean sacrificing, or less comfort. And (choice #49) the right attitude can make supposed sacrifices painless. Or better, turn what might be thought of as a sacrifice into a "good feelings knowing you're doing your part for the greater good" experience. Consider American presidents' past and future efforts in this regard.

President Carter's responses to a 1970s energy crisis included turning the thermostat in the White House down from 65°F to 55°F, and putting on a sweater. This turned off many (choice #45) More is Better Mentality and (choice #49) production technology-oriented Americans. Some say this ill-advised conservation publicity helped elect Ronald Reagan. And that informing Americans as to how much money and energy they could save by increasing insulation / weatherizing their homes—using the White House as a back drop for such a campaign—would have been better. Others say Americans childishly lacked the right attitude. President Biden will soon need to convince Americans to trade in their gasoline-powered cars for electric ones. How will he overcome a problem: time challenged people may complain about slow electrical energy fill-ups? Might we be seeing he and Jill leaving a presidential limo EV to relax with a sit down meal while the vehicle is charging? (Some companies are investigating simply swapping out uncharged for charged batteries.)

Decisions to have smaller families can be approached with an attitude of resolve to produce quality, not just quantity. I've counted as both feel good and environmentally responsible (choice #40) limiting the number of children I've brought into the world to (zero population growth associated) two. While I admire those with zero, one—or who've adopted children—for me, the two-child decision was the right balance between personal responsibility and not diminishing the richness of life. I also feel good about my 1974-1975 decision to learn to fix tasty, (choice #21) healthy natural / vegetarian food and give up eating red meat. I was recently congratulated for making this choice by an environmental activist local young couple I much admire who just had their first child.

Inspired by a number of books I read in my twenties, having reached age seventy I believe (choice #45) an enoughness-based / attempting to minimize environmental impacts lifestyle has served me well. I say this while at the same time receiving occasional comments that suggest otherwise. These include a) I shouldn't always "do things the hard way," b) I should consider relaxing my standards and enjoying life more, and c) Recalling Kate Soper's (chapter 6) philosophy, I should tweak my lifestyle so that it's less "alternative" and more (choice #21) "hedonism." Seems I increasingly tell them it's no fun just throwing money at buying something neither I, nor the planet need, or paying for someone else's labor. And counter that the flip side of "labor-saving" is "cheating me out of getting healthy, needed exercise."

So much for general reflections—let's commence a tour of where I live, focusing on practices / ways I choose to live I'd like to see others adopt. Before I continue, I need to clarify some things. First, I live alone (like 28% of American households) in a small (900 square foot) manufactured home. Second, the sunny southwest mountain climate I live in has much bigger winter heating demands than summer cooling ones. Third, the use of solar energy I'll describe is, in many respects, a frugal / poor person's one—not something the pampered 10% will gravitate toward.

Set back a scant twenty feet from the street, my house has a decided lack of curb appeal. The roughly eight foot tall by fourteen foot wide cross-section it presents—with central twelve square foot window, masonry brick foundation beneath and slightly pitched roof above—impresses only with its (choice #3) humility.[33] In front of, and surrounding the house, various vehicles are typically parked. A 2008 Toyota Prius sits in front, a 1993 Saturn small wagon around to the right, and three bicycles sit near the front door, under the covered patio to the left.

As you head from the patio to the backyard, you encounter the first of two small outbuildings I've built: it has a sign "The Observatory" above the door.[34] This outbuilding is technically a "warm room." It houses the computer where I examine images the outside platform-mounted telescope provides—the basis for the variable star photometry behind my citizen science activity. As with much basic scientific research, ordinary people may struggle to connect such efforts with what matters to them. I previously covered this ground (near the beginning of chapter 5.) The essence of that justification is that it's only by studying other stars that we have confidence in the prospects for our Sun continuing to gift the Earth with its energy for billions of more years. And some idea as to the constancy associated with this energy's delivery to Earth.

In the last chapter I described the food production aspects of the second building, my greenhouse. Within, two compost piles and a few concrete blocks soak up extra heat on sunny winter days, adding thermal mass that helps keep plants warm during winter nights. I've recently spent $70 in building a three foot wide by twenty-five foot long walkway / deck (with stairs on each end) to connect house, greenhouse, and telescope. The limited $ outlay illustrates my use of free and second-hand materials: one hundred feet of 2x6 + ten feet of 2x10 floor joist lumber: $16; decking boards: free; forty-five concrete blocks for piers: $35; six pounds of nails: $3; exterior paint: free; sand & cement: $15; ten anchor bolts: $1.

Behind the greenhouse, and slightly beneath it as the backyard slopes downhill, you'll see the property's most eye-catching structure: the 840 watt (=0.840 kilowatt) ground-mounted solar photovoltaic panel array. This produces an average of 90 kilowatt-hours (kWh) of electrical energy each month—which roughly equals my average monthly utility bill based consumption. I use a portion of that solar electricity to reduce that electric company bill. That averages $9 / month above the minimum service charge, based on usage of roughly 90 kWh / month. Much of that runs a conventional refrigerator. The solar array also reduces my natural gas consumption. My gas bill averages a laughable $6 / month over the minimum service charge, based on 8 therms / month usage.

Natural gas powers my whole house heating system furnace. And powers a domestic hot water tank, which I only use in winter with pilot light on and set to lowest setting. Photovoltaic solar electricity meets 90% of my hot water needs. And—in further reducing gas consumption—it also powers my innovative "solar kitchen." This provides a nice, very easy to use, sunny midday alternative to regular outdoor solar ovens—which I've used, but haven't warmed up to!

My photovoltaic (PV) panels are series-connected to provide 120 volts direct current (VDC). As such they power electric resistance heating elements in a) a separate water tank for hot water, b) various ones in solar kitchen appliances which cook a significant fraction of my food, and c) two baseboard heaters, which strategically bring small amounts of heat to where I need it. They can also charge a small battery bank. I select where the solar electricity goes by manual switching. The choices are to 1) heat water, 2) the solar kitchen, 3) the living room 800 watt baseboard heater, or 4) to the battery bank.

This last choice sends solar array output to charge a one kilowatt-hour (kWh) capacity 120 VDC lead acid battery bank, which cost around $140 including shipping. Note this battery bank is very small. Off-grid, larger houses need much bigger ones (at least 12 kWh capacity) to meet demands for cloudy periods without sunshine. I use my 120 VDC battery bank to meet two quite different needs. First, it can power 12 VDC LED lights, fan, and small appliances (radio, CD player, laptop, phone charging, etc.) by employing a 120 DVC to 12 VDC converter (cost under $15). Second, I use it to power a 400 watt heater in a special location as part of my "solar-assisted zone heating" I'll describe shortly.

Before doing that, I wish to tout the (choice #46) DIY practicality and economics of how I use solar electricity. It is a very simple and inexpensive. If you know where to buy them, you can pay just $300 for solar panels equivalent to, or better than my array.[35] By finding a hot water heater with a defective electrical heating element and installing a new one, buying two new electric baseboard heaters, and going to a thrift store for used toaster oven, slow cooker, waffle-maker, and toaster, you can keep investment in appliances to around $100. I've likewise used some ingenuity to keep solar panel mounting and electrical distribution and wiring related costs under $100.[36]

I have not tied my solar array into the utility company. That connection requires a pricey ($1500 or so) grid-tie inverter, specialized knowledge beyond many DIY folks, and dealing with lots of red tape. Nor have I invested in a large, expensive battery bank. But unlike grid-tied, larger solar systems, my setup works during utility electrical power outages. Then, its daytime operation is normal; at night during short (one day or less) outages I still have some electrical service—including lights, radio, CD player, phone, laptop computer, cooling fan or limited spot heat.

Having described my use of solar electricity, I should point out that the sunshine I most enjoy using streams in through glass, or strikes the wet clothes hanging on my clothesline to dry. Although I have an electric dryer, I use it rarely (once a year?) I prefer the roughly ten minutes of sunshine, fresh air and exercise I get hanging my (often thrift store purchased) clothes in the sun to dry. This often gets me thinking of my grandkids' future, and thoughts like "I just spared the atmosphere about four pounds of CO_2 associated with the fossil fuel the utility company would have burned to make the 4 kWh my electric dryer would have used." This becomes a labor of love in thinking that I'm doing this for the futures of all the boys and girls around the world.

In general, I use solar energy in a sometimes labor-intensive fashion to be environmentally responsible, and make most efficient use of dollars invested. I work to minimize fossil fuel use and keep utility costs low. What I do in that regard would be unacceptable to many Americans. Beyond all the usual energy-saving measures you commonly read about, I do a couple of things that deserve mention. First, I put DIY insulating panels in place over many windows to retard night-time heat loss[37], and remove them to storage in closets or elsewhere during the day. Second— and more important—I employ what I call solar assisted zone heating.

Zone heating is about putting heat where you need it. Where I'm hanging out, I like temperatures at or above 70 °F. I insure that in three ways: first with day-time direct gain sun, second with battery-bank supplied targeted "solar" heat at night, and third, on cloudy days with small low wattage electric (utility company powered) heaters. Accordingly, my winter days are typically spent working inside taking full advantage of sunshine. Mornings I sit in an office chair working at a computer staying warm with solar energy streaming in through the adjoining east-facing window. By afternoon, I've moved to a computer at a desk in my bedroom where sunshine through a southwest facing window warms me.

On cloudy cold days, I'll sometimes take my laptop to work in—or perhaps hang out reading or watching television—in what I call my "Boutique Capsule" (BC). Before describing that, note that as long as the zone I occupy is heated, the rest of house can stay at 48 degrees or so. Of course if I have visitors, I can easily turn the thermostat up. Inspired by my stay at a hostel in Amsterdam full of these private sleeping compartments, I built a BC up above the queen size bed in my bedroom. Think of it as a very well-insulated sleeping loft with a sliding, one-inch thick, four x eight foot foil-faced insulated panel serving as door.

From a heating perspective, whereas my whole house volume is roughly 7200 cubic feet, the BC has but a 7 ft x 2.5 ft x 2.5 ft = 44 cubic foot volume. Inside my BC I have a 400 watt electric heater—which can run on either utility company 120 VAC power or 120 VDC from my battery bank. But most of the time waste heat from a 13 watt reading light and my body keep it warm. (Revisit my back of the envelope calculation in chapter 5 for the quantitative details.) On very cold nights, I stay warm with waste heat from the laptop or occasionally turning on the electric heater. I'll power that from the battery bank if voltage permits. To prolong battery life, I run heater for no more than one hour on any given night—typically, on the coldest nights, for five twelve-minute on, forty-eight minute off intervals spread out over five night-time hours.

Enough of the technical details I've most wanted to share about my lifestyle. I realize what I've described is not for everyone. And that it's easy to scoff at individual actions people take to save energy—like simply opening curtains in winter to let sun in, closing them in summer to keep sun out, turning off lights and appliances when they aren't needed, etc. But, multiplied by millions and millions of people doing this in a worldwide growing trend, they add to both lots of energy (and money) saved, and lots of love for a better future for our children.

Again, I note it's easy to pooh-pooh the value of the things individuals do in (choice #31) changing their lifestyles to help cut greenhouse gas (GHG) emissions. Such putdowns contrast the relatively tiny GHG amounts the atmosphere is spared by these changes, with the vastly larger savings that can be realized through successful political action to change national policies (recall Figure #27.) In truth we need both approaches. We need people living lives based on using energy wisely, using solar, choosing (choice #45) enoughness, and occasionally sacrificing for the common—and the planet's—welfare. The latter can pave the way, with minimal resistance, for institutional changes and laws that ideally mandate much of what many folks are already doing.

As I conclude describing how my lifestyle is shaped by climate change concerns, you'll note that I have not said much about my transportation related fossil fuel energy use, nor food production. Decreasing the first and increasing the second are future goals. In the 18 months I've put 5200 miles on the Prius, 400 miles on the Saturn, and have not been on an airplane. My best garden edible food production in recent years has been 134 lbs / year. As this book goes to press, my 2021 garden output (at 121 lbs with some growing season remaining) should easily beat that.

Ideally a small electric car with battery bank charged by another array of solar panels is in my future. Right now I'm excited that better bike tires that withstand thorn-caused flats have decreased bicycle down time. And that my long-time building garden soil fertility, acquiring increased know-how, and building infrastructure (greenhouse, water catchment, etc.) is beginning to pay off with more garden produce harvested. Do I look forward to a day when everything my lifestyle needs is finished, and I simply have to enjoy using the infrastructure I've put in place? Not necessarily, I'm happiest when I have projects to work on.

F. Solar Power for the People

Starting with a topic name and adding the ending "for the people"—as was done in forming this section's title—may unavoidably give a political left leaning flavor to something. Having attacked many right-wingers, fair play suggests I find another target on the left. I've settled on filmmaker Michael Moore. His recent film *Planet of the Humans* generally showcases a lack of scientific literacy and critical thinking skills. It specifically fails to appreciate solar photovoltaic panels.

Moore's film claims this (choice #49) technology places heavy silicon mining demands on the Earth, and in doing so reveals that he totally misses the (choice #52) "free fuel" and other values of renewable resources. To illustrate, compare, two 500 megawatt power plants, solar and coal. In its fabrication, the solar electricity generating facility would require 20,000 tons of silicon, but with free solar energy will need no more resource input over its estimated 40 year lifetime. In contrast, after its fabrication, a coal plant of that size would need 20,000 tons of fuel in the form of coal <u>every four days!</u>

Current photovoltaic technology depends on abundant silicon dioxide (sand), of which roughly 60% of the Earth's crust is made. It looks good resource availability and extraction-wise. Good, not just when compared to coal, but when compared to another renewable energy source: hydroelectric power. For example, building the Glen Canyon dam on the Colorado River required mining 200,000 tons of the cementitous, water-proofing mineral pozzolan and other materials to make the required 10 million ton concrete dam structure. It provides 1320 megawatts of electrical generating capacity.

Putting data for coal, hydroelectric, and solar together, the Figure #35 chart shows the resource extraction advantage of solar. Thus, besides essentially zero air pollution and greenhouse gas production when compared to coal generated electricity, solar is not associated with huge mining scars, mining accidents, black lung disease, water pollution, waste tailings piles, high mercury levels in eagles, etc. While this solar technology has some environmental impact (what doesn't?), in comparison with coal, it's extraordinarily healthy. This is a great reason to think of it in "power to the people" terms—but there are others.

Figure #35

technology	Resource needed to generate 1 MW electric over 40 year lifetime of the power plant
Solar	40 tons of silicon (=roughly 80 tons of silicon dioxide / sand)
Hydro	7600 tons of concrete (from an even greater amount of mined minerals, aggregate, etc)
Coal	146,000 tons of coal

(Note: my review of Moore's *Planet of the Humans* film is at www.projectworldview.org/reviews.)

Recalling the history of groups like the United Mine Workers and other unions, coal can be thought of in power to the people terms. I connected with coal a decade ago in China. My wife and I had just come down from walking along a stretch of the Great Wall with a group of tourists and British / American expats, when we missed a turn on a trail. Before we knew it, we were lost. Other than difficulty in communicating, I remember two things about the rural Chinese family who rescued us. First, before making calls, they had to climb a nearby hill to get cell phone reception. Second, their heating stove was fed from a large pile of coal stacked outside their house.

Like many Americans, I'd been intrigued by China after Nixon's visit there in 1972. I still have a book I bought in 1974, *China: Science Walks On Both Legs*. This report was the work of an American organization that's still going strong: Science for the People. When I look over this book today I think of two things. First, those Americans who toured China, and later reported, were apparently carefully shielded from certain later revealed truths. I conclude this since the book treats what started there ten years after "Liberation," namely The Great Leap Forward (see chapter 6,) as a successful program.

Second, in 1974, when I first got excited about solar photovoltaic technology, only solar cell modules designed for spacecraft were available. They cost around $100 per watt. From the *China: Science Walks On Both Legs* book, it seems back in 1974 the biggest thing China had going for it (choice #49) technology-wise was its decentralized health care manned by the barefoot doctors.

It boggles my mind to think that not quite fifty years later China is by far the world's bigger producer of photovoltaic panels, they are very high quality, and extraordinarily cheap.[38] A recent story in the *Guardian* headlined "Insanely cheap energy: how solar power continues to shock the world"[39] tells the story. Thank you, Chinese industrial might. The few made in America are higher priced—something needs to change fast.

Science for the People publishes a similarly titled magazine. A recent (volume 23, #2) article celebrates "the people of Som Energia, a green energy consumption co-operative with more than 65,000 members, which provides [sustainable, mostly solar]... electricity to 113,000 homes and organizations throughout Spain..." This is a (choice #34) co-operative principles-based group seeking "to address situations of energy poverty." In relatively affluent Spain everyone has access to electricity. In contrast, in parts of sub-Saharan Africa—in three countries, Central African Republic, Democratic Republic of Congo, and Malawi, with total of 110 million people —less than 20% have access to electricity according to World Bank 2019 data

I can imagine the world's 2755 billionaires contributing less than one-ten thousandth of their $ 13.1 trillion net worth (based on 2021 *Forbes* list data) to fund a $1.3 billion project. This would buy 20 million packages of 100 watt solar panel, 100 watt-hour battery, LED light, and hookup wire. It would greatly improve life for these poor Africans. Contrast this with Solar United Neighbors (SUN), a solar co-op Americans can join. Homeowners can get a professionally installed solar system working on top of their regular utility service. They get a bulk purchase discount— although I note the SUN people get $600 per contract signed. The overall cost seems high: around $2.75 per watt—or $11,000 for a 4 kW system. The investment eventually pays off in reduced electricity bills.

Were I to pick up with what I was doing forty years ago—when I organized what was possibly (as speculated by *Solar Age* magazine) the first bulk co-operative purchase of photovoltaic panels in America by a bunch of end users—I'd take a different approach. Like I did back then, I'd involve the local community college. They could offer a program to train electrical journeymen types to help homeowners hook up solar panels to certain appliances and electric vehicle (EV) batteries. Similar to what I've described in the previous section, these would be stand-alone systems, without expensive grid-tie inverters. Utility companies need not be involved.

The type of hookup I'm talking about is fundamentally simple. The electric heating element in my water heater tank essentially hooks to two wires coming from positive and negative terminals of my solar array. The same is true for the 120 VDC power outlet in my kitchen, that runs my solar kitchen appliances; and for electric baseboard heater in my living room. While I have a small (1 kWh) battery bank as described, I eventually hope to charge a much bigger battery bank that lives in an EV.

Rather than three solar panels hooked in series to provide 120 VDC, twelve of them could furnish 480 VDC. In theory, this could directly charge the EV battery bank in a Nissan Leaf. Again, this is simple in principle—pretty much like the hookup to jump-start a car with a dead battery. Two wires coming from positive and negative terminals of the solar array attach to the positive and negative terminals of the EV battery. After a charge controller sensed this battery was fully charged, solar output could be directed across a heating element in a large water tank. This could meet both hot water and some space heating needs[41]. Adding a simpler (not gird-tie) inverter, the EV battery bank could power the house during utility power outages.

There are safety concerns—and that's where a trained person could help DIYers. Such a person could also provide panel-mounting suggestions—but that actual job is again fundamentally simple. It, and hooking panels together, is something a typical (choice #46) DIYer can handle. Of course, many would not choose the DIY route. Then the locally available trained person could be put to work doing the installation—not just being a consultant. The EV charging application could be facilitated with help from vehicle makers providing their battery bank terminal / interface pin out wiring diagram details, and suggested DC charging specs, to qualified individuals. I'd love to see a technically-minded teacher partner with a community college in writing a grant to get government funding for a demonstration project.

Even in sunny Arizona, based on the recent SUN presentation numbers I saw, payback time for a homeowner investment in such a turnkey system is typically ten to fifteen years (less if tax credits help.) As I've described it both here and in the previous section, I believe a good amount of useful solar electricity can be had with payback times in the two to three year range. Nice, when you consider the panels typically have twenty-five year warranties. I'd like to see "Solar for the People" happen as I've just described. I still believe in the solar energy education / community college / local business partnership like I did forty years ago when I had U.S. Department of Energy and Arkansas Dept. of Energy funding. (Thank you, President Jimmy Carter and Governor Bill Clinton.)

Notes

1 Bendix, Aria "Disturbing before-and-after images show how parts of San Francisco could be underwater by 2100" *Business Insider* February 6 2019

2 East Palo Alto, next door to Silicon Valley, already has a problem from rising San Francisco Bay waters.

3 How long to count to one billion? At a one per second rate: 32 years!

4 San Francisco's all time high temperature of 106 °F was on Sept 6 2017.

5 from US National Oceanic and Atmospheric Administration (NOAA)

6 according to NASA's Global Climate Change climate.nasa.gov

7 Krulwich, Robert "How Humans Almost Vanished From Earth in 70,000 BC" *NPR* story October 22 2012

8 a total of 46 million acres burned according to "2019-2020 Australian bushfire season" *Wikipedia* article accessed April 23, 2021

9 according to the rule of 72, 72 divided by 3 = 24 years doubling time

10 a dry toilet that depends on composting to break down human waste. Ours was "flushed" by putting in a dipper full of sawdust before closing the lid.

11 Understanding the limiting reactant concept from chemistry can help here.

12 Bill Gates is the wealthiest, most visible example of this.

13 Geoengineering can massively alter the global environment to cut warming. Three dangerous, expensive schemes: 1) using space-based mirrors to reflect sunshine back into space, 2) adding iron to oceans to feed plankton, increase CO_2 absorption, and 3) adding sulfates to atmosphere to create haze, blocking sunshine. Much better: plant lots of trees, paint lots of building roofs white.

14 Watts, Jonathan "Climate Change made Siberian heat wave 600 times more likely-study" *The Guardian* July 15, 2020

15 Global CO_2 emissions fell in 2020 by nearly 6% due to the pandemic according to the International Energy Agency (IEA), but they projected 2021 missions would grow by 5%. Previous annual changes have been +1.5% in 2018; in 2019 it was +2.7%)

16 These USA values are higher than the 16 metric tons per person per year cited elsewhere since they include emissions due to deforestation / land use

17 The *UN Environment Programme* estimates a 7.6 % decline per year every year for the next decade is needed to prevent warming above the hoped for limit of 1.5°C above pre-industrial global temperature levels.

18 Nield, David, "A Major Ocean Current Could Be on the Verge of a Devastating 'Tipping Point'" article on sciencealert.com February 25, 2021

19 At www.projectworldview.org/climate_change.htm you can find information about "Climate Dialogues" or "Carbon Conservations."

20 Groups such as the *Citizens Climate Lobby* and *Climate Leadership Council* have detailed plans (Chapter 6 section G sketched one) Many have garnered

bipartisan support. One proposed plan was backed by Al Gore with the slogan "Tax what you burn, not what you earn!" This "not penalizing work approach" has potential to widely appeal to those on the political right and reshape our economic system to their liking. The fee and dividend rebate plan can fight inequality by benefiting the poor more than the rich. Regardless of political motivation, song #15 (Appendix B) might help inspire action.

21 Needed are more: 1) options for choosing small, affordable, renewable energy powered / energy-efficient housing, 2) options for choosing small, affordable, electric and renewable energy powered vehicles, 3) options for choosing from affordable, widespread mass transit options, and 4) people pursuing safe, energy and cost saving, often technically simple DIY solar / renewable energy-based / home retrofit projects—which regulations in many jurisdictions often currently preclude or make needlessly expensive.

22 Hydrogen produced using renewable energy (splitting water via electrolysis, etc.) can do what methane currently does—and power cars (via fuel cell technology). But, methane delivery infrastructure leaks must be stopped—as must methane escaping from underground drilling or coal mining activity. This is a priority given that methane is a potent greenhouse gas. One ton of it causes 86 times more warming than a ton of CO_2. Fortunately it only lasts only about ten years in the atmosphere, whereas CO_2 lasts hundreds of years.

23 Two comments. First, due to the pandemic I did not fly or ride buses / trains. This past behavior of mine has certainly increased my carbon footprint. Second, given my investment in planting an acre of trees which soak up 100 tons of carbon dioxide per year, I could claim my lifestyle is carbon neutral.

24 With this choice "a person would trim their carbon footprint by a whopping 58.6 metric tons / year —about the same emissions savings as having nearly 700 teenagers recycle as much as possible for the rest of their lives." So writes Sid Perkins in his report of the study.

25 Front wheels of bikes inexpensively purchased second hand can be replaced with wheels having motorized hub / controller linked add ons available at reasonable prices. The typically 36 volt electric motors employed can be powered by three series connected 12 volt batteries. Lithium batteries are preferred due to reduced weight, but lead acid ones are practical, cheaper, recyclable and perhaps safer. Either way the DC output of household photovoltaic solar panels can charge them.

26 see "How to Buy Carbon Offsets" in the *New York Times* July 24 2019

27 Her study may understate the environmental impact of coffee in that it doesn't consider the growing prevalence of single serve coffee brewers using coffee pods / K cups which now are a $5 billion industry. While potentially offering some environmental benefits, negatives in the form of resource use and filling landfills with nonbiodegradable and potentially human health concerning plastic garbage far outweigh them.

28 These can be nothing more than a cast-off water tank painted black and placed in a well insulated box with glass or transparent cover facing south.

Plumbed as   part of a cold water in line feeding a regular hot water tank, existing water pressure provides motive force. Note they may need to be covered or drained in winter to avoid freezing.

29 These can be nothing more than a piece of metal painted black placed in a well-insulated box with glass or transparent cover facing south . Inlet / outlet openings are cut, and ducts, blowers added; heat storage provisions involving rock bins, concrete blocks, etc. can be added for larger collectors.

30 According to Mesa, Arizona based World Tree (www.worldtree.info), investing $2500 in planting one acre of such trees can capture nearly 1000 tons of CO_2 in 10 years. This could offset an average American's remaining lifetime GHG emissions —since such folks, at 20 tons per year, would need 50 years to put 1000 tons into the atmosphere. But, this may not be the main benefit attracting some investors. They may be looking at the projected return of $33,578 with the sale of lumber harvested from the trees. (That's with 25% of the revenue from the timber sale: 50% goes to the farmer, and 25% to World Tree). Sounds too good to be true? It may be— but realizing a fraction of such projected benefits could be nice.

31 Solon, Olivia "Drought-stricken communities push back against data centers" *NBC News* June 19, 2021

32 cited in *Wikipedia* article "Cat Predation on Wildlife" accessed March, 2021

33 Taking an affluent faulty colleague to visit my small house near ATU in 1994, upon seeing it he asked, "Where's the rest of your house?" This guy lived in a large all-electric house that back then had $400/month electric bills.

34 My dad made the sign for my observatory and first building project in 1966

35 The cost will be more if they have to be shipped a long way. Neighborhood groups could rent trucks to haul several pallets of panels and split the costs. Sun Electronics (sunelec.com) in Miami, FL has very good prices.

36 For example, instead of paying more than I wanted to for small specialty switches (since DC switching can cause dangerous electrical arcing,) I've employed cheap ($6 each) large manual push in / pull out AC disconnect switches (meant for air conditioner applications) to select which of four circuits my 120 VDC solar power output goes to. My batteries are sealed, glass gel bladder types that can't be overcharged, don't vent gases, and safely live in a closet. Manual control is not advised for forgetful types.

37 These can be made from four foot x eight foot sheets of rigid foam insulation cut with a cheap razor blade drawknife.

38 Earlier in the year, one could buy pallets (from Sun Electronics) of "for export only" panels at a Miami warehouse for 16 cents a watt!

39 Kurmelovs, Royce "Insanely cheap energy: how solar power continues to shock the world" *The Guardian* April 24, 2021

40 I'd like to see USA electrical co-ops versions of Som Energia in Spain.

41 Strategically located, solar heat in this water tank could meet all the space heat needs of a tiny, well-insulated house—the type of affordable housing we should be building—not large, energy-guzzling, million dollar structures. (Note: waste heat from my solar water tank helps keep my bedroom warm.)

Chapter 8: Skepticism and Reverence

A. Introduction

The previous chapter referred to my recent participation in what could be called protest marches. A frequent sign I've carried at such events urges, "Build Bridges, Not Walls!" In a sense, the overriding theme of this chapter is to build a bridge across a particular chasm. It seeks to bridge the wide gulf between science and spirituality. Allowing a generally (choice #4) skeptical attitude (until convinced otherwise) to stand in for science, and the word reverence to stand in for spirituality, we have our chapter title: Skepticism and Reverence.

Skepticism and reverence are (choice #49) attitudes. An attitude refers to a characteristic evaluative orientation and / or response tendency toward something previously experienced or encountered. The associated evaluation can be positive (like), negative (dislike), or neutral (no opinion.) Whereas reverence provides an example of a positive attitude, skepticism is generally associated with a negative one. Skepticism is often tied to being critical of religious faith—certainly the choice #4 pairing of Skeptic and True Believer themes makes this connection.

Many associate reverence with religion, or generally with a positive regard for spiritual matters. In contrast, blasphemy refers to speaking irreverently with negative regard for something others hold sacred. In depicting the (choice #8) battle between secular humanists and religious fundamentalists, Douglas Preston's fun, fast-paced 2007 science fiction novel *Blasphemy* is full of irreverent speech. Yet it ends by reverently putting words in God's mouth, pointing the way to a new religion. "This is your destiny: to find truth. This is why you exist. This is your purpose. Science is merely how you do it. This is what you must worship: the search for truth itself." I think Carl Sagan would like these words.

Frank J.Tipler is both searching for truth and has an attitude. Referring to atheists, he once said, "If they want a war, I intend to win it!"[1] Who is this now seventy-three year old man—a Baptist preacher, Protestant minister, or someone with faith-based community credentials? No, he's a highly respected Ph.D. physicist and author. His books[2] cover topics you wouldn't expect someone to take on from (choice #1) an evidence-based perspective. These include the physics of immortality, resurrection of the dead, the physics of Christianity, and apocalyptical embrace of the coming technological singularity.[3]

I mention Tipler for three reasons: 1) to illustrate that it's simple-minded to link (choice #4) skepticism with scientists putting down true believers, 2) in relation to renewing discussion of Teilhard de Chardin's ideas, and 3) to dispel fears of some readers, that in such conflict, I'll strongly argue on the side of science against spirituality. In this latter regard, note the *Project Worldview* mission statement: "We strive, where possible, to show respect for a wide range of (sometimes contradictory) beliefs, values and behaviors, and abide by a "Neutrality Pledge" constrained by a commitment to call out lies and misinformation." Thus I'll be on the side of (choice #1) facts and evidence, and against those (choice #43) "Spreading Disinformation..." Where facts or their interpretation are in dispute, I'll present both sides.

One can feel reverence for things far removed from religion. It's been said that engineers revere (choice #49) the power of technology to solve problems. Likewise, many theoretical physicists (like Albert Einstein) readily admit they feel reverence for certain mathematical equations, and attest to their beauty in representing some aspect of reality deemed important. Whereas scientists strive to keep emotions and biases out of laboratories and interpretations of evidence they gather, some see what they are doing as a spiritual pursuit. But this is spirituality as broadly defined (in chapter 4) as "the domain at the intersection of what both our thinking heads and our feeling hearts tell us is fundamentally important."

While often thought of as something negative, skepticism can also be seen as a positive attribute possessed by a scientifically literate person. Such a person understands the (choice #10) methods science employs and its important concepts. Furthermore, he or she is able to link science's fantastic success to an attitude: a generally skeptical one. When confronted with significant challenges to its conceptual framework, I can imagine a generic defender of this science-based status quo turf initially taking a hostile stance. He or she might proclaim, "I'm skeptical. You'll need to work to convince me!" If you question scientists as to their preference for choice #4 themes, I'd say the vast majority would prefer the Skeptic theme. (See Song #2 in Appendix B.)

Whereas skepticism can be connected with an arrogant (choice #3) "...I Know What's Best" expression putting down someone's beliefs, careful reading of the Skeptic theme description shows it can also be connected with what humble folks possess: doubt and uncertainty. Likewise the True Believer theme cites those it describes as possessing belief "free from doubt." Thus we see the science-minded skeptic on the side of humility, and the religious faith zealot on the side of "I have found the answer!" type arrogance. In describing the science vs. (narrowly-defined) spirituality conflict, this chapter humbly tries to make peace and find common ground. Sir John Templeton (1912-2008), American-born British investor, fund manager and philanthropist, also sought to do this.

I first visited the Templeton Foundation website in late 2010, when they sponsored a conference *"Quantum Physics and the Nature of Reality"* in honor of Cambridge physicist and Anglican priest John Polkinghorne (1930-2021) to coincide with his 80th birthday. A Foundation November 3rd press release began "For centuries, Western science and philosophy has been built on the bedrock understanding that there is a clear difference between the material and the immaterial —or, in theological terms, between the natural and the supernatural." It then provocatively asked, "What if new scientific findings hinted that the distinction might present an inaccurate view of reality?" The press release went on to suggest that quantum information theory might "dramatically blur, if not collapse, the distinction between "immaterial 'ideas' and material reality"—a distinction with (choice #9) implications.

Along the way it mentioned founder John Templeton's book *Possibilities for Over One Hundredfold More Spiritual Information.* I was immediately intrigued (choice #3) by this book's subtitle *The Humble Approach in Theology and Science.* Templeton captures the essence of this approach with the phrase: "How little we know, how eager to learn." And by describing "spiritual information" as involving "concepts from religion which have proven beneficial...[and] basic invisible realities such as love, purpose, creativity, intellect, thanksgiving, prayer, humility, praise, thrift, compassion, invention, truthfulness, giving, and worship." No doubt atheistic types valuing (choice #9) Scientific Materialism will object to the Templeton Foundation's founder's apparent embracing of Vitalism and (choice #6) Mysticism. And find fault with his spending millions of dollars on "rigorous verifiable research" into such things as purpose and prayer. But most will agree the world needs more of the "invisible realities" in Templeton's list.

After Sir John died, I was surprised to learn he and I had things in common. Like myself, John Templeton joined the Christian Presbyterian Church at a young age [4] Unlike me, he never left it. Like me, he also (choice #45) practiced thrift and frugality. Of such behavior, a friend laughingly characterized Sir John as something of a Calvinist with respect to wealth, saying, "He believes it's okay to make money so long as you don't enjoy it." Whatever his motivation, John Templeton gave away most of his money: his (choice #32) serving others philanthropic gifts reportedly totaled $1 billion over his lifetime. Given his interest in scientifically rigorous investigations into (narrowly-defined) spirituality, late in his life Sir John gave $6.2 million (with "no strings attached") to set up The Foundational Questions Institute. Its mission is to "catalyze, support, and disseminate research on questions at the foundations of physics and cosmology." Its advisory board includes some of the world's leading physicists.

Later in this chapter I'll describe related science and spirituality / paranormal excursions into what I'll term "forbidden territory." I'll use knowledge gleaned from that—and from my seven decades of life—to first personally delineate, and then land on, "sacred ground." From there I'll send "dispatches from the front lines in the battle to find meaning in life." And end by imagining entering "the promised land" at my life's conclusion. But first—perhaps to bolster credibility with you, the reader, I'll encourage our taking some skeptical looks. We'll then go on to consider what skeptical non-believers have called "skyhooks."

B. Four Skeptical Looks

The list of seemingly incredible things many people believe in without (choice #1) real evidence—some to the extent of building their lives around them—is a long one. The list began long ago with people needing explanations for what they didn't understand, and often found disturbing. Thus (choice #5) a Creator / Personal God, who some thought of as also (choice #16) dispensing justice, was conceived. As were (choice #6) beliefs in lesser gods and things like (choice #9) vital spirits, ghosts, angels, etc. Today—despite our fantastically successful science-based understanding of how the world works— spiritual (choice #31) tradition-based institutions, dating from ancient times when people didn't know any better, are still well entrenched.

While pushy church folks, evangelists and proselytizers try to (choice #3) recruit new believers in ancient, narrowly-defined spiritual traditions, another effort seeks people to believe in other things. In contrast to the faith-based effort, this more secular one promotes belief in what has been called pseudoscience. This refers to something that seemingly has a scientific basis, but, upon closer investigation, does not.

Pseudosciences have typically been much investigated using (choice #10) scientific methods and (choice #4) thoroughly debunked as lacking in truth, in useful application, or both. Many pseudoscientific beliefs persist because 1) they typically offer simple answers to complex issues, 2) people lacking training in science uncritically believe in them without (choice #12) doing their own analysis of the merits, and 3) those promoting such beliefs—often through "sensationalism" and sometimes (choice #43) disinformation campaigns— profit from doing so.

Young people—who perhaps more readily engage in (choice #1) wishful thinking than adults—are often targeted for recruitment. So are people who (choice #21) are sick and looking for a cure to what ails them. The latter might be bombarded with appeals from hustlers, modern snake oil salesmen, quack doctors, those peddling crystals with healing power, pitches for homeopathy[5] remedies, etc. Given the (choice #3) loud advertising barrage from these folks, uneducated, perhaps increasingly hopeless, sick people may never encounter quiet sober appeals. Sadly, appeals to reason—by those who value the substantial evidence as to why one should be (choice #4) skeptical of what is so heavily promoted — often fall on deaf ears. So gullible people fall prey to those hawking what is essentially magic.

Before continuing, we review the two viewpoints of choice #7 with excerpts from theme descriptions.
excerpt from the Orderly & Explicable theme
"I believe we can eventually greatly comprehend how the world works if we only "Dare to Understand." From a 6th century BCE Ionian Enlightenment success predicting when a solar eclipse would occur— increasingly people have found natural and rational causes for observed events…"
excerpt from the Magic theme
"…instead of attempting to understand, magic enthusiasts celebrate mystery. They seldom try to explain paranormal gifts, spirit communication skills, …[or abilities]… they feel healers/ shamans/ witches / astrologers possess. …"

With respect to supposed cures for sick people, controlled scientific studies (choice #10) can readily determine what works and what doesn't—what is worthy of believing or investing in, and what isn't. Thus, from the viewpoint of sophisticated salespeople, the market for what they're pushing is limited to sick people ignorant of evidence-based medical recommendations. In contrast, for those seeking new recruits to any of a huge offering of pseudoscientific beliefs, the market is much bigger—although it still depends on uneducated consumers.

In examining efforts to win (choice #3 and choice #4) new True Believer followers in conceptual frameworks not built around narrowly-defined spirituality or science, we offer four skeptical looks: at 1) Atlantis / visits by aliens, 2) astrology, 3) Noah's flood-based geology explanations, and 4) promoters of the idea that the Earth is flat and does not rotate. We can put True Believers in these four things into three different categories: fans of the first two go into the pseudoscience box, promoters of flood geology go into the (choice #8) sacred book faith-based box, and flat Earthers go into the crazy (choice #38) conspiracy theory box.

Skeptical Look #1: Belief That Advanced Civilizations Have Left Their Mark on Human History
Prisca sapientia refers to sacred ancient wisdom regarding the nature of things. Pythagoras (570 – 495 BCE) and Plato (424 – 348 BCE) are part of a group of sages who supposedly passed it on; Issac Newton may have been one who sought it through his little known (choice #7) occult studies. In our modern day, many New Age enthusiasts seemingly follow in this seeker tradition.

Many are excited by two ideas used by some to interpret long-ago human history and explain features found at certain archaeological sites. One is belief that an advanced civilization flourished over 10,000 years ago on the continent of Atlantis—only to be destroyed by some catastrophic event that submerged it. A second posits other advanced civilizations— extraterrestrial (ET) ones—have periodically visited Earth. Numerous books, (choice #38) wild conspiracy theories, TV programs and movies often loudly promote these notions. Those promoting beliefs in Atlantis and ET type *Chariots of the Gods* books want you to see the investigations they report on as part of (choice #7) science's continuing effort to explain what were once mysteries. While their books undoubtedly get people thinking and promote (choice #12) curiosity, they typically employ more (choice #1) wishful thinking than scientific rigor. Rather than starting (choice #2) with an open mind, they often are biased by trying to fit evidence to their beliefs that an advanced civilization existed long ago, or in ET visits.

Atlantis based theories interpreting human prehistory can be traced to what many conclude is a literary device Plato used—creating a fictional nation to contrast with the real Athenian city state. He did this, they say, to bolster his ideas about the organization of society. Dim memory of the destruction of a civilization with the eruption of the volcanic island of Thera (now called Santorini) around 1600 BCE perhaps aided believability. Suffice it to say that geological understanding culminating with (see chapter 5) plate tectonics theory totally discredits the notion that whole continents can sink.

Graham Hancock is one of the more serious investigators in the field that scientific mainstream consensus labels pseudoarchaeology, a branch of pseudoscience. Trained as a journalist, he is the accomplished author of lengthy volumes such as *Fingerprints of the Gods* and *Magicians of the Gods*. He argues that after a comet struck Earth around 10,800 BCE destroying an advanced civilization, its survivors dispersed and became the magicians who helped construct amazing monuments throughout the world. The website theoriesofatlantis.com describes Hancock as "the loudest voice in the argument against the accepted chronology of the development of civilization."

One can go to the scientificamerican.com website—or to the June 2017 issue of *Scientific American* magazine— to find a "No. There Wasn't an Advanced Civilization 12,000 Years Ago" rebuttal to Hancock's claims. There, along with other arguments, author, noted skeptic, and scholar Michael Shermer finds it inconceivable that the comet strike Hancock and others hypothesize would have destroyed all evidence of such a civilization. He asks, "Are we to believe that after centuries of flourishing every last tool, potsherd, article of clothing, and presumably from an advanced civilization, writing, metallurgy, and other technologies— not to mention trash—was erased?" He and others basically challenge Hancock to produce convincing evidence. While supporters of Hancock point to scientists like Alfred Wegner who were long ridiculed before being accepted—recall from chapter 5 Wegner's continental drift claims led to plate tectonics—few, if any, of them are researchers respected by the professional archaeology community.

As for ET, one of the most famous questions in science is "Where Are They?" Nobel Prize physicist Enrico Fermi (1901-1954) asked this as the flying saucer craze of the early 1950s was getting attention. Fermi's question—which is even more relevant decades later—refers to the fact there is no reputable scientific evidence that intelligent beings exist anywhere else in the vast universe. Certainly there is no physical artifact documentation —nothing to convince (choice #4) scientifically trained skeptics— that such beings have visited Earth.

Skeptical Look #2: Belief in Astrology
Long-ago night sky watchers noted the (choice #7) orderly workings of the heavens—and that it was sometimes disturbed by unexpected events: shooting stars, new stars (novae), the northern lights, eclipses, comets, etc.   People tend to (choice #18) fear what they cannot understand. Sometimes explanations with no basis in fact are concocted to allay these fears: solar eclipses result when a dragon tries to eat the Sun, (choice #17) the Devil sends comets, or plague is due to a conjunction of planets.

Throughout history, people have sought celestial explanations for events on Earth. Even today the ancient practice of astrology seeks to provide this based on a supposed connection between the positions of stars and planets at some time of interest. After pseudoscientific calculation, astrologers might cast a horoscope that predicts an aggressive personality for someone born when the red planet Mars—associated with blood and the (choice #6) God of War—is in a prominent position.

Claims that the planet Mars has such influence can be investigated by considering the forces involved. The gravitational forces are minuscule. Similarly, light, radio signals, or magnetic effects reaching you from planets are hundreds of millions of times weaker than effects produced by household lights, household radio outputs, or permanent magnets in loudspeakers. To illustrate how scientifically literate folks with critical thinking skills can assess such claims, we provide a summary of a relevant back of the envelope calculation that involves proportional reasoning (described in chapter 5 section B) It shows the gravitational force exerted on you by Mars, when it's closest, is ridiculously small compared to the gravity the Earth exerts on you. ******************

Earth is roughly nine times more massive than Mars, so Newton's Law of Gravity says, other factors being equal, it will exert nine times stronger gravity. But even when closest, Mars is roughly 40 million miles away. By comparison, on Earth's surface you're 4,000 miles away from Earth's center. (To simplify calculation we assume all Earth's mass is concentrated at its center.)   So Mars is 40 million divided by 4 thousand = 10,000 times farther away from you than Earth is. So its gravity force is much weaker. Newton's Law of Gravity is an inverse square relationship—so gravity is not just 1/10,000 as much, it's (1/10,000) x (1/10,000) = (1/ 100 million) as great. Meaning Earth's gravitational force on you is 100 million times greater than what Mars exerts on you when closest. Now combining both factors—9 times greater due to mass, and 100 million times greater due to distance, we conclude Earth's gravity force on you is 900 million times stronger than what Mars puts on you when closest. ****************************

Astrologers can argue that the forces involved are unknown to science. Fine, what are they, what are their properties? Give us some hypothesis about how they work, scientists ask. Give us a hypothesis written in a way that it can be tested and shown to be false. They have no reply.

Harvard graduate and cultural historian Richard Tarnas is an unusual example of someone who—many would say—should know better than to believe in astrology. Writing in the October/November 2019 issue of *The Mountain Astrologer*, he describes the Copernican revolution as "the light of reason's triumph over the darkness of the ancient night, of superstition and ignorance, of myth, mystery and the unknown." I have no problem with that description—it could have come from his 1991 book *The Passion of the Western Mind,* which was highly praised by influential academics and widely adopted by various universities.

But, just as his 2006 book *Cosmos and Psyche* revealed his heavy intellectual investment in astrology, so too does this recent commentary. It goes on to assert, "Astrology offers to the modern mind and soul a royal road across the threshold of the disenchanted universe." From both his celebrating "reason's triumph" and use of "disenchanted" — suggesting freed from (choice #7) magic, etc. — you might conclude that traveling the "royal road" of astrology is (choice #1) an evidence-based and reason-based pursuit.

But is it? The framework astrology provides is not logical since, in making cause and effect claims, it fails to identify any responsible force or mechanism. And, in testing the (often very vaguely worded) predictions made by astrologers, no evidence of divining the future type success has been found. Instead numerous analytical studies by responsible scientists support the null hypothesis. Meaning there is no correlation with any statistical significance between astrologer's predictions and what actually happens. It seems that astrology proponents like Tarnas are basing their enthusiasm for supposed links between important events on Earth and celestial events, on wishful thinking. And I suspect many profiting from astrology operate with (choice #43) some amount of deceit.

Given today's knowledge, it's easy to put down modern astrologers as ignorant, deluded, wishful thinkers. But astrology is truly ancient. Once it was hard to separate it from astronomy, creation myths, and religious beliefs. The three Wise Men of the *New Testament* may have been astrologers intrigued by a highly visible conjunction of planets (perhaps Venus and Jupiter)—although many scholars dismiss the story as fiction created by the author of the book of *Matthew*. Nonetheless Jesus' birth was an important event of 2000 years ago.

Today, one might point to the events of September 11, 2001 and search for astrological explanation. In *Cosmos and Psyche* Tarnas provides us with one—and it's downright embarrassingly laughable! For starters, the event Tarnas cites—a supposed lineup of Saturn, the Earth, and Pluto referred to as the Saturn-Pluto opposition— was not something someone could observe for two reasons. First, Pluto is small and far away (recall officially it's no longer considered a planet but rather a dwarf planet). So it's very faint—roughly fourteen magnitudes or 400,000 times fainter than bright, readily visible Saturn. It takes a substantial telescope, dark skies, and a determined observer to even see it. Second, an opposition event puts the two objects in opposite parts of the sky, so when one rises above the horizon as seen from Earth, the other sets below it.

And it was nothing special. As a post on the astrology website astrograph.com soon after the event said, "The Saturn-Pluto opposition runs for a relatively long period of time, in this case up to a year. It was exact last August 5th, it will be exact again on November 2nd, and again in late May 2002." Given this event's lack of "smoking gun" significance, other astrologers (like those behind the above web page) noted arcane planetary position alignments in identifying supposed triggering influences of Mercury and Jupiter. What I've cited is classic pseudoscience: there is no real evidence to link the 9/11/2001 tragedy with any special celestial event. (See "Dispatch #4" to come for an example of a special celestial event and the meaning I found in it.)

Richard Tarnas doesn't limit his making astrological connections to this tragic event. According to the *Wikipedia* article about him, his book

Cosmos and Psyche "claims that the major events of Western cultural history correlate consistently and meaningfully with the observed angular positions of the planets." That he uses astrology to interpret events like Napoleon's 1812 invasion of Russia, the 1914 start of World War, the September 11, 2001 tragedy, etc. is an outrageous insult to both astronomers and historians.

Skeptical Look #3: Belief in Noah's Flood Geology

Many (choice #8) sacred book faith-based leaders and (choice #16) Moralistic God devotees also ridicule the 9/11/2001 explanations of astrologers. But explanations they typically offer are equally incredible. American Christian fundamentalist Rev. Jerry Falwell placed the (choice #24) blame on those he disliked. Thus, after connecting the attack with the behavior of the supposedly (choice #6, choice #37, choice #42) ungodly (pagans, abortionists, feminists, gays, lesbians,) he said, "If we decide to change all the rules on which this Judeo-Christian nation was built, we cannot expect the Lord to put his shield of protection around us as He has in the past."

Many with extreme worldviews similar to Falwell's believe in something called flood or creation geology. This tries to explain geological features as due to the flood of Noah's Ark fame. One operation advertises "See Flood geology for yourself with the world's #1 Grand Canyon Christian tour."[6] You can pay up to $129, board a van and join a day-long excursion that interprets Grand Canyon geology from such a perspective.

I suspect that, when paying customers approach the National Park's Geology Museum at the Canyon's south rim, tour operators tell them to ignore what they encounter. They should not look at the educational walk / placards / timeline that provide a scientifically accepted account of the formation of the rock layers and the magnificent canyon that cuts through them. (Recall we used Figure #20 in sketching that story in chapter 5.) But the tour operators are the ones to ignore. In claiming an earlier global flood event—one with no evidence in the geologic record —created the Grand Canyon a few thousand years ago, they are perpetuating nonsense that represents an arrogant insult to geologists.

Skeptical Look #4: Belief that the Earth is Flat

I'd say some of the people who accept what they hear on that Flood geology tour are also candidates for succumbing to pitches from (choice #38) the goofy flat Earth conspiracy theorists. According to flat Earth promoters, those doing the conspiring are scientists—especially those working for NASA. Pictures that NASA provides clearly showing the Earth's curve / its spherical nature are fakes, they say. As are time-lapse photos or Foucault Pendulum demos showing Earth's rotation. They discount all of the basic observations and history (described in chapter 5) that displaced a fixed, immobile Earth from the center of the universe.

Suppose you asked one of them to put aside disgust at the supposed massive effort NASA has made to perpetuate the hoax that the Earth is round and both rotates on its axis and revolves around the Sun. Put aside their disgust and accompany you in traveling a couple of hundred miles. Perhaps in an airplane where, under the right conditions, the Earth's curvature can clearly be seen. Or traveling with you on the Earth's surface to conduct chapter 5's "Discovering the Sky" exercise #9.

On the latter trip, with you as interpreter, they could see with their own eyes the movement of a celestial object (the bright star Canopus) that, independently of supposedly deceitful NASA, could confirm the Earth's spherical shape and size. Would they do this? I suspect small-minded prejudice (recall chapter 2) — built on themes Mind Narrowly Focused, and The True Believer—would dictate their refusing to take part. Just as Catholic priests refused to look through Galileo's telescope long ago.

You may dismiss this flat Earth thing as involving the beliefs of crazy wackoos, something we shouldn't be spending time with, right? I would agree except for what a November 18 2019 *CNN* story headline says, "The flat-Earth conspiracy is spreading around the globe." It goes on to report, "A YouGov survey of more than 8,000 American adults suggested last year as many as one in six Americans are not entirely sure the world is round." And reports of life in Fantasy Land continue.

A similar percentage, 18%, based on a May, 2018 survey by Pew Research, believe "Humans have existed in their present form since the beginning of time" —a view consistent with Biblical Creationism. No doubt many of these folks lack critical thinking skills needed to separate fact from fiction. As such, to the extent they're willing to follow some authoritarian demagogue, they represent a threat to (choice #29) democracy. The same survey found 48% believe "Humans have evolved over time due to processes that were guided or allowed by God or a higher power," and only 33% assert "Humans have evolved over time due to processes such as natural selection; God or a higher power had no role in this process." Such data trouble political activists battling (choice #8) religious fundamentalist views in battles such as teaching creationism in public schools, or (choice #42) a woman's right to choose.

In the next section, we again turn attention to the wildly successful theory of biological evolution (see chapter 5.) Recall natural selection is the process that has the effect of allowing the survival and reproduction of individuals best adapted to their environment. It operates at genetic, individual organism, and group/species levels over long time periods. It can explain the appearance of design in nature without invoking the presence of a Designer. (Aside: males suffering prostate problems aren't fans of Intelligent Design given the male urinary tract's poor layout.)

C. Skyhooks (and Old Biology Meets New Physics)

Most challenges to what might be called standard evolutionary thinking proceed from a religious, faith-based perspective. Certainly William Jennings Bryan, the famous "attack dog" prosecuting belief in evolution in the 1925 Scopes trial, repeatedly showcased his Belief in a Personal God. Few, if any, reputable scientists embrace this choice #5 theme, with its acceptance of an activist God violating the laws of physics and performing miracles. But some accept the other (Monotheistic Deism) theme in this pair. I won't use this belief—or belief in Intelligent Design[7] —in discussing evolution.

I'm not comfortable with either of these themes. So if I had to mount a challenge to evolution as currently explained, I'd do so— hesitantly— from the choice #7 perspective of trying to bring "magic" into the Orderly & Explicable category. I'd suggest a quantum mechanics based extending of the scientific conceptual framework, following physicists trying to explain mysteries using what they call nonlocality. They invoke entanglement and what Einstein called "spooky action at a distance." Could these be behind mechanisms that somehow inform evolution?

In looking at evolution with a (choice #4) skeptical eye, I'd begin by recognizing that natural selection based biological evolutionary theory plays such a fundamental role in explaining so much about the history of life on Earth that it must be essentially correct. Then, from a (choice #10) Scientific Method based perspective, I'd urge evolutionary biologists to consider evidence that raises a question. How do standard mechanisms account for the evolution of certain seemingly very unlikely things— beginning with the origin of life itself? In following up on this concern,

I'd appeal to the poorly understood physics (especially that associated with nonlocality / random processes at the boundary between the classical and quantum realms) as applied to biology. Before continuing in that direction, let's pause to develop some background.

In his 1995 book *Darwin's Dangerous Idea*, Daniel Dennett distinguishes between what he calls "cranes" and "skyhooks" to account for the evolution of life on Earth. In the words of Richard Dawkins, in *The God Delusion*, "Cranes are explanatory devices that actually do explain. Natural selection is the champion crane of all time. It has lifted life from primeval simplicity to the dizzy heights of complexity, beauty and apparent design that dazzle us today." Dennett notes that skeptics of evolution are sure that, somewhere, God or divine intervention or "a helping hand (more accurately a helping mind) must have been provided a skyhook to do some of the lifting."

Dawkins emphasizes that, unlike skyhooks, cranes do their work slowly. He answers skeptics of the notion that highly improbable, blind, mindless, random processes could have produced seemingly purposefully designed complex structures. In *Climbing Mount Improbable* he uses an analogy emphasizing the power of accumulation. "On the summit sits a complex device such as an eye or a bacterial flagellar motor. The absurd notion that such complexity could spontaneously self-assemble is symbolized by leaping from the foot of the cliff to the top in one bound. Evolution, by contrast, goes around the back of the mountain and creeps up the gentle slope to the summit—easy!"

If Dawkins is right—and he may be—I should not proceed. Yet, something physicist Roger Penrose wrote in 1989 continues to bother me: "There seems to be something about the way the laws of physics work which allows natural selection to be a much more effective process than it would be with just arbitrary laws." This raise questions like, "Is evolution an informed rather than random process?" And "Could evolution be informed by information beyond what it obtains from the environment with feedback as to an organism's short-term fitness? Many who believe evolutionary processes are guided in long-term fashion toward end results refuse to accept the universe is devoid of meaning. Physicist Frank Tipler[8] is such a person. He likens one of Penrose's diagrams to a diagram (Diagram 4) in Teilhard de Chardin's previously mentioned book *The Phenomenon of Man*. Both involve the so-called Omega Point—where physicists' heat death of the universe is realized.

The heat death is based on the Second Law of Thermodynamics, where the universe—treated as a physically isolated single system—naturally tends to increasing disorder (entropy). That, combined with the universe's observed continuing expansion, unavoidably results in matter in equilibrium with insignificant temperature differences. Without these, no large-scale energy exchange can happen / no significant work can be done. To overcome this grim fate, Catholic mystic Teilhard de Chardin postulated two modes of energy: tangential energy that physicists can measure and a radial energy. This latter energy is not subject to the Second Law. (Choice #9) vitalists connect this with spiritual energy or consciousness. Teilhard envisions consciousness evolving and growing, culminating with a Divine consciousness / Omega Point final state.

About Teilhard's ideas, Tipler—writing in 1985 with coauthor John Barrow—says "His original theory has been refuted, or perhaps we should say has become obsolete. However, the basic framework of his theory is the only framework wherein the evolving Cosmos of modern science can be combined with an ultimate meaningfulness to reality." He says this, recognizing that if all life dies in a heat death at the end of the universe, "all meaning must disappear."

I don't need to believe there is a design or purpose inherent in everything (teleology.) I'm not bothered by a universe without meaning other than what we give it. But I am bothered by calculations that suggest classical physics mechanisms can't explain matter self-organizing in highly complex ways which biological evolution requires. The calculated probabilities of molecular assembly are far too low, or time scales much too long, to be believable. Seems another mechanism must be involved.

In my 2012 "Imagining a Theory of Everything for Adaptive Systems" contribution to the Springer published volume *Origin(s) of Design in Nature*, I suggested quantum random walks are involved—though at the time there was no evidence they actually operate in the biological world. These would metaphorically allow doing better than what a drunk person moving in random directions accomplishes due to dumb luck. Or to use a different metaphor, that such quantum processes would "seemingly allow systems to do something analogous to what a good chess player does: analyze all possible moves and pick out the best one before it is made."

Does this happen in nature? A recent finding suggests it does. As a September 12, 2019 *MIT Technology Review* report puts it, "[it] may explain the genetic code, one of the greatest puzzles in biology." The report describes the first evidence (from a French research group) that a particular recipe for searching through a database of N entries, first published in 1996 and based on the quantum computing random walk, is an actual naturally occurring phenomenon. Is a God-provided skyhook involved? No. Conceivably this quantum process could (choice #7) explain something otherwise mysterious that seems like magic.

The extent to which life depends on uniquely quantum phenomena is unknown, but researching this may shed light on other difficult to explain biological mysteries. Recall in chapter 5 we discussed the ability of birds to navigate long distances, and mentioned the discovery of a particular protein in birds' eyes that allows them to literally see the Earth's magnetic field. Now, as reported on January 8 2021 in *Nature* (based on a paper appearing in the *Proceedings of the National Academy of Science*,) University of Tokyo researchers have linked this to "a clever trick of quantum physics and biochemistry." This involves photoreceptors called cryptochromes—present in the eyes of migratory birds, dogs, humans, and other species. Now, for the first time, researchers have shown cryptochromes respond to magnetic fields.

While spins of electrons have long been associated with magnetic fields, the new research shows that "the spins of two individual electrons can have a major effect on biology" in the words of a biophysicist member of the team. High school chemistry says that unpaired electrons, part of so-called free radicals, are highly reactive. Now we know these electrons can hook up with similar electrons in other atoms to form what are called entangled pairs. Once their history becomes linked in such a fashion, their spins correlate so that changes in one are somehow transmitted to the other. This happens instantaneously no matter how far apart they are. While the entanglement is believed to be fleeting in the microscopic cellular environment, it nonetheless seems to last long enough to provide a macroscopically significant magnetic component.(Previous researchers had failed to find iron or other magnetic materials in the brains of birds.)

The complete explanation of both the quantum computing connection with the origin of the genetic code, and the ability of birds to sense the Earth's magnetic field using a quantum process associated with cryptochromes in their eyes, could involve nonlocality. This refers to objects transcending space, making concepts of place and distance meaningless. In a quantum entanglement, two particles separated by what can be a vast distance—even light years apart—co-ordinate their behavior instantaneously without signals.

How does that relate to flipping quantum coins or changing electron spins? Possibly through a concept, popular with science fiction fans of movies such as *Interstellar*, known as a wormhole—also-called an Einstein-Rosen bridge or ER. As *Scientific American* contributing editor George Musser writes in his 2015 book *Spooky Action at a Distance*, "Such a link might join entangled particles. If two quantum coins are the two mouths of a wormhole, there'd be no mystery as to why they land on the same side when you flip them." His book gets its title from Einstein's characterization (in his famous 1935 EPR paper) of quantum entanglement nonlocality. The connection Musser describes is concisely referred to as the ER=EPR possibility.

While complete understanding is currently lacking, many think that the growing field of quantum biology will eventually explain what have long been mysteries. That would take them out of the realm of magic as described in the choice #7 theme, since "magic enthusiasts celebrate mystery!" I'd love to see the still rather speculative nonlocal physics related quantum biology mechanism (that I've done lots of hand-waving in trying to concisely describe) become an accepted part of evolutionary biology. And personally, I rather like considering the fuzzy explanations of phenomena—ones that are not yet part of the accepted body of science but rather are there lurking at the edges.

The "Holy Grail" of physics is finding a Theory of Everything that reconciles quantum mechanics and general relativity. Of many proposals, I like those requiring gravity and spacetime emerge from quantum entanglement linking the universe's every particle. (My 2012 paper cited in note 15 chapter 5 is based on this.) One, from University of Minnesota professor Vitaly Vanchurin, has recently intrigued me and the physics community. In an August 4, 2020 paper[9] he proposes that, like human brains, the entire universe can be understood as a neural network—one that extracts information, learns from interactions, and changes accordingly. Long a fan of "Quantum Darwinism[10]," I perked up when Vanchurin said, "If the entire universe is a neural network, then something like natural selection might be happening on all scales from cosmological and biological all the way down to subatomic scales." His twenty-two page paper ends with a one sentence acknowledgement: "This work was supported by the Foundational Questions Institute."

While some scientists are intrigued by unexplained phenomena, others purposely stay away from any association with whole areas of them. They especially avoid investigation of paranormal, psychic (known as psi) phenomena, reincarnation, near death experiences, UFOs, etc. (Being very skeptical, my thoughts on otherwise unexplained UFO accounts steer toward unusual natural phenomena, flaws in human perception, parapsychology, and even perception of a defect in space time and avoid ET /alien visits.) Some feel threatened by investigations of such strange phenomena; others dismiss, in (choice #2) closed-minded fashion, the possibility they may be real. Also in the former category are religious true believers, including academics, who take anything they perceive as possibly necessitating a change in their rigid beliefs, or narrowly defined area of religious expertise, as a personal attack.

Most scientists deny the reality of these phenomena. The hostility is such that, Edward F. Kelly, University of Virginia professor and psi researcher, feels that study of not only psi, but another important class of mental phenomena — namely mystical states of higher consciousness— have become "taboo" subjects. Their scientific investigation is the focus of the 600 + page book *Beyond Physicalism*, published in 2015, and partly edited by Kelly. He also spearheaded a related collaborative research project. What follows, with occasional interruption, is a brief report on this book. Alas, while some might see it as a book scientists would be (choice #12) curious to read, many scientists—especially those in academic positions without tenure—see it as forbidden territory.

A Forbidden Book

This book's subtitle, *Toward Reconciliation of Science and Spirituality*, suggests it seeks to move science beyond (choice #9) Scientific Materialism. Referring to the science vs. religion conflict, with the volume Kelly hopes "to open up a third way" that would "expand science" and take "seriously the possibility that the world's mystical traditions disclose genuine empirical truths about the nature of reality." Prompted by Kelly's remark, consider words from this choice #6 theme:

excerpt from the Mysticism theme

"I...think that personal religious experience has its roots and center in mystical states of consciousness...this feeling of Oneness...<u>Not</u> sensing distinct gods or deities, in rare perfect moments I feel union with an undifferentiated whole."

Kelly feels that perhaps "the major obstacle to wider acceptance of psi is the absence at present of a conceptual framework or theory in terms of which these phenomena make sense and do not conflict with other parts of our scientific understanding of nature." What is sought, he writes, is "an empirically justified, theoretically satisfying, and humanly useful 'big picture' of how things really are and how we humans really fit in."

Part II of this impressive volume presents "...New Worldviews That Accommodate the Targeted Phenomena"—including (choice #9) two chapters with a psychobiological perspective, and two with a psychophysical one. The former includes what are called ROSTA (for "Resonant Opening to Subliminal and Transpersonal Assets") models— which (sadly) currently may be "incapable of generating potentially falsifiable predictions."[11] The latter include contributions from highly respected UC Berkeley physicist Henry Stapp,[12] and Columbia University mathematical physicist Bernard Carr.

Stapp's "Mind/Brain Connection" theory builds on the consciousness-based Copenhagen view of quantum mechanics. He cites Cornell University psychology professor's Daryl Bem's 2011 experimental findings (since replicated by others) that appear to show backward in time causation. Bem's experiments involve subjects initially selecting one of various possible actions, only to later have random number generated outputs appear to be biased by those choices. While leaving room for mystery, Stapp feels "nature's choices are not actually random, but are positively or negatively biased by the positive or negative values in the minds of the observers that are actualized by... (nature's) choices."

Edward Kelly makes good progress in attempts to reconcile Stapp's "quantum-theoretic account" with a "widely heralded 'integrated information theory' of..."Caltech neuroscientist Christof Koch and colleague Giulio Tononi (IIT, discussed at the end of chapter 5.) Tononi believes "consciousness is a fundamental part of the universe—just as fundamental as mass, charge, etc." Kelly argues the neuroscientists' "view of ordinary perceptual synthesis ...now comes within a hair's breadth" of Stapp's account.

Carr imagines a higher dimensional psychophysical information space he calls the "Universal Structure." Of it, he writes, "This space has a hierarchical structure and includes both the physical world at the lowest level and the complete range of mental worlds—from normal to paranormal to transpersonal—at higher levels. The assumption that mental phenomena require a communal space is tantamount to positing some form of Universal Mind." How does this connect to (choice #9) Vitalism and (choice #6) Mysticism? With respect to the former no details are offered other than the observation "the notion that spirits resided" in the fourth dimension was "particularly fashionable" in the 1890 to 1905 period. Regarding the latter Carr writes, "A common feature of mystical experience is a feeling of 'unity,' and this might be a natural manifestation of the higher dimensional connection implied by the Universal Structure proposal."

We're about to leave the new physics / nonlocality /quantum biology / skyhooks / magic = mystery territory we've been in. We're about to do this given 1) perhaps appetites have been whetted to explore the God = the "Oneness" of mystical experience possibility, and 2) as Kelly puts it, "the central notion of something God-like at the heart of individual human beings and of nature itself." Given this, and, given how ripe it seems for all sorts of exploration, why don't we linger?

We don't spend more time with this because most physicists feel (choice #1) lack of real evidence means those arguing to attribute some separate reality—an arena in which paranormal phenomena play out—other than just perceptions generated by and confined to our brains alone—are engaging in wishful thinking. Others call it "quantum flapdoodle."[13] In celebrating life, love, and appreciating mysteries the universe presents, sacred realm adventures to follow won't be presented as seeking meaning and purpose put there by God.

D. Sacred Ground

Recall, from chapter 1, a visionary Carl Sagan imagining science and religion coming together in the future, and inspiring "reverence and awe." And, from chapter 4, our description of reverence as "profound respect mingled with love and awe," which brings with it these and other feelings, including humility and sanctity. Sanctity, the quality or state of holiness, sacredness, or inviolability that something possesses, is a word carrying lots of emotional baggage. This stems from (choice #42) the abortion controversy and The Sanctity and Dignity of Life. This is unfortunate as there is much to appreciate here. Some other words of Carl Sagan get at this, "The time has come for a respect, a reverence, not just for all human beings, but for all life forms —as we would have respect for a masterpiece of sculpture or an exquisitely tooled machine."

Chapter 4's definitions of religion and, as broadly defined, spirituality, suggest these are places to look to find meaning in life. While we'll have more on say on these topics, our starting point and focus here, inspired by James Carroll, is choice. In his 2011 book *Jerusalem, Jerusalem* he writes, "Meaning is the discovery of the relationship between choice and consequence." Taking this to heart, the *Choices We Make* booklet (Appendix A) can play a significant role in a search for meaning—and for sacred ground. There, the only references to this latter phrase are in choice #42 and, in a "sacred text" context, in choice #8.

These sacred texts are typically ancient—with parts of the *Bible* and *Torah* that "inform" our conception of Earth and Sky written 2500 years ago in the Iron Age. Even the *Qu'ran*, transcribed roughly 1300 years ago, is hardly modern. Indeed, given how the world has changed—and the knowledge we have now that was lacking then — many don't find these ancient texts particularly relevant to what we as individuals or human society need now. This, and other complaints—including "What do you say when your sacred book depicts God as behaving evilly?" (pondered in chapter 4)—provide reasons for rejecting "Religious Fundamentalism" and preferring the modern "Secular Humanism" theme in choice #8 as we search for meaningful sacred ground

That theme's rejection of Belief in a Personal God constrains our selection in choice #5—and in making another choice. Without a Personal God living inside one's head, the Moralistic God of choice #16 won't be welcome there either. Staying with relevancy criteria, certainly the choice between the two offerings in choice #13— apocalypticism inspired by a vengeful ancient God and modern computer-aided planning tools based Dancing With Systems—is obvious. Likewise we can frame choice #11 as between Fatalism, with an ancient, resigned feeling of powerlessness, and Free Will, with our modern technological attempts to wrest power and control from Nature, and whimsical gods. Besides modern relevancy, psychology dictates preference for the latter theme.

There are other ways to approach God / religion and choices involved. One can start with honesty— something at the heart of two choices: choice #1 between Evidence-Based and positive expectations / wishful thinking themes, and choice #43. This latter choice— between Valuing Honesty, Learning and Spreading Disinformation / Tactical Deception — should be essentially secular. Sadly, the world of preachers has its share of liars and con-men.

With respect to choice #1, I think religion—especially the part about God—involves lots of wishful thinking. It's about faith, not evidence. If we honestly distinguish between what we firmly know and don't know about God based on real evidence, I think it's not farfetched to say we know nothing. Put another way: God =Unknown. So, adopting this view, Weston LaBarre in his 1970 classic *The Origins of Religion: The Ghost Dance*, concludes, "...Theology is a science without subject matter, and the theologian is one who does not know what he is talking about."

Ignoring this insult, theologians and those with a religious perspective, may prefer Magic to Orderly and Explicable in making choice #7. Magic connects with mystery, and, according to LaBarre, so does religion. In fact he begins page one of his 600+ page classic by saying, "There is no mystery about religion. The genuine mysteries lie in what religion purports to be about: the mystery of life and the mystery of the universe."

Even if you share my disdain for religious fundamentalism, you may nonetheless take strong exception to the conclusions I've reached above. That's fine. As Weston LaBarre puts it, "The difference between sacred dogma and the secular hypothesis suggests that the religion of an individual is an autobiographical statement, defended in the same way and with the same means that he defends his personality. A man's religion is what he feels about the Unknown; and what he feels is based on what he has experienced in his emotional growth and individual life history, his own positive and inescapable 'truth'."

Likewise what we hold sacred may differ significantly. I like what LaBarre writes, "...The sacred is the realm of adaptation to anxieties, to crises both social and personal, and to common unsolved problems like death. The sacred is the realm of high emotional potential." James Carroll notes this word's root in Latin means " to make holy," and links "sacred" to "sacrifice" and "giving up something valuable out of the impulse to do good for others." Thus our search of where to look to find meaning involves the philosophy behind (choice #45) Enoughness.

Pondering that—and avoiding bringing God (the Unknown) into our definition of sacred—we're left with the following. "Sacred: what can inspire sacrifice and feelings of awe and reverence; what is considered worthy of spiritual respect, devotion and emotional investment." With spirituality as "the domain at the intersection of what both our heads and our hearts tell us is fundamentally important" — we have a map.

Figure #36 My Personal Sacred Realm

1) Being there for those I love when they need me—and celebrating / honoring / letting them live on in my memories after they are gone— including those who died in military service
2) Serious yet relaxed conversation with family and friends — especially with respect to the human condition and questions of fundamental importance
3) Listening to a wise (based on learning and experience), caring, someone speak passionately and eloquently about something I also care about
4) Learning about and gaining new appreciation of the human experience—especially with respect to questions of fundamental importance
5) Sharing, sometimes through teaching, what I've learned with others— especially with respect to the human condition and questions of fundamental importance
6) In responding to feeling wronged or confronting injustice, maturely choosing peaceful, non-violent means— when others might childishly opt for revenge and violence
7) Learning about and gaining new appreciation of the natural world — especially with respect to questions of fundamental importance
8) Being outdoors on a journey in a land different from where I live. This can involve interacting with people of a different culture, appreciating their heritage, seeing natural beauty, unexpected encounters with wildlife while hiking, or star-gazing under a dark sky or from a different latitude. (See Figure #38 as well)
9) Working, especially with others, defending the biodiversity and integrity of nature and / or fighting threats to environmental quality or human health
10) Working hard: losing myself in manual labor— especially when it's connected to something worth producing, promoting the common good or something I believe in
11) Being at archaeological sites connecting with life long ago
12) Enjoying museums and appreciating historical treasures skillfully presented, or being outdoors where historical heroes of mine have lived, worked, or are being celebrated
13) Listening to music that evokes strong feelings in me — especially as part of celebratory performances or occasions
14) Peak experience in transcending feeling of wholeness /connectedness —I especially value love-making for its potential in this regard.

"What is sacred?" Each of us will answer this in our own way. I've done this by listing in Figure #36 fourteen activities and settings that help me find meaning in life. They describe my personal sacred realm. Items 2) and 5) in this list mention the human condition. Bringing in item 6), we note that once "people lived by killing." In *Jerusalem, Jerusalem*, James Carroll argues that, seen as the story of how the human conscience deals with this realization, (choice #17) "violence is the problem the *Bible* is addressing." Seems Jesus' (choice #14, choice #18, choice #19) preaching love and non-violence is a key problem-solving contribution.

What else? Frustration with flaws can elicit our (choice #32) cynicism. Operating in the sacred realm can suppress that negativity Not only are we imperfect creatures but we are discrete, separate entities. This can bring some profound feelings of loneliness. A strong ego may only exacerbate them. In the worst cases, when we fail to come to terms with imperfections, this can bring (choice #26) profound alienation.

Sometimes, if we're able to somehow turn off our egos—lose our small individual selves in, or to, something much bigger—we can overcome the loneliness / alienation and exist in the belongingness space that item 14) above identifies. Carried to an extreme, (choice #6) mystical, ultimate feeling of Oneness, experiencing cosmic consciousness can result. With such feeling, can come great (choice #20) passion. With the inclusion of passionate love-making in my sacred realm, comes a vow to never cheapen it with casual engagement. Leaving down to earth needs and alternative hedonism pursuits behind, one could only seek partners with whom a transcending "touch the Sky" experience was possible.

This last term—from an old song[14] by the band Chicago—and the above context, brings to mind another song from the same era: Led Zeppelin's "Stairway to Heaven." Per item 13) in Figure #36, this classic, loved by so many, is one of my favorites. Taken literally, one might naively think it's not only about "getting high" but also about looking to the sky or "on high" for God. But the last verse's lyrics: "where all is one, and one is all: to be a rock and not to roll," suggests we attain that mystical feeling (choice #6) of Oneness here on Earth (as a rock). We do this by losing our ego / looking within. For a rock and roll song—where rolling is often linked to sexual activity—this song's use of "not to roll" is notable. I see rolling as an activity in 3D space, and —if we get to where this song tries to take us (to Heaven?) —we transcend that in merging with something bigger (God?) Something we seek within ourselves—not up in the sky.

Besides the Zeppelin classic, another winner in the "music that evokes strong feelings in me" contest is the Rolling Stones' song "Gimme Shelter" —also revered by fans worldwide. I rather unexpectedly involved it in particularly memorable sacred realm experience in an item 11) archaeological setting in February 2018. The next section provides an account of that Earth-centered spirituality adventure. This Stones' song is about feelings of fear—uncomfortable feelings in a reality we try to escape. The Zeppelin song, in contrast, stirs feelings we want to embrace. It's a celebration— something we occasionally need.

Sasha Sagan concurs. In her 2020 book, *For Small Creatures Such as We*, she describes growing up as the daughter of Carl Sagan and Ann Druyan. "As a secular home, we had some traditions carried on from our ancestors. The philosophy was wonderful: it fulfilled some deep philosophical and intellectual needs. But what it lacks is celebrations, holidays, and rites of passages." After losing her father at age fourteen, she's been searching for them.

As I write, I have yet to read Sasha's book, which reports on that search. Rather I offer results of my (choice #21) alternative hedonism efforts to fill that celebratory void. Note my previous Figure #36 list —while alluding to personal celebrations—omits holiday celebrations to be widely shared, and potentially sacred rituals and journeys. These are something any religion, especially a new one, needs to have if it's to attract followers. Note the lists in Figures #37 and #38 are separated by a comment on ceremonies involving drums—attention-getting devices.

Figure #37 Activities / Rituals w/ Profane ➔ Sacred possibilities

Celebrating Holidays: Since 1970, **Earth Day April 22** has been celebrated on John Muir's[15] birthday—a great day for (choice #41) affirming Respect for Nature. And increasingly people recognize **October 12** as **Indigenous Peoples' Day**—not Columbus Day. In recent years math and science-minded folks have begun celebrating two special days. One is **Pi Day March 14.** Written 3.14, we have a two decimal approximation of the ratio of a circle's circumference to its diameter. March 14 is also the birthday (in 1879) of the person many consider to be the greatest thinker since Issac Newton (whose birthday was Christmas Day, 1642): Albert Einstein. It's a great day to celebrate the (choice #7) Orderly and Explicable universe and our "daring to understand" it. The second special day is **Mole Day October 23**—a great occasion for honoring (choice #2) global vision that spans space and time. A mole can be thought of as a conversion factor between the microscopic world of atoms and the macroscopic world—ten raised to the 23rd power, written 10^{23}. So it's celebrated on October 23—also a day to appreciate geologic time—something no one did in 1650. That's when Irish Bishop James Ussher announced God created Earth in a six-day process that began at 9:00 AM on October 23rd in 4004 BC. Beyond this breaking constraints imposed by those with vision limited in time, Mole day recognizes (choice #1) evidence-based knowledge triumphing over wishful thinking.

Celebrating by Making Cards—I like giving people personalized— often humorous—birthday or other special day cards that I (choice #46) make, rather than just buying some consumer offering. Finding a way to make them laugh challenges my (choice #47) creative expression skills.

Singing / Music: Instill meaning into celebrations with music—perhaps music you perform, songs you've written, etc. See Appendix B for a church service built around such songs. Other examples appear elsewhere in this text; more are on the *Project Worldview* website.

Gardening: establishing one in your backyard for growing your own food or in a public spot in a community effort; composting to build garden soil; catching rainwater for watering the garden; celebrating—and being (choice #19) grateful for— a fall harvest of garden produce.

Cooking: expressing your creativity in the kitchen with tweaking recipes you find or inventing new ones—all with the goal of putting healthy (and sometimes delicious in alternative hedonism fashion) food into your body. Sharing your creation with others adds to your enjoyment—as does using your own garden produce.

Planting Trees: for fruit, shade, or use as a Christmas or other holiday tree to decorate. (Harvesting figs from trees I plant is on my bucket list.)

Getting out in Nature: a) hikes with naturalists, for bird watching, identifying plants, viewing wildlife; b) geologist guided interpretive talks and walks / fossil digs / rockhound adventures at local sites; c) volunteer trail—building / clean up litter / pick up trash around local streams

Indoor Education / Celebration: museum / planetarium visits and special school / outdoor park programs. These can also be places to join others in Earth Day, Pi Day, and Mole Day celebrations

Discover the Sky Education a) guiding children, perhaps over many months, through the ten observing exercises presented earlier; b) going to star parties with sky tours—either naked eye or telescopic—conducted by skilled astronomy educators; c) watching— possibly counting / charting— meteors, especially during showers

Discover the Sky Celebrations: celebrating the Sun at special times: partial and especially total solar eclipses; celebrating the Moon at special times: notable full moons, thin crescents, harvest moons, lunar eclipses; celebrating close conjunctions of the moon and planets, or two planets— pointing out to children that these are line of sight alignments and have no special significance other than helping us identify objects and appreciate beauty; celebrating the appearance of bright comets visible to the unaided eye—this can be an occasion to talk about long-ago superstitious fears and put modern understanding to psychological use.

Citizen Science: Opportunities abound for gathering ecological data on plants, birds, insects, fungi, etc. and studying fossils, stars, galaxies, etc

Energy Use or Climate Action Related: Hanging out clothes to dry in the sun; engaging in energy-saving treatments, retrofits or do-it-yourself solar projects; getting people together for carbon conversations; Earth Day can expand into Earth Week to raise awareness; joining others in groups like the Sierra Club can make environmental activism fun.

Charity: with money or volunteer labor, supporting non-profit organizations and causes that are dear to your heart

Worldview Related: making *Choices We Make* playing cards / booklet; playing educational games associated with these; using *Project Worldview* website-based tools to assess your worldview and others'.

Comment on ceremonies involving drumming

Consider a ceremony—perhaps an indigenous peoples' one— involving drumming. Certainly the sound of drums can attract curious folks to this event. But, before continuing, I direct attention to the (choice #12) Imagination, Curiosity, and Intellectual Freedom theme. Once our curious individual decides to stay and watch this hypothetical ceremony, the drums take on another role—one that connects with the other theme in choice #12: The Group Think Imperative.

Drums fit in an induction procedure that serves to narrow consciousness by providing something for the mind to focus on. The procedure is what Princeton psychology professor Julian Jaynes—in his 1976 book *The Origin of Consciousness...*—called The General Bicameral Paradigm. Others (like Eckhart Tolle in his 1997 book *The Power of Now*) might say a drum beat focus keeps the mind from wandering. It can help tune out cerebral noise and achieve a goal: kill the ego, live completely in the moment, and dwell in state of cosmic consciousness. Some seek such (choice #6) mystical experience to obtain knowledge of the Unknown / God —perhaps through divine revelation. (See Song #3 in Appendix B.) Short of such ectasy, a drum beat can keep the mind immersed in a song.

The Group Think Imperative is almost the anti-thesis of the scientific method, so you wouldn't expect it to be part of "a religion that stressed the magnificence of the universe as revealed by modern science." You're mostly right. Drumming can be part of pagan, Earth-centered spirituality rituals based on ancient knowledge / misconception, whereas I want to promote rituals that build, reinforce and celebrate modern understanding—especially those with Earth / Sky connections. Yet unlike other practitioners whose efforts have the same effect of turning off our analytical minds, good drummers can be appreciated for the efficient operation of their brains. As one recent study concluded, "Professional drumming is associated with a more efficient neuronal design of cortical motor areas."[16] (Aside: we'll miss you Charlie Watts!)

I close this section with the list in Figure #38—one of sacred journeys. Unlike "the hero's journey" described by Joseph Campbell, entries here are more focused in space and time. And in the next section I present "dispatches from the front lines in the battle to find meaning in life."

Figure #38 Earth & Sky centered Spirituality Sacred Journeys

Discover the Earth journeys: regional field geology outings —some can be built around auto road trips using widely available roadside geology guides; to the Grand Canyon and other national and state parks with extensive geology interpretive displays
Getting out in nature journeys a) to hike the most famous USA long trails—the Continental Divide trail in the Rockies, the Pacific Crest trail in the Sierra Nevada, the Lewis and Clark National Historic Trail, and the Appalachian trail; b) to visit national parks— note some have junior ranger educational programs for home schooled or other kids; c) to visit World Heritage Sites; d) climbing high mountains (say peaks exceeding 14,000 ft. elevations, or the highest in a particular state or region;) e) floating long stretches of scenic / challenging white water rivers
Special Discover the Sky journeys a) to view celestial events: most notably total eclipses of the Sun, the Northern Lights, etc; b) to dark sky preserves or simply to get away from city lights and show city kids the Milky Way; c) to celebrate particular celestial objects—for Canopus as previously described, or to sites celebrating Venus / Aphrodite, etc.
Ocean / Marine Life journeys: to the sea shore for the marine life experience or to large aquariums with interpretive guides and displays
Visits to sacred places of the ancients: to megalithic sties, archaeoastronomy sites
Visits to places important to the history of science

E. Four Dispatches in Battle to Find Meaning in Life

**Dispatch #1: Report of July 2018 Talk I Give
at UU Church in Prescott, AZ**

What follows is an edited excerpt from the script I used for this talk. It was accompanied by many slides—one being Figure #39—and music. (Note: for this book, I added the figure #, choice # references.)

Figure #39: The View from Inside Menga Dolmen Antequera, Spain

＊＊

The inspiration for my talk this morning—entitled "Life Begins Where Your Comfort Zone Ends" — came while I was underground in what was once used as a tomb. The title is a bit deceptive because a lot of what I'll talk about centers on the concept of creative destruction. It will build on the Lovers Leap Story I told earlier.[17]

Let me take you back to a day last February… I awoke a long way from home on the Mediterranean coast in Malaga, Spain, and caught a bus for Antequera. Disembarking, I entered the town early in the morning through a colorful arch. I proceeded to walk two miles or so to the relatively deserted Menga Dolmen, part of a megalithic World Heritage site. I'm traveling by myself in a country where I don't speak the language. If that isn't enough to get me out of my comfort zone, I soon find myself underground in a structure built 6000 years ago, underneath huge megalithic slabs.

I walk fifty feet or so to the back of this underground dagger-like penetration of the earth, and having an idea, I take a seat. I plan to summon my earth-centered spirituality inner child, and meditate…Alas, I'm unable to shut off my mind, so I decide on another way to calm my restlessness, soothe feelings of insecurity and honor where I am: with a song. Pulling out my iPhone, I'm soon listening to a favorite song—and thinking…

…About the region's brutal, (choice #17) violent past—especially during the early 15ᵗʰ century; about (choice #50) war-torn hell on Earth that exists today for refugees in places like Syria struggling to escape; of my own growing up memories of (choice #18) fearing nuclear war; of children today worrying about climate change. As I listen, I think of the climate disruption of the last year: of a flood in Houston brought about by a North American record of fifty-three inches of rain in the short time of a couple of days; of a hurricane that brings unprecedented death, blackout and misery to Puerto Rico; of heat and drought induced, outrageously high winds driven, wild fire that burns many thousands of homes around Santa Rosa, California.

The (choice #13) apocalyptic song I'm listening to is the Rolling Stones' "Gimme Shelter" —a song many associate with death and the grim end of the 1960s love in / flowers in your hair era. This music ends. I walk up toward the entrance and, looking out, have a strong feeling that the view of Lover's Rock—what's been called "the most important archaeological view in the world" —celebrates death in a way that has nothing to do with our tragic lover's leap story. And directs attention to sacred ground.

This is the only megalithic structure in Europe whose axis points (Figure #39) to a terrestrial, not celestial, landmark. Why was it honored? Inside looking out at Lovers Rock that morning, I had a strong feeling as to why its builders aligned it that way 6000 years ago. They wanted to celebrate the death that gave life to an ancient tribe. I sensed they were honoring what I imagined happened on that mountain long ago: the tribe founders executing a new (choice #47) survival strategy. They'd learned to kill big animals—or herds of them—by driving them off the cliff. I imagined the conception / execution of this creative destruction was a (choice #49) technology advance worth recognizing, and loss of life worth honoring.

Lover's Rock was already famous when Christopher Columbus set sail on his famous voyage. In the voyage's log he likens a landform seen in Cuba in late October 1492 to a specifically named "Pena de los Enamorados" —the Spanish name of "Lover's Rock." This profit-driven adventure began the creative destruction that one author has called "The Conquest of Paradise."[18] Of course much destruction is less creative and more pointless. Some is tragic—certainly the legendary leap off this dramatic cliff was. ***

I have three comments, beginning with one about the song "Gimme Shelter." If "Stairway to Heaven" suggests finding Heaven, this dark, foreboding song has you worrying about a future in which humanity has descended into a Hell on Earth. Second, Columbus is not a hero of mine—not surprising given my (choice #51) anti-colonial, anti-imperialist preference for Ethical Globalization. Third, you'll recall I used LaBarre's book *The Origins of Religion: The Ghost Dance* to help introduce the exploration of sacred ground. The second part of that title takes one back to a final tragic episode in four centuries of western hemisphere violence that began with Columbus. I'm thinking about the massacre recounted by Dee Brown in *Bury My Heart at Wounded Knee* and what followed shortly after. That was, in LaBarre's word's, "...the Great Ghost Dance of 1890...[which] provided the crashing climax to the collapse of American Indian culture."

Dispatch #2: Report on November, 2019 Talk I Hear in Flagstaff, AZ from an Inspiring Native American

That first dispatch sets the stage for a second report of a sacred realm experience. It connects with my sacred realm lists in several ways, but most notably through Figure #36 items 3), 6) and 9). Specifically on November 15, 2019, I joined roughly 400 people at a Flagstaff Arizona conference. The event was titled "Climate 2020: Seven Generations for Arizona," —a name recognizing Native American planning tradition.

The title inspired part of my (chapter 7) *Love in a Time of Climate Crisis.* family letter. There I went back to 1785 to highlight a span of over seven generations of my family history—also noting how atmospheric CO_2 climbed with growing population and industrial activity during the years spanning those generations. Bill McKibben, in *The End of Nature*, says "[I] can think back five generations in my family," and only "265 generations ago, Jericho was a walled city of three thousand souls." Before people started to gather in such cities, they were hunter-gatherers.

My grandkids can say seven generations ago Neverson Cook established the Cook family plantation— built on land indigenous Americans (of the Cherokee tribe) had tragically been forced off, and onto a trail of tears. Now I was settling in to hear Xiuhtezcati Martinez, a nineteen-year-old, long black haired indigenous climate activist, hip hop artist, and author, give the conference keynote address. Speaking from his heart, I realize this guy is both sacred representative of, and has semi-legal standing in speaking for, people whose humiliation gives them every right to hate.

Growing up in Boulder, Colorado, the son of an environmental activist mother and a Mexica / Aztec father, he began speaking internationally on those issues at the age of six. Xiuhtezcati soon cites threats to cultural traditions—and to our planet's environmental health— and urges people to (choice #31) work for change based "on your passion—what you love enough to defend." He wants to remind the world of the old ways his ancestors practiced, based on (choice #41) respect for the land. To that, he tells us, we must return. Noting that ultimately we have all come from somewhere—that we are all indigenous people—he cites the "threat to all of our cultural survival." He urges all of us to defend the sacred.

Addressing an Arizona crowd that includes professional planners concerned about water availability in a warmer future world, he notes water has always been sacred to Western native peoples. Recalling memories of "riding on my Dad's shoulders," he credits this man with helping him in "contextualizing my life, my voice, my path." This he sees as finding "a way to leave something beautiful behind in honor of those who came before me; in honor of those who struggled through (choice #24) oppression and genocide, helping me to recognize that we are here now because our ancestors fought for us to be here. Now I carry that responsibility for future generations."

Echoing an earlier Navaho speaker's call to "warrior up" to battle climate change —a woman who had said, "Great Spirit, we know you hear us!" — Xiuhtezcati tells us to "hold onto your love—anchor yourself with it, for the going will get harder." His talk—titled "Imaginary Borders"—emphasizes that, armed with love for the Earth, we are all "collectively in this together." He sees the "mindsets" of the powers that be as the (choice #51) same ones that can be traced "back to the colonization of America." As such he sees those people as promoting "illusions that work to separate us." He ends telling us that this "shared responsibility we hold" to come together to collectively defend the Earth we love, could turn out to be "humanity's most unifying moment," and "our finest hour." I instantly rise to applaud, having been truly moved.

I ponder what I've learned about Xiuhtezcati's worldview with respect to three choices. In choice #36, he manages to represent and promote both Proud Identification & Tribalism and Global Citizen themes. Per choice #24 building bridges, not walls / culture of tolerance, he adds we should "build bridges across generations." His words help me bridge, both the fifty years of age difference between us, and generations of "us vs. them" — as in white man vs. Indian —cultural divide played out long ago in my family history. Finally, a choice #19 related question, "Why so much bitterness and hate from white-privileged folks like Trump, and talk of unity/ forgiveness/ love from minorities they've historically oppressed?"

Dispatch #3: I Unexpectedly Encounter a New Age Christ-like Figure in Sedona, AZ February 2021

Famous for its stunning red rock scenery, Sedona might also lay claim to being the "New Age Capitol of North America." Recalling my chapter 1 characterization of this movement, you know I've been exasperated with some of its adherents. Yet, as both my report on "A Forbidden Book" earlier in this chapter, and the "Strange Events That Shake Worldviews" ending to my 2015 book *The Worldview Theme Songbook* show, I try to maintain an open-mind with respect to many New Age beliefs. Certainly my closest friend these days—Leena, who played a key role in the story the earlier book ended with—challenges me in this regard.

Thus on a gorgeous, warm, sunny Friday in mid-February 2021, I relaxed while Leena meditated nearby. She sat at the base of Kachina Woman, a striking red rock prominence rising roughly seventy-five feet above a nearby so-called "energy vortex." We'd driven to a surprisingly crowded trailhead a few miles out of town. After hiking a mile, as the path started a steep climb to our destination, I began to hear a flute playing. Looking up, I realized the music was coming from a person who'd somehow made a seemingly impossible climb. He was perched at the top of Kachina Woman.

The music was nice, but I cringed when this person began speaking. I wasn't close enough to hear the words, but I muttered something to Leena about not wanting to listen to "a preacher... ranting like a crazy man," to use a phrase from the Rolling Stones' song "The Back of My Hand." I'd been prepared for the afternoon to present challenges to my

worldview. Already Leena had added to my conception of kachinas as
being Native American dolls, by also connecting them with (choice #9)
spirit beings—ones who travel between dimensions. I could handle
hearing that from her—but I wasn't ready for a sermon from a stranger.

After Leena headed in closer, I found a place to sit on a ridge. To the left
I could see the protected natural beauty of the Secret Red Mountain
Wilderness area. Below to the right were scars on the land— the homes
and facilities of the Enchantment Resort—reminders of the threat that
developers pose to ecological integrity. Straight ahead, roughly 200 feet
away, was the precariously situated flute player. He wasn't delivering
sermons after all.

What we—me and the roughly thirty people in the area—got from him
were pleasing melodies, punctuated by a sentence introducing each song.
While I'd captured enough words before I got seated to suspect the guy's
theme was unconditional love, it was the first complete sentence I heard
him offer that got my attention: "This song is for courage—courage to
release the consciousness and see with your heart."

Courage—I'd told Leena weeks earlier in a New Year's Resolutions
discussion—was what I needed to muster as much of as I could to meet
the challenges the year would bring. As the "concert" continued, I slowly
traded my (choice #4) skepticism and (choice #32) cynicism for a
(choice #1) positive longing for a world built around a (choice #14)
Relaxed, Generous, Loving mindset. Had the flute player been urging us
to follow him and his (choice #16) Moralistic God, I'd have been out of
there. But I couldn't dispute his (to use another old song's title) "What
the World Needs Now is Love"[19] message.

The music ended. The flute player descended. I'd assumed he was a
young man, so I was surprised to see he looked about my age. He began
talking individually with people and giving out hearts of some sort. I
figured these were made of plastic and—despite his assurances—were
definitely not full of the Creator's energy, which he said was love. As we
started down the hill, Leena gave me the heart he'd handed her. She put
it into my daypack. While I grudgingly appreciated the forty-five minute
experience I'd had, only later did I begin to realize that I'd witnessed
something extraordinary.

The first clue came when Leena told me, as we approached the car, that I could keep the heart. She had the one the same guy had given her roughly eight years earlier, when she'd last meditated at Kachina Woman on a overcast, drizzly day. The second clue came that night when, almost as an afterthought, I reached into my daypack to have a look at the heart. I was surprised to find a hand-crafted one-quarter inch thick, heart-shaped red rock, with two nicely fashioned two inch long lobes. It had been carved from the rock formation the flute player had been sitting on.

It wasn't a petrochemical polymerization process plastic product —it was ancient. It came from the Earth itself. How old was it? From my knowledge of northern Arizona geology, I recalled that many of the rock layers exposed in the Grand Canyon (chapter 5) are also visible in the Sedona area—with one stunning red rock scenery addition. Sandwiched in between the Coconino Sandstone and Hermit Shale layers (in Figure #20) is an 800 to 1000 foot thick layer known as the Schnebly Hill Sandstone. It was laid down 270 million years ago.

Placing this reddish piece of sandstone between my fingers and stroking its face with my thumb, it felt soft and smooth, with just a hint of grit. Even though it was just 8:30 PM, I was tired, and soon after enjoying the pleasing sensation stroking the rock provided, I fell into a deep sleep. I awoke near midnight with a burning question, "Who is this flute player?" A Google search quickly provided answers, and I found several inspiring accounts written by those who'd encountered him. Most notably, someone had posted a video account of an experience at Kachina Woman—first listening, then climbing to interview the flute player at the end of his performance from the lofty perch. This *You Tube* offering is titled "Robert the Reiki Flute Player of Sedona's Boynton Canyon." Robert, it reports, has been giving flute concerts twice a day, seven days a week, from the top of Kachina Woman since June of 2011.

As I write, I'm soaking up this five-minute music video—feeling (choice #19) grateful to its producers—stroking the rock, and reliving my experience. I'm seeing and hearing Robert say things like, "The whole idea is to spread unconditional love around the earth, one heart at a time. This is how we're gonna change everything on the Earth." And "This song is about releasing…If it's negative and it does not serve you, let it go!" He's articulate, charismatic, radiates caring good intention. He comes across as, not a crazy man preacher, but as an inspiring (choice #31) "Let's make it happen," and "No more plastic Jesus" type person.

After viewing the video, my (choice #4) inner skeptic directs my attention to the *Wikipedia* article about Reiki. Reading this, my mood changes. It jolts me out of an unconditional love mindset, and into one built around the other choice #14 theme: Cautious Processing. After identifying Reiki as "a Japanese form of alternative medicine called energy healing"—where the energy involved comes from the chi life force (see choice #9 Vitalism)—it labels Reiki as pseudoscience. Without actually saying it's dangerous, it says, "There is no proof of the effectiveness of reiki therapy compared to placebo." The skeptic in me turns back on. But I also try to imagine—as choice #7 Orderly and Explicable, and Magic themes suggest—fitting what Robert says into an (choice #1) evidence and (choice #10) science-based framework.

As I stroke the rock Robert lovingly fashioned, I have no doubt that I'm transferring atoms and molecules that were recently part of his body to my own. Might such connection extend to somehow entangling me and Robert via the (admittedly hand-wavingly described) quantum level mechanisms sketched earlier in this chapter? After pondering this, I'm disturbed by the complexity I've introduced into analyzing Robert's simple message. I could just say something like, "When I listen to Robert, see him on the video, and stroke the rock, I feel his loving kindness commitment. It moves me. I want to embrace it. I'm in awe of how he has touched me with his simple message and with the courageous, unselfish, dedicated way he reaches people with it.

In contrast, the way I approach wanting to help people in "making sense out of the confusion of existence," is laughably complicated. In trying to simplify talking with others about aspects of reality, I'm nonetheless still working with 104 worldview themes. As a communicator, Robert seems to embrace a KISS philosophy: "keep it simple stupid." As measured by Tolstoy's "There is no greatness where there is not simplicity, goodness, and truth," I link Robert with greatness.

If I silence the (choice #4) Skeptic in me, my True Believer and my (choice #1) Inner Positive Thinker won't question what Robert says. His message can be distilled down into spreading love or loving energy. I can explain it by saying it's centered on the (choice #14) Relaxed, Generous, Loving theme, and related to other themes listed in the (see chapter 4 Figure #8) description of the Christian Love / Stewardship generic worldview. And to a New Age Spirituality / Mysticism one.

In encountering Robert, I feel like I've encountered Jesus as I've long imagined him. The Jesus who lives inside me—in my heart with loving kindness and positive, generous, (choice #18) Good Samaritan, Golden Rule impulses. Not someone who lives far away in a pie-in-the-sky Heaven with God. Not a "believe in Him or burn in hell" character that many evangelical Protestant Christians worship—and the Christian Salvation / Having Dominion Over generic worldview of Figure #7 characterizes. Not the guy worshipped by those small-minded prejudice folks who seem to be more on the side of hate, than love.

Encountering Robert took me back to a long-ago "highest high" peak experience I described near the end of the *Coming of Age...*book. "It was May 10, 1975 at a Hollywood theater. Annie and I were there to see the rock opera *Tommy* in which a deaf, dumb, and blind boy is awakened to his hidden potentialities, becomes a self-actualized leader and then a Messiah." I remember "getting high from the music and the story and merging with the reality on the screen." I remember "leaving the theater feeling like a resurrected Tommy." And this memory is relevant today.

Thank you Robert for giving me "excitement at your feet.[20]" Thank you, brother, for urging us to find the "guts to leave the temple," and your commitment to making the world a better place. I shall treasure the heart-shaped rock you provided, which I now think of as imbued with meaning. The kind of meaning I've long sought to find in life. I've come to see this 270 million year old heart-shaped piece of the Earth as calling out to all of us, "See me. Feel me. Touch Me. Heal Me."

Dispatch #4: My Worship of Another Celestial Object
and Thoughts of Death

I've long worshipped the Sun. During the 1978—1985 period this worship was particularly intense. I built a passive solar house, became an early user of solar PV panels, got involved in solar energy education at a local community college, then ran a solar energy engineering consulting business called compuSOLAR. Lack of political support for solar in the USA— and associated economic reality —killed that effort...But things have changed—and solar has come roaring back. This book's pushing sun worship culminated in chapter 7 with description of my use of solar-assisted zone heating, and the "Solar for the People" essay. But this dispatch isn't about the prominent, life-giving Sun. It's about a much more obscure celestial object—indeed it's only fleetingly visible from where I live and have lived. Mostly it's invisible below the horizon—as if it's dead. I associate it with death—as in remembering those who have died. But unexpected glimpses of it nurtured growing worship Before revealing this object's identity, I'll share thoughts about my death.

I've finally decided what I want done with me after I die. After I'm cremated, I want my ashes put in a cheap but durable container that might reasonably be called a canoptic jar.[21] I'd like this ecologically sensible effort to continue with the jar's burial in some meaningful and practical location that remains to be determined.[22] In the middle of that jar, surrounded by my ashes, I'd like two things. First, the six-inch diameter pyrex telescope mirror[23]I grew up with. Second, the SBIG CCD imager which, when coupled with a telescope, sent so much star-filled enjoyment my way for so long. I just went out to the outbuilding where this lives to verify its diameter and the mirror's are roughly the same. And I saw a dandelion plant with yellow flower in bloom outside the entry door, above which "The Observatory" sign my dad made long ago is mounted. What does this have to do with "another celestial object?"

That object is Canopus, the far southern star and second brightest in the sky after Sirius. My connection with this object began on September 9, 1964. That was the day my father and I brought home a new telescope made by The Optical Craftsmen Company in Northridge, California. Dad—concerned that I might buy, sight unseen, a mail order telescope— had found this company's listing in the phone book. A trip out there got me the company's catalog. This identified what was perhaps their second best-selling telescope as the "Canopus" model—the first one being designated the "Sirius" model after the brightest star.

Soon after I brought home that Canopus telescope—and spent months delivering newspapers with an after-school paper route to pay off the $200 bank loan that financed it—I'd forgotten the model designation star name. This was made easier by the fact that the Hollywood Hills prevented my glimpsing this far southern star from the Burbank backyard where I used the telescope for many years. But I never forgot seeing the rings of Saturn that night after my Dad and I brought home my new six-inch reflecting telescope.

That same "summer of the telescope" of my junior high years began with my mother disciplining me for some transgression I can't remember. My penance involved weeding the front lawn of dandelion plants—a job that initially seemed overwhelming, both in perceived time commitment and unappealing nature of the work. Looking back, I see that this task—which took many hours spread out over many days—helped me realize how much I love "digging in the dirt." I now connect it with my later digging triumphs, especially in house-building excavation work. Those exploits later earned me "The Human Backhoe" nickname.

I think I first actually saw Canopus while driving on Interstate 40 in the California desert one night when I was in my thirties. It wasn't until I moved to the (latitude 32° south) mountains of southern New Mexico that I began seeing it more often. One night, when I wasn't even thinking about viewing it, especially stands out. On December 21, 2010—the night of the winter solstice—I anticipated viewing a lunar eclipse. I was aware that this was a special celestial event: the last time a lunar eclipse occurred on the day of the winter solstice was 372 years earlier in 1638. I suspected many astrologers out there practicing their ancient craft could tell you exactly what this modern event supposedly portended.

As it turned out, something totally unexpected made that night's special celestial event personally meaningful. Soon after midnight I noticed a bright star close to the southern horizon. As the lunar eclipse progressed, and the Moon faded, this star—Canopus—steadily gained altitude as the Earth turned. By the time Canopus reached its culmination—and shined a mere 5° above the southern horizon, —sunlight that had been lighting up the Moon was no longer doing so. Blocked by the Earth's shadow, the Moon had disappeared—but there, nearly due south, was Canopus. That night cemented Canopus' status as my favorite star.

I'd previously developed an astronomy educator's appreciation for the possibilities that Canopus offers for expanding worldviews—especially those of people who live where this star just briefly appears above the southern horizon. As described earlier in (chapter 5, Figure #15) the changing altitude of this star from different locations can be used to determine the size of the Earth. The Greeks, Erathostenes and later Poisidonius, first did this over 2000 years ago. In 1153, observing from Marrakesh, Morocco and vicinity, Spanish-Muslim astronomer Ibn Rushd similarly employed Canopus.

A few hundred years later, a number based on observation of Canopus changed history. Had Poisidonius' ancient, but rather accurate, numerical value for Earth's circumference been properly converted to the right units by Ptolemy as recorded in his ca. 150 AD classic *Almagest*,

Columbus's famous voyage might never have occurred. In setting sail, Columbus believed Earth's circumference to be only 18,000 miles—an error of 6,000 miles that overlooked the existence of whole continents in between the Atlantic coast of Spain and the Pacific coast of China.

My December 21, 2010 experience got me thinking about a "religious pilgrimage" involving Canopus. There are well-established precedents for such journeys. Every year, thousands of Christians and Moslems travel—sometimes long distances by foot—to the Santiago de Compostela in Spain, to the Holy Land around Bethlehem / Jerusalem, or to Mecca in Saudi Arabia. Where might such a journey celebrating Canopus be set? Answer: between northern latitudes 35° and 32° where its greatest "demonstrating Earth is round" potential exists. And where greatest (choice #2) global vision expanding prospects exist.

In this regard I can imagine annual "Walk for a Small Planet" or "Bike Ride for a Small Planet" early March celebrating Canopus events. Certainly these could give participants a wonderful, personal experience-based sense of the Earth's size. Conceivably such 220 mile or so long treks might span two weeks (including camping) if you're walking—or three to six days if you're riding a bike — in the American Southwest. All the while, night after night you'd watch the bright star Canopus slowly climb higher in the sky as you journeyed south. A good route in New Mexico—mostly along Highway 54—could involve a slight mid-journey detour to camp at the Three Rivers Petroglyph site.

I like to think that long ago some Native American creative thinker—say one headed south and similarly watching Canopus—might have had an "Aha!" moment. Say, after years of annual journeys as part of trade or seasonal relocation, he or she thinks about what an ant moving on the surface of a round object would see. And makes the imaginative intellectual leap to being the ant, the round object being the Earth, and changing positions of the star Canopus being what's observed. I've looked for petroglyph depictions of this at Three Rivers with no success.

Like my December 21, 2010 experience, my next significant encounter with Canopus was also unexpected. After moving a bit farther north to my new home in Arizona, with Canopus even lower in the sky, I'd assumed mountains would block my viewing it. But one early March night— nearly five years after moving to this location—I happened to notice a star-like object just above the mountains when looking straight out my front entryway. I initially figured it was a new or overlooked light for some telecommunication setup. But given its southerly direction and the time of year, I investigated. I was stunned—it was Canopus.

I ended up honoring what still seems like an amazing synchronicity. I built something of a sky temple—a shrine to Canopus that celebrates its unexpected visibility from the front door area of my house. I enclosed a portion of my front patio, and mounted a small, little used telescope there. For the base of this mounting, I used what for me represents a canoptic jar—a ceramic planter pot filled with rocks. I've imagined holding a Canopus viewing party from there on some future night. September 9th would be a logical date for doing this. In fact, on September 9, 2014 I celebrated the 50th anniversary of bringing my Canopus model telescope home by again using it to view Saturn. But Canopus itself rules out September 9th —it simply won't be visible. Likewise on my Dad's May 3rd birthday. My Mom's January 7th birthday would work—but the star of the show won't appear until 11:30 PM. So I've tentatively settled on a early evening celebrating Canopus party in some future year on my oldest grandchild's March 3rd birthday.

If you glance back at it, you'll see "My personal sacred realm" Figure #36 list begins with something like "ancestor worship." This spurs thoughts of love, fear of loss, death and why many people need something like religion. And why religions that promote life after death are so popular. The new "religion" this book has sketched, partly based on "reverence for what Earth and Sky teach us," (choice #16) disdains thoughts of literally dying and going to Heaven based on judgment of a moralistic God. But there's another way to live on after death: to do so in memories. I'm thinking of this as I wind up this final dispatch from the front lines in the battle to find meaning in life.

Thus, every September 9th—as diehard native Californians celebrate an admission day holiday—I return to memories that give the day we brought home the telescope a uniquely personal meaning. My father is a big part of those memories, just as sights of dandelion flowers trigger recollections of my mother. These memories allow my parents—my Sky parent and my Earth parent—to live on, to transcend death.

F. The Ending of this Book—Three Alternatives

I've written three endings to this book. Alternate Ending #1 continues the seeing celestial sights / death theme of Dispatch #4. Alternate Ending #2 appeals to cutting-edge physics and builds on the very earliest (from Chapter 4) of "Stories from My Own Experience" to bring closure. Alternate Ending #3 builds on both of these alternatives. I can't decide which I like best—so I ask you to read them all and decide.

Alternate Ending #1

The comets I've been most impressed by and involved with showing off were Hale-Bopp in 1995 and Hyakutae in 1996. But Halley's comet is the most famous one. And viewing it as a youngster presents a wonderful possibility: living long enough to—seventy-six years later—see it again in old age. The *Coming of Age...* book imagines my own children, who saw it at ages three and five, seeing Halley's comet again in 2061. And their thinking back to Dad, showing it to them with that old telescope back in 1985. I've even written a song that connects my family history, Halley's comet, and death. It's called "Caring Respect."[24] It's to be sung to the tune of the theme from *The Music Man*—my Dad's favorite musical—namely the song "Seventy Six Trombones."

While the song's first verse starts in a very celebratory upbeat way as you might expect from this rousing music, the enthusiasm dampens so that its fifth and last verse is sung in steadily softer, slower, subdued, then almost barely audible fashion. It ends (with apologies to poet T.S. Elliot) "not with a bang, but a whimper" in the form of these words:

"Helpless when we enter this world
That's how we leave
Humbly, humbly we end up where we start
If I'm helpful to others along way
With caring respect
I'll die having done my part"

Looking back on a life of intellectual curiosity, it would be nice to imagine concluding at its end (again with apologies to T.S. Elliot), "I did not cease my exploration. And the end of all my exploring has been to arrive where I started, and know the place for the first time." Might death reveal some secret to life? Might a part of me (choice #16) live on after the death of my body? I have strong doubts.

Yet, from a (choice #3) Humbly Unsure perspective I can't rule out this possibility with 100% certainty. I can conceive of a "holographic blueprint" or (higher dimensional?) "Universal Structure" (Cosmic Mind?) in which individual consciences continue to exist in some form.

Seems my (choice #1) internal Positive Thinker demands such a conception. And, given my intense curiosity, it's just the sort of thing that could provide a reason to welcome death: to learn the answer to such ultimate questions. I have another (choice #7) reason for toning down my (choice #4) skepticism in considering such questions:

I like pondering the mystery=magic component of efforts to make sense out of existence—to dwell there in reverence, to stand in awe and wonder.

Alternate Ending #2

I've spent nearly a lifetime defending the (choice #11) Free Will notion that we control our own fates, and pooh-poohing those who say things like "everything happens for a reason." Perhaps the closest I get to allowing for any deterministic possibilities not consistent with my "I'm in charge" free will belief, comes when I consider physicists' efforts to put together a so-called Theory of Everything (TOE). Looking at current paths to arriving at such a theory, I'm most intrigued by those employing the holographic principle, suggesting the universe is like a hologram.

A hologram is an image created using lasers, mirrors and knowledge of how light waves interfere with each other. This image can be recorded on a glass plate. When it's projected, the viewer experiences a three dimensional image. Interestingly, if the glass plate is broken into smaller pieces, each piece is capable of recreating the same three dimensional image exhibited by the whole intact plate, although the clarity and resolution of that image is reduced. It's as if there's no localized storage of the image on the glass plate, the image is stored all over the plate.

Conceivably the universe is like this: the whole is contained in every part, albeit at a reduced resolution. Teilhard de Chardin seemed to think so, although the technology for making holograms wasn't invented until after his death. In an introduction to de Chardin's book, Julian Huxley describes Teilhard's vision. "He thus envisages the world-stuff as being 'rolled up' or 'folded in' upon itself, both locally and in its entirety." Ervin Laszlo is another who has imagined a holographic blueprint behind the encoding of a fundamental space-time information field.

If you like such models, then you can readily imagine that literally the whole universe is inside the smallest grain of sand—and inside you. Thus, conceivably, in a (choice #6) mystic trance, you might experience "outer space" by looking within and exploring the "inner space" of your mind. You might likewise believe that the entire life history and accumulated wisdom of a very old person is accessible to the very young person residing in the same body and sharing the same brain.

As I write I am the proverbial biblical (*Psalms* 90, verse 10) three score and ten years. Looking back on my earliest memories as a three and a half year old—of my parents leaving me for three weeks, and the young Sunday School teacher / babysitter telling me about Jesus and warning me I needed to behave to avoid Hell fire—I wonder what would seventy-year old Stephen have said to that child to comfort him? In the context of this book, I can imagine the following communication.

"Relax, Steve. Be patient. Your parents will be back, so until then be as comfortable as you can with yourself. That relationship is something you'll always have—whether young or old—so work on (choice #26) building a good one. As for believing in Jesus, you know it's easy to be skeptical and find fault. I've learned that you can usually find evidence to tear down just about anything or anybody. And that we're all imperfect creatures—including those who promote Him. I have no doubt that those folks surround this character Jesus—if He ever existed at all—with all kinds of baloney (to avoid using a stronger word.) I'd advise being selective, and —where evidence is not overwhelming in choosing what to believe—consider engaging in a tiny bit of (choice #1) positive thinking to the extent you need to be comforted."

"You miss your parents and their (choice #25) unconditional love. But as you grow, you'll realize that (choice #14) love is all around. You'll meet people who seemingly have it in such abundance they might remind you of an idealized Jesus=God=Love conception. Some will seemingly have it for you. You'll recognize they too are imperfect creatures. Hopefully that realization won't come painfully when they let you down. If you feel alone, it can't hurt to (choice #6) imagine we are all connected. And that your parents, Jesus, God, and all the love you've experienced or suspected is there inside you—for you to draw on and be comforted by."

"Finally, you'll learn that love has both receiving and giving aspects. I know as you grow up you'll increasingly try to be like those who have loved you and who you see as being full of love to give. Try to be one of them—to spread the love. And try to avoid, or minimize, letting people down and hurting them. And realize that the more people feel 'We're all in this together,' the accompanying sense of belonging will grow and overwhelm the alienation of those walled off by (choice #32 and choice #33) cynicism, greed and self-interest. You can promote that feeling by building bridges that promote belonging, not walls alienated people hide behind. Above all, **choose to live in a way that maximizes the love you give back to the world, and in a way that makes it a better place.**

Alternate Ending #3

It's been said that all people really need in life are three things: work to do, someone to love, and something to look forward to. As I age, besides the usual things grandparents look forward to seeing, I've other reasons for wanting to hang around. Given my (choice #12) intellectual curiosity, I'd be (choice #19) grateful for definitive answers to two big questions— one spurred by looking out into space, the other by looking within.

First, "Where are they?" The odds are overwhelming— recall the Drake equation in chapter 2—that we are not the only intelligent beings that have ever existed in the spatial vastness of the universe. But the universe's history also spans a vast time—and intelligent civilizations eager to communicate don't live forever. Nonetheless, most likely our counterparts are out there right now likewise wondering, "Where are they?" Some think UFO sightings and reports of alien abductions are evidence they've visited us. I think those things can be explained in other ways.[25] Likewise I'm skeptical of those channeling gurus who claim telepathic communications with extra-terrestrials (ET). I suspect this is nothing more than mental illness and / or fraud. I could be wrong.

If definitive proof of contact with ET is to be had, I'd say radio telescope signals will most likely provide it. But however it comes, as the *Childhood's End* title of Arthur Clarke's 1950s science fiction classic suggests, this could mark an important transition in the human experience. It could help people finally shake off (choice #41) the childish notion that we are special, that some (choice #5) Personal God watches over us, (choice #8) provides sacred words to live by, (choice #13) might reek apocalyptic havoc if we collectively misbehave, and ultimately (choice #16) sits in judgment of us.

A second big question I'd like answered builds on previous imagining and is best stated as three smaller questions. "Is the universe something like a hologram, with the whole contained in every part? If so, does this provide information that informs both evolution and choices individuals make? If so, how is information that we might say is elsewhere in space / time—in the distant future, once stored inside the brain of someone who lived in the distant past, in a Cosmic Mind, etc—transferred? I can imagine waking up to stunning experimental confirmation of some physicists' theory of everything—one built around a holographic priciple, spacetime emerging from quantum entanglement, and pointing to information transfer mechanisms.[26] This too would be a key transition in the human experience. While marking a stunning triumph of (choice #1 and choice #10) evidence-based methods and science, it could also validate something quite different: the (choice #6) mystical, (choice #7) magic, (choice #9) vitalistic, and (choice #10) Non-Rational experiences that have long informed peoples' spirituality.

Answers to these questions will help humanity realize its potential. With technical details beyond the grasp of most, the discoveries could rekindle a childish conception: God is love. Putting to rest the notion God dwells in some physical place in the sky—and New Age imagining of minds "ascending" to merge with ET minds— the discoveries could promote something else. That God is found by looking inward, just as the gospel of *Thomas* had Jesus urging us to do. Looking to love inside you.

Thinking of love as life believing in itself, with life-affirming spirituality infused by feeling (choice #16) "the moral arc of the universe bends toward justice" and "we're all in this together." Imagine those feelings—and (choice #14) loving kind-heartedness and choice #41 respect for nature —are widespread. **Imagine living in a time when we, as a species, feel good about choices we've made in the global village.**

Notes

1 from franktipler.com/about
2 his notable book: *The Anthropic Cosmological Principle* w/ J. Barrow 1985
3 a term generally related to the future creation of artificial intelligence of such magnitude and capability that irreversible changes in human civilization result
4 I was baptized in a Presbyterian Church at age 12 and married in one at 25
5 a pseudoscientific medical practice based on belief the cure for something in sick people is to be found by extreme dilution of the agent that makes healthy people sick. Often the dilution is so extreme that no molecules of the causative agent would be expected to remain in the homeopathic medicine.
6 canyonministries.org
7 the belief that the features of the universe and its life are best explained by a directed intelligent cause (i.e. God), not natural selection
8 with John Barrow in their 1985 book (note 2 above) as found on page 203

9 "The World as a Neural Network,"arXiv:2008.01540v1 [physics.gen-ph]

10 Zurek, W. "… the quantum origins of the classical" *Rev Mod Phys* 75: 715

11 Recall a theory's ability to generate hypotheses that can be tested is critical

12. I met Stapp after a presentation I gave in Budapest a decade ago.

13 Physicist Murray Gell-Mann (1929-2019) used this term.

14 The full line is "Cry sweet tears of joy, touch the sky" from the song "Make Me Smile" on the Chicago album released in 1970

15 Muir has long been revered for his communicating the sacredness of nature. Sadly, words of his have surfaced that, to quote a Sierra Club statement, "continue to hurt and alienate indigenous people and people of color." Without condoning Muir, I note that he, like the rest of us, was an imperfect creature.

16 Newman, Tim "Drumming Makes Your Brain More Efficient" *Medical News Today* December 16, 2019 This reports the cable connecting the two brain hemispheres is altered in drummers. Their anterior corpus callosum cable has fewer, but thicker fibers—promoting more rapid transfer of nerve impulses.

17 a tale of forbidden love between Moorish princess and Christian soldier in 14th century Andalucia. It may have inspired Shakespeare's *Romeo and Juliet*

18 Sale, Kirkpatrick *The Conquest of Paradise* Penguin Books New York 1990

19 DeShannon, Jackie "What the World Needs Now" 1965 song

20 Given the "feet" involved, Leena told me I needed a footnote here.

21 Made of limestone /pottery, these were used by ancient Egyptians to preserve human organs. Canopus was the boat captain who took Menelaus to Troy.

22 Someone could sneak into Forest Lawn Cemetery, not far from where I was born, quickly dig a hole between my parents' gravesites, and bury this jar. Maybe I'm naïve enough to imagine they might get permission to do this?

23 To preserve telescope for use by family, the damaged original finder scope — which pointed me to so many celestial sights—can replace the mirror.

24 This is the last song, on page 100 in *The Worldview Theme Songbook.*

25 the best UFO accounts could be explained by something as common as debris entering the atmosphere, or as rare as perception of a space-time defect (understood by analogy w/ gravitational lensing?) I can even imagine visits of technically-advanced humans from the future. Alien abduction stories are most likely psychological attempts to deal with human-caused trauma.

26 See page 341 for my current favorite as to Theory of Everything approach.

APPENDIX:

Appendix A frames 104 worldview themes by pairing them to make fifty-two choices, as has been done in *The Choices We Make booklet*, itself based on *The Choices We Make* playing cards. (Note: the cards can be seen as a low tech form of social media.) Version 5.0 themes are used. An index has been added. Numbers following entries like "Index CH #1" represent page numbers in the text where discussion of themes related to the particular choice occurs. Those contemplating a particular choice could benefit from reviewing all of the indicated page references.

#201A   **A♦**   Choice #1   **A♦**   #201B
EVIDENCE-BASED	**POSITIVE EXPECTATIONS**

#201A	#201B
EVIDENCE-BASED	**POSITIVE EXPECTATIONS**
I trust in a rational belief system, built on facts and concepts, ultimately linked to observation and experience, which fit together in a coherent way as part of a useful (for making good predictions) logical framework. Whether it be my own worldview —or a collective product of a multitude of minds (scientific consensus)—I see this framework as steadily evolving (improving!) based on feedback. If they pass certain tests, I'm generally able to accept psychologically disturbing features of Reality (example: the finality of death) rather than deny them. I strive to separate fantasy from reality and not deceive myself.	If hope means having only positive expectations, I'm a hopeful optimist. I can firmly believe, with complete confidence and trust, in something for which there's little or no evidence, and certainly no proof. I can deny evidence and believe in something if doing so provides hope or useful psychological advantage (example: belief in an afterlife.) I sometimes interpret events / actions of others, and make decisions, based on what I'd like to be true, rather than what is true. I can delude myself. I see it as adopting healthy beliefs which promote my and perhaps my family's or loved ones continued psychological well-being.

Index CH #1: 5, 31, 34, 35, 54, 64, 67, 72, 80, 87, 95, 100, 101, 109, 127, 129, 130, 139, 150, 151, 168, 170, 171, 177, 179, 181, 183, 191, 218, 219, 222, 256, 290, 323, 324, 326, 327, 329, 332, 342, 344, 350, 357, 360, 365, 367, 369
Index CH #2: 25, 26, 42, 43, 46, 55, 72, 80, 85, 146, 149, 151, 152, 162, 169, 173, 175, 183, 185, 191, 192, 201, 215, 237, 251, 256, 275, 290, 329, 334, 340, 348, 363

#101A   **K♦**   Choice #2   **K♦**   #101B

#101A	#101B
MIND OPEN, VISION GLOBAL	**MIND NARROWLY FOCUSED**
I'm capable of great foresight, am open-minded and curious. Since my mind ranges freely over the intellectual terrain, my worldview extends in space & time. I respect evolutionary change, natural cycles and the web of existence of which I'm part. I appreciate cosmic distances, geologic time and statements like "Our bodies contain atoms once inside ancient stars." I know the past provides insights into dealing with today's problems; that future consequences of what we do must be considered. I realize the world is complex and sometimes understanding it requires simultan- eously holding conflicting beliefs.	I can live in the moment and let stimuli and experiences pass by without judgment. Other times, in "pre-meditated ignorance" fashion, I avoid exposing myself to beliefs / values that would necessitate some revising of my worldview. If I nonetheless encounter them, I've been known to ignore facts that produce psychological discomfort. I don't like facts, beliefs, and values that are inconsistent with each other. And I like to "keep it simple, stupid," and often refuse to deal with issues requiring my mind range widely in space and time, or the complexity of simultaneously holding conflicting beliefs.

#1A　　Q ♦	Choice #3　Q ♦
HUMBLY UNSURE When it comes to knowing what's right, what's best, the true nature of things, or having answers to life's important questions, I feel inadequate. While others most assuredly promote their beliefs with black and white certainty, I am silent and see shades of gray. I can't forget the complexity of the world or the smallness / ignorance of any one person. I'm not sure enough of anything to lay it on everyone else. I trust not in high principles, but in small experiences. (Note: This person enters arguments hesitantly, but after presenting facts and uncertainties may confidently seek the truth and express an opinion.)	**I KNOW WHAT'S BEST** I feel I have found "the answer" (what to believe, buy, how to behave, the best way to do something, etc.) And I feel obligated to share what I've found with you, so you too can benefit! Please bear with me if it seems my evangelizing, persuading, etc disrespects your beliefs, values, or feelings — I have your interests in mind! (Note: Some see these people as selfless leaders willing to helpfully step up and point the way forward, others see them as dispensers of propaganda who selectively use facts / emotionally charged language to promote a self-serving agenda.)

#1B　　J ♦	Choice #4　J ♦　　　#2A
SKEPTIC I believe knowledge is generally accompanied by uncertainty and doubt. I like where doubting can lead: to questioning, debating, reconsidering, testing, new knowledge, and eventually to the truth. I am suspicious of faith-based beliefs. In deciding what to believe, I prefer reason and critical thinking, to emotion and wishful thinking. In putting down "true believers"— sometimes treating them with contempt— I lack humility and can be arrogant. (Note: critics charge that, in efforts to "debunk," skeptics can be closed-minded, and too eager to dismiss evidence not supportive of what they believe.)	**THE TRUE BELIEVER** My faith in what I believe is free from doubt. If you'd had my experience, you'd also believe! I understand what it is to be a Believer. I like to think of myself as devoted to a noble cause in the fight for justice or search for Truth. I too can overcome obstacles through courage, persistence, and Shining Purity. I define who I am, magnify my identity, and recognize my enemies through my crusades. (Note: Faith is used here in a broadly defined spiritual context. Critics say true believers have an "excess of certitude" and / or cite their "irrational persistence" in holding "untenable beliefs.")

#8A	10♦ Choice #5 10♦	#8B

MONOTHEISTIC DEISM

I rather tentatively believe in a God who might be called "The Creator of the Universe" or "The First Cause" and who may be the ultimate source of a creative dynamism ("vital spark"?) that seemingly energizes life. Beyond that initial moment (which some link to "The Big Bang") I believe God does not interfere with the workings of the universe—which proceed according to physical laws. I believe humans' conception of God can only be informed indirectly through observation and rational investigation of the natural world— not directly through divine revelation or mystical experience.

BELIEF IN A PERSONAL GOD

I believe, not only did He create me, but that God is concerned with human beings personally. I conceive of Him as a personal being (perhaps a father) with a personality. I value talking with God through introspection / praying. I believe God listens to prayers and watches over us. I believe that, given His personal interest in the world and its people, He will intervene on behalf of worshippers (performing miracles, etc) or to reward / punish. Some conceive of God in terms of forgiveness and love, others in terms of vengeful, judgmental punishment.

#7A	9♦ Choice #6 9♦	#12A

MYSTICISM

I, like William James, see personal religious/spiritual experience having its roots and center in mystical states of consciousness. If, like me, you've had this (belonging to the universe feeling of Oneness?) experience, you'll respect my characterization: 1) it can't be adequately described in words, 2) it provides insight into fundamental Truth—perhaps that perception of discrete objects and the passage of time are illusions, 3) it can't be sustained for long, 4) it makes me feel passive—as if grasped by a superior power (God?) Not sensing distinct gods or deities, in rare perfect moments I feel union with an undifferentiated whole.

POLYTHEISM, ANIMISM, PAGAN.

I believe in the existence of many gods. While not all deities are thought to have physical bodies or even be worthy of worship, some certainly are. Like humans, these deities are seen as having their own personality traits, needs, desires, etc, but with additional powers and, in some cases, supernatural attributes. Many of us worship gods associated with particular objects (Sun, Moon, water, etc,) events (birth, death, etc,) or character types (hero, trickster, muse, etc.) Animists talk of gods inhabiting special places. For them nature is alive, with spirits animating both living and non-living things.

#6A **8♦**	Choice #7 **8♦** #7B
ORDERLY AND EXPLICABLE I say we can eventually greatly comprehend how the world works if we only "Dare to Understand." From a 6th century BCE Ionian Enlighten-ment success predicting when a solar eclipse would occur, increasingly people have found natural and rational causes for observed events. Progress has come with appreciating cause and effect, solving problems by breaking complicated wholes into smaller parts, forming concepts and using them in frameworks, testing hypotheses and learning from feedback —all in building and refining an extraordinarily useful structure for explaining, predicting, creating.	**MAGIC** Like science and technology, magic seeks to control nature. Instead of attempting to understand, magic enthusiasts celebrate mystery. They seldom try to explain paranormal gifts, spirit communication skills, ability to right wrong relationships, etc they feel healers / shamans / witches / astrologers possess. Some see "magical rites & beliefs" as "expressions of an act of faith in a science yet to be born." Some are confident scientists will eventually explain things like the healing power of faith—whether in God /gods /drug/placebo or doctor. Others feel many aspects of Reality will always defy understanding.

#9A **7♦**	Choice #8 **7♦** #10
RELIGIOUS FUNDAMENTALISM As an orthodox follower of the _____(insert name of religion)__ religion, I believe that human behavior should not deviate from that called for in my religion's sacred text: __(insert name of sacred text)_ This I see as the unerring word of God. I hold it to be literally true, and believe that it provides an absolute basis for morality. I believe that God can and has personally intervened in the lives of people in ways consistent with stories in this sacred text.	**SECULAR HUMANISM** I don't believe in a personal God. Without faith in a divine purpose for human existence or absolute moral code, I aim to put meaning, notions of good and evil, and universal values into my life. While troubled by ignorance and injustice, I accept human imperfections. I value learning. I champion self-realization through reason, and responsible living through brotherhood. Overcoming "the anxiety of nothingness," in asserting the inherent dignity and worth of all of us, in helping us appreciate our place, I maintain a hopeful, optimistic, outlook on life.

#5A 6♦	Choice #9 6♦ #5B
SCIENTIFIC MATERIALISM I say the universe, life, humans had no Creator—their existence is due to forces acting on matter and random chance. The universe has no purpose, or notion of good and evil, other than the meaning and value we give it. Life involves only matter, physical / chemical processes (physicalism) — not vital spirit. Someday scientists will create it in the lab. Spirituality exists only in the mind, a product of processes in brains. I discount knowledge not based on observation and reason. (Note: some connect life with interacting with the environment to get information /structurally coupling with it.)	**VITALISM** I see life as holistically endowed with something special: spirit, soul, life force (Qi in China, Prana in India.) Most religions involve belief in spiritual beings: living things with souls, disembodied spirits, ghosts, angels, that natural objects are conscious (animism), etc. Traditionally the self-awareness called consciousness (home of conscience) is thought to reside in souls. (Note: While disdaining the above, some link life with a creative/ organizing principle. They see it as emerging from the collective behavior of a complex system, and as something more than the sum of its parts.)

#6B 5♦	Choice #10 5♦ #12B
SCIENTIFIC METHOD I value solving problems by scientific methods: gathering data (I like numbers), making testable hypotheses (I like equations) to fit data, testing (I like statistical tests,) refining, publishing for others to verify. Scientists work to avoid bad experimental design, faulty controls, selection effects, bias, prejudice, errors, etc. A complex problem may require reduction to many simpler ones and sorting out multiple causes / effects. Science works better than anything else when it comes to making good predictions and solving problems. If there were something else that worked better, I'd be for it!	**NON-RATIONAL KNOWING** More than most people do, I trust intuition, gut feeling, instinct, and unconscious knowledge— where I respect my brain's power of pattern-matching. I don't discount dreams and synchronicity to the extent others do. I value the collective unconscious and brief glimpses I've had into Reality "with the curtain pulled back." More wholistic than reductionistic, I appreciate what can't be measured. I find science limiting. I'm a visual thinker, sensitive to environmental cues—sights, sounds, smells, tactile insights—and to feelings! I'm especially alert to signs of danger and am good at detecting deception.

#11A   **4♦**   Choice #11   **4♦**   #11B

FATALISM

I believe that events are fixed in advance so that humans are powerless to change them. I say it's naïve to think that—in the big scheme of things — we control our own destinies. Whether you call it "God's plan" or "the will of God" — or call it determinism and involve factors beyond human control—I'm resigned to believing that my life's course is fixed as part of the larger scheme.
(Note: deterministic predictability depends on natural / physical laws, genetic and epigenetic endowment, the (predictable) response to environmental stimuli, etc.)

FREE WILL

I believe that humans have the power to freely choose between alternatives, exercise rational control over their actions, and generally shape their destinies.
I believe those who preach "whatever will be, will be" and claim "the future's not ours to see" are fools. I see resigned helplessness, and waiting for God to solve problems people could solve themselves, as dangerous.
(Note: Appreciation of quantum mechanics and chaos theory has led many scientists away from the notion that complex events always unfold in rigidly determined, predictable ways.)

#15   **3♦**   Choice #12   **3♦**   #30

GROUP THINK IMPERATIVE

If stimulated / stressed, I give up choices I'd otherwise make. I suspend thinking/narrow consciousness and passively transfer control of myself to some real or imagined authority. I put my faith and trust in, feeling obligated and beholden to, this authority. The authority is associated with a culturally agreed on expectancy behind a setting or belief system. This giving up control happens most often where peer pressure to conform is strong, or when rituals trigger trancelike behavior — even hallucinations. (Note: a wide variety of folks, from indigenous people to teenagers to cowardly politicians, can behave this way.)

IMAGINATION, CURIOSITY, INTELLECTUAL FREEDOM

I value free inquiry unconstrained by authority—as the best way for gaining knowledge and perfecting society. I promote maximizing individual liberty of thought, belief, and questioning. Unlike many, I am especially curious. I value the freedom to let my imagination run wild. I'm driven to seek out and explore new territory in pursuing intellectual rewards. I get a thrill acquiring new knowledge, making new connections— even out of mustering courage to not conform. I'm especially productive working at the interface of internal imagination and external experience.

#9B 2♦	Choice #13 2♦ #13
SIMPLY IN GOD'S HANDS: APOCALYPTICISM	**COMPLEXITY—IN OUR HANDS: DANCING WITH SYSTEMS**

SIMPLY IN GOD'S HANDS: APOCALYPTICISM

I think the end of the world, or some catastrophe after which life won't be the same, is imminent—perhaps in my lifetime. While my belief is based on a hopeful expectation— God's victory (led by the return of a beloved religious leader / prophet) and the final triumph of good over evil— I realize there are other possibilities. The end could come with the triumph of evil, or God's disgust with His Creation and decision to start anew with a clean slate by means of His choosing.

COMPLEXITY—IN OUR HANDS: DANCING WITH SYSTEMS

Complex systems are difficult to model due to interacting parts and distinct properties that can arise unexpectedly. Modeling physical systems with many levels of organization, even ecosystems, is much easier than tackling social systems. That task, applicable to a wide range of problems, should involve 'dancing': humbly gathering and valuing data, learning, being mentally flexible / alert to how the system creates behavior, and to feedback. We plan and anticipate. Trends ➔ Predictions ➔ Policy Changes. Averting catastrophe to create a future we choose.

#202A A♥	Choice #14 A♥ #202B
CAUTIOUS PROCESSING	**RELAXED, GENEROUS, LOVING**

CAUTIOUS PROCESSING

Metaphorically my mindspace contains unfamiliar, potentially unfriendly, dangerous places, so I'm cautious. I draw out as much information from it as I can, and perhaps am not as "giving back" as some. I often feel unsettled, stressed, anxious. My caution is due to past a) unpleasant, distressing sensory experiences, and b) physical and emotional stress caused by hurtful incidents or encounters. Given my self concept and memories, with my fear of a) and b) I sometimes feel angry and mean. (Note: some subjected to prejudice, bullying, or unwanted sexual attention may abandon caution and hit back.).

RELAXED, GENEROUS, LOVING

Metaphorically my mindspace is like a pleasant, warm, loving, family home where I am calm and relaxed. Perhaps lack of stress or fears of being unable to cope, makes me more giving / generous. Besides being helpful / kind, I often give others "the benefit of the doubt." Given this mindset, I feel lots of love. This I connect with feeling affection such that imperfections are overlooked and that others' —or another's—happiness, is critical to one's own. (Note: Many who believe "God is Love" have a similar viewpoint, which some call God-centered.)

#102A K♥	Choice #15 K♥ #102B
CONSCIENTIOUS, EFFICIENT STEWARDSHIP	**EASY-GOING, DISORDERLY, CAVALIER**
I try to do what is right or fair. I try to meet work obligations and other duties carefully, thoroughly, and efficiently —minimizing wasted materials, energy, money, time or effort—and taking responsibilities / commitments to others seriously. I anticipate and plan for emergencies. If entrusted with managing what someone cares about, I'm a good steward. I pay attention to details. I'm a good listener. When I feel stressed because I know something isn't right, I typically feel I must fix it. So, I'm often putting things in order or am in task-oriented mode. I'm happiest when I'm busy.	I'm typically relaxed and tolerant in how I approach work, duties I have, or responsibilities I've accepted. I'm not easily upset or worried about obligations I have to others. I can generally live with an associated lack of planning, careful organization or irregularities in how I go about my activities. I try to minimize stress in my life, <u>not</u> "sweat the small stuff," and filter the stimuli coming at me so as not to feel overwhelmed. As such I've acquired a reputation (undeserved?) for being lazy, and having a cavalier attitude. So, seldom am I asked to manage what others value.

#14A Q♥	Choice #16 Q♥ #14B
SALVATION & MORALISTIC GOD	**MORAL ARC OF UNIVERSE / KARMA / REINCARNATION**
Guided by conscience / wishing to minimize or avoid punishment (including self-administered), I seek to live in accord with God-given moral standards. I believe that every person is born with soul condemned to suffer, but by behaving properly one's soul can be "saved." So I often ask myself, "Am I good enough to go to heaven?" (Note: Some believe that a moralistic God's favorable judgment can "save" someone. Upon death these souls spend a blissful eternity with God in heaven or paradise. Those souls with unpardonable sins spend an eternity in hell.)	Without involving guilty conscience God or divine judgment, I feel the moral arc of the universe somehow bends towards justice —perhaps in a spiritual version of action / reaction or cause / effect. (Note: Some extend this with "cosmic justice" where a person's actions in one life produce karmic forces with consequences in future lives. This requires believing a non-physical essence (soul, consciousness, etc.) in each of us survives death and is part of a continual cycle of birth & rebirth. Some believe that over-coming desire and ego allows escaping this cycle➔ Nirvana.)

# 25　　　J♥	Choice #17　　J♥　　#29B
EVIL IS OUT THERE I believe evil exists separately from us. Have you ever wondered what might happen if your conscience—through no fault of your own—was captured by a demon? If, directed by an evil force, the anger and hate inside you was not restrained but instead loosed on others? If—without that inner voice restraining you—you could do anything you wanted to? Given our flawed, sinful nature, I think the potential for this happening exists in all of us. So we must fight all manifestations of the Devil's work. And support harsh punishment of criminals as a deterrent. (Note: critics call this "the myth of pure evil.")	**TAKING CHARGE➔ VIOLENCE** I can be powerful. I can often get what I want by intimidating and instilling fear, by verbally and / or physically threatening. Since this only succeeds if the threat is believable, I've got a reputation associated with verbal abuse and resorting to actual physical violence — even condoning torture. (Note: some who lack restraint use the old threat system, based on "Give it to me or I'll hurt you" or "Pay me and I'll quit bothering you." A more modern approach is to file / threaten a lawsuit. Of course sometimes abandoning restraint—even going to war— can be justified.)

#16A　　**10♥**	Choice #18　**10♥**　　#16B
CULTURE OF FEAR I view society, to some extent, as threatening my security and well-being—so I take precautions to minimize risks. I often ask "Will someone hurt me if I do this?" Far from wanting to interact with and trust them, I generally fear strangers, especially those who seem clearly different. I lock the door to my house at night. I own a gun to protect myself and loved ones should the need arise. I try to align myself with those who have power. I believe those who break laws should expect harsh punishment—especially if they are poor or powerless.	**GOLDEN RULE, VILLAGE ETHIC OF MUTUAL HELP** I see all humans as worthy of special treatment. I believe society would work best if all people obeyed The Golden Rule: that is, treat others as you would want them to treat you. I don't lie, cheat, steal, discriminate, or arbitrarily restrict, because I don't want people doing this to me. If I see someone suffering, beyond empathizing / feeling their pain, I give them compassion. If I see someone in need, I practice a "village ethic of mutual help": I help them because someday I may similarly need help from someone.

#17A   9♥   Choice #19   9♥   #17B

BITTERNESS, VENGEANCE

If my current state is less than desired, I often focus on what's wrong, feel bitter, angry, resentful or jealous, and look to assign blame. My response to feeling victimized is often to seek revenge and punish those responsible. (Note: Some report that, until they get justice or enact revenge, they feel as if they're held captive by the need for it. Bringing religion into this, those worshiping a spiteful Old Testament God may opt for vengeance and "an eye for an eye, a tooth for a tooth."

Some vengeance is shame or scapegoating related. This can span a wide range: anything from ostracism to honor killing, murder / genocide.)

GRATITUDE, FORGIVENESS

If my current state is less than desired, I try to focus on what's right, feel grateful that I am alive, hopeful that my plight will improve, and become determined to make it so. When I'm feeling victimized, I try to make peace with what happened.

When appropriate, I offer forgiveness, unload emotional baggage, and perhaps even make some good flow from evil. Forgiving can trigger a cathartic feeling of moving out of captivity into freedom. (Note: Bringing religion into this, those worshiping a loving New Testament God "turn the other cheek" and are lenient /forgiving.)

#18A   8♥   Choice #20   8♥   #18B

PASSIONATELY IMPULSIVE

I know that some people carefully, rationally weigh alternatives when they come to a fork in the road. I'm typically not like that. Often my needs seem urgent and my actions are guided by powerful feelings— fear, anger, jealousy, love, lust, frustration, intuition, sympathy, courage, possessiveness, insecurity, sociability, hostility, sorrow, etc. (Notes: 1) Rather than acting in goal-oriented, measured fashion, primitive urges or childish reactions often spur this person's actions.
2) Undoubtedly, rash, risky, "do without thinking actions" lead to early, sudden death for many.)

RATIONAL, DISPASSIONATE

I typically make decisions after carefully considering the costs, risks and benefits—choosing from alternatives available. I do this free from passion, unaffected by emotions, and when necessary can resist instant gratification and wait. (Notes: 1) No doubt some differences in dispassionate and passionately impulsive people can be traced to brain biochemistry.
2) Learning /feedback/ memories of past experience all shape the mature worldviews that are behind making good choices—ones consistent with beliefs and values and that result in living a long, fulfilling life.)

#28A	7♥	Choice #21	7♥	#28B

HEDONISTIC ORIENTATION

I live life to maximize my own pleasure / happiness, and minimize pain, suffering, and doing without. I seek whatever brings me pleasure: food, drink, consumer goods, exotic travel, interactions with friends, sexual gratification, gambling, music, sports, games, recreational drug use, etc. (Note: hedonists are short-term oriented and neglect their health in embracing "eat, drink, and be merry—tomorrow we die." Some, the more affluent, may even more selfishly indulge in pleasure seeking but do so by finding/creating another world where they can escape from painful realities poor folks face.)

HEALTHY ORIENTATION

I like this advice: "You only get one body. How well you care for it—or don't care for it—makes a big difference in the length and quality of your life." (Note: those who value health need to take care of their body's immediate physical & mental health needs. And educate themselves as to long-term needs based on sound medical science. Good nutrition, exercise, plenty of sleep, etc can lessen both fear of, and likelihood of, illness. Meditating, having friends/ emotional support can help with stress (which can cause illness.) This is wise from both coping and, with high health care costs, financial perspectives.)

#29A	6♥	Choice #22	6♥	#33B

THE SELF-RESTRAINED PERSON

Beyond taking full responsibility for all my actions, I heed my conscience, and, to some extent, incorporate self-denial and adherence to behavioral guidelines into my life. (Note: the origin of such guidelines, whether from work schedule, legal, marriage vow, military, financial, health, family, environmental, ethical, or religious considerations, can vary. And commitments differ. Monks and nuns commit to a life of asceticism, others to voluntary simplicity. For dieters, those battling addiction, athletes, those working a less than enjoyable job, etc, restraint may only last until a goal is attained.)

ADDICTION

I have failed to restrain myself. Increasingly I feel trapped by my own behavior, and that —in my despairing moments—I have no choice to behave otherwise. I am, to some extent, imprisoned by my brain biochemistry. Simply put: *I can't stop doing certain things, even though I need to, or must, to survive.* (Note: Such people are addicted to certain substances and/or behaviors. These include addictions to tobacco, alcohol, illegal drugs, painkillers, caffeine, food, sex, sugar / sweets, carbonated soft drinks, gambling, video gaming, shopping, etc.)

#32A   5♥   Choice #23   5♥   #33A

HUMAN RIGHTS

I wish for all law-abiding people: "life, liberty", equality before the law, legal recourse when rights or privacy are violated, presumption of innocence until proven guilty, and the right to appeal conviction. I'd outlaw discrimination (by race, sex, color, nationality, language, sexual orientation), arbitrary arrest, torture, imprisonment due to poverty, inhuman treatment and enslavement. I'd grant freedom— of movement, speech and creative expression (exempting what is hateful or hurtful to society), assembly, religion, to fair compensation for work, and to choose a marriage partner.

SERVITUDE—SUFFERING, ENABLING, OR ENSLAVING

It's abhorrent, but like others, my life is severely constrained. The cause of this powerless condition may be quite different: extreme poverty, massive debt, harsh environmental conditions, ignorance, prejudice against us, disability, the authority or greed of some dominating individual who exploits us, kidnapping, dogmatic beliefs, imprisonment, restrictions of authoritarian government, etc. (Note: none choose this for themselves; an enabling many—perhaps including you?— indirectly choose it for others; an enslaving few directly choose it for others.)

#32B   4♥   Choice #24   4♥   #39B

CULTURE OF TOLERANCE

I respect, accept and appreciate the rich diversity of our world's cultures, our different forms of expression and different ways of being human. Rather than using differences in appearance or behavior to exclude, I aim to celebrate them and include where appropriate. For such diverse people to live in harmony, whether on the world or local stage, educational efforts are needed. At the local level, such education helps others appreciate both the challenges diversity poses and benefits it brings to neighborhoods. (Note: several groups have "Teaching Tolerance" projects.)

BLAMING / SCAPEGOATING

Angry over outrage / hurt I've suffered, I may single out person or group to blame. (Note: scapegoating often involves discriminating by unfairly blaming others for real or imagined offense. It happens at all levels: from sport fans blaming a player for a loss, parents targeting unwanted child, to prejudiced people targeting those whose looks, skin color, or sexual orientation they don't like, to organized groups committing hate crimes, to nation states targeting whole populations for genocide. Some scapegoaters are racists; some are bigots; some are misogynists; some are just insecure childish adults.)

#38   **3♥**   Choice #25   **3♥**   #39A

LOVE AS FAMILY GLUE
I see love as the glue holding together families—including loosely defined ones and those not linked by genes or legal ties. And I associate families with life's great joys. Inside the family home, unconditional love can provide unmatched comfort / security feelings. Meeting what some may call family obligations—like spending quality time together, parents nurturing /sacrificing for growing children, children respecting (even honoring) parents / grandparents despite their faults and helping comfort / care for them as they age, etc. — should flow naturally out of this love.

TOUGH LOVE
I think tight knit monogamous families are where children acquire high moral standards and discipline through continual reinforcement and parental modeling. In parenting— and teaching children to accept responsibility— I believe kindness can do more harm than good. We shouldn't pamper, spoil, or indulge. We should allow for some independent discovery— even if that means children learning from mistakes. When my child's or spouse's behavior falls short, rather than accept excuses, he /she should be confronted with my expectations as to their rectifying it.

#41   **2♥**   Choice #26   **2♥**   #52

STRUGGLING WITH A BASIC NEED: SELF ESTEEM
Psychologically challenged, I'm struggling to find the road to emotional maturity and make peace with myself. I seek a sense of my own intrinsic value, self respect, confidence in my ability to see life as a challenge—not a threat—and being able to enjoy it in relaxed fashion. I want to leave behind what's inside me too often now: feeling alienated, unworthy, shame, that I can't cope, that I'm a failure; too concerned about what others think of me; anxiety, fear, and self doubt. When I'm really down on myself, with this battle raging inside, I lose hope.

PHYSICALLY CHALLENGED → INDEPENDENT LIVING
Perhaps like you, I value self-determination, self-respect and equal opportunity —but unlike you I have a handicap. This makes my fully functioning and achieving difficult, if not impossible. Even when I seemingly overcome this condition, I'm conscious it exists. I'm aware that people and /or technology "crutches" often help me. I'd like to depend on these less, and more often function independently. In rising to challenges posed by old age, illness, pain, impairment, etc, I've overcome obstacles I once thought insurmountable. I continue to hope!

#203A　　　　A♣　　Choice #27　　A♣　　　#203B

HIERARCHICAL RIGIDITY	EGALITARIAN PROGRESSIVE
This title names the conservatism that's part of my worldview: it's associated with a social dominance orientation in which a social hierarchy is maintained via discrimination-based legitimizing tools (paternalism, meritocracy, race-based, wealth-based, etc.) Believing it's consistent with a natural order and fosters social stability, I accept the inequality inherent in such social ladder society—and its often centralized organizational /power structure based on adhering to rules, conforming in a cultural / moral sense— and value property rights and the status quo.	This title names the social justice path valuing equality my worldview is built on. I believe all humans should have the same rights, opportunity / privileges. Where their goals are consistent with this belief, I support collective struggles against centralized power that seek to reform church, state, political, and economic institutions. I generally don't like discrimination / exclusion. I support 1) social movements that are hierarchy attenuating (not enhancing) – feminism and affirmative action are examples, and 2) empowering the powerless.

#103A　　　　K♣　　Choice #28　　K♣　　　#103B

INDIVIDUAL GLORY	CELEBRATING TEAM ACCOMPLISHMENTS
I am competitive and prefer "I win, you lose" zero sum game outcomes. I can be egotistical. I have something of a pioneering spirit and at times am comfortable being "a lone wolf." I will sometimes seek credit for contributions I make to group efforts, rather than just remaining anonymous. I value a social philosophy / belief system that places individual interests and rights above those of society—and individual freedom, self-reliance and independence above any social contract obligations. Where applicable I'll more often say "I" than "we" and "me" instead of "us."	I am a team player. I love being part of co-operative efforts. I like "win-win" outcomes and think there's enough glory to go around. I suspect that my self-esteem benefits from the community groups I belong to, and to a "sense of belonging". I value a social philosophy / belief system that emphasizes the interdependence of every human being and promotes co-operation over competition. I'd say I'm more spiritual and value connectedness, than egotistical. Where applicable, more often I'll say "we" than "I", or refer to "us" instead of "me."

#20B   Q♣   Choice #29   Q♣   #31

AUTHORITARIAN FOLLOWER	**EDUCATION FOR DEMOCRACY**
I could live in a non-democratic authoritarian system — accepting subjugation, losing some freedom and the vote. I'd like law & order maintained, duties & rights of citizens spelled out, and trouble-makers (incl. the press) reigned in. I'll follow strong leaders —whether from single party, military, church, aristocracy, etc. — and charismatic individuals. (Note: Followers favor authority / uniformity / obedience / over freedom /diversity /independence, can be manipulated by fear mongers, and accept simple answers to complex problems. At some point when followers submit too much, democracy ends.)	I like the feedback that well-educated citizens provide elected officials in a democracy with their votes. I don't think this will work without them, as they're, as Jefferson put it, "ultimate guardians of their own liberty." So, free K—12 state supported education for all should promote 1) skills to make valued workers, and lifelong learners / critical thinkers, 2) people skills / community values, 3) understanding of technologically and ethically complex issues they may one day vote on, and 4) their ability to ultimately select good leaders.

#20A   J♣   Choice #30   J♣   #21A

ELITISM	**IDEALISTIC POPULISM**
I have problems with democracy. I say most people are ill-prepared to vote /decide what's best for society. I don't trust assemblies of such people; I fear their collective strength. Society is best served by a select group of leaders. Highly educated, trained, and groomed to wield power—perhaps even manage centrally planned economies— they should maintain law and order, promote production of wealth, and guide the masses. (Note: Elitists often identify with capital not labor, and with experts not the people's collective wisdom. In democracies, some use money to magnify their voices and manipulate outcomes.)	"The People—Yes!" sums up my trust in people's collective wisdom, resourcefulness, and ability to overcome defeats and cynicism. I have faith that, after struggle, they'll triumph over forces wanting to fool them with misinformation, divide them with prejudice, dominate workplaces, and wrest power from communities seeking to control their own affairs. I recognize their hard work / promote their continuing education. We need inclusive institutions that serve people, not extractive ones. Like Jefferson, I see the common people as "the most honest and safe depository of the public interests."

#34   **10♣**   Choice #31   **10♣**   #35B

VALUING TRADITIONS / STATUS QUO	**WORKING FOR CHANGE**
I believe that the rules and customs of any long-lived society deserve respect. This glue, shaped by challenges of untold demands, holds society together. While those guided by self interest may not like limits on behavior that society imposes, accepting them is a responsible choice. (Note: Those who respect authority, law & order, and value the hard work / sacrifices of their ancestors, will be comfortable with this theme. So will many who value traditional gender-based roles and long-lived religious institutions. Some prefer the status quo to pre-serve advantages they possess.)	I'm dissatisfied with the status quo. Three factors— gauging 1) my dissatisfaction, 2) the perceived gap between how things should be and how they are, and 3) my belief in the need for and/or rightness of the change I'm working for— determine the strength of my commitment. (Note: Activities the dissatisfied pursue can include raising public awareness, political campaigning, lobbying, building social movements to reform the system from within, filing lawsuits, organizing strikes, boycotts, civil disobedience, violent revolutionary / terrorist tactics, hunger strikes, etc.)

#21B   **9♣**   Choice #32   **9♣**   #36A

SERVICE TO OTHERS	**CYNICISM**
I admire those who serve others — either out of sense of civic / patriotic duty, desire to give back, or just because they care about people suffering /struggling and want to help. While not all of us can choose military service, run for public office, work for a community service organization or volunteer to help the sick, deprived, uneducated, etc—we can support dedicated public servants and non-profits. At times I've felt good about giving my own time, energy or charitable contribution to aid such efforts. (Note: "Service is the rent we pay for being…the very purpose of life" as Marian Wright Edelman put it.)	Once I thought people could be trusted, had good intentions, were decent, caring, honorable. Now I think otherwise: humans are self-serving; many are corrupt: fraud / bribery follows them! Those who embrace altruism are deluded, not seeing misguided self-interest for what it is. Many "do gooders" are hypocrites, too stupid to see themselves as such. I was once more accepting and forgiving. Now I am critical—sneering at, and finding fault with, much of what people do and say. Most politicians are crooks. I don't support "public servants"!

#42   8♣   Choice #33   8♣   #43

ETHICAL ORIENTATION

I'd say ethics starts with honesty and respect for laws, extends in earning a living to adhering to professional ethical codes and avoiding conflicts of interest, and for those especially concerned with social justice, comes to include applying principles which involve asking questions, like
1) Greatest General Good Principle: "Will this benefit the greatest number of people?"
2) Principle of Fraternal Charity: "If tables were turned, could I live with the consequences of my decision?"
3) Principle of Universality: "What would be the results if everyone acted in this manner?"

SEEKING WEALTH & POWER

Here's my "ethics": "Pursue your own gain, otherwise predators will eat you. The strong survive, the weak don't —it's natural law —just as maximizing happiness and pleasure comes naturally— not sacrificing for others. Acting out of envy or upon 'I want' desires means you're master —no one is pulling your strings. Do what it takes— lie, cheat, steal, spread misinformation —to succeed. Celebrate success as evidence of superiority. The meek won't inherit the Earth. 'Those who have the gold make the rules!'" (Note: capitalist greed seemingly drives creating wealth better than state non-market system planning.)

#19A   7♣   Choice #34   7♣   #48B

COMPETITIVE CAPITALISM

I believe in individuals and small businesses rationally behaving in a diverse, self-interest based economy with widely spread ownership. As availability of resources, jobs, products and market conditions change, workers, employers, producers, buyers, sellers, etc. compete to maximize gain. Competition, for the most gain, best job, etc, promotes efficiency, lower prices, and anticipating changes. It stimulates people to work hard, innovate, take chances. Capitalism is built on commodification and market transactions based on the exchange values of things.

LIKING CO-OPERATION-BASED COMMUNITIES

I prefer cooperation to competition, since the latter can bring out the worst in people. I prefer locally controlled economic arrangements involving a mixture of co-operative, employee-owned, and private businesses. I like community-based voluntary, democratic organizations in which people join hands in promoting community, common good, and local self-reliance. I dislike big, authoritarian, centralized; I like face to face barter, recognizing experiential value, and distinguishing goods from commodities.

#19B　　6♣　Choice #35　6♦　#49A	
CORPORATE CAPITALISM	**SOCIAL WELFARE STATISM**
Large corporations are superior to small business, with limited liability, greater ability to get capital, exploit natural advantages, enjoy economies of scale, lobby and shape government policy. Those that have grown by consolidating with rivals may face little competition. I'm awed as they harness production forces, satisfy consumers, and create wealth.(Note: optimists see corporate leaders increasingly putting stake-holders (workers, the community, the environment, etc.) above short-term profits for share-holders. Pessimists fear corporate greed, unethical use of power, self-serving disinformation, and environmental recklessness.)	I believe in reining in corporate power / concentrating economic controls / planning in the hands of a highly centralized government (statism). I prefer government that: 1) takes responsibility to ensure that everyone is looked out for by providing extensive social services; 2) assures environmental quality, workplace safety / societal stability through appropriate regulations; 3) maximizes spending to promote peaceful social harmony, and minimizes military spending; (Note: While social welfare states heavily tax private property, they don't challenge its sanctity as socialism does.)

#37A　　5♣　Choice #36　5♦　#37B	
PROUD IDENTIFICATION & TRIBALISM I take pride in being a(n)	**GLOBAL CITIZEN** I do not primarily identify with any particular nationality, religious or ethnic group. I think of myself first
_____ (insert name of nationality, religious / ethnic group, tribe, etc). I identify with other members of this group, and sometimes favor them as I interact with people in general. Proudly I display symbols of this affiliation and will fight or otherwise serve our cause in battles where our interests are at stake. (Note: Tribalism also lives here! Besides "us" and "them," this involves thinking / behaving / voting based on loyalty to social group not larger whole.)	as a global citizen, and try to be knowledgeable of people, customs and culture in regions of the world beyond where I live. In ethical issues involving "people" and "place," I identify all human beings with the former, and planet Earth with the latter. No one is excluded from my ethical concerns tent— everyone is inside, all are family. (Note: global citizens seek to think / behave / vote based on protecting our planetary home and the well being of all its inhabitants.)

#35A	4♣	Choice #37	4♣	#48A

SHARING WHAT MANY CONSIDER VERY PRIVATE	**PRIVACY**
I assert personal autonomy, flaunt societal convention, and protect my sense of identity / authenticity as follows: I publicly acknowledge one or more of the following: 1) my sexual orientation deviates from what has traditionally been socially (and in some cases, legally!) acceptable — typically meaning… I'm homosexual, 2) my gender identity (female or male) does not correlate with the sex assigned to me at birth, 3) you should think of me as neither male nor female but rather of indeterminate gender. 4) I am not monogamous.	I value privately asserting personal autonomy, perhaps flaunting societal norms, and secluding myself — hiding behind walls, hiding information about myself from others' scrutiny or their technology-based tools / databases. I seek to avoid disturbance (serenity compromise), embarrassment (confidentiality compromise), injury (security compromise) and /or bodily integrity compromise by others (including corporations seeking profit or governments failing to respect my body.) The extent I'm able to do this depends on socioeconomic factors and my relative power / powerlessness.

Index CH #37: 31, 38, 139, 221, 224, 275, 335

Index CH #38: 10, 33, 58, 60, 67, 68, 69, 83, 108, 111, 114, 117, 131, 134-35, 144, 224, 227, 231, 232, 271, 274, 330, 335

#36B	3♣	Choice #38	3♣	#49B

CONSPIRACIES	**IDEALISTIC SOCIALISM**
Some say I'm paranoid and deluded, that I play fast and loose with facts in an anti-social way. I am cynical. I don't trust power. My suspicions of others' motives often extend to imagining a few evil individuals with a hidden agenda conspiring to infiltrate institutions, manipulate events and shape outcomes to their liking. (Note: While some involved with conspiracy theories are in it for entertainment, others are "culture warriors" unethically pushing their values, beliefs, and practices. While occasionally a conspiracy is real— the typical internet spread conspiracy is mostly fiction.)	I'm idealistic—some say deluded. I can imagine ethical, honest, altruistic people conspiring to infiltrate institutions, manipulate events, and shape outcomes. They believe in a centrally planned economic system with the state controls of means of production /distribution designed to meet human needs. Common good, not private profit / growing wealth, is valued. Such a conspiracy would not disturb me. (Note: socialists can be democrats, authoritarians, even communists wanting common ownership of property. All see labor as the chief source of wealth, deplore its exploitation, and link this to injustice/poverty.)

#50A 2♣	Choice #39 2♣ #50B
LIBERTARIAN	**LEFT ANARCHIST**
I oppose 1) taxes beyond those needed for law enforcement /national defense, 2) government interference with free market forces, and 3) laws limiting individual freedom—restricting speech / public expression, limiting firearms, requiring military service, making certain acts crimes where there's no victim, restrictions on private property use, etc. Freedom is protected by such property, so governments should not appropriate it for public welfare. Like Ayn Rand, I see "the virtue of selfishness" and value "the non-aggression principle."	My brand of libertarianism abolishes the state altogether, and abandons or vastly reduces private property rights. It values egalitarianism—empowering the powerless —and order. It replaces government with free associations. Co-ops and communes would be key units in this ideal way to organize society I imagine. (Note: Left anarchism comes in different forms. One is collectivist anarchism where means of production are collectively owned and managed by producers themselves with labor-based compensation; another emphasizes need-based distribution.)

#204A A♠	Choice #40 A♠
FREEDOM FROM LIMITS	**LIMITS AND ETHICS**
I value individual freedom and don't like regulations that restrict it. Regarding freedom of speech, the only limitation on it I accept is on speech urging immediate hurtful action. If my actions don't directly bother or harm other human beings—or negatively impact their property—I believe I'm free to do whatever I want with my body, my machines or my property — including land I own. I don't think we live on a small planet since it's big enough to seem mostly devoid of human presence over vast areas. If we ever do run out of living space / resources on Earth, we'll simply go elsewhere in space for them.	I support common sense regulations that protect people and the environment. I support limiting freedom of speech to prohibit speech that is clearly hateful / hurtful to society—including knowingly spreading false information. Rather than acting as I please, I must respect the bigger whole I'm part of—whether it's family, village, ecosystem, etc. —and limit my impacts based on ethical, scientific, and other considerations. I believe we live on a small planet and increasingly our collective actions threaten our planetary home. Going elsewhere to live is a fantasy: If we ruin Earth, we have no viable Plan B.

#104A **K♠**	Choice #41 **K♠** #104B
HUMAN CENTERED Humans are special. I'd say we have dominion over the natural world (some say it's God-given) So I believe the natural environment should be used, developed, and enjoyed— in short, nature should serve people. I am comfortable with the increasing commodification of everything and valuing things based on usefulness to people. Creatively making land more to my liking and using its resources, wildlife, etc, is part of being human — not something I should apologize for or feel guilty about. (Note: some extend this in worshiping a Personal and Moralistic God and highly valuing their own ultimate salvation.)	**RESPECT FOR NATURE** I say humans are part of nature, not its rulers. I think animals and nature also have rights—even legal ones. People should cherish, revere, stand in awe of natural beauty, not despoil it or threaten integrity of ecosystems. This interconnected unity should be valued without regard to usefulness to people. Feeling Respect for Nature can come from living in wilderness, working the soil, and indigenous religion. Natural pantheists identify God with a self-organizing, ever evolving, perhaps self aware universe. Pantheists don't recognize a Personal God, but typically equate God with the sum of all existence.

#44A **Q♠**	Choice #42 **Q♠** #44B
SANCTITY & DIGNITY OF LIFE I say life is a sacred, mysterious gift. I stand in awe of its conscious feeling, vibrant expression. Thus, I will not engage in any behavior nor sanction any act that ends such life, or needlessly inflicts pain on living things. My respect for the integrity of life is such that I oppose medical, biotechnological, or agribusiness practices that I see as tampering with or degrading it. I especially value human life. (Note: vitalists believe "Life begins at the moment of conception." In worshiping a Personal God, some further restrict the scope of this theme in claiming, "Abortion is an insult to God.")	**HANDS OFF MY BODY** I say the most basic human right is having control of what you do to your own body. So I say to narrow-minded moralists, lawmakers, etc. seeking to restrict this right: "Hands off my body!" Steps a young woman takes to insure that her body does not give birth to an unwanted child are her business, not yours. Steps a sick suffering man takes to end his life with dignity are his business, not yours. (Note: from an ecological viewpoint we see "Some things have to die for others to live," and that "Our crowded planet needs fewer people, not more." Value <u>quality</u>, not quantity, of life.)

#3 ♠J Choice #43 ♠J #4	
VALUING HONESTY, LEARNING I like sharing "Today I learned…" and later using my new knowledge in teaching others. I'm honest, value facts, and can distinguish between the role of genes and memes in human evolution. I want to advance cultural evolution and shape healthy worldviews by promoting memes I value, and encourage learning from experience of Reality. Feedback this provides can guide humanity adapting to its global environment, promote worldviews associated with better predictions, and encourage honesty. I value exposing lies /deceit, countering false information, and teaching critical thinking skills to others so they can do this.	**SPREADING DISINFORMATION / TACTICAL DECEPTION** I'm an imperfect human being, so I will occasionally lie. Given my ambition and desire to "win," I will spread false information if that's what it takes. Is this evil or sinful? I don't know. I do know long ago my ancestors lived in a "kill or be killed" world! "What if everyone values the truth so little?" you ask. I'd say we're living in that world today and many of us are doing fine. (Note: knowingly spreading lies, computer viruses, deceit, etc. is something honest people typically don't do. If this hurts innocent people and is done for hateful reasons, most would say it's evil.)

#22A 10♠ Choice #44 10♠ #23A	
ECONOMIC GROWTH I'd say economies are healthy when they're growing, creating lots of jobs, and there's good public / private sector cooperation. Investing in infrastructure and better access to information improves productivity and decision -making. Investing in human skills leads to new ideas, new technologies—and new markets. The benefits of growth and free trade will overcome poverty. While environmental problems can be formidable, government and corporate planners —backed by scientific and technological expertise—are up to the challenge. Growth is good!	**SUSTAINABILITY** Unrestrained growth threatens Earth's biosphere. I believe we need sustainable development: meeting present needs without compromising the future. Each generation should leave the next at least as much wealth per capita as it inherited, where wealth includes both manmade and natural capital. Economies should be based on people and environment friendly technologies, renewable energy use, and resource recycling. Their health should be gauged by indicators of sustainability and well-being. We need to move beyond thinking "all growth is good!"

#23B **9♠** Choice #45 **9♠**

ENOUGHNESS	MORE IS BETTER MENTALITY / ABUNDANCE
I aim to maximize well-being, while minimizing consumption and ecological footprint. I like the five "R"s: reusing, repairing, recycling, refusing to buy what I don't need, and reducing waste. I like voluntary simplicity, and "small is beautiful" appropriate technology —which has no significant environmental impact and takes advantage of what is abundant (including human labor). I don't think "more is better" and like the freedom to take personal responsibility and say "I have enough!" (Note: many have no choice and practice enoughness out of necessity, beginning with frugality / "making do.")	I prefer experiences / things that are richer, bigger, louder, longer, faster, stronger, with more features etc. It's human nature to seek status and prefer winning over losing; being associated with powerful things— whether they be machines, houses, cars, human body parts etc—rather than feeling small, weak, and powerless. I like freedom to generally have more! (Note: With "prosperity theology" or "abundant life," some connect this with religion / New Age thinking. Critics point to traditional religious vows of poverty, asceticism, "live simply so that others may simply live.")

#26A **8♠** Choice #46 **8♠** #27

THE CONSUMERIST	THE SMALL PRODUCER
I value freedom to spend money and buy things. If I like what a product can do for me—and its image/ associated message— I will buy it. I like pretty things. If I am envious of something someone else has, I will work to get one for myself. When I tire of a possession, I discard it for something new. Often, I express who I am through what I buy. I find my needs can be met if I shop around, and I like to shop. (Note: many shoppers give no thought as to resource use, chemical residues, packaging / waste disposal issues behind products they buy.)	I'm not happy just buying what others—like big corporations — provide. I like expressing who I am through what I make with my hands and small tools. Whether producing food, shelter, clothing, arts & crafts, etc— for my use or others'—I'm happiest doing this type of work — although earning a living this way is challenging! If I can't have both, I value function more than pleasing form. I like societies based on families working land as small producers. They have great incentive to protect it /maintain its productivity out of self-interest, etc. (Note: many have no choice: they must produce to survive.)

#24A   7♠   Choice #47   7♠   #24B

STRUGGLING WITH A BASIC NEED: SUSTENANCE

Seldom feeling playful / creative, my life is dominated by drudgery and struggle to provide necessities so I /my family can survive. This struggle often leaves me in a weakened state, but sometimes I pause and ask, "Are sustenance needs being met, and are prospects good they'll continue to be met in the future?" If the answer is no, then I must make changes. I fear the day when I have no choices, and death lurks nearby. (Note: poor people, especially those confronting injustice, may not accord people or nature the respect that they would if their lives were more rewarding.)

CREATIVE EXPRESSION

I see life as playground, where I express creativity, not prison where I struggle to survive. As living space designer—or as chef—I go beyond shelter or taste: I bring taste/form/ function together in pleasing ways. As writer/artist/designer/composer, my creations come to life when creative thinking, passive observing, listening—and sometimes emotionally painful experience— ends, and active describing, sharing, storytelling begins. Seems suffering brings out my best art: imposing structure on transient chaos —presented not in isolation but as part of an interconnected fabric that touches the divine!

#45A   6♠   Choice #48   6♠   #45B

BORROWING MENTALITY

I prefer having/doing something now — borrowing money (becoming obligated) to make that possible— rather than waiting until a future time when I've saved enough money to (or can otherwise) have / do it. In general, I have no problem with individuals or governments contracting monetary, personal or ecological debts against tomorrow so that I (or society) can have / do something today. (Note: many employ leverage: using borrowed funds to purchase an asset, having that asset appreciate in value, and selling it at a big profit!)

WORK, PLAY, PAY AS YOU GO

I need work to do, someone to love, and something to look forward to, to be happy. I avoid going into debt to buy what I don't really need since in the long run this will maximize fun, freedom, and choices, and minimize guilt, worry about bills, and interest charges. Pay as you go also means giving back to society— ideally with meaningful, socially engaging work—not mortgaging your future with risky bets, and not incurring ecological debt by leaving future generations with a mess to fix, and yourself with guilt. (Note: the young should foster relationships with those able to help them get started; the old should help others do this.)

#46A 5♠ Choice #49 5♠ #47A

TECHNOLOGICAL FIX

In confronting big problems or minor human inconvenience / irritation, I look to technological ingenuity / engineering design / problem solving skills. I trust engineers / planners using technology assessment to find technology-based solutions to such problems. Such efforts have steadily brought nature under control greatly increasing human comfort. (Note: critics say labor-saving "advances" have promoted unhealthy sedentary lives, social media etc. have promoted virtual interactions over in person, real ones, and out of control technology threatens both ecosystem and planetary environmental health.)

ATTITUDINAL FIX

In confronting big problems or minor human inconvenience / irritation, I look to changing attitudes / behavior with education, drawing on existing social institutions. Defusing anxiety / mistrust conflict brings is a good first step (humor can help!) I trust people coming together and cooperating; in their willingness to learn from each other —sharing worldviews, articulating values/goals. This can resolve conflicts and find non-technology or human labor /soft technology based "win, win" imaginative solutions. (Note: critics say this democratic, transparent process is too time-consuming to tackle big urgent problems.)

#46B 4♠ Choice #50 4♠ #47B

MILITARY BACKERS

I think of militarists as exalting military virtues / symbols, being comfortable following orders and with the military chain of command, advocating military preparedness, being the first to call for war, etc. — and I call myself one with some hesitancy. While I don't doubt that waging modern war is the ultimate technological solution to problems essentially based on disputes between people, I know that great military leaders can nonetheless prefer diplomacy and see war as something to be avoided. Sometimes that isn't possible. Sometimes evil is so entrenched that war is the only way to eradicate it.

PACIFISM / NON-VIOLENCE

I think of pacifists as 1) opposed to using guns, war, violence to settle disputes and 2) preferring use of non-violent means to fight evil— rather than vengeance, capital punishment, etc—and I call myself one with some hesitancy. While I see fighting violence with more violence as both morally wrong /contradictory, and don't believe good can come out of evil, I worry that if evil is not punished, not countered with strong action, then more evil will result. (Note: avoiding war through diplomacy, something pacifists applaud, is the ultimate attitudinal fix.)

#22B 3♠	Choice #51 3♠	#51A

IMPERIALISM

I welcome affluent nations / multi-national corporations extending power and influence over developing nations, and believe everyone benefits. The big rich entities benefit from new markets for products, resource extraction, etc; poor regions from economic development and exposure to values / lifestyle /culture of the affluent world— which I view as superior to those they supplant. I view favorably the nation building that sometimes accompanies military interventions, and may even accept territorial expansion of the more developed at the expense of less developed world.

ETHICAL GLOBALIZATION

To insure globalization proceeds ethically, I think we need nation transcending authority. This could be provided by strengthening / democratizing existing institutions (UN, IMF, FAO, WTO, WHO, etc) and creating new ones. It would mediate disputes, do peacekeeping, promote health, regulate international trade— intervening when worker exploitation, environmental / health crises or economic upheaval warranted. It would regulate capital flow, bust monopolies, promote wealth / technology transfer aiding the poor—and protect unique cultural heritages and diversity of all sorts.

#40 2♠	Choice #52 2♠	#51B

ENVIRONMENTAL ECONOMICS

Holes in market capitalism must be fixed! Prices must include life cycle environment health impact fees. Fossil fuel subsidies must end. Renewable energy based efficient industrial activities like natural processes (matter recycling in closed systems) should be promoted— not waste /polluters. Use of Earth's commons (air, water, land, soil, trees, minerals) should be linked to responsibility to protect it. Incentives should encourage producing necessities (small affordable housing, plant based food, clean water), valuing and protecting biodiversity and natural capital (especially soil), and reducing inequality.

BIG BUSINESS PUSHES GLOBAL LIMITS

I value market-based pricing and corporations' profit motive. Their resource extractive (fossil fuels, mining, etc.) endeavors should speed up as growth demands. Their government partners should push "top down" approaches to meet big challenges: climate change and need for new infrastructure / cybersecurity and "brittle" infrastructure. As we run into resource / carrying capacity limits, we need ambitious (fusion, geoengineering, space-based solar power, asteroid mining, etc), capital and energy intensive, high tech solutions.

APPENDIX B: "Love in a Time of Global Crisis" –
a church service built around songs
Earlier I quoted Carl Sagan imagining science and religion coming together at some future time. Special program lay-led services in secular or existing liberal religious settings can provide a route for bringing them together in memorable, global education fashion. Below I outline one such program built around music. While science students are warned to leave their emotions behind when entering the lab, in appreciating the music-based program that follows there are no such constraints

Music manipulates emotions: it plays on our heartstrings. While we are thinking, feeling, joining, and doing creatures, no one doubts that strong emotions can turn our lives upside down. Despite efforts to steer our lives in a direction guided by reason, we often end up going where our feelings lead us: our emotions have the last word! In choice #20 terms, you might expect the songs that follow—largely built around (choice #14 and choice #25) a theme that includes "love"—to appeal more to passionate, rather than dispassionate types. Yet the "crisis" part of that theme begs for clear thinking associated with those who display a stoic serenity under pressure. And while stoics are often described as free from passions, they can be linked to tranquil good feelings of uplifting joy, cheerfulness, good intent, cherishing—and by some definitions, love.

Songs can inspire even the stoics among us. Most religions make heavy use of them. Accordingly, below you'll find fifteen songs—with new lyrics typically to be sung to the music of old favorite songs. Fourteen of these songs— identified with lyrics by S. Cook*—originally appeared in *The Worldview Theme Songbook* by Stephen P. Cook published by Parthenon Books ISBN 978-0-9627349-4-6 and used with permission. This is a collection of eighty-one songs—one for each of *Project Worldview's* version 3.0 worldview themes. (Note: they can also be found on the *Project* Worldview website.) While lyrics there come with many footnotes, the lyrics presented below have just a few.

The Church Service: Love in a Time of Global Crisis
Imagine…as people enter the sanctuary of a progressive church, they are given three things: 1) their own copy of *The Choices We Make* booklet; 2) an order of service: this lists the songs the congregation will sing, keys them to the related choice # in the booklet, and offers a brief introduction that will be read before each song is sung, like what follows; 3) double-sided, small print, stapled sheets with song lyrics, like what follows.

SONG #1: "The Doubt" lyrics by S. Cook* choice #3 / intro[1]
sung to the tune of "The Weight" by Berry, Stipe, Buck, Mill
inspired by recording of The Band

Made it here Sunday morning
But a war rages inside
To many questions I've no answers
And my beliefs often collide
Oh my God can you tell me
Where I might find certainty?
He looked at me and held my hand
And said "Seek humility!"

Honk if you love Jesus
Don't if you're unsure
Honk if you love Jesus
Oh, Oh, Oh
I've got the doubt back in me

Humble Mother Teresa[2]
Helped the poor for seventy years
A candidate for sainthood
Her soul was full of fears
Jesus God Mary where are you
Inside I feel a lack there of
She touched me and whispered
"Find me in your love"

Honk if you love Jesus
Don't if you're unsure
Honk if you love Jesus
Oh, Oh, Oh
I've got the doubt back in me

I seek love and belonging
To be part of a greater whole
I'm a small imperfect creature
But have trouble playing that role
How can I find peace
Lose myself, become truly free?
From within comes an answer:
Don't preach, don't judge, just be

Honk if you love Jesus
Don't if you're unsure
Honk if you love Jesus
Oh, Oh, Oh
I've got the doubt back in me

SONG #2: "The House of Skepticism" lyrics by S. Cook* choice #4 / intro[3]
sung to the tune of "The House of the Rising Sun" trad. / The Animals

There is a part of my worldview
I call it skepticism
If you wanna meet this part of me
Just tell me 'Christ Has Risen'

I've been trained in science
Its methods fill my head
But it's common sense that tells me:
When you're dead, you're dead

I like reproducible results[4]
Without them I will doubt
So the faith-based claims
you make my friend
For me don't have much clout

Doubting leads to questioning
Questioning to debate
But until we leave our biases behind
Finding the truth must wait

Hypotheses should be tested
Predictions verified
I'll put my faith in these my friend
Non-testable ones I'll deride

I don't much care for dogma
Or conflict with reason and fact
So if you cite this authority my friend
I won't let you relax

There is a part of my worldview
I call it skepticism
If yours is built on faith alone
Please escape that prison

SONG #3: ""Words Get in the Way" lyrics by S. Cook* choice #6 / intro[5]
to be sung to the tune of "The Games People Play" by Joe South

How words get in the way Piece by piece we have our say Mighty tough to put away And get your head free We see the world part by part[6] Not as a whole work of art Naming things gave it a start Describing Reality	Your ego's like a bright sun It dims if words you shun Glimpse the Eternal One[8] If you get your head free
Then we had to step outside Being apart, Oneness died With words we hit our stride They've served us well They helped us make maps[7] Put on our thinking caps Meet goals, take victory laps Compile stories to tell	If ego baggage you sell And give into nature's will If in the now you can dwell You'll find the Over Soul If with words you don't fight Subject and object unite In wise silence[9] take delight Meet the soul of the whole
With words we relive the past Chart events from first to last Time begins with a blast To eternal Reality	What if you really tried Banish thoughts, from them hide Trade apart for back inside Feel the power of now[10] Sail sea of joy far from port[11] To the Mind of God pay court To describe it words fall short I'll use only one: wow!

SONG #4: "Rational World Dreaming" lyrics by S. Cook* choice # 8 / intro[12]
sung to the tune of "California Dreaming" by Mamas & Papas

The God delusion[13]'s gone It's been swept away Our childhood has ended With helpless yesterday Life built on learning In both work and play Rational world dreaming Of such a brand new day	Religion fueled hate No longer on display Faith-based nonsense Has no place today Tolerance and sharing Brotherhood please come stay Rational world dreaming Of such a brand new day
No holy books and church No God or need to pray With ethical caring Love in new array Life full of meaning Put there our own way Rational world dreaming Of such a brand new day	Take responsibility For your life today Help others where you can You got dues to pay With reason and caring Let us find our way Rational world dreaming Of such a brand new day. Rational world dreaming Of such a brand new day.

Choices We Make in the Global Village page 401

SONG #5: "Fatalism" lyrics by S. Cook* choice #11 / intro[14] to be sung to the tune of "Lodi" by John Fogerty / Credence Clearwater Revival	
Many many years ago A notion in my head I was powerless—God's will I couldn't put it to bed I don't control my own life This got planted in my brain Oh Lord, stuck with fatalism And pain Often I hear people Meekly accept poverty Saying don't question God's plan You know it's meant to be Hard work doesn't matter I'm resigned to my fate Oh Lord, stuck with fatalism Sad state	If I got reality cash[15] Whenever someone said to me This bad thing that happened, You know it was meant to be I'd get on that free will train Ride 'til my head got clear Oh Lord, stuck with fatalism Up here [vocalist smiles and to points to his brain]

SONG #6: "Grateful" lyrics by S. Cook* choice #19 / intro[16] to be sung to the tune of "My Girl" by Smokey Robinson and Ronald White / The Temptations	
I've had trouble, been suffering pain When I'm down like that, dark clouds can dump rain Tears now all spent In my head this new mindset Grateful, feeling so grateful Not blaming you, I forgive and forget Not backing resentment, not a good bet Who's my sweet pet? And why is life now no sweat? Grateful, feeling so grateful	Expecting sunny days, my outlook bright Running with a kind heart, traveling light I just won't let Dark clouds make me cold and wet Grateful, feeling so grateful Less anxiety to get in my way I'm grateful With positive thoughts I now play I'm grateful Feeling so, feeling so, Feeling so grateful, yeah grateful Life is good again and I'm grateful…Grateful

SONG #7: "Be Change" lyrics by S. Cook* choice #31 /intro[17] to be sung to the tune of "Dream On" by Steven Tyler / Aerosmith	
Every time someone considers me Just what is it I want them to see? I think I know-oooooooooooooo Seems I want my life to show Others the right way Toward a better future someday- aaaaaaaaaaaa	Well..llllllllll—today so many think So much sits on the brink[18] Could be without your pledge We find it falling over the edge

Every time I want something to be
What if making it so is up to me?
Here's what I'll do—oooooooooo
Work so hard, to recruit you

Work with me, work for the change
Work with passion
the world to rearrange
Join with me: let us show 'em today
Let's bring the change
to sweep the past away-aaaa

Work with me, work for the change
Work with passion
the world to rearrange
Join with me: let us show 'em today
Let's bring the change
to sweep the past away-aaaa

Be change, be change, be change
Be the change you want to see
Be change, be change, be change
Be the change you want to see
Be change (Repeat six times)
Oh-oooooooooooo

Work with me, work for the change
Work with passion
the world to rearrange
Join with me: let us show 'em today
Let's bring change
to sweep the past away

Work with me, work for the change
Work with passion
the world to rearrange
Join with me: let us show 'em today
Let's bring change to sweep the past
away-aaaa

SONG #8: ""Hey Help Us Out Pal" lyrics by S. Cook*   choice #32 / intro[19]
to be sung to the tune of "Hey Look Me Over"
by C. Leigh, Cy Coleman / Bing Crosby, Rosemary Clooney"

Hey help us out pal,
lend us a hand
Service to others,
doing what you can
Help pound the pavement,
help with the phone
Volunteer, feel good,
change your life's tone

And your effort will help us
give something back
It will lift those who need it,
get them back on track
We'll all feel good inside,
knowing that we tried
And in helping out we take pride!

Hey help us out pal,
write us a check
Charity can help lives
that are a wreck
If you're grateful for what you've got
Show it and share with the have nots

And your gift will help us
right life's wrongs
Cheering those sufferin'
like favorite songs
We'll all feel good inside,
knowing that we tried
And in helping out we take pride!

Hey help us out pal,
in government
Some must carry the ball,
all can't punt
Stand for election,
apply for selection
Public servant,
a noble profession

And your work can help us
right what is wrong
Doing our part
to make government strong
We'll all feel good inside,
knowing that we tried
And in helping out we take pride!

SONG #9 "Ethical Man" lyrics by S. Cook* see choice #33 / intro[20]
sung to the tune of "Piano Man" by Billy Joel

Share your wisdom you're an ethical man Principles for living today Help us to ask the right questions Help us to find our way Find a home in your head for honesty Install it there on a throne Learn to value the truth Don't be aloof With good conscience you're never alone Respect the law or work to change it Abide by professional code Give it your best Avoid conflict of interest March for justice don't be slowed	Apply the Greatest Good principle With a question to ask before you act Perceived social benefits All those good hits Will they reach great numbers in fact? Apply the Fraternal Charity principle With a question about the affected If I'm in his shoes Would this I choose Given consequences and what's been neglected? Apply the Universality Principle Consider this question from the first What can you say If all acted this way Would it be for the best or the worst? Share your wisdom you're an ethical man Principles for living today Help us to ask the right questions Help us to find our way

SONG #10: "Building The Common Welfare" lyrics by S. Cook* choice #35
to be sung to the tune of "I Heard It Through the Grapevine" intro[21]
by N. Whitfield and B. Strong / Marvin Gaye

I'm tired of hearing you Talking 'bout the free lunch crew[22] Putting down the welfare state Jesus preached love, not hate If your son was hungry poor, Would you slam the kitchen door? Building the common welfare To lift up some, we must share Building the common welfare Someday you may need our care Please don't you bitch to me 'Bout that housing subsidy Valuing your tax dollar Putting down those in squalor If your daughter was homeless, Would you ignore her duress?	Building the common welfare To lift up some, we must share Building the common welfare Someday you may need our care You put down markets not free And social security You'd shred the safety net On big business stake your bet Damn your socialism scare We need national health care Building the common welfare To lift up some, we must share Building the common welfare Someday you may need our care

SONG #11 : "My planet 'tis of thee" lyrics by S. Cook   choice #36 / intro[23]
sung to the tune of the patriotic songs "America" and "God Save the Queen"

My planet 'tis of thee Sustainability Of this I sing	Long may we keep what's whole Accepting steward's role Humility our goal Our love the queen
Long may our world be bright With nature's holy light Power us by thy might Our Sun the king	Our choices show we care With them we do prepare A safe just space
My planet 'tis of thee Responsibility Of this I sing	May we defend our earth Providing life a berth And sing with heart and mirth Our love we bring

---

SONG #12: "Amazing Place" lyrics by S. Cook*   choice #41 / intro[24]
to be sung to the tune of "Amazing Grace" by John Newton / traditional

Amazing place, our Earth profound Its cycles, its ecology Tread softly on its fertile ground Let its ecosystems be	Live lightly on the land and share With all creatures great and small[25] Your lifestyle says that you care When through you nature stands tall
Leave, not take, and you can belong To biotic community Wilderness how sweet its song Life's dynamic harmony	Our species had a million years Belonging to Nature's scheme Now standing apart the time nears To live a sustainable dream

---

SONG #13: "Stingy" lyrics by S. Cook*   choice #49 / intro[26]
sung to the tune of "Cloudy" by Paul Simon and Art Garfunkel

Stingy More hoarding, less giving I call it stingy It's not the way I want the world to be Greed and giving just don't mix We need an attitudinal fix Not money gaming tricks Those with gold rule or Golden Rule take your pick **REFRAIN =** Hello what's right I haven't seen you through the dark night Can't you come out into the light? ************************************	Stealing Taking what you've no right to that's stealing It's not the way I want the world to be Rip-off and right-on just don't mix We need an attitudinal fix Not pirate plundering tricks Me first, our children's future take your pick *********REFRAIN***************

Lying
Saying what you know is false
that's lying
It's not the way I want the world to be
Uncouth and truth just don't mix
We need an attitudinal fix
Not muddying the waters tricks
Bullshitting or enlightening
take your pick
*********REFRAIN***************
Prejudice
Not giving someone a chance
that's prejudice
It's not the way I want the world to be
Not my kind and kindness
just don't mix
We need an attitudinal fix
Not ethnocentric tricks
Racist or color blind justice
take your pick

*********REFRAIN***************
Bad Karma
Bad comes back to bite
that's bad karma
It's not the way I want the world to be
Hard knocks, soft kisses just don't mix
We need an attitudinal fix
Not hard sell huckster tricks
Wham bam or thank you, ma'am
take your pick

*********REFRAIN***************
So my friend please don't lie
And let's divide that pie
Give the ol' Golden Rule a try
Lets remake the world,
not let our dreams die

*********REFRAIN***************

SONG #14 "Patience At Its Limit" lyrics by S.Cook* choice #51 / intro[27]
sung to tune of "Take It To The Limit" by Henley, Meisner, Frey / The Eagles

Protesting at the World Economic Forum
Where the fat cats meet in the snow[28]
I was reading 'bout inequality—
that new report
It got me feelin' looooooooooooooow

The world's richest eighty-five people
Holding outrageous wealth
While billions of poor arrange
Lives in squalor and filth
Hey this troubles me greatly:
Unfair, don't stare, please care, gotta share
Something's gotta change

So we fight for what's right
Our emotions are raw
Our patience at its limit: the last straw

We got capitalists making big money
We got failure to spread it around
If the have-nots revolt tomorrow
They'll have the high ground[29]

And when you're trying to stay alive
Somebody needs to care
You can't find enough food
But there's plenty elsewhere
With some help you could break in
So you're looking round for higher ground
And planning to intruuuuuuuuuuuuuuuude
So we fight for what's right
Our emotions are raw
Our patience at its limit: the last straw

Patience at its limit
Patience at its limit
Patience at its limit: the last stray

Patience at its limit [Please!]
Patience at its limit [Come on!]
Patience at its limit: the last straw

Patience at its limit [Please!]
Patience at its limit [Come on!]
Patience at its limit: the last straw

[starts to fade out] Patience at its limit Patience at its limit Patience at its limit: the last straw	[fades out still more] Patience at its limit [Please!] Patience at its limit [Come on!] Patience at its limit: the last straw
[fades out more] Patience at its limit [Please!] Patience at its limit [Come on!] Patience at its limit: the last straw	[fades out to barely audible] Patience at its limit [Please!] Patience at its limit [Come on!] Patience at its limit: the last straw

SONG #15 "Battle Hymn of New Economics" lyrics by S. Cook* choice #52
to be sung to the tune of "The Battle Hymn of the Republic" intro[30]
by William Steffe/Julia Ward Howe / traditional

Let us join together To enact a carbon tax And to hard working poor people Rebate this money back At greedy corporations and polluters We'll aim our attack Fight greenhouse gases and inequality	Sustainability Forever Earth First Forever Solidarity Forever United We are Strong
Sustainability Forever Earth First Forever Solidarity Forever[31] United We are Strong	Economic indicators should not rise As more and more we trash If we keep ignoring hidden costs Our economy will crash Measuring sustainable economy Isn't something rash Value environmental integrity
Let's proclaim renewable energy Based economy as our goal And put a stop to building power plants Fired by dirty coal Stop C O two levels from rising That we shall patrol Value nature and biodiversity	Sustainability Forever Earth First Forever Solidarity Forever United We are Strong

NOTES for the Songs

1 Song #1 intro: British philosopher Bertrand Russell once said, "The whole problem with the world is that fools and fanatics are always so certain of themselves, but wiser people are full of doubts. "

2 Mother Teresa (1910-1997) had a "dark night of the soul" lasting many years

3 Song #2 intro: Michael Shermer in his book *The Science of Good & Evil* wrote, "The balance between doubt and certainty, between open-mindedness and closed mindedness, is what I call skepticism."

4 facilitating these is a goal of scientific investigation, made possible by careful adherence to, and documentation of, experimental or other procedures so others can repeat the work and verify it

5 Song #3 intro: David Steindl-Rast, Benedictine monk, in the 1991 book *Belonging to the Universe* which he co-authored with physicist Fritjof Capra, wrote, "Faith...is a matter of trust. Courageous trust in that ultimate belonging which you experience in your religious moments, in your peak moments. Faith is that inner gesture by which you entrust yourself to that belonging."

6 this line appears in Ralph Waldo Emerson's essay *The Over-Soul.*

7 conceptual maps

8 phrase I like to think Einstein used (although what he wrote is translated from German "the old One").

9 Emerson's phrase

10 *The Power of Now* is the title of a book by Eckert Tolle.

11 this line honors two 1960s' songs with mystical overtones: the Stevie Winwood / Blind Faith song "Sea of Joy," and the Gary Brooker / Keith Reid / Procol Harum song "A Salty Dog."

12 Song #4 intro: Valerie Tarico, in her essay "Six Reasons Religion May Do More Harm Than Good," wrote "Religion trains believers to practice self deception, shut out contradictory evidence, and trust authorities rather than their own capacity to think."

13 the title of a book by evolutionary biologist and famous religious skeptic Richard Dawkins

14 Song #5 intro: Two comments: 1) An Italian researcher's paper targeting the origin of fatalistic tendencies concluded "People with low income and considering themselves at the bottom of the social class tend to be more fatalistic, and 2) As reported on *CNBC* in February 2021, a survey of 10,000 USA millionaires found that 97% of them believe they're in control of their own destiny—a much higher number than the 55% of the general population who also believe this.

15 reality cash is metaphorically what you spend in the Reality Marketplace–an imaginary place (made real on the *Project Worldview* website) where important ideas, beliefs, values, and worldview themes are bought/ sold.

16 Song #6 intro: Two comments: 1) a bumpersticker asks, "Humbly Grateful or Grumbly Hateful?" and 2) New Age philosopher Francis Story Talbot, also known as Manitongquat meaning "Medicine Story," says "God Is Love...[and] Love is life believing in itself"

17 Song #7 intro: African-American political activist Cornel West said, "Justice is what love looks like in public."

18 a tipping point reference

19 Song #8 intro: Marian Wright Edelman, Children's Defense Fund founder, has said, "Service is the rent we pay for being...the very purpose of life."

20 Song #9 intro: According to Robert Fulghum, in *All I Really Need to Know I Learned in Kindergarten*, in that setting children learn things like "Don't take things that aren't yours," "Don't hit people," "Say you're sorry when you hurt somebody," "Play fair," "Share everything," and "Clean up your own mess."

21 Song #10 intro: American founding father John Adams said, "Government is instituted for the common good for the protection, safety, prosperity and happiness of the people, and not for the profit, honor, or private interest of any one man, family, or class of men."

22 free lunch is often applied to poor people using state provided welfare program services. The more general economics term is free rider, where people benefit from resources and services they don't pay for.

23 Song #11 intro: Adam Daniel Finnerty, in his book *No More Plastic Jesus,* wrote "This growing awareness that we are part of a global system —a global village—is a tremendously revolutionary concept...capable of remaking our entire planet."

24 Song intro #12: Kate Raworth, British economist and author of *Doughnut Economics*, writes, "Humanity's 21st century challenge is...to ensure that no one falls short on life's essentials...while ensuring that collectively we do not overshoot our pressure on Earth's life-supporting systems."

25 this line is from Cecil Frances Alexander's old Anglican hymn

26 Song intro #13: Winston Churchill said, "We make a living by what we get. We make a life by what we give."

27 Song intro #14: News item: As the 2014 World Economic Forum started in Davos, Switzerland, an Oxfam report said the world's richest 85 people control as much wealth as the world's poorest half—its 3.6 billon poorest people.

28 phrase used by rock star/ humanitarian Bono in describing the World Economic Forum meeting in Davos, Switzerland

29 the moral high ground or ethically superior position

30 Song #15 intro: Oystein Dahle, Norweigian business person and former oil company executive, has said, "Socialism collapsed because it did not allow the market to tell the economic truth. Capitalism may collapse because it does not allow the market to tell the ecological truth."

31 title of 1915 song written for labor unions , used for progressive causes

Appendix C:
Carbon Footprint Calculation

Here we present the details behind doing your own carbon footprint calculation and illustrative examples. (See chapter 7 section D for an overview.) Your carbon footprint C will be found by adding three impacts: $C = C_H + C_N + C_L$ These three quantities are defined as follows.

C_H is the part of your carbon footprint based on your documented
   household residential and transportation energy use

C_N is the part of your carbon footprint representing your share, based on your income and relative C_H, of the **national** energy footprint

C_L is a correction factor based on two important **lifestyle** factors

You start by assembling your energy use and income data.

E_H and C_H calculation—Instructions for completing worksheet:
Col. 1: if you have natural gas used in therms, multiply by 100 to get cubic ft; if you have miles traveled by gasoline powered vehicle, divide miles by average miles / gallon to get gallons used—example: my Prius went 4300 miles, averaged 43 miles / gallon, divide 4300 by 43 = 100 gallons of gasoline used
Col. 3: divide entries in col. 1 by values in col.2 and put result in col.3
Col. 5: multiply entries in col. 3 by values in col.4 and put result in col.5
Col.6 : divide entries in col.5 by 2200 to get metric tons put in col. 6 , Finally, complete additional steps indicated in body of worksheet

Figure #40 Worksheet for E_H and C_H carbon footprint calculation

	Col.1	Col. 2	Col. 3	Col. 4	Col. 5	Col. 6
Source / units	my amount	Unit /MBTU	MBTU	1bs CO_2 /MBTU		
Natural gas / cubic feet		975		117		
Electricity / kWh		95		88*		
Home Heating Fuel oil #2 / gallons		7.25		163		
Coal / lbs		75		210		
LP Gas / gallons		10.35		139		
Gasoline, gallons		8		157		
Add up the values in Col. 3, enter result ➜				←this is your personal energy use		
Air travel	Enter data in online carbon footprint calculator, such as calculator.carbonfootprint.com or others, enter result➜					
Bus & Rail	Enter data in online carbon footprint calculator, such as calculator.carbonfootprint.com or others, enter result➜					
	C_H Add up all the values in Col. 6 in tons of CO_2 and record result here ➜					

* based on 2019 EIA figures for USA mix from all sources (62 % fossil fuel + nuclear + renewables) ** divide col. 5 entries by 2200 lbs / metric ton to get col.6 values

Example: The completed worksheet for my carbon footprint calculation appears as Figure #28 in chapter 7. From the Col.3 total in the worksheet, my E_H value for fossil fuel derived energy is 36.3 MBTU and Col. 6 value for C_H is 2.02 metric tons of CO_2.

E_N and C_N **calculation—Instructions**: After completing the E_H calculation, you'll need your income data. If you live outside the USA you'll need to go online and find databases that provide national income and energy use information. Americans can follow my example and use values I provide. From national energy use information, you'll need E_{ave}, the total primary fossil fuel derived energy per capita for your resident nation in millions of BTUS (MBTU) / person-year. To get the W_1 correction factor, divide your annual gross adjusted income by national average (per capita) annual income. Make sure same currency and basis of figuring is used for each. To get the W_2 correction factor, divide your E_H value, representing the total fossil fuel derived energy you've used in the last year from the sum of Col. 3 worksheet entries—by a national per capita personal fossil fuel derived energy use in residential and transportation sectors for the last year. Make sure units used are the same. The fraction f of national primary energy use attributed to residential and transportation sectors is needed. You'll then plug your data into the equation $E_N = W_1 \times W_2 \times (1\text{-}f) E_{ave}$.

Finding CO_2 emissions associated with this indirect fossil fuel energy use, taking the national carbon dioxide emissions in metric tons from non-residential and non-transportation sectors and dividing by the nation's population will give CO_2 emissions per capita. Dividing that by the national non-residential and non-transportation sector fossil fuel derived per capita energy, which is $(1\text{-}f) E_{ave}$, gives metric tons of CO_2 associated with every one million BTUs of energy. Finally, multiplying by your value for E_N gives C_N the metric tons of carbon dioxide emissions associated with your indirect fossil fuel energy use.

Example, continued: my 2019 gross adjusted income as reported to IRS was $32,942. For the USA, according to Census Bureau data, for 2019 a corresponding national per capita income is $39,156. From USA Energy Information Administration (EIA) data, E_{ave}, the total primary fossil fuel derived energy per capita, = 271 MBTU / person – year. So W_1 = $32,942 / $39,156 = .841. My E_H value for fossil fuel derived energy is 36.3 MBTU. The best available data from the US EIA puts the national per capita personal fossil fuel derived energy use in those sectors at 95 MBTU / person-year. So W_2 = 36.3/ 95 = .382. Based on EIA figures, the fraction coming from residential and transportation sectors, f = .35. Plugging in, E_N = .841 x .382 x (1-.35) x 271 = 56.6 MBTU

Total USA carbon dioxide emissions from non-residential and non-transportation sectors in 2019 was 2267 million metric tons. Dividing by a population of 328 million, gives 6.9 metric tons per person. Dividing that by the corresponding $(1\text{-}f) E_{ave}$ value of 176 MBTU/ person-year of such fossil fuel energy use gives .0392 metric tons per MBTU. Multiplying by E_N, I get C_N = 56.6 MBTU x .0392 = 2.22 metric tons.